A BETTER WORLD

THE GREAT SCHISM:
STALINISM AND
THE AMERICAN INTELLECTUALS

WILLIAM L. O'NEILL

SIMON AND SCHUSTER
NEW YORK

Published by Simon and Schuster
A Division of Gulf & Western Corporation
Simon & Schuster Building
Rockefeller Center
1230 Avenue of the Americas
New York, New York 10020
SIMON AND SCHUSTER and colophon
are trademarks of Simon & Schuster
Designed by Edith Fowler
Manufactured in the United States of America

10 9 8 7 6 5 4 3 2 1

Library of Congress Cataloging in Publication Data

O'Neill, William L.
    A better world.

    Includes bibliographical references and index.
    1. Soviet Union—Foreign opinion, American.
2. United States—Relations—Soviet Union. 3.
Soviet Union—Relations—United States. 4. Radi-
cals—United States—Attitudes. 5. Intellectuals—
United States—Attitudes. 6. Progressivism (Unit-
ed States politics) 7. Public opinion—United
States. 1. Title.
E183.8.S65053 1982   973.91   82–12547
ISBN 0–671–43610–4

193260

To Alan R. Mendelsohn

Acknowledgments

I am grateful to the American Philosophical Society for travel money, to the National Endowment for the Humanities for one of their splendid fellowships, and to the Rutgers Research Council and Rutgers University for their generous support of my work over the years. The following institutions gave me permission to examine and quote from their document and manuscript holdings: the Boston University Library, the Lilly Library of Indiana University, the Newberry Library, the Princeton University Library, the Schlesinger Library of Radcliffe College, the Archives of the Wisconsin State Historical Society, the Yale University Library. I thank them for their assistance, and my thanks also to the following for permission to quote from their own unpublished writings, or from material they control: Joseph Alsop, Edward L. Bernays, Malcolm Cowley, Thomas I. Emerson, John W. Finch, Sidney Hook, Alfred Kazin, Corliss Lamont, Max Lerner, Mary McCarthy, Dwight Macdonald, the estate of George Orwell, the Honorable Claude Pepper, William Phillips, James Roosevelt, Morrie Ryskind, Arthur Schlesinger, Jr., David Sinclair, Stephen Spender.

My agent, Georges Borchardt, has been, as always, wise and steady. Alice Mayhew of Simon and Schuster provided good criticism and a rich flow of suggestions. I appreciate their aid. It is a pleasure to dedicate this book to my friend Alan Mendelsohn, who helped by disagreeing with me on the main points.

Contents

	Preface	11
I	In Shock: August 24, 1939–June 22, 1941	13
II	The "People's War" Begins: 1941–1943	43
III	The Revival of Anti-Stalinism	75
IV	The "People's War" Falters: 1943–1945	98
V	In the Postwar	116
VI	The Rise and Fall of Henry Wallace	142
VII	The Eclipse of Progressivism	161
VIII	The Blacklist	212
IX	China: Progressive Paradox	252
X	The Question of Liberal Guilt	284
XI	The Academy and the Crisis of Liberalism	324
XII	Rewriting the Past	351
XIII	Conclusions	376
	Notes	387
	Index	428

In any view of the American cultural situation, the importance of the radical movement of the Thirties cannot be overestimated. It may be said to have created the American intellectual class as we now know it in its great size and influence. It fixed the character of this class as being, through all mutations of opinion, predominantly of the Left. And quite apart from opinion, the political tendency of the Thirties defined the style of the class—from that radicalism came the moral urgency, the sense of crisis, and the concern with personal salvation that mark the existence of American intellectuals.

—LIONEL TRILLING

The thirties was a period of radicalization, to be sure, but it was mainly a radicalization controlled and manipulated by the Stalinist party-machine. Hence one can scarcely discuss this decade without also characterizing it as a period of ideological vulgarity and opportunism, of double-think and power-worship, sustained throughout by a mean and crude and unthinking secular religiosity.

—PHILIP RAHV

Preface

THIS IS A BOOK about the struggle among non-Communist leftists and liberals over American relations with the Soviet Union
from 1939 through the 1950s. As everyone knows, the quarrel
began earlier, during the "red decade" of the 1930s, but it did
not end then. No later decade was as red. The Communist Party
was never again as strong. Hopes for a second American revolution died out. What did not perish, and actually became
stronger after Germany attacked it, was the faith among many
seeking to make a better world that Russia led the way. So long
as the United States and the Soviet Union were allied, most
Americans conceded the point, or at least withheld disbelief.
It was the best time ever for progressives, as they often called
themselves. By this was meant not believers in progress as such,
or voters for the Progressive Parties of 1912 and 1924, but
rather those Americans who were pro-Soviet without being
members of the Communist Party. Their enemies among liberals and independent leftists preferred to be called anti-Stalinists, because "anti-Communist" was a blanket label that covered
moderates and rightists also. These are the terms that will be used
here.

Though some feel strongly about Russian-American relations
today, few care as violently as people once did. Most of the
period we will be looking at was a time of extravagantly high
emotions. It mattered greatly to liberals and leftists what was
said about Russia. To a degree this was because the lives of
nations and peoples were involved. But unlike now, progressives
had additionally a large emotional investment in the Soviets.
From 1935 to 1939 literally millions of Americans had joined
the "Popular Front" of pro-Soviet organizations. And, though
shattered by the Stalin-Hitler pact of 1939, after Russia entered the war it came together again and was bigger than ever,

owing to support from government and the business community. The general agreement that Russia was a fine ally and could be trusted made life extremely difficult for anti-Stalinists, who found themselves an isolated and sometimes embittered minority. It was unsettling to know truths about Russia that no one was willing to hear.

After the war, when public sentiment turned against Russia, and the Popular Front collapsed, this time for good, emotions continued to run high. Progressives, eager to avert the Cold War, tried feverishly to stem the tide of adverse opinion. Anti-Stalinists, though now aligned with the majority of Americans, found it hard to keep their balance just the same. Almost everyone said or wrote things they would later regret, or should have regretted. Both sides were injured in various ways. Many persons even now bear scars acquired at the time.

Yet, despite all that has gone by since then, some survivors remain at odds. Old progressives admit, sometimes, to having been wrong about Russia, but insist that they meant well and should have been listened to accordingly as advocates of peace and reform. It was the anti-Stalinists, they insist, who are to be faulted, since by attacking Communism and Russia they helped bring on McCarthyism and even the Vietnam War. Anti-Stalinists reject the accusation, and in turn blame progressives for lying about Russia and putting its interests ahead of their own country's. Further, anti-Stalinists believe, as one said, that beyond foreign policy "freedom of the mind and all its fruits" was at stake. It was in defense of cultural freedom at home that anti-Stalinists were most active and vocal, opening themselves to the charge made later that they had gone too far.

In one sense a history, this book concerns today also, and not just because so many participants have survived. The issues live on, too, and always will so long as we care about the way in which political opinions are formed and advanced, the relation between politics and culture, as also between ends and means. Few any longer defend the Soviet Union. Almost everything else about the great debate over it still matters. Here, especially, to know the past is to know ourselves.

WILLIAM L. O'NEILL

Highland Park, New Jersey

I

In Shock:
August 24, 1939–June 22, 1941

ON AUGUST 24, 1939, Russia and Germany announced that they had signed a nonaggression pact the previous day. Each country promised not to attack the other and to increase trade. Hitler then invaded Poland, and Britain and France declared war on Germany. By agreement Russia and Germany divided up Poland and absorbed it. The USSR also seized the Baltic States and later invaded Finland. Hitler, his eastern flank now secured by the pact, overran Western Europe, aided by large quantities of raw material from Russia. The pact and its aftermath threw progressives the world over into confusion and despair. In America as elsewhere they had been following the Soviet lead in foreign affairs because Russia seemed to them the most antifascist of the great powers. Indeed, from 1936 on, as sole supporter of the doomed Spanish Republic and leader of the Popular Fronts, it seemed to be the *only* antifascist power. Stalin had manipulated this belief deftly, persuading millions of Americans that they had to rally behind the USSR whatever its flaws. These were obvious enough and rapidly became more so. The period of greatest enthusiasm for Soviet policies, 1936 to 1939, coincided with a great terror that reduced the population of Russia by at least ten million. Still the American faithful hung on, claiming that few were being purged (even Stalin's harshest critics greatly underestimated the actual death rate) and assuring themselves that so forward-looking a regime would not be executing, among others, heroes of the Bolshevik Revolution without good reason. The truth could not be known, they insisted, and even if knowable should not be allowed to weaken antifascist unity.[1]

The Stalin-Hitler Pact destroyed that unity in an instant. It also demonstrated Stalin's contempt for progressive opinion. Non-Communists in the Party's front organizations had assumed that communications with Russia went both ways. The Soviets had encouraged this delusion by paying lip service to progressive concerns and bestowing flattering attentions on progressive visitors to Russia. Accordingly the pact shocked progressives in at least three ways. It showed that the Soviets put national interest ahead of everything else, and that they had an unnerving lack of regard for the feelings of sympathetic Westerners. Further, it supported the charge of anti-Stalinists, hateful to progressives, that Communism and Nazism were both totalitarian systems.

Progressives fought against this to the bitter end. In 1939 Sidney Hook, a philosopher and erstwhile Marxist, organized a Committee for Cultural Freedom opposed to dictatorships of both the left and the right.* To Hook's surprise, Freda Kirchwey of *The Nation* attacked them for sinning against unity. Hook still thought of *The Nation* as an open forum of the liberal left, which it had been since 1918 under the direction of Oswald Garrison Villard. But in 1937 Kirchwey took control as owner and editor, making *The Nation* an organ of the Popular Front. Though Hook had not noticed this earlier, Kirchwey's critique opened his eyes. He wrote Kirchwey that her statement "brings the *Nation* that much closer to 13th street [Communist Party headquarters] in the public mind; some members of the committee have told me that after reading your editorial they felt as if the *Nation* had died."[2] Similar attacks followed, in the Communist *Daily Worker* and, in its issue of August 26 (which had gone to press before the Stalin-Hitler Pact was announced), in *The Nation* again. A letter signed by four hundred leftists and progressives described the Committee for Cultural Freedom as an effort to split the "democratic front." Praise of Russia was mingled with abuse of committee members. "With the aim of

---

* Members included Thomas H. Benton, V. F. Calverton, John Chamberlain, Merle Curti, Babette Deutsch, John Dewey, Max Eastman, Morris Ernst, John Haynes Holmes, Suzanne La Follette, Sinclair Lewis, Claude McKay, John Dos Passos, James Rorty, Norman Thomas, Dorothy Thompson and Oswald Garrison Villard.

turning anti-fascist feeling against the Soviet Union they have
encouraged the fantastic falsehood that the U.S.S.R. and the
totalitarian states are basically alike."[3]

Overnight the pact made signers of this statement look foolish and led some progressives to examine their consciences. I. F.
Stone, a fellow-traveling journalist, confessed that he was as
surprised as anyone by Stalin's change of heart. He reminded
readers that conservatives had been predicting for over a year
that Stalin and Hitler would get together. Though he ignored
them, anti-Stalinist radicals had been saying so, too, Max Eastman in a general way since 1934 and the independently leftist
magazine *Common Sense* at least six months before the fact.[4]
No one Stone knew, he continued, had paid any attention to this
kind of reactionary propaganda. But Stone confessed to having
ignored a reliable source. *The New York Times* issue of October 10, 1938, included a crucial dispatch from its Moscow
correspondent, Walter Duranty. Duranty had been sent to Russia in the early twenties to counteract the notoriously inaccurate and anti-Bolshevik stories it had been receiving. With
Duranty's help the *Times* went on misleading readers as before, though in the opposite direction. Stone did not exaggerate when he called Duranty "an unofficial spokesman for the
Kremlin." Duranty's cable of October 10 said that nothing
stood in the way of a Russo-German pact except Hitler's prejudice against "Judeo-Bolshevism." This was not so great an obstacle as one might think, according to Duranty. "But Hitler is
not immortal and dictators can change their minds and Stalin
has shot more Jews in two years of purges than were ever killed
in Germany."[5] Though Jewish, Stone only understood this
"cynical and shocking" prediction after it came to pass. Such
blindness was the curse of progressive journalism. It was one
thing to be partisan and ignore unwanted information when
delivered by enemies or outsiders, as, for example, *Common
Sense*. No one in the opinion business could be faulted for this. It
was quite another to ignore a Duranty, who was pro-Soviet and
hence, to progressives, trustworthy. Stone sensed the problem
presented by their refusal to accept unwanted information
whatever the source, but could do nothing about it. He and
other progressive journalists were committed to the left's always
being the right side, even when plainly wrong. Their position

could be sustained only by ignoring the worst features of Soviet life, which led to further mistakes. Failure to see the pact coming was only the most embarrassing of these.

Progressives, and even some anti-Stalinists, compounded their error by accepting Moscow's rationalization of the pact as a defensive move inspired by Western appeasement of Hitler. The opposite seems to have been true. In a brilliant article for *The Nation* Louis Fischer, its formerly pro-Soviet Moscow correspondent, explained Stalin's reasoning. The pact arose not from fears that the Allies might refuse to stop Hitler but out of certainty that they would fight. Once the Allies announced, on March 31, 1939, that they were willing to go to war in defense of Poland, Stalin saw his chance. "Thus as long as the Allies followed a policy of appeasement and surrender to the fascist aggressors, the Bolsheviks were pro-Ally. And the moment the Allies took a firm stand against a fascist aggressor, the Bolsheviks made a pact with him. That is what is called dialectics," Fischer wrote sardonically.[6] The Allied decision to fight Hitler meant there would be a western front and consequently no German attack on Russia, giving it freedom of choice. If it sided with the Allies it would have to go to war against Germany with no prospect of gain. But if Russia sided with Germany it could have what it wanted without war. Stalin had been shrewd but mistaken, in Fischer's view. For Hitler the pact meant the difference "between certain defeat and a chance of success." Nothing Hitler conceded to Stalin offset this advantage. Fischer was right. The capture of Soviet documents in German archives later provided evidence supporting his thesis.[7] Events themselves justified Fischer's claim that Stalin had made an error, one so great, as it turned out, that Soviet Russia would barely survive it. Later Soviet apologists would excuse the pact on the ground that it bought Russia time to prepare for war.[8] This argument was false in several ways. The time would not have been needed if Russia had backed the Allies, because Germany could not, as of 1939, have fought a two-front war successfully. And, in any case, the added time was a liability because during it Germany's strength, in relation to Russia's, grew. The Soviets were worse off in 1941 than in 1939, having outsmarted themselves to an almost fatal degree.

Freda Kirchwey did not endorse Fischer's grim and accurate

view of Stalin's motives. But she admitted, with other disillusioned progressives, that the Soviet "experiment," as they used
to call it, had failed.[9] Villard spoke for the magazine in reviewing his long history of sympathy and open-mindedness. He had
been fair, but it was clear now that Stalin's dictatorship "is not
only just as bloody as the others but just as crooked, treacherous and criminal."[10] Kirchwey shrank from admitting the
worst, until Russia's invasion of Finland brought this concession: "The Finns are fighting for their lives and for the independence of their country. And whether they are conscious of
it or not, they are fighting to resist a conception of revolution
that threatens every ideal that the working-class movement has
stood for."[11] Though she gave them no credit, what the anti-
Stalinists had been saying for more than a decade was true.
Stalinism was the betrayal of the Russian Revolution, not its
fulfillment.

Reinhold Niebuhr, a distinguished Protestant theologian then
entering on the years of his greatest influence among liberals,
went further, arguing in *The Nation* that those Marxists "who
wrongly assume that the mass organization of society is the sole
source of ideological pretension" must be unmasked. So also
must Russian claims of "transcendent disinterestedness in the
field of world politics . . ." He concluded:

Thus Russia has graduated into the position of a completely modern state. Not only does it engage in the general
rationalizations of which all nations avail themselves and
which consist in interpreting facts from a particular national
perspective, but it has learned the art of the tyrannical
state, which so controls all organs of opinion that it can
manufacture, rather than merely interpret, facts to suit
its purposes.[12]

The *New Republic* was less sure. It had been founded during
the Progressive era by three prominent intellectuals—Herbert
Croly, Walter Lippmann and Walter Weyl—as an organ of
cerebral liberalism. Though it changed hands more than once,
the *New Republic* would never entirely lose this character. In
the politically lifeless twenties the magazine, with Weyl dead
and Lippmann gone, turned more toward culture, keeping this

interest even when re-politicized in the thirties. Its literary editors, Edmund Wilson and then for many years Malcolm Cowley, were influential critics. Beyond intelligence and taste lay a further asset. The *New Republic* did not struggle with deficits, the scourge of liberal journalism. Its losses were absorbed first by Willard Straight, an investment banker, and then by his widow, Dorothy, even after her remarriage in 1925 to an Englishman, Leonard Elmhirst. Croly died in 1930, and for the next fifteen years policy at the *New Republic* was shaped by Bruce Bliven, a former newspaper editor, and the economist George Soule, who together wrote all the unsigned editorials. Their *New Republic* continued to pride itself on being thoughtful and realistic. Less emotional than *The Nation*, it reacted less strongly to immediate events. During its progressive years the *New Republic* was generally as wrong as *The Nation*, but in a loftier way. It too joined the Popular Front, and misinformed liberals about conditions in Russia. "George Soule and I were unforgiveably slow to realize what was happening," Bliven admitted later, but they had a good excuse.[13] All the anti-Stalinists were either conservatives or followers of Trotsky and, in either case, unreliable. Like most progressives Bliven paid no attention to the independent critics of Russia. He too preferred sources who agreed with him and thus heard only what he wished to hear.

The *New Republic*'s response to Stalin's about-face in 1939 was instinctive. The editors made clear at once that only people lacking in worldliness and sophistication were surprised by this turn of events. It was time for these innocents to grow up. "European affairs are still full of insincerity, devious methods, secrets and surprises, and we should not be taken aback at any treachery or weakness. The utmost possible realism and wariness must govern our action in relation to foreign affairs."[14] Though the *New Republic* counseled readers not to stampede out of united-front organizations, they did so anyway.[15] The editors then decided that where the common herd had gone wrong was not by leaving Popular Front organizations after the pact, but by welcoming Communists as allies earlier under the wrong impression. It had been unwise of progressives "to regard the communists as dependable allies or to expect them not to shift when the interests of the movement demanded a new line." Similarly, people "who are morally outraged at the behavior of Soviet Russia are so because they have been naive enough to take communist propaganda at its face value."[16] The editors congratulated themselves for never having been so simple-minded, which accounted for their admirable balance after the pact was signed.

Russia's invasion of Finland destroyed this pose. Forgetting their own strictures against moral outrage and overreaction, the editors wrote:

> By a brutal assault on a well governed intelligent nation that has the admiration of the world for its sturdy and progressive culture, the Soviet Union has unleashed the dogs of hate that were already straining to tear it to pieces. It has made defense of its action impossible on the part of those who were friendly or were willing to reserve judgement. It has provided a strong moral case for those who wish to destroy communism and all its works.[17]

Luckily for them, the editors stopped just short of embracing anti-Communism. Later, when the desire to swallow Soviet crimes overcame them again, even this much moralizing was not something they would care to remember.

Like Bliven and Soule, Malcolm Cowley found it hard to give up old loyalties. Cowley belonged to the famous Lost Generation of writers. A poet as well as a critic, he became also the first historian of his literary generation. His *Exile's Return* (1934) was both a memoir and a collective biography. In it he accomplished the feat of simultaneously glamorizing the literary culture of the twenties and exposing it as morally and intellectually bankrupt. There was almost no politics in the book, yet it was political in the extreme. A chronicle appearing in the 1930s that showed how the religion of art, as Cowley termed it, had failed during the 1920s was by its nature a political statement. Cowley drew the moral more clearly in a later edition of the book than he needed to at the time. "It was an easy, quick, adventurous age, good to be young in; and yet on coming out of it one felt a sense of relief, as on coming out of a room too full of talk and people into the sunlight of the winter streets."[18]

In the more bracing air of the thirties Cowley exchanged the religion of art for the religion of socialism. A few years after the pact he recalled what it had been like in the good old days just ended.

> All through the 1930s the Soviet Union was a second fatherland for millions of people in other countries, including our own. It was the land where men and women were sacrificing themselves to create a new civilization, not for Russia alone but for the world. It was not so much a nation, in the eyes of Western radicals, as it was an ideal, a faith and an international hope of salvation.[19]

Cowley was an active Popular Fronter in the thirties and wrote slashing reviews of books hostile to Russia, greatly offending anti-Stalinists. But, he remembered much later, he had begun to feel uneasy even before the pact.[20] As a leftist he resented having to compromise revolutionary ideals for the sake of unity with progressives. At the same time, Russia kept getting harder to defend. After the pact Cowley retreated. He, with the *New Republic*, was hostile to it, telling a writer who had composed a poem hailing the pact, "You are almost the only poet submitting his work to the *New Republic* whose poems are turned down for political reasons—in this case the political reason being that we can't share your feelings about the new Russian policy."[21] Yet he went on believing that the Russian purge victims were guilty, and writing what Edmund Wilson told him was "Stalinist character assassination of the most reckless and libelous sort."[22] Cowley answered that he was not ready to embrace his former enemies or turn on his former allies. Must he now believe, he asked Wilson rhetorically, "that Communists I saw working hard and sacrificing themselves are really, without a single exception, un-principled careerists?"[23] Cowley did give up working for left organizations, but allowed them to go on using his name—a compromise that satisfied no one and had, finally, to be abandoned.

Such ambivalence was not unusual. Communists and fellow-traveling intellectuals whose loyalties had been formed during the ultraleft years were least affected by the pact and its consequences. After Poland was invaded, twenty thousand of the Party faithful rallied in Madison Square Garden. James

Wechsler, an ex-Communist, reported that though the new line had not yet jelled, enthusiasm ruled the day: "There was a good deal of singing and cheering, and old revolutionary songs, reminiscent of the 'third period,' were once more restored to prominence."[24] Many Communists were glad to find themselves revolutionaries once more. There were still enough of them to maintain a private social world, insulated against the disapproval of outsiders.

Fellow-traveling intellectuals who lived in that outer world had a harder time. Few defended the Soviet's about-face openly, and those who did were ostracized, according to Samuel N. Harper, a Russian historian at the University of Chicago. Young Harper had been in Russia when the Bolsheviks took over, and he admired them loyally ever after. Having to follow the twists and turns of Soviet policy was difficult, since he had to keep forming and publishing new opinions. But it was never harmful to him until after the pact, when defending Russia isolated him. He was deeply hurt by the angry reactions of people to his continued Stalinism and died a lonely death the following year, too soon to profit from the Russo–German war.[25] For Carey McWilliams also this was "a nightmare season. Name-calling and denunciations became the order of the day; old friends ceased speaking; new political alignments emerged."[26]

Most Popular Fronters took the majority view. Antifascism was their main concern, and Stalin's betrayal of it outraged them. Granville Hicks left the party soon afterward. Richard Rovere of the Communist *New Masses* resigned his editorship. Robert Forsythe, *New Masses* film critic (as also of *Collier's* under his real name, Kyle Crichton), took his name off the masthead. Heywood Broun, a noted journalist, Paul de Kruif the medical writer, Joseph P. Lash and numerous others dropped out of the Popular Front.[27] These steps were less decisive than they seemed. The Popular Front was dead, killed by Stalin's new policy and the hostile reaction to it. Whether one resigned publicly or, like Cowley, gradually drifted away made little difference. The question was what to do next, and to this there seemed no answer. After leaving the Party Granville Hicks met with prominent left intellectuals, including Max Lerner, to see if a common ground for action existed. Lerner wrote Harold Laski, an old friend, that he believed "we can undo the suspicion and hatred and provincialism that grew up between the factions of the Left during the 30's." A fresh start seemed possible because recent events had cleared the air of cant. "You can scarcely think nowadays because of the noise made by those who are eating their words."[28] Lerner was mistaken on both counts. Old enmities could not be overcome. Events moved so rapidly that it was not easy to form a settled opinion. For many, waffling seemed best.

This was the course taken by Upton Sinclair. He had been a famous radical since his best-selling exposé of meatpackers, *The Jungle*, was published in 1906. During the thirties he gained fresh laurels by running for the governorship of California on his semisocialist EPIC (End Poverty in California) platform, which he came close to putting over. He also joined the Popular Front and spoke favorably and often about Soviet Russia, despite his lack of reliable data. When war broke out Sinclair favored the Allies, as he had the last time. "I am with you heart and soul in this fight," he wrote an English friend.[29] Yet he did not wish to break the Soviet connection, even though Russia was aiding Germany. Nor was he willing to rethink past positions. Sidney Hook urged him fruitlessly to criticize Stalin. James T. Farrell, an ally of the Trotskyists, asked if in view of recent events he still believed that the Russian purge victims were guilty. And what about Sinclair's old certainty that the great dictators would not get together? During Stalin's terror Eugene Lyons, another former radical turned anti-Stalinist, had asked Sinclair if he did not think that Germany and Russia might end up on the same side. Of course not, was the reply; during the purges, by shooting Marshal Tukachevsky and most of the Red Army's high command, who were pro-German, Sinclair knew from reading Soviet propaganda, Stalin had laid this question to rest. Farrell asked about Sinclair's earlier claim that critics of Russia suffered from "an anti-Stalinist obsession." I don't know now, answered Sinclair, ducking all the questions.[30]

Actually, Sinclair had not changed his mind. His faith in Russia was based, he wrote a friend, on the strongest possible footing.

> But I have hopes of Russia in spite of bureaucracy and dictatorship, and the reason is because I have been

watching their education for twenty-two years. That education has been Democratic in the broad sense and in spite of their dictatorship [*sic*] and Socialist, and I do not believe that millions of people who have read my books and Gorky's and all that enormous mass of revolutionary material are going to forget it entirely.[31]

This was to say that no nation which consumed his books in prodigious quantities could ultimately go wrong. Given the natural vanity of authors, Sinclair's reasoning was less curious than it seemed. Who can easily find incurable faults in people who seem to love one's work? By the same token, a nation that read millions of copies of books by Upton Sinclair had to be united. "On the subject of discontent in Russia," Sinclair wrote Eugene Lyons, "you are mistaking the foam for the beer."[32]

These conflicting emotions—affection for his Russian fans, disappointment in Stalin, support for England and France, nostalgia for the united front—made Sinclair erratic. In October the *New Masses* asked Sinclair to alter a piece he had sent in so it would fit the new Party line. He had erred by implying that "we favor Britain and France as against Germany, and as you know our position is that this is an imperialist war with no justice on either side."[33] Sinclair promptly made the change. But though a habitual signer of Front documents, when the League of American Writers asked him to sign a statement urging writers to promote American neutrality, Sinclair refused.[34] Seven months later when the *New Masses* asked Sinclair for an article supporting peace he said no. His views would not please the *New Masses,* Sinclair explained. And he asked Joseph North, the magazine's editor, what did he think would take place if Hitler conquered Britain and France? Sinclair's guess was that Hitler would be in Moscow by the next summer, that is, the summer of 1941, as nearly happened.[35]

Thus, when Sidney Hook attacked Sinclair in *The Call* for betraying socialism he was not quite on the mark. *The Call* was the Socialist Party's official organ, to which Sinclair contributed. Hook argued in a letter that Sinclair no longer believed in socialism because he had abandoned democracy, an essential feature of it. This was not unfair. Hook had no trouble finding antidemocratic statements in Sinclair's vast outpourings. And

Hook could produce a letter in which Sinclair had said that if Hitler ever eased up on Soviet Russia because it had become counterrevolutionary "I will admit that Stalin has sold out the workers."[36] But Sinclair had admitted no such thing. "Tomorrow, he will find other reasons for believing in Stalin. And this in the name of socialism and scientific method," wrote Hook.

Though right about many fellow travelers, Hook was wrong here. Sinclair had been shocked when Russia abandoned Britain and France. When Russia was forced into the war Sinclair felt relief. He answered a request from TASS, the Soviet news agency, with a friendly note, but Sinclair had learned a lesson. He wrote his English friend that it would "be very amusing to see how the Communist strikes all over the country will come to an end, and Churchill and Roosevelt will become heroes in the Communist press."[37] As late as October 1943 Sinclair was willing to endorse close relations among the Allies for the National Council of American-Soviet Friendship.[38] But this was out of a desire to win the war, not from any faith in Stalinism. Slowly, almost invisibly, Sinclair was changing sides. His days of apologizing for Soviet crimes were over. Having loyal readers in Russia no longer seemed enough. In 1948 he would support Truman against Henry Wallace, passing the acid test.

Sinclair demonstrated that a person's reaction to the Stalin-Hitler Pact was not a reliable guide to future conduct. Sinclair swallowed the pact, acquiring indigestion only later. This was by no means usual. But taking the more popular course of rejecting the pact and its consequences was an even poorer omen. Raymond Robins is a case in point. He had joined the Alaskan gold rush as a young man and had come out of the wilderness alone, with a small fortune acquired under mysterious circumstances. The rest of his active life was devoted to social reform and Christian evangelism. Robins was a leader in the settlement-house movement, as also of Theodore Roosevelt's Progressive Party. He was in Russia with the Red Cross when the October Revolution broke out. After the American ambassador left Moscow Robins became a semiofficial emissary between Washington and the Bolsheviks, to whom he became deeply attached. After the war Robins stayed a Republican. Yet he also worked for diplomatic recognition of the Soviet government. When it was achieved in 1933 he paid a triumphant last visit to Russia, where he got undeserved credit for a step President Roosevelt had taken on his own. Though Robins did not participate in great events again, his papers are instructive because of a personal misfortune. Several years after visiting the Soviets Robins fell from a tree on his Florida estate, breaking his back in two places. He was confined to a wheelchair after this, and mail became his lifeline. As a result Robins not only corresponded more than most people but, cut off from all his old friends, wrote more intimately.[39]

Robins managed to agree with Soviet foreign policy most of the time and even to accept the purges. When John Dewey investigated Trotsky, Robins tried to set him straight. Robins had met Trotsky and thought the great exile, out of egotism and bitterness, was urging dissidents to collaborate with Germany and Japan "for the overthrow of what he considers a traitorous Soviet Government." In any event, the main point was that

> the one effective barrier to the triumphant march of military imperialism over Europe and the Orient is Stalin and the Soviet Government. Trotsky and the Trotskyites weaken the Soviets and aid the Nazi and Fascist dictators. This threat to human freedom and democratic social control seems to me of vastly more consequence than the fortunes of Leon Trotsky.[40]

Soviet sympathizers were always saying that the guilt or innocence of purge victims did not really matter, but, as the terror dragged on, Robins, who was a Christian and knew some of the victims, revolted. In June 1939 he confided to his sister-in-law Mary Dreier, an old Progressive reformer like himself, that he had written to a former associate asking him if in light of the terror he might want to rethink his hostility to religion. As in Germany, the lack of it had led to "the *Stalin purge,* which was just as evil as the Hitler purge, and germinated from the same stem of a ruthless materialism and a denial of the sacredness of the human soul."[41]

Robins had doubts about Soviet foreign policy even before the pact. Stalin's appointment of Constantine Oumansky as ambassador to the United States was a bad sign. It meant that Stalin, having been rebuffed by Britain and France, "now will try isolation on his own."[42] This, Robins understood, would enable Hitler to invade Poland, resulting in war with Britain and France. Though Robins was correct, like most Soviet sympathizers he had difficulty clinging to hateful opinions, no matter how well founded. A month later he was writing to Mary Dreier that Prime Minister Neville Chamberlain of Great Britain was about to make a deal with the Axis powers, freeing them to attack Russia.[43] A month after this Robins was fearing the worst again. "But if Stalin plans a selfish isolation in this world struggle . . . and the establishment of a permanent semi-oriental despotism I would no longer be interested in the maintenance of the Stalin regime."[44] When the blow fell, though prepared for it to a degree, Robins was crushed. The pact and the war proved to him, he wrote Mary Dreier, that "THE HUMAN RACE IS NOT WORTH SAVING."[45] He acknowledged that the Soviets had their reasons. They were mistaken just the same. "Now they need to watch their step, for they are isolated in Europe and beset by Japan in Asia."[46] When Russia invaded Poland it meant the end, Robins told his sister-in-law, of "LENIN'S GREAT DREAM, AND THE SOVIETS WILL BECOME AN ORIENTAL IMPERIALISM—AND THE FAIREST HOPE IN OUR DAY OF THAT 'MORE ABUNDANT LIFE' FOR WHICH THE LORD CHRIST DIED SHALL BE DIMMED AND GO OUT IN A WAVE OF HUMAN BLOOD."[47]

But old habits died hard. On the twenty-second anniversary of the Bolshevik Revolution Robins celebrated. In a note to himself he said that he felt privileged to have been there for it, and to have witnessed later its results. "I have seen mechanized-industrialized COLLECTIVE AGRICULTURE vitalized by young 'Conquerors of the Fields' where for unnumbered generations there had been individual strip farming with primitive tools . . ."[48] Forgotten again were the millions of peasants shot or starved to death so that private farming might be abolished. Still, events could not be ignored. After Russia invaded Finland Robins told friends that Communism was finished as a world movement. Stalin resembled Hitler, and was equally wicked.[49] He urged his friend Claude Pepper, a U.S. senator from Florida, to work for maximum aid to "the fighting free men of Europe."[50] Robins apparently believed that the work of decades was over. Nevermore would he defend the Soviets or lend his name to Communist activities. If so, he was wrong. When the train of history drove by next time Robins would climb aboard.

Frederick L. Schuman was a different kind of Soviet sympathizer. Robins was the sentimental type like many Popular Fronters. It excited his heart to think of collective farms, Soviet nurseries and the glorious soul of Lenin. Schuman was his opposite. Though not, it seems, a Party member, he was a true Stalinist who worshiped at the altar of Soviet power. According to *Partisan Review,* which hated him, Schuman had fellow-traveled as early as 1932, when he belonged to the League of Professional Groups for Foster and Ford, the Communist Party slate. He denied this under oath in 1935, when the University of Chicago was investigated by a committee of the Illinois State Senate. Though found not to be subversive, he left Chicago, becoming Woodrow Wilson Professor of Government at Williams College, a small, aristocratic men's school in Massachusetts. In the Popular Front years he defended the Russian purges, attacked Trotsky as a renegade, and hailed Soviet democracy. Schuman always claimed to be a liberal, which did not mean much, since he regarded Stalinism and liberalism as compatible.[51]

Power politics was Schuman's religion, not only during the Stalin era but afterward. A student of his in the 1950s wrote that "the thing that most impressed me about Schuman was that despite his liberalism, he was an advocate of a tough power-politics approach to international diplomacy."[52] Armed with this advice, Jeb Stuart Magruder went forth to become a Nixon man, one of those who fell at Watergate. What Magruder did not understand about the Schuman version of liberalism was that its love of force was no anomaly but the key ingredient. Soft progressives such as Robins were unnerved at times by Stalin's ruthlessness. Schuman reveled in it. Accordingly, the Stalin-Hitler agreement delighted him. This was power politics of a high order, he wrote in the *New Republic.* First Stalin had cleansed Russia of fascist traitors, along with many innocents, admitted Schuman, which was too bad but didn't matter. Then when Britain and France refused to meet Stalin's terms for a collective-security agreement, he turned around and got them from Germany. "With Berlin's assent Moscow has now built the barriers against Berlin which Britain and France were unwilling to concede."[53] Cleverness could scarcely go further. Of course it was a dirty trick, but so what? "Power politics is beyond sentiment." If liberals could not see this they deserved to fall. Their task now was to study Machiavelli and prove to Stalin that they would make worthy allies.

This was too much realism even for the *New Republic*. The editors were not interested in establishing their bloody-mindedness to Stalin's satisfaction. They took issue with Schuman's cynical point of view. Morals did matter in politics, they insisted. "The leadership of a popular movement must, on pain of defeat, retain the confidence of the people. To act like Bismarck or Napoleon may bring nothing more than a Bismarckian or a Napoleonic success."[54] That was not the liberal way, they said, directing attention to Vincent Sheean's attack on the Soviets which they had printed earlier.[55] Actually, Sheean was overreacting, too, they added (remembering the Golden Mean), but in the right direction.

Schuman was not entirely without a moral sense. He wrote carelessly and often, making his ideas hard to pin down. In one mood he despised moralizers, in another he moralized. *Partisan Review* said that his conduct exhibited patterns "of ethical indifference one day and hortatory fervor the next, old dogmatic predictions quickly denied by history and replaced not by modesty but by new predictions."[56] So it was that after the invasion of Finland Schuman wrote *The New York Times* a letter repudiating Stalinism, though with no admission of having been a Stalinist. He also wrote to the *New Republic,* defending himself against the charge of cynicism made earlier. After worrying a bit about the limits of realism and the question of means and ends, Schuman confessed that Stalin's latest move was "an utterly indefensible criminal act that is at once politically stupid and morally monstrous." Power politics was no longer beyond sentiment. "The nausea and indignation which all liberals feel in the face of this outrage is [*sic*] completely justified. For the first time Moscow has deliberately and wantonly broken its own solemnly pledged word, and this without a shadow of justification, legal, ethical or political." Doing so was not Realpolitik, Schuman insisted, defending his taste for Machiavelli, but rather the lack of it. Stalin had "given way to a blind brutality, as devoid of political intelligence as of legal and moral scruples."[57] This raised for the first time, and possibly the last, a question in Schuman's mind as to whether Russia would make a trustworthy partner in the effort to build a world order founded on justice and law. To regain his confidence Russia was going to have to withdraw from Finland with apologies, and pay for the damage. In the end Schuman settled for less. Like Robins, he would embrace Stalin again when Russia was invaded.

At the war's low-water mark, when Britain alone was fighting fascism, Schuman exchanged letters with the neofascist intellectual Lawrence Dennis, whom *The Nation* described as a "champion of dictatorship." They were published in *The Nation* with a commentary by Max Lerner, and reveal the essential Schuman. The topic was a new book by Dennis, *The Dynamics of War and Revolution* (1940), which Schuman admired.

Let us grant, to use his [Spengler's] terminology, that "capitalism" and "democracy" are doomed by the rise of "Caesarism." The state form of tomorrow is "Caesarism" with all that this implies in social and economic terms. Caesarism means both "socialism"—that is, military totalitarianism resting on a dynamic faith and a will to action— and "internationalism"—that is, the end of national sovereignty in favor of a world state or a small number of world empires. Both are necessary for the survival of Western civilization in the age of its fulfillment and decline.[58]

Schuman complimented Dennis for recognizing the inevitability of this kind of socialism, while faulting him for not seeing that internationalism was equally certain to prevail. In Schuman's view the United States was going to either be conquered or become totalitarian and international, fighting to the death with the other "totalitarian imperialisms." Regrettably, New Dealers and liberals were failing to measure up. Perhaps the lead would pass to someone like Father Coughlin—a demagogic Catholic priest who was popular in the thirties. That would be unfortunate, Schuman wrote, not, he wanted to make clear, because he harbored anything resembling "moralistic or humanitarian scruples," but because Coughlin and the "new barbarians" lacked ability. Schuman was frustrated beyond measure that no one in America seemed to have the "realism or leadership" to do the job.

Max Lerner's response took the form of a letter to Schuman, whom he knew well, having also taught at Williams College. No doubt Lerner had often heard Schuman go on in this vein, as otherwise he would have been more indignant. Lerner was a sentimental leftist, spiritually akin to Raymond Robins, but with a lot more bounce. In the past Lerner had rationalized the crimes of Stalin, and he would do so again. But unlike Schuman he had to deceive himself before misleading others. Lerner was a democrat, as *The Nation* said, and his pro-Soviet enthusiasms were nourished by his odd belief that he and Stalin thought alike. Lerner disagreed with Schuman that socialism and fascism were similar. With Schuman he wanted plenty of American aid to Britain, but he asked how could people be expected to support this if told that the moral and ideological features of Nazism were unimportant? Similarly, if Caesarism is inevitable, why should people risk their lives fighting it? Declaring that Schuman shared his ends and values, a misconception he would entertain for years, Lerner urged the Woodrow Wilson Professor of Government to be more careful about means. Do not suppose, Lerner warned Schuman, that you and Dennis can be comrades because you both speak the language of Machiavelli, Marx and Spengler—though in fact this would seem to make a powerful bond. Lerner objected that Schuman seemed to be against right-wingers only because he could not depend on them to succeed. A better reason was the harm they would do to democracy and humanist culture. Finally, Lerner urged Schuman not to feel like an unheeded Cassandra. In the fight for a new and better world,

> we are, as thinkers, not alone. We have the people as allies. In Spain, in Czechoslovakia, in Poland, in Norway, in Holland, in England, they have shown knowledge of the meaning of the struggle and a desperate heroism waging it. They have been betrayed by the capitalists, the politicians, the generals, the diplomats. But in the face of all that they have not let us down.[59]

Here was the voice of the Popular Front again, proclaiming the unity of opposites. Spenglerian gloom and liberal cheer were to go forward together, held up by faith in the struggling masses. The voice of the past, to be sure, but of the future also.

The events of 1939–40 made many intellectuals eager to explain what had gone wrong, and sometimes even where they had gone wrong personally. Some resisted this temptation. *The Nation*, whose capacity for introspection was nonexistent, did not apologize for past errors. Except when nursing grudges it had almost no memory, the world being born anew in its pages every week. The *New Republic* was endowed with partial recall. Yes, it admitted under fire, there had been some resemblance between *New Republic* policy and that of the Comintern. This was unintentional. It was not the magazine that fellow-traveled but the "Communists [who] at that time adhered in large part to the *New Republic* line."[60]

Rewriting history did not satisfy everyone. Max Eastman produced a great book explaining what was wrong with Soviet Russia and why it had taken him so long to see it—though he had gotten off the train of history earlier than most.[61] Granville Hicks, distinguished while a Communist by his honesty, was equally candid after leaving the Party. In a brilliant essay he laid out the reasons why intellectuals like himself were attracted to Communism. "We were a good lot, but rather stupid," Hicks confessed, having shown that there was much more to it than this.[62] Roger Baldwin, an ardent Popular Fronter, admitted nothing beyond defeat. "Though the record of the united front and the liberals in the face of the superior forces of fascism and war has been one of universal failure, the method has proved sound in principle as the only practicable means of uniting popular forces with any chance at all of overcoming reaction." Baldwin did not explain how a method that failed in practice could still have proven itself sound in principle. Instead he wrote that the lesson to be learned was that Popular Front organizations must be officered by liberals. Though not mentioning it, Baldwin had already acted on this belief by purging his American Civil Liberties Union of Communists. Suspicion of totalitarians was vital, Baldwin continued, but "the fight for unity takes first place."[63]

Malcolm Cowley agreed. On no point were liberals more sharply divided than over the need for unity. In theory everyone favored it. The real question was how much should be sacrificed for unity's sake. This was the heart of the long struggle over relations with Soviet Russia. Except for hardened fellow travelers, pro-Soviet intellectuals did not deny entirely Stalin's crimes. They knew that he was brutal and that there were no civil liberties or political freedoms in Russia, or at least not enough. But before the pact, and after Russia was invaded, many would argue that liberals had to accept Soviet imperfections for the sake of joint action against common enemies. Even during the pact era hopes for unity survived, at least among non-Communists. Thus, Malcolm Cowley wrote to Felix Frankfurter in 1940 on the familiar theme. Liberals and progressives had been defeated everywhere in the world save England, he wrote.

> In part their defeat was due to their tragic inability to agree among themselves. I have lately been working on a book about the history of the American intellectuals during the last ten years, and one of the points that impresses me most as I go over the story is the amount of bickering among them and how it weakened all parties and opinions and factions. Unfortunately a catastrophe does not seem to have drawn the liberals any closer together, except in England where they are faced by immediate danger.[64]

If the intellectuals could not get together, Cowley said, they would "play a very small part in the building of a new world." There was something to this, as also to the anti-Stalinist view that no unity worth having could be gained by pushing aside the truth. Even after the pact, it was still not clear which way intellectuals would finally go.

Some intellectuals saw the problem in more cosmic terms, adopting grand, Schumanic overviews of the human condition. This was the way of Lewis Mumford and Archibald MacLeish, who provoked a long murky debate on the sins of liberalism and modern civilization that ground on until America entered the war. At the age of forty-five Lewis Mumford was already a noted architectural critic, urbanist, and historian of culture. An absolute pacifist in 1935, he had come to favor American intervention in the war and was disgusted with liberalism for dragging its feet.[65] In the *New Republic*—and in his book *Faith for the Living* (1940)—he denounced intellectuals and liberals and all their works. They had sold out to Stalin earlier, now they were betraying civilization in the name of peace. It all went back to the eighteenth century, when the false god of "pragmatic liberalism" raised its head. Mumford favored "ideal liberalism," a robust ethic unintimidated by science, uncorrupted by materialism, unafraid to fight. Ideal liberals like himself saw that isolationism was a sign of the growing rottenness and barbarism of pragmatic liberals.[66]

Archibald MacLeish, poet and Librarian of Congress, thought so, too, adding that the Ph.D. thesis symbolized, and possibly even caused, this moral and intellectual decline. "It is work done for the sake of doing work—perfectly conscientious, perfectly laborious, perfectly irresponsible."[67] He too wrote a book embellishing this theme—*A Time to Speak* (1940)—which became known as the Mumford-MacLeish thesis. Waldo Frank took the same line in the same way. His *New Republic* article, and his book *Chart for Rough Water* (1940), decried American materialism, liberal corruption, "empirical rationalism," lifelessness, godlessness and isolation.[68]

Attacks this sweeping and shapeless were hard to refute. The *New Republic* did not shirk its duty even so. Lewis Mumford was all wrong about their values, which were admirable, the editors complained. Mumford was acting like a sorehead because so few liberals were interventionists. He did not understand the situation. "It is not a mark of barren isolationism to believe with all one's heart and soul that the best contribution Americans can make to the future of humanity is to fulfill democracy in the United States."[69] Malcolm Cowley was offended also. In reviewing Mumford's book he accused it of expressing a humane form of fascism, to which Mumford naturally took exception. It required three letters for Cowley to make himself clear. What he had meant to say, Cowley finally managed to get out, was that while Mumford was not a fascist, he had something in common with Catholic fascists "who think that the world has to be reordered and regenerated, that we have lost the tragic sense of life, that society must become organic, that 'ideal liberalism' is fine, but historical liberalism has got to be attacked and destroyed."[70] MacLeish was off base as well, and never more so than when calling on intellectuals to assert leadership. They had been beaten, perhaps for a generation. According to Cowley, MacLeish was in the position of a football coach who at half time, with the score forty to nothing against them, tells the players "they can still win the game if they go out on the field and fight. The team knows better."[71]

It seemed to Edmund Wilson that in blaming writers for the present mood of defeatism MacLeish was calling for censorship, or at least self-censorship. In a talk before the American Association for Adult Education MacLeish appeared to say that writers should not question desirable propaganda, even if it was wrong. Wilson feared that MacLeish, who was a government official, had a darker purpose in mind. Was he not, Wilson speculated, preparing the way for a new set of official moral purposes, as in the last war? It was discouraging to hear the Librarian of Congress speak of "dangerous books."[72]

New Republic editors Bliven and Soule were inspired by this confused debate to moralize again. Part of the heat in these exchanges, they wrote, arose from the generation gap. While the faculty of Eastern colleges and universities had already declared war on Hitler, students, judging by recent petitions, were lukewarm about aid to the Allies and opposed to American intervention. The professors were thinking "in moral terms, sometimes at the expense of practical considerations." The students, contrarily, avoided moral issues and seemed to distrust words in general. Though disagreeing with the professors over intervention, the *New Republic* felt they had the right attitude. Students were failing to see that "moral issues have become more important to national defense than armies or navies." Mumford-MacLeish did have one valid point. Some writers had erred by treating war and peace cynically, "reducing everything to propaganda and back-stage maneuvers . . ." "If this magazine has sometimes published writing of this type," the editors said in a rare mood of contrition, "which we have tried to avoid doing, we hereby do penance for our sins."[73] The task now, the magazine declared more typically, is to open our eyes and see the world as it is.

This did not solve the problem, which was that liberals could not agree on what, once their eyes were opened, people were supposed to see. Many felt that the Mumford-MacLeish indictment of liberalism was wrong, or at least too extreme.[74] The editor of a group of postmortems and prophecies that appeared in 1941 was representative. Yes, he wrote, the present crisis owed something to intellectual unpreparedness. "Futilitarian"

intellectuals had, as Mumford-MacLeish said, done considerable harm. Ignoring all evidence to the contrary, he then explained that "it is to the liberals that people everywhere are
turning in this crisis for leadership and guidance."[75] In the
same volume Malcolm Cowley suggested that maybe what liberals needed to become more effective was a new faith rivaling
the false teachings of fascism and Communism. Possibly the
"religion of humanity that has for a long time been developing
in the West" would do. If the better postwar society everyone
wanted "is to be a planned society, then its religion will also
have to be planned, no less carefully than its economic system
or its governmental structure."[76] Lewis Corey, an economist
and former Marxist, took a more usual line. Marxism was a
rational set of ideas that merely happened to be in error. The
challenge was to develop a new system of checks and balances
combining rational planning with democratic controls. It was
still possible to have a "world of greater democracy, welfare,
and peace."[77]

Max Lerner never tired of sounding this note. Mumford-
MacLeish were wrong to say, he announced in a characteristic
piece, that "our moral faculties have atrophied because we have
been worshipping the false gods of materialism and creature
comforts." The failure, rather, was "the effect of our social will
and organization." The solution was to press on again, but more
resolutely. "For myself I see no way of our surviving the harsh
age except by further collective social effort—more dynamic
than before, more sophisticated, determined to promise less and
fulfill more."[78] Lerner held that in spite of undemocratic excesses, "the core" of Marxism remained useful. This theoretical
taste was not evident in his own writings, where sociohistorical
analysis was always giving way to uplift. He was liberalism's
cheerleader, also its evangelist. For years he played this role in
the *New Republic,* where he always seemed out of place.

The main division for intellectuals, as for Americans generally, was not over morals but over foreign policy. Communists
and fellow travelers did not figure in this debate. They were
estranged from their progressive allies by the new Comintern
line. When the Communist-backed American Peace Mobilization was formed in Chicago on September 2, 1940, only hardened fellow travelers—Vito Marcantonio, Paul Robeson, Joe

Curran of the National Maritime Union, Carl Sandburg, Richard Wright, Theodore Dreiser—would lend their names to it. The Communist brand of left-wing isolationism gave rise to a curious journalism, and not only in the Party press. An example was the newsletter *In Fact*. It was established by a free-lance journalist named George Seldes. He had become a newsman at the age of nineteen and, according to his memoirs, was shocked to discover the immorality of newspaper owners. Seldes developed a hysterical need to expose their partisanship and lack of ethics, which, as it happened, he shared, differing from William Randolph Hearst only in point of view and effectiveness. Though he visited Russia during the 1920s, Seldes claimed not to have become political until the Spanish Civil War. He revered the Loyalists and was abjectly grateful to Russia for supporting them. When Russia invaded Finland he was stung into action by, as he saw it, the false and one-sided newspaper treatment of Soviet affairs. He established *In Fact* to remedy this defect with false and one-sided reporting of his own. Starting with six thousand subscribers in 1940, *In Fact* rose to a peak circulation of 176,000 in 1947—making it the most widely read left publication.

Seldes opposed the presidential campaign of Wendell Willkie in 1940, offering readers this exclusive information: "*In Fact* believes the reason the big press is for Willkie is because big business is for Willkie: *In Fact* calls attention of its readers to the fact that almost all the big advertisers are pro-Willkie."[79] *In Fact* observed the Popular Front custom of referring to its political enemies, who were legion, as fascists. Resisting labor unions was fascistic, as was racial prejudice. President Roosevelt was very nearly a fascist for scheming to enter the war. "No ruler can take a nation into war unless he breaks a militant propeace labor movement," wrote Seldes, revealing a nonexistent presidential conspiracy to destroy the CIO.[80] William Allen White's Committee to Defend America by Aiding the Allies was fascist, as was *The Saturday Evening Post*. Ambassador Joseph P. Kennedy would have been a fascist, but was redeemed by his isolationism. Kennedy had warned President Roosevelt, Seldes reported, that England was going fascist.[81] In May 1941 Seldes ran the following headline, capturing several obsessions at

once: "Hess Peace Flight to Hitlerite Duke of Hamilton Over-
shadows US Plan to Enter War in a Few Weeks."[82] In June,
six months ahead of time, Seldes announced that the United
States was now at war. "We are at the beginning of a dictatorship which . . . may prove as terroristic as that practiced by the
nations we are fighting."[83]

Seldes' lack of restraint was typical of the Communist-led
"peace movement." In 1941 the Almanac Singers, left-wing
folk artists of whom the best known were Woody Guthrie and
Pete Seeger, released an album called *Songs for John Doe*, in
which antiwar lyrics were imposed on familiar tunes. One was
called "Plow Under."* In it the artists claimed that the government meant to have American boys slaughtered, as hogs had
been during the New Deal.[84]

President Roosevelt did not take an agricultural view of
human life as this song asserts. It was the weakness of their
policy that drove Communists and fellow travelers to such
lengths. They had attacked appeasement before the pact with
considerable success. Now they were obliged to practice it, ignoring fascism and abusing democratic leaders they had formerly endorsed. It was a strategy that won them few friends.

High feelings kept many intellectuals from thinking clearly.
Mumford-MacLeish were terrified that American aid to Britain
would be too little and too late—as almost happened. Blinded
by passion, Mumford-MacLeish could not see that something
besides moral decay kept Americans from reacting quickly to
Europe's need. This led them into denunciations of liberalism,
the intellectuals as a class, and modern culture generally, which
missed the point. The real reasons for Americans' slow response
to the crisis were historical. American entry into the First World
War had produced few of the benefits claimed for it. It did not
make the world safe for democracy, end all wars or free all
peoples. More than that, American entry made things worse.
It prolonged the war, weakening Russia and allowing the Bol-

---

* These songs were to haunt the Almanac Singers, not only after
American entry into the war—which by then they favored along with
the rest of the old Popular Front—but afterward too. Both they and
their successor group, the Weavers, would be mercilessly red-baited.

sheviks to take power. Intervention resulted not in the peace without victory Wilson once called for, but in a victorious peace that embittered Germany and paved the way for Hitler.

After the armistice many came to feel, and with reason, that Americans had died in vain. Pacifist propaganda between the wars was often fatuous. Yet it was actual experience, not brainwashing, that made Americans wary. Most Americans, as polls showed, favored neutrality. In this they were mistaken. Nineteen forty was not 1916. Hitler was not the Kaiser. Dead ideas ruled the living until dangerously late. Even so, name-calling did no good. Intellectuals, still less the American people, were not going to war because Mumford-MacLeish thought them cowardly and immoral. But events were educating them, as also, strangely enough, the progressive weeklies.

With the advantage of hindsight we know that America should have entered the conflict, if not in 1939, surely in 1940. But this course, so evident to Mumford-MacLeish, was impossible. Public opinion was not ready for it, neither were progressive journalists. Thirties radicalism had combined a sterile antifascism with intense suspicion of Britain and France. For some time after war began the one canceled out the other. Hitler must be stopped by the Allies, progressives held, but without treacherously drawing innocent Americans into the quagmire. Germany's invasion of Norway shook the *New Republic* without weakening its resolve. There was no point to American intervention, as nothing more could be done for the Allies than was already being done. Anyway, it was more important to press for reforms at home. "If we can prove to the world and ourselves that we mean business about democracy, we need have no fear that we cannot defend it against external enemies. The chances are that in that case we shall not need to."[85]

Why progressives thought that social reforms would defend them against Hitler remains a mystery. It was an article of faith just the same, frequently invoked to bolster morale after German victories. The *New Republic* cited it again when Norway fell, though also calling for stronger coastal defenses.[86] When France surrendered, the editors confessed that they had shared the false popular view that the Allies would defeat Hitler. But having been wrong was no reason to alter policy. Aid to Britain must increase, they wrote, forgetting earlier claims that this couldn't be done; otherwise things should go on as before. They kept on sniping at Allied leadership, blaming the ruling classes of Western Europe for being backward and incompetent, while at the same time demanding that they stop Germany. When a conscription bill was introduced the editors protested, standing by their belief that an army of half a million was all America needed to protect itself. And they kept insisting that anything more than a defensive force would lessen aid to Britain. But they soon had to admit that this position was obsolete. "It is with heavy hearts that the editors of the *New Republic* endorse the principle of compulsory service at this time. . . . For many years they have fought militarism in every form."[87] But defense now had to come before progressive scruples. In the same mood they endorsed Franklin Roosevelt for President. The *New Republic* always criticized Roosevelt, and always concluded that there was no better choice for President. After his reelection the editors wrote that despite his defects, and the fact that the Republican candidate, Willkie, was not so bad, Roosevelt's defeat would have been taken as a sign that the American people were endorsing appeasement. And it would have restored to power the very business and commercial interests whose opposite numbers had misled Britain and France.[88]

The worse things got, the better Britain looked to *New Republic* editors. By the start of 1941 they were saying it was time to put aside suspicion of Britain, though no one had been more suspicious than they.[89] The *New Republic* printed more and longer articles, spelling out in detail the strengths of Germany, the needs of Britain, the challenge facing America.[90] When the Lend-Lease bill was passed the editors had to admit that it brought the country a step closer to war. But readers need not worry. When America intervened it wouldn't be because of "secret machinations of bankers, foreign propagandists or domestic dictators."[91] The people themselves would decide, they affirmed, ignoring the fact that America never had gone and never would go to war as the result of a popular vote. By May the *New Republic* was urging that belligerent steps be taken. It called for more active naval patrols, armed convoying all the way to Britain, and the acquisition of foreign bases. Forgotten was the old belief in coastal defenses, a short-range navy, and a small professional army. "Either we should do nothing, which is to say that we should accept Nazi domination of the world, or we should do everything."[92] The *New Republic* was tired of carping from the sidelines, tired also of complaints that Britain was not a fit ally. Since Poland fell, though the editors had not noticed this at the time, "it has been the will of the people of England, not the self-interest of the few ignoble and selfish men who remain in power, that has turned every defeat into victory."[93]

There is no way of telling when the editors came to favor intervention, as they felt constrained all along by public opinion. Even after Germany and Russia went to war they hesitated. In July they said again that the people would not accept a declaration of war. The effort to get one, even if successful, would leave the country divided. But the people had shown they would accept the President's policy of easing into the conflict by degrees. This was clearly the right strategy.[94] A month later they changed their minds. Public opinion was moving too slowly and events too fast. The *New Republic* abandoned its claim that the United States would enter the war democratically and arrived at a new theory. It was now the President's duty to mold public opinion by declaring war on the Axis. This would still be a democratic act because if the public disapproved it could retaliate at the polls in 1944.[95] On this slippery basis they stated publicly what they had felt privately for some time, it would appear. Aid to Britain, and even Russia, was not enough. The country must go to war. The *New Republic* had done everything a responsible journal could do. In trying to firm up liberal opinion behind intervention it had offered a thousand facts and figures. The editors had worked for many months to show, on the basis of hard evidence, that isolation wouldn't work. The magazine failed in the sense that American entry was not brought about through force of logic. But it failed in the right way, some tricky reasoning excepted, having tried hard to enlighten and inform. Freed by Russian neutrality from the need to dissemble and evade, the *New Republic* wrote a bright page in the history of progressive journalism.

So also did *The Nation,* and in much the same way. The

difference, as always, was mainly one of style. *The Nation* was less self-important than its rival, and less substantial too. Lighter in weight, it moved faster. Freda Kirchwey endorsed conscription months before the *New Republic* and was more eager to see Roosevelt reelected.[96] This led Villard to end an association of forty-six years with an angry letter to Kirchwey and a final column. He predicted that someday the editors would see that the policies they supported would lead to "dictatorship and turn us into a totalitarian state."[97] America was to be saved not through armaments but by making democracy work. Villard was defending appeasement, Kirchwey replied in the same issue, a doctrine more dangerous than fascism.[98] This was brave of Kirchwey, as Villard had many admirers who sent in an "avalanche" of canceled subscriptions.[99] Kirchwey didn't care. The lost subscriptions were soon replaced. Villard's later course would have forced the break, anyway. He joined the America First Committee, an isolationist united front that included conservatives like Henry Ford and Charles Lindbergh, liberals such as Chester Bowles, and even the Socialist leader Norman Thomas. Just before the presidential election of 1940 Villard wrote in *The New York Times* that he supported the Republican ticket. If Willkie's election meant a period of reaction at home, so be it. "I am not sure whether today there can be that reaction, but if it came it would be a small price to pay for peace and efficient, clean-cut administration."[100]

For a time *The Nation* favored Roosevelt's policy of backing England and antagonizing Germany. When Hitler failed to take the bait *The Nation* grew impatient. In May 1941, though Americans as a whole still preferred neutrality, *The Nation* called for war. Its basic war aims, published when Russian entry was still a dream, were simple. Hitler must be defeated by force of arms. The democratic social revolution must go forward. Indeed, according to Freda Kirchwey, these constituted a single goal, for "Hitler can only be defeated by revolution."[101]

The progressive weeklies had done all they could to aid Britain and prepare Americans for war. And they had done so for the most part honorably. But in changing their minds about the war they retained old assumptions. In the thirties they had opposed war because it threatened the revolutionary movements to which they were committed. When they embraced war it was for the sake of these same causes. Predictably, when Russia came in the progressive weeklies would see it once again as an ally in this struggle. The Popular Front, with all its fatal delusions, would be reborn in a sense. And the progressive weeklies would revert to type, sacrificing honesty once more upon the altar of hope.

II

The "People's War" Begins: 1941–1943

THINGS DID NOT GO WELL for the Communist Party after war broke out, and particularly after the Soviet invasion of Finland, which outraged almost everyone. A Gallup poll found that among Americans having an opinion on it, ninety-nine percent favored Finland.[1] Though some Communists preferred the new ultrasectarian line as being more revolutionary, the Party suffered otherwise. In 1938 it had recruited four thousand members a month. After the Stalin-Hitler Pact fewer than one thousand a month signed up. In January 1940 Party Chairman Earl Browder was sentenced to four years in prison on charges of passport fraud. Anti-Communism, not justice, was responsible for this. In March, Communist leaders of the Fur Workers Union were indicted on antitrust charges. An officer of the Communist-led National Maritime Union was arrested for libel. Party members suffered in numerous other ways.[2]

No doubt a witch-hunt would have followed had Russia not been attacked. When the invasion began, the Communist "peace" movement was holding a continuous vigil at the White House. On June 21 the call had gone out for a national "Peace Week." The next day Germany invaded Russia. No more was heard of Peace Week. The White House pickets melted away. Communists discovered the imperialist war to be actually a struggle against fascism. No one now exceeded them in support of national defense. Communist-led unions stopped going on strike. John L. Lewis, whom Communists had applauded for acting like a labor leader after the war began instead of making emergency compromises, fell from grace. In 1943 Browder would accuse him of belonging to the Nazi-led Fifth Column.

Not only did Communists bar strikes, they endorsed incentive pay and piecework, which earlier they had rejected as speed-up devices. Many progressives took a sardonic view of this turnabout, especially at first. When the Communists supported aid to Britain, *New Republic* editors warned them off. It was hard enough to persuade conservatives of Britain's need without Communist endorsements "such as not even a mother could love."[3]

The main victim of the stillborn red scare of 1940–41 was the Trotskyist Socialist Workers Party. It was very small compared to the Communist Party, but had a strong labor base in Minneapolis, where Troskyists had become prominent in Local 544 of the Teamsters Union. This annoyed Daniel J. Tobin, head of the Teamsters, and in the spring of 1941 he attempted to take personal control of the local by appointing a receiver with absolute power over its four thousand members. Local 544 voted to leave the Teamsters and affiliate with the CIO. Tobin, an important Roosevelt backer, then appealed to the White House. In a matter of weeks United States marshals raided Socialist Workers Party headquarters in Minneapolis. Twenty-nine Trotskyist leaders of Local 544 were arrested and charged under a seditious-conspiracy statute that had been enacted in 1861, and also under Title I of the Smith Act, a repressive law whose passage the year before had gone largely unnoticed. Eighteen of the Trotskyists were found guilty and sentenced to prison on December 8, 1941. Twelve were given sixteen months in prison, six got a year and a day. These were considered light sentences inasmuch as the charge involved conspiring to overthrow the government. Perhaps someone in power had a guilty conscience. It was clear that the convicted men's real offense had been to challenge Daniel Tobin. Attorney General Francis Biddle denied in his memoirs that Roosevelt had instructed him to do Tobin a favor. Biddle insisted that his real aim had been to test the constitutionality of the Smith Act, hoping the courts would nullify it.[4]

A Civil Rights Defense Committee was formed, with James T. Farrell as chairman, to overturn the convictions. Though Farrell was a Trotsky sympathizer, most committee members were not. John Dewey was a vice-chairman, as was the anarchist Carlo Tresca. Sponsors included John Chamberlain, Waldo

Frank, Clement Greenberg, Margaret Marshall of *The Nation,* Professor F. O. Matthiessen, Mary McCarthy, Edmund Wilson and other prominent intellectuals. The committee had thirty active locals and raised $50,000. The ACLU filed an amicus curiae brief in support of the committee's appeal. The Trotskyists went to jail anyway. The Smith Act survived—to Biddle's dismay, it seems; though hundreds of cases were subsequently referred to him, Biddle authorized only one more wartime sedition trial.

The significance of this affair was unclear at the time. The Trotskyists had few supporters. Most outside the SWP who helped them were civil libertarians rather than admirers. Liberals as a group displayed little interest in the case. The Communist Party welcomed it. Stalinists were among those who testified in court as to the SWP's subversive nature. The Party press repeatedly endorsed the prosecution.[5] As usual, Communists were not thinking ahead. They hated the Trotskyists, and never more so than during World War II, as the Trotskyists stood aloof from it. But the key fact was not that their enemies were being punished, but that the Smith Act was holding up. One day it would be used against themselves. Joseph Starobin, who was for many years a Communist, wrote later of the Trotskyist case that "the failure to make civil liberties a principle, the failure to abide by principled behavior, cost the Communists dearly." John Gates, another Party worker, agreed. In the McCarthy era, he came to believe, "we reaped the harvest of the seeds we ourselves had sown."[6]

The invasion of Russia changed everything, though not at once. British intelligence knew it was coming, and Churchill was on the radio within hours expressing sympathy and promising aid to Russia. This helped crystallize American opinion. Most American newspapers followed his lead, even though as a practical matter neither England nor the United States had anything much to send. A Gallup poll in July 1941 found that seventy-two percent wanted a Russian victory, while only four percent favored Germany.[7] Even so, memories of Stalin's treachery were not at once erased. The *New Republic* had struggled to remain neutral about Russia in 1940. It attacked the anti-Stalinist intellectuals, calling them the "I-told-you-so gang" and the "Monomania Squad." Anti-Stalinists were still falsely equating Nazism with Communism. They cared nothing about reform. "In the fights on the home front for civil liberties, for helping the underprivileged here, for wise domestic policies in many fields, they are conspicuous by their absence."[8] But as Stalin drifted closer to Hitler the *New Republic* changed its mind. In May 1941, without giving them credit, it decided that the anti-Stalinists were right, Communism was Nazism. Stalin's cooperation with Hitler showed the value of the "liberal philosophy of instrumentalism," which held that "a body of doctrine is to be judged not so much by its absolutes as by its outcome, and that the choice of means often determines the end, rather than vice-versa." Thus, despite differences in ideology, the Communist and Nazi movements were as "alike as two peas in their means—the technique of disciplined conspiracy, the one-party state, the complete contempt for anything that stands in their way, the primacy of power, the acceptance of all evil so long as it may be used, as they think, for a good end."[9] This made them natural allies.

When Germany invaded Russia the *New Republic*'s first instinct was to remember the lesson so painfully learned. It agreed with Churchill that everything possible should be given Russia to keep her in the war. Even so, the chickens had come home to roost. "The Soviet Union under Stalin has sacrificed one by one practically all the principles which made the Russian revolution twenty-four years ago flame like a glorious hope across the heavens for millions of suffering people."[10] This mood did not last. It was only weeks before Max Lerner was discovering virtues in Russia again. True, Stalin had behaved badly and, in a sense, deserved what was coming to him. But the United States could not afford the luxury of a Soviet defeat. Anyway, the war had changed things. "For now that Russia has been drawn into the war on England's side, even if she survives she will be a responsible partner in a common peace."[11] This non sequitur was typical. There was no necessary connection between entering the war and becoming responsible afterward. Lerner was always tacking a hope onto a fact, as if the one determined the other. His real reason for believing that Russia would behave well in the future was the same one he always had, and owed nothing to recent events. Despite perversions, he continued, the Soviet system was better than Germany's because it was rooted in the "humanist and life-affirming doctrines of mass progress and human worth, the Marxian conviction that men can build a world through rational effort, that by transforming their social universe they can transform themselves."[12] So much for the instrumentalist belief that a doctrine is to be judged by its outcome.

Lerner was followed the next week by Samuel Grafton, a columnist for the *New York Post,* whose thinking was even more confused. Why is it, he asked, that we are so afraid of Russia? If readers imagined that fear of Russia had something to do with Soviet actions they were mistaken. "Our fear of the Russian ideology is linked with our own disastrous failure to solve our own employment problem. This may translate itself into the second failure of inadequate assistance to the Soviet Union. We are not free to act because we are frightened."[13] On the face of it this made no sense. Americans did not fear Russia because of unemployment. The "Russian ideology," as Grafton called it, alarmed people because murderous acts were committed for its sake. The *New Republic* had been clear enough about this before June 22. Now the vision was fading. The magazine seemed unable to promote a Russian-American alliance on its merits. Instead of arguing that Russia and the United States had a common interest in defeating Germany, the *New Republic* was soon at work proving that Russia was not only useful but admirable as well.

Bruce Bliven addressed the question of why Russian morale was higher than America's. It went back to the depression, he explained, when relief and assistance were given out so grudgingly. Recovery efforts did not give enough people a stake in the country. The free-enterprise system made Americans materialistic and callous to the sufferings of others, qualities unknown in Russia, he appeared to think. Then too, the schools had failed to promote democracy. Americans, unlike Russians, did not know what they stood for.[14] Bliven's curious belief that Soviet citizens were fighting well for political reasons owed nothing to the facts. Nor did his equally strange beliefs about American morale and the national character. Habit was reclaiming the

New Republic. For years it had enjoyed comparing Russian virtues to American faults, on the theory, seemingly, that doing so promoted reform. Russian entry into the war, though forced, allowed the editors to resume congenial old ways.

In November 1941 the *New Republic* ran a special section, "Russia Today," which established that it had learned nothing from history. Roger Baldwin took up, for perhaps the last time, his old work of whitewashing Soviet denials of human rights. In the narrowest sense, he admitted, there were no civil liberties in Russia. But if we took a more spacious view we saw in Russia industrial democracy, freedom from racial discrimination, equality, and respect for the rights of national minorities. There was no political democracy, but "the evidence over many years reveals a form of industrial democracy which gives fairly free play to critical faculties . . ." The same evidence allowed Baldwin to claim that the "Soviet citizen thus has apparently a substantial voice in correcting immediate grievances on his job." And, though the people could not challenge basic policies, a "Russian citizen has at his disposal nearly as much objective foreign information as an American." Domestic news was heavily censored. Still, there was no racial or cultural discrimination and Soviet women were equal to men, not only in theory but in practice. Baldwin admitted that he had been wrong thirteen years before in *Liberty Under the Soviets* when he predicted growth toward democracy. That had been canceled by the purges. But with war came opportunity. "If the forces represented by our imperfect democracies survive, the Soviet Union, whatever its immediate fate in the war, seems likely to follow more closely the pattern of the western world to which it is in part committed by its own tentative professions of belief."[15]

In Baldwin's defense it must be remembered that he had not been to the Soviet Union in many years and was speaking from ignorance. John Scott, an American who had lived in Russia during the terror, lacked this excuse. He set out to defend Stalin anyway. The purges had been necessary because many top officials were against Stalin's plan to create a new industrial base in the Urals and Siberia. Had they prevailed, Russia would not now have a protected base from which to supply the Red Army. Thanks to the purges also there was no internal fifth column in

Russia to collaborate with the Nazis, as happened elsewhere. "It is likewise clear that the effectiveness of Stalin's administrative machine, regardless of its failings, has been an important factor in making possible Russia's heroic defense."[16] All this was as fantastic as Baldwin's discovery of equality and industrial democracy in the Soviet Union.

Fellow travelers would repeat these assertions time and again. Soviet military achievements would excuse everything Stalin had done. The purges would be said to have strengthened Russia, though actually they had weakened it and nearly destroyed the Red Army. Millions of Soviet citizens did in fact welcome the Germans at first, resisting only when it became clear that Hitler's rule might be worse even than Stalin's. Soviet apologists paid no mind to these inconvenient truths. Stalin's highest crimes and greatest blunders would henceforth be invoked to justify cooperation with Russia.

Nobody was better at turning political water into wine than Max Lerner. His assignment in "Russia Today" was to show how being invaded disproved what everyone knew to be true about Russia. First, it gave the lie to the slander, expressed by the *New Republic* only months before, that there was no essential difference between the two totalitarian systems. If this were the case, he asserted, Germany would not have attacked, the Russians would not have fought so well, and the *New Republic* would not now be endorsing aid to Russia. Soviet resistance proved that a socialist state could be strong in military and administrative terms, "fit for survival in a harsh world," he said, as if anybody doubted this. It also showed the ability of people to "break through political forms even when those political forms are unfavorable and oppressive." The Russians were able to do so because they "have been given a sense of participation in a process of social and economic reconstruction. The great reason why the Russian people are fighting as they are is that they are fighting in defense of something they believe they themselves have had a hand in building, and something that they believe belongs to them."[17] In other words, the Soviet system gave people strength to break through the Soviet system, the worst thing in Russia giving rise to the best. If true, this would have been the most remarkable of Stalin's achievements.

The Nation also reverted, though more slowly. By October Freda Kirchwey was remarking favorably on the "release of revolutionary spirit and energy that followed the invasion of Russia," in defiance of the facts, which were that Stalin was playing down ideology and promoting nationalism.[18] With a logic worthy of the *New Republic* the editors explained why aid to Russia should not be made conditional on reforms. "Those who refuse now to help Russia because they fear its communism and irreligion are quite certainly the enemies of both religion and freedom. Because Russia needs our help, the American plea for greater religious toleration and a greater measure of democracy within Russia is likely to be listened to."[19] The truth was that placing conditions on aid simply would not work. Either the Soviets would reject the aid or, more probably, they would accept it and ignore the conditions. *The Nation,* like the *New Republic,* avoided this line of thought because it did not square with their dream of Russia as a state capable of enacting reforms voluntarily out of gratitude. Readers who could swallow such a fantasy would not balk at naked propaganda, which *The Nation* gave them as well. According to Anna Louise Strong, there was no religious problem in Russia to worry about. "Today Young Communists are not allowed even to scoff at their parents' religion . . ."[20] To *The Nation* Russia was alternately revolutionary and liberal—or sometimes both at once—as the need of the moment required.

Thus, even before America went to war, the failure of progressive journalism was assured. *The Nation* and the *New Republic* decided to be disingenuous about Russia. Apart from token regrets over the lack of political freedom, both magazines would behave for years as if willing Russia to be better made it so. Later some progressives would claim that they had misled others about Russia because they had been mistaken themselves. This is not much of a defense. During the Stalin-Hitler Pact era *The Nation* and the *New Republic* had written honestly about the Soviet Union. Like everyone else the editors failed to realize the extent of Stalin's crimes. But they understood the Soviet system well enough. When Russia was invaded, progressive journalists put this knowledge aside. No summit meeting appears to have been held at which they voted to apply a coat of whitewash. None was needed. The moral and intellectual corruption of the thirties was deeply rooted. It needed only a Russia at war to flourish once again, more extravagantly than before.

When America took up arms, the *New Republic* was not what it had been in 1917, or even 1937. Malcolm Cowley still wrote for it but was no longer in charge of the book section and no longer deeply political.* In 1942 Alfred Kazin, then an unknown young writer and critic, went to work for the *New Republic*. It was his lack of distinction at the time that commended him, Kazin was later to write. The magazine was only a shadow of its former self, having been reduced to about thirty thousand subscribers. The famous names on its masthead were seldom seen. "The magazine was left entirely to Bliven, who dominated but showed no joy. He felt inferior to the *New Republic* tradition."[22] This was the view of litterateurs envious of *Partisan Review*. Politically the *New Republic* was far from dead. It still had influence and the old pretensions. And, thanks to the war, its period of greatest growth lay just ahead.

Bliven and Soule, like Croly, Lippmann and Weyl before them, were determined to make war justify their support of it. To this end Soule wrote a long essay, "The Lessons of Last Time." He sought by reviewing the past thirty years to determine what progressives should stand for now. Two great mistakes had been made, he thought. A peace had been imposed on Germany that was too harsh to last and too mild to prevent Germany from rising up again. The second failure had been for Europe to continue operating a world system based on power politics and colonialism. These errors caused the present war. Soule believed, echoing Freda Kirchwey, that this war differed from the last in being revolutionary. The old order was doomed whatever happened. The challenge, accordingly, was not just to defeat the enemy, but at the same time to build "a democratic, rationally managed, fully productive world order, without which

* Cowley had left the *New Republic* just before Pearl Harbor to work for Archibald MacLeish at the Office of Facts and Figures, a new war propaganda agency, later absorbed by the Office of War Information. But his years of fellow traveling made government service impossible. Congressmen attacked him so fiercely that he was obliged to resign. This marked the end of Cowley's active political life.[21]

the military struggle cannot result in victory, and without which the fruits of victory cannot be realized."[23]

The Soviet Union was, he admitted, a threat to this new world. Soule did not expect Marxists to give up their ambitions, whatever they said during the war. "But we can render them powerless to effectuate their aim, and relegate their dogma to the limbo of disembodied ideas, by conducting our own affairs in such a way that their propaganda is harmless."[24] Soule's essay was the only one of its kind to appear in progressive weeklies during the war. Though too optimistic, Soule's hopes were not based on wishful thinking. He saw problems and did not imagine that because the Soviets needed help now they would always be compliant. Nor did he think that because most people wanted peace, freedom and prosperity the conflict had become a people's war.

Such realism was hard for progressives to sustain, and after 1942 almost impossible. Instead they searched out evidence that history was moving in their direction, or, when nothing could be found, made it up. In 1941 Henry Luce, publisher of *Time, Life* and *Fortune,* had called for an "American Century" during which this nation would lead the world in the name of brotherhood and free enterprise. Max Lerner explained why Luce was mistaken. The people did not want an American-dominated capitalist world order. They favored the "People's Century," a time of revolutions calling not for American primacy but "a federation of nations in which, if we are leaders, we are leaders among equals, with their consent, pooling our resources of wealth and intellect and will with theirs."[25] This was the dream also of Vice-President Henry Wallace, with which the *New Republic* agreed. Churchill and Roosevelt distressed progressive journalists sometimes by appearing to believe in an Anglo-Saxon war. The *New Republic* urged them to overcome error and get in step with Wallace, who was calling it the "common man's war" and proclaiming the "century of the common man." *The Nation* too held these beliefs.[26]

Fear usually gave way to hope. In November 1942 Michael Straight of the *New Republic*'s funding family said that the people's war was incomplete. Russia and Britain were having a people's war, but not Latin America, the Middle East and India. China was in danger of falling into an unpopular war, as the Nationalist government seemed more worried about Chinese Communism than about Japanese imperialism. Only more aid to Chiang Kai-shek would, in some unexplained way, halt the backward slide.[27] The next week Straight warned that actually there was no turning back. "This war is no incident! It is part of an immense world revolution, the people's revolution! It is bringing into being a new kind of democracy in which every citizen is mobilized in the general welfare; it is creating a new world order in the United Nations."[28] But then again, maybe not. State Department inertia was a threat. Only the right kind of United Nations could save the people's war.

Some progressives knew that Russia's role in the people's century could not be taken for granted. Early books and articles tended to skirt this difficulty, as by making vague appeals for a permanent collective-security organization.[29] More often the way out involved plans for a world organization made up of regional federations.[30] The advantage seemed to be that it put America and Russia in the same building after the war, but in separate rooms. Even Frederick Schuman, who had not yet forgiven Stalin, liked this approach. His *Design for Power* (1942) advocated a Federal Union of the Atlantic embracing the United States, Great Britain, certain British dominions, antifascist Latin-American states, and Western Europe.

G. D. H. Cole, a noted British socialist, in his book *Europe, Russia and the Future* tried to face the problem squarely by dividing up postwar Europe. Eastern and Central Europe would benefit from "socialist" revolutions on the Russian model. Workers' parties in Western Europe would establish democratic socialism. Both regional systems would then cooperate for the greater good. To fellow travelers this did not go far enough. Alan R. Sweezy, an economist, said in the *New Republic* that Cole admirably justified the Stalin-Hitler Pact and Russia's invasions of Poland and Finland. Cole's vision of a sovietized Eastern Europe was a "realistic and courageous analysis. But Mr. Cole's German and Eastern European comrades may quite justifiably resent his implication that, while a soviet revolution is likely to be necessary and a good thing for Germany and Poland, England has some better (and presumably nicer) way of achieving socialism."[31] The anti-Stalinist *New Leader* took an opposite view. Ralph Abramovich held that Cole's plan for dividing Europe was based on false assumptions. One was that Russia was moving toward a genuinely socialist order. Another was that two systems so radically different could peacefully coexist in Europe. This fundamental disagreement between progressives and anti-Stalinists was to contine well beyond the war.

As the Sweezy review indicates, the doubts and fears of progressive weeklies did not keep them from running pro-Soviet propaganda. This was often done by Ralph Bates, an English novelist who had fought with the Loyalists in Spain. He was sorry to inform *Nation* readers in 1942 that many liberals were finding it difficult to overcome their suspicion of Russia. Liberals feared that a victorious Soviet Union might overrun Europe, or, conversely, that it might make a separate peace with Hitler. If the Russians did fight on they might not abide by the peace treaty. Maybe they would gain permanent influence in the Balkans and elsewhere. Bates called upon readers to overcome doubt. It was such negative thinking that had invited the Stalin-Hitler Pact. A close study of the natural laws of international politics had persuaded Bates that "earnest collaboration and unstinted help" to Russia "are likely to be repaid with honest partnership."[32] This was the customary leap of faith that enabled fellow travelers to put reality behind them.

Bates was a great believer in the theory, propounded by John Scott and others, that the Russians fought well because of pride in what Stalin had accomplished, even if not too thrilled by his means. In the *New Republic* he said that "it was a new Russia, and one with the lineaments of grandeur, that the Russian people knew they were being persuaded, tricked, or driven into creating. It is the grandeur of the vision they remember now, as the invader threatens their decades of invested labor." Despite lack of freedom and government mistakes "the Red Army astonishes the world because the Russian people have a vision, and believe themselves able to realize it."[33] Bates owed his deep knowledge of the Russian mind to books by fellow travelers and Soviet apologists, the usual source of fantasies such as this.

Bates was willing to concede that Stalin had erred in the past. It was just as likely to find progressives arguing that Russian military success proved that Stalin's decisions in the thirties were the right ones after all. Reviewing two books by friends of the Soviets, Joachim Joesten wrote in *The Nation* that they clarified three beliefs entertained by liberals at the time. Liberals had attributed the human costs of the Five-Year Plan to the "ruthlessness and despotism of the Stalin regime." They had believed that the purges of 1936–38 were a "desperate attempt of a dictator to crush all opposition to his rule." Liberals had opposed the Soviet attack on Finland out of a "dogmatic horror of aggression and natural sympathy for the under-dog." As usual, liberals had been wrong. Of course these were nasty moments in Soviet history, Joesten noted in passing, but now we could see that they were all "preventive measures which subsequently were justified by the course of events . . ."[34] This judgment was supported by Maurice Hindus, who had written a book explaining how Stalin's apparent crimes built up the Soviet defense industry, and by Walter Duranty, who showed that the great purges, especially of the Red Army, "eliminated in time a fifth column of the first magnitude. France might still live today if it too had carried out a timely purge of its generals."[35] Joesten was in the hard-boiled, Schumanic tradition, one of those who preferred to look at Russia "realistically," which meant saying in effect that no Soviet act was too vile if it could be shown to aid the war effort. In practice, everything always turned out to have had this result. Achievement was considered necessary, doing so was easy.

The progressive weeklies liked to balance tough-minded statements with tender appeals to sentiment. Alexander Werth was notable because his reporting combined both. Werth had been born in Russia in 1901. Though his father was Russian, his mother was English, which enabled the family to move to Britain in 1917. After graduation from Glasgow University he worked as a journalist, helped by his knowledge of the Russian language. In 1941 Werth entered the Soviet Union as a correspondent for Reuters, the British news service, contributing also to progressive weeklies and the London *Sunday Times*. Werth was an effective propagandist because he seemed not to have prejudged all issues, unlike most apologists for Stalin. He opened *Moscow War Diary* (1942) by reviewing his prewar judgments of Soviet policy.[36] Werth had approved of the aggressions. Russia had to seize eastern Poland, the Baltic States and part of Finland to keep them out of German hands. Actually, he implied, Russia had not gone far enough, having wrongly allowed Germany to invade the Balkans. Werth had described Russia's course in the year or so before it was attacked as one of appeasement and "timid opportunism." Had the adventures been bolder, one gathers, he would have liked them more. Werth brought up this criticism to show that he had entered Russia with an open mind.

Upon arrival he was at once struck by the West's distorted view of Stalin, owing to the fact that most books about the great man were written by his enemies—Trotsky, Max Eastman, Boris Souvarine and other malcontents. They obscured the central point, that "on vital issues, Stalin got things done, however unpopular they might be." As usual, the guilt of purge victims did not matter. "And even if they had not committed the crimes with which they were charged, would not these old Bolsheviks have undermined or delayed the growth of Russia's military strength had they continued to play an important part in military affairs?"[37] In obedience to custom, Werth offered no evidence—there wasn't any—that the old Bolsheviks did not believe in national defense. Nor was there proof that but for collectivization "would not certain peasant elements today be acting as a Fifth Column?"[38] Probably Werth had in mind the alleged kulaks, butchered or sent to die in the Gulag Archipelago years earlier. It certainly was true that dead persons did not become fifth columnists, though Werth was tactful enough to leave the point unstated. And the generals, of course, had to be shot because they were potential fifth columnists also and wanted to make a deal with Hitler. Why Stalin had to kill generals for advocating a policy he soon embraced was another question Werth did not ask. Nor was the absorption of Baltic states a problem. Perhaps Stalin seized them because they had too many fascist leaders, or maybe, Werth added, "Estonia and Latvia aren't really countries." In any case, they did not matter either.

Once the disagreeable task of explaining away Stalin's crimes was finished, Werth grew lyrical. Political commissars had been restored in the army, and none too soon, for "the political commissar sometimes acts in much the same way as a regimental chaplain."[39] The Russians were fighting well for their government because "though it is ruthless in some ways, even the most critically minded feel that, at least *potentially,* it is a good regime, with the Stalin Constitution as a basis for the future."[40] Looking ahead, Werth guessed that the "post-war competition (and the ultimate choice for Poles, Czechs, and even Germans) may be not between capitalism and Communism, but between two forms of democracy—capitalist democracy and Soviet democracy (with a progressive application of the Stalin Constitution)."[41] Werth believed that Russia and England would converge, with England becoming more socialistic and Russia more libertarian. The United States, he feared, might lag behind because of attachment to outmoded capitalist ideas.

But before the glorious future there was the glorious present. Thanks to the war Russia was producing "a rich crop of great music and great books." "I am told," Werth said, having no need to hear it for himself, "that in Leningrad, Shostakovich is already writing greater music than he has ever done before."[42] Russians were always telling Werth how democratic they would be after the war, and they were always displaying greatness of soul and character. The Russians, he assured readers, were a splendid people, closely resembling the English. Thus Werth scooped all those American reporters who would soon be finding numerous similarities between the Russians and their own countrymen. Later Werth had second thoughts. In his classic *Russia at War* (1964) he would say that as Russia was so unprepared when war came, Stalin had not made very good use of the twenty-two months when he was at peace with Hitler. And Werth would declare that the Red Army did not reach the German level of professionalism until 1943, doubtlessly because Stalin had put so many officers to death. At the time, though, he had no doubts or, if he had any, suppressed them in the usual manner of antifascist journalists.

Despite differences over past events, there was general agreement among progressives on current issues. Whatever its faults, Russia was a worthy ally, they were sure. Even the more independent monthly *Common Sense* believed this, along with the related notion of the war as something good for people. "The great significance of having Russia as our ally is that it is the home of the great twentieth century revolution of the common man."[43]

What Russia needed from the West in 1942, everyone agreed, was a second front. By this was meant an Anglo-American invasion, preferably of France, but maybe of North Africa. J. Alvarez del Vayo of *The Nation* was reliably informed that the common man wanted the second front to be launched against Spain. Vayo was Spanish, a former official of the republic, which accounts for his unique reading of popular sentiment.[44] Progressives were always criticizing the State Department for failing to see that this was a people's war. Diplomats were always hand in glove with conservatives abroad instead of promoting revolution. It was a mystery to progressives why Roosevelt put up with this, though there were encouraging signs in the summer of 1942 that he was whipping State into line. "The threat of rival agencies challenging its sacred jurisdictions has stirred the department out of its ancient lethargy and forced it, as the recent pronouncements of Hull and Welles have demonstrated, to spread the language of a people's war."[45] *The Nation*'s optimism was misplaced. It would have to go on flaying State for its backwardness, a duty Kirchwey relished. Arthur Upham Pope told her that a friend of his had heard Sumner Welles denouncing Kirchwey for criticizing him all the time. She passed this news on to I. F. Stone, hoping it was true.[46] Bruce Bliven too was annoyed that the State Department was continuing to appease reactionary governments, but urged progressives to bear in mind that President Roosevelt "is the spiritual leader of all mankind" and would set things right in the end.[47]

The elements of a new Popular Front were beginning to coalesce. Like the old one it would seek unity on the liberal left to promote reforms at home and combat fascism abroad. As before, close ties with Russia would be the keystone of its foreign policy. There would be important differences. In one way the second Popular Front would be narrower than the first. Many liberals and intellectuals had gotten off the train of history for good and, while supporting the war effort, would not entertain false hopes about Russia or join with those who did. In another sense the second Popular Front was broader, owing to the American-Russian alliance. Unlike in the thirties, Washington encouraged people to admire the Soviets. Then, too, many Americans were impressed by Russia's stubborn defense of itself. According to Roper polls, in the five months from October 1941 to February 1942 some fifteen million Americans were won over to the view that Russia should be treated as an ally on the same basis as Great Britain. Press criticism of Russia died out. Large groups of businessmen heard government notables hail the Soviets. Some twenty-five movies portraying Russia favorably were made during the war.[48] Much of this enthusiasm was shallow and would not last. But while it did progressives could not help feeling that the common man, and even the uncommon man, was on their side. Anti-Stalinists became an isolated minority.

Most progressives were willing to forgive and forget past Soviet sins, but they often remained skeptical of American Communists. The *New Republic*'s Washington columnist TRB (at this time Kenneth Crawford) held that the American Communist Party was an obstacle to Soviet-American friendship.

> What also needs saying is that Russia might make a substantial contribution to the mutual good will and understanding without which no treaty means anything, by cutting off every remaining vestige of connection, or appearance of connection, with the irritating connivers who run the Communist Party of the United States and who continue to bask in reflected Russian glory.[49]

Not everyone felt as strongly, but the idea was heard enough so that when Earl Browder gained the privilege of writing directly to President Roosevelt he filled his letters with attacks on progressive friends of Russia, including periodicals such as *The Nation,* the *New Republic* and *PM,* a liberal daily newspaper in New York. They were not to be trusted, was Browder's view, a parochial one arising mainly from their criticism of him and his party.[50]

For a time the mass media equaled or outdid progressives in glorifying Russia. In 1943 an issue of *Life* magazine was devoted entirely to pro-Soviet gush. *Life* declared editorially that

> no nation in history has ever done so much so fast. If the Soviet leaders tell us that the control of information was necessary to get this job done, we can afford to take their

word for it for the time being. We who know the power of free speech, and the necessity for it, may assume that if those leaders are sincere in their work of emancipating the Russian people they will swing around toward free speech—and we hope soon.[51]

This was the issue's most unfriendly statement. Looking backward, *Life* held the Stalin-Hitler Pact to have been justified, and the purges also on account of the Trotskyist fifth columnists—it now being gospel in the United States, as in Russia, that Trotsky was allied with fascism. No effort was made to square this contention with the next point, that with Trotsky gone Russia was no longer interested in world revolution and other radical practices. Former Ambassador Joseph E. Davies, the highest-ranking apologist for Soviet Communism, explained yet again that Russia was a worthy partner and in the future "will not promote dissension in the internal affairs of other nations."[52] Collective farms and various Soviet institutions received the customary praise. The Russians, *Life* had discovered, were very much like Americans.

Even conservative businessmen joined the chorus. Typical was airline president Edward V. Rickenbacker, a World War I flying ace. He returned from visiting the Soviets to announce that their bad reputation was the fault of local Communists who had misrepresented them. Instead of being revolutionary the Soviets were moving the other way. Indeed, if they kept on, Russians were going to achieve democracy, whereas if America did not change, Americans would lose it. Rickenbacker was especially taken with Soviet labor policy. The Russians had "iron discipline in industrial plants, severe punishment for chronic absenteeism, incentive pay, and compulsory overtime work." The Red Army also had the right idea. "Nowhere in the world have I seen so much respect for rank."[53] (This was too much even for *The Nation,* which observed sarcastically that Rickenbacker "has seen the future, and it works.")[54] A *Fortune* poll in 1943 discovered that of all occupational groups it was business executives who had the most confidence in Russia. Whereas only thirty-one percent of the whole population thought that Russia would be cooperative after the war, forty-eight percent of executives believed that the Soviets "would not

try to bring about Communist governments in other countries."
But they were not alone. Congressman Rankin of Mississippi,
the most racist and anti-Semitic figure in government, hailed
Stalin as a Gentile and a conservative. Monsignor Fulton Sheen
said that "the family is higher in Russia than in the United
States, and God, looking from heaven, may be more pleased
with Russia than with us."[55]

At the very least, as Ralph Barton Perry, a professor of
philosophy at Harvard, explained it, America and Russia had a
common respect for human dignity that made their alliance
moral as well as practical. Even Catholics could unite with
Marxists against "the party of cynicism, injustice and inhumanity," said Perry, thereby drafting Stalin into the camp of
human decency.[56]

These are not isolated examples. In an important article published during the fifties Paul Willen surveyed the popular press
of the war years to show how widespread the enthusiasm for
Russia had been. Reviewing public-opinion polls taken at the
time, he concluded that only seven percent of those questioned
foresaw that Russia would play an aggressive role after the war.
Collier's magazine ran many articles showing the Russians to be
much like Americans. In 1943 it declared editorially that Russia had developed a "modified capitalist set-up" and was evolv-
ing toward American democracy.[57] *The Saturday Evening Post*
thought so, too. Its expert on Soviet affairs was Edgar Snow,
who admired both Russian and Chinese Communism, which he
had done more to publicize in America than anyone else, notably in his popular book *Red Star Over China* (1938). During
the war's last three years the *SEP* published nothing on Russia,
with one exception, that was not written by Snow. Even *Reader's Digest,* despite an article by Max Eastman critical of
Stalin, took much the same approach. Its correspondent in Russia during the war was Maurice Hindus, author of numerous
books acclaiming Soviet practices. *The Rotarian* published articles by such fellow travelers as the English historian of Russia
Bernard Pares. And its book review editor recommended pro-
Soviet works including Davies' *Mission to Moscow* (1942) and
the even more fatuous *Maxim Litvinoff* (1943) by Arthur
Upham Pope.[58]

Against this backdrop the progressive weeklies do not seem

quite so bad. They offered some variety of opinion, and in beating the drum for Russia they did not always avoid unpleasant facts. *The Nation* opened 1943 with two thoughtful essays by Reinhold Niebuhr, who tried hard to present Russia in a favorable and yet realistic light. There were differences between Communism and Nazism that offered grounds for hope. "The fact is that though communism uses dictatorship brutally, it does not exalt it as an end in itself. Nor does it worship either race or war. Its moral cynicism is only provisional, and it is never morally nihilistic, as the Nazis are. It is, in fact, ultimately utopian in morals, just as is the liberal-democratic world."[59] The great difference between democrats and Communists was not so much over ends as over means. This was important but not decisive, Niebuhr then believed, especially as Russia had given up exporting revolution. It would favor peace and the status quo when victory was won. Dissolving the Communist parties outside Russia would remove lingering doubts about the Russian alliance.[60]

There was already a difference between liberals such as Niebuhr, who wanted assurances that the Soviets had given up promoting revolution for good, and those, like Freda Kirchwey, who believed that revolution was inevitable. Ralph Bates, in one of his frequent *Nation* reviews, argued that even if Russia dissolved every Communist party there would still be a revolution in Europe, and the Tory element would then want to attack Russia anyway. It was unreasonable to expect Russia to disband the foreign Communist parties, and unnecessary too, as they were so useful and progressive. Communists had been invaluable in the Spanish Civil War. And in America funds for Loyalist Spain were raised almost entirely by Communists and those willing to work with them. What the situation demanded was not dissolution of the Comintern but a new united front. Not so, answered Niebuhr. Liberals were right to demand that Russia stop interfering with the internal affairs of other countries through its puppet Communist parties.[61]

A few months later Stalin dissolved the Comintern. All the national Communist parties were now supposedly on their own. In a *Nation* symposium liberals expressed guarded pleasure at this move. Progressives were more enthusiastic. Vayo said it was a real blow to the Axis and a great opportunity for even more unity among labor and progressives. Though Bates had not wanted it, he welcomed Stalin's act just the same, calling again for a reborn united front, since Communists had become even more dependable than before. Only Louis Fischer broke ranks. It seemed to him that this move, while good because it strengthened the alliance, showed Russia to be acting out of a narrow nationalism that could be dangerous later. His only hope was that foreign Communists would be antagonized and give up their slavery to the Kremlin, "where communism and idealism have ceased to dwell."[62]

More characteristic was Malcolm Cowley's response. He reviewed four books in the *New Republic* that had come out at about the same time carrying the same heartening message.

All four of them agree that there is no serious point of conflict. Russia wants her boundaries as they were in 1941. She wants severe penalties for the German leaders who have enslaved and massacred her people. But she does not want to rule Western Europe and she does not want to convert the world to communism.

Though written before the Comintern's dissolution, the books showed it was practically inevitable. "It was a development out of everything that has happened in Russia for the last fifteen years. Socialism in one country is a slogan that means exactly what it says."[63]

When Russia abolished the Comintern Max Lerner too was delighted. Though only a gesture, later taken back, this, he was sure, was a momentous step, a sign of Russian self-confidence, a move "toward dissipating the bogey of a post-war Bolshevik revolution." It might foreshadow a true Russo-American alliance. Maybe now there would be unity among progressives everywhere.[64] In the *New Republic* he said again that this showed Russia's goodwill. There were three reasons now for believing that the Russians would be a healthy force in the postwar world. One was that Russia was fighting an antifascist war. Another was that Russia had solved her economic problems and would not need foreign adventures for gain. Thirdly, the Russians had been changed by the war, Lerner was certain, having read this somewhere. "The thoroughgoing organization of the war economy, the civilian resistance, the guerilla warfare could only be achieved in a war that had become democratic in its inner nature."[65] Through the magic of the people's war, every Russian military advance became another step toward democracy, so far as progressives were concerned.

In July 1943 *Reader's Digest* published an article on Russia that aroused Lerner's deepest feelings. It was written by Max Eastman, who had lived in Russia, knew the language, and was about as well informed on Soviet affairs as an outsider could be. Eastman's piece was entitled "To Collaborate Successfully We Must Face the Facts About Russia."[66] It was short on collaboration, long on the unpleasant facts about Russia that justified diplomatic caution. Lerner and *PM* sensed danger and gave over half a page to averting it. Eastman had called Henry Wallace, Wendell Willkie and Joseph E. Davies "apologists for communism." To the contrary, said Lerner, when the history of present foreign relations was written theirs would be "shining names in it." Lerner resented Eastman's characterization of pro-Soviet Americans as softheaded and sentimental. Not true, explained Lerner, we are the true realists. This claim was undermined a few passages later when he wrote:

As I read Eastman on Russian poverty and the subjection of the people, I kept thinking: if these people are slaves, why do slaves fight so well? Why do starving people form themselves not just into a nation with an army, but a *nation in arms*? Why do Russian children, as Maurice Hindus described them in *Mother Russia*, die for their country with a deep joy that would do honor to grown and mature men? Why do Russians have the sense that they are fashioning a new world, with new meanings—a sense that we in America seem sadly to have lost?[67]

So much for realism.

The reference to Maurice Hindus explains a great deal. Hindus was born in a poor Russian village. His family arrived in the United States in 1905, when Hindus was fourteen. After graduating from high school he spent three years as a farm laborer in upstate New York before entering Colgate. He completed his education at Harvard, where he studied writing. His first book, *The Russian Peasant and the Revolution,* was published in 1920.[68] Having spent much of his youth among Russian peasants and American farmers, knowing the Russian language, and being extremely well educated gave Hindus unique qualifications, which he made the most of. Interpreting Russian peasant life to the English-speaking world became his career. He returned to Russia in 1923, the first of a series of long visits that were the material for many books, *Mother Russia* being his thirteenth.

Though well equipped for his unusual profession, Hindus suffered from a condition afflicting all journalists whose careers were based in the Soviet Union. Reporters who did a tour of duty in Russia and then moved on could say what they pleased afterward. But Hindus and others needed to stay. Accordingly, what they wrote had to pass inspection. Unlike Soviet journalists, they were not required to whitewash everything. But they had to accept the fundamental law of Stalinism, which was that the end justified the means, however terrible. For Hindus this law was especially onerous because the peasantry suffered more than most Russians from Stalinism. The imposition of collectivized farming was disastrous. Upward of five million peasants were starved, slain, imprisoned or exiled, with the most successful (called kulaks) faring worst. By 1934, when it was over, collectivization had reduced the country's livestock by half. The production of other foodstuffs declined also, so that even today Russia, which once exported grain, must import it.

It fell to Hindus more than any other Westerner to explain away this blunder and this crime. He did so unflinchingly even before the war, which, however, made things easier. In *Mother Russia* (1943) Hindus reported that his latest visit had shown him a country united in defense of its principles. This redeemed all the violence and atrocities of Stalin's reign, even the deaths of enthusiastic Russian youngsters which Lerner found so moving. Most of the unpleasant aspects of Stalin's rule, it could now be seen, resulted from the urgent need to prepare for war, Hindus declared, though collectivization began before Hitler at a time when Russia and Weimar Germany had good relations. "Now, in the light of war and Russia's fierce resistance, the Plans loom as one of the most farsighted and astounding achievements of all time."[69] Even those Russians who had been against the Five-Year Plans when they were going on, many skeptics had told him, realized they made possible Russia's successful defense. Thanks to war and Stalinism, "uncertainty and chaos have given way to sober reflection and to deep-rooted stability. Class hate and class warfare, so flaming in former years, have yielded to love of country, love of the past, love of the people—and to immeasurable faith in the future."[70] Russia was a dictatorship, but it was the dictator who made all this happen. Democracy would come later when Russia could afford it. The resemblance here to Lerner, including even the language, was not accidental. A generation of progressives had learned from Hindus how to drown the horrors of Soviet life in a warm bath of sentiment.

Progressives differed from fellow travelers in that to the latter the horrors did not exist. In this spirit Henry Pratt Fairchild, a professor of sociology at New York University, wrote to Lerner after reading his column on Max Eastman's *Digest* article. In refuting Eastman, Lerner had admitted that large numbers of Russians were imprisoned in camps and, worse still, there was no freedom of thought. Fairchild wanted to know how Lerner could say such a thing, given the fact that "restriction on thought seems to be inherently contradictory to the whole Soviet conception." Fairchild pointed to the spread of education and the publication of books and the reverence for science, all of which he knew about personally, having been to Russia in 1933 and allowed to think freely. Of course, there was the small matter of limitations imposed by ideology. But "the ideology itself is unreservedly devoted to the upbuilding of the individual personality as a functioning member of a social group, and to me it is inconceivable that when the system feels itself sufficiently secure it will not be just as ready to welcome criticism and free analysis as any other on earth.[71]

This was the voice of the true believer, as was that of Arthur Upham Pope, author of *Maxim Litvinoff* (1943). Not himself a Communist (he thought the Party was un-American), Pope was faithful in every respect to the Soviet line. Though Litvinoff was the progressives' favorite Russian diplomat, Pope did not take the easy way of keeping to the popular aspects of Soviet diplomacy. He praised Stalin for moral courage and modesty. The pact with Hitler became necessary, he explained, when

Prime Minister Chamberlain of England tried to involve Russia in a war with Germany. Russia invaded Poland to keep part of it out of German hands, and Finland to suppress fascism. Readers learned all about the people's war again and the need for a second front. What they did not hear about was the forced famine that accompanied collectivization, nor the purges, still less the Gulag Archipelago. "Firmness" was Pope's word describing Stalin's harsh ways, made necessary, of course, by threats to Russian security.

Fellow travelers liked to get away from nasty little specifics, preferring instead to dwell on the big picture and the train of history. Robert Lynd, a noted sociologist, tried to get Dwight Macdonald, editor of the left-wing *Politics,* to do this. Rather than harping on Stalin's defects and going in for "reckless, complacent name-calling," why didn't Macdonald realize that in Russia, as presumably elsewhere, the movement toward centralization and planning necessarily involved mistakes and excesses of authority. Macdonald could see this on some subjects, "but when it comes to the Soviet Union you fly off in a rage, personalize all the sins as malevolent acts of Stalin, and generally refuse to view the situation as a difficult institutional situation full of coercions that force the hands of administrators."[72]

Macdonald declined to view mass murder as an understandable response to institutional difficulties. This obliged Lynd to perform greater feats of euphemism. In a letter bristling with political and professional clichés "centralized national planning," "bureaucracy," "giant technology" and "special circumstances" led to "problems" that had to be dealt with "bluntly." Lynd was sorry that Russia did not have the "kind of pure socialism that fulfills all our dreams."

> But the thing that I am stumped by is the apparent imputation of nothing but malevolence to the Kremlin by some of you fellows. It's all "crafty," "drunk with personal power," "ruthless"—a matter of personal deliberate intent, with no quarter even for mistakes, the tight coercions of circumstances, and with the Sov. Un. constantly measured vs. a perfectionist yardstick.[73]

On the other hand, critics often wondered why to the faithful the crimes of Stalin were never his fault.

. . .

Fellow travelers like Vayo and Bates, who admired Russia because it was revolutionary, if only by example, were probably less influential than those who admired it to the degree that it was not. Prominent among these was the historian Bernard Pares, who in 1944 brought forth an entire book to ease liberal fears.* He had first visited Russia in 1898 and had gone on to found the program of Russian studies at the University of London. Pares had been in Russia when the liberal revolution, which he favored, took place. He had not liked the Bolsheviks, who killed some of his friends, but was satisfied that their methods had later been discarded. In *Russia and the Peace* (1944) he asserted that "the Communists would never have remained in power if they had continued in the practices with which they started."[74] Pares had it the wrong way round. Under Lenin mass murder and forced labor camps were, to a degree, incidental, byproducts of crisis. Stalin institutionalized them. Pares reversed the true order of things because it was what progressives wanted to believe, and because Stalin helped them out with his doctrine of revolution in one country and by laying down conservative policies to govern sexual conduct, family life and education. These enabled Pares to say that advocates of revolution were now to be found "more easily in America than in Russia."[75]

Having gone to all the trouble of eliminating Trotsky and the doctrine of permanent revolution, Stalin was hardly likely to revive it after the war. It was out of date, continued Pares, and no one in Russia was interested in it any longer. Seemingly the idea of revolution no longer applied even to the Soviets. "The present regime in Russia makes no claim to be communist," Pares had disclosed in the *New Republic*. The Soviets never pretended to have achieved communism, only to be working toward it. After the war Stalin would cultivate his own garden, plus good relations with the independent states of Eastern Europe.[76] This would be good for the world, and for Russia too on account of

---

* This and other examples listed here date from later in the war, but retain the euphoric spirit of the early years.

that bracing up of the individual which was so long missing. That is the chief difference which I have noticed since the revolution. I will even venture to guess that this is perhaps a nearer approach to true democracy than the liberal movement before the revolution; for then liberalism was a theory where the sense of its responsibilities was lacking, and now we are beginning to see that material of character and purpose out of which a true democracy can be made.[77]

For Dr. Harry Ward, a Protestant leader, former chairman of the ACLU, and devoted fellow traveler, Soviet democracy had already arrived. In *New Masses* he explained that of the two forms of democracy, capitalist and socialist, Russia was blessed with the latter. It was the higher form "because it spreads democratic principles and practices over more sections of the people and wider areas of life."[78] He scourged liberals for entertaining the false idea that "the Soviet Union is a totalitarian state ruled by the small minority who compose the Communist Party."

More typical was Richard Lauterbach, a popular journalist who had been sent to Moscow in 1943 by Time-Life. He was full of the customary enthusiasm for Russian dedication, heroism and steadfastness. The people were bursting with faith in their leaders, about whom, he confessed, they knew very little, not that it mattered. As the Russians were so terrific and had such fine achievements to their credit, peace would be certain were it not for the anti-Soviet press in America, which continued "to distort the Soviet Union's true aims and policies, making understanding and friendship almost impossible."[79] There was a danger that reactionary governments in Britain and America might gang up on Russia after the war. But there was a common ground also.

We like our way of running things, and I think the Russians understand pretty well that we won't tolerate outside interference. The average Russian is not interested in world revolution, and as I've already said I don't think Stalin is going to "export" revolution either. He would much rather export fur and import our heavy machinery.[80]

And so to bed, with visions of fur and heavy machinery dancing in the reader's head.

Russia Is No Riddle was the title of a similar book, by a journalist with much experience in the Soviet Union. He too believed that Russia and America would get along, thanks to the "ruggedness, honesty, and warmheartedness of the common man in both countries," a surer basis for accord, no doubt, than even furs and heavy machinery.* And then again, there was the common bond of democracy, firmly rooted locally in collective farms and such. Nationally, "the Soviet leaders expect to build the future edifice of Soviet democracy around the frame of the Stalin Constitution."[82]

No one was better at this sort of thing than Edgar Snow, *The Saturday Evening Post*'s authority on Russia and China, who visited Soviet-occupied Eastern Europe while the war was still on. In the magazine and his book *The Pattern of Soviet Power* (1945), he reported that, judging by Rumania, Eastern Europe had little to worry about. No revolution was being imposed. People had a degree of liberty, considering the war, that was "astonishing." "Reforms" were going on throughout Eastern Europe, of course, making it resemble the Soviet Union in desirable ways. And German prisoners of war enjoyed such good treatment in their Siberian factories, he was assured by a Soviet friend, that their wages made Russian workers envious.

Snow did not know Russia as he did China, which may account for the gush. Stalin was a wonderful person, Snow had learned—modest, realistic, simple, dignified, and yet fun-loving.† He lived simply, too, in a six-room Kremlin flat, setting a

---

* The answer to this had been given earlier in *The Nation* by an American Socialist, Travers Clement, reviewing a book by Harold Laski, who had said that the West had no quarrel with the Russian people. "That is quite true. But unfortunately there can be no unity, on an organizational basis, with the people of a police state over the heads of their rulers. If there were an independent, that is, a real labor movement in Russia, if there were opposition working-class parties, such unity would be possible. If, as Mr. Laski claims, the Soviet Union is 'the central support upon which the future of the working-class depends,' then God help the working-class!"[81]

† Lerner thought so, too. "The men around Stalin have learned his sense of power, but they have little of his saving humor and flexibility," he wrote, showing an intimate knowledge of Stalin's jolly ways.[83]

good example. After much disingenuous reasoning, Snow ended his book by saying that both Russia's conduct in Eastern Europe and its need to repair war damage made another war unlikely. The Russians, they hoped with American aid, were going to be busy reconstructing and achieving a high level of consumption.

> Once that becomes a fact, *but only then*, and once the Kremlin feels reasonably secure in a peaceful world, it may become possible for the Russian people to enjoy the freedoms of political democracy—a democracy more in line with our own best traditions—side by side with the Soviet system of economy. Until then, the doors between Russia and the advanced capitalistic countries will not fully open. But now they are at least ajar. It is our responsibility, as much as it is Russia's, to see that they are not again slammed shut.[84]

For a progressive this was good. Snow conceded more than most who wrote about Russia and, though sentimental and slippery in the way of "soft" progressives, was realistic about power politics and did not expect the millennium.

Even so, he remained a Soviet apologist, and the *New Leader* assigned his book to Eugene Lyons, a conservative anti-Communist, who treated it harshly. Bennett Cerf, Snow's publisher, objected. He compared Lyons with Gerald L. K. Smith and Senator Bilbo, notorious racists and reactionaries. Lyons answered that this showed he had always been wrong about Cerf. He used to think of Cerf as a fellow traveler with a certain "muddled honesty." But in his letter to the *New Leader* Cerf had used the Communist "amalgam" technique, according to which the name of a person to be smeared was bracketed with hateful names so that something would rub off. "If Mr. Cerf were not an emancipated comrade who holds bourgeois decencies in contempt, he would be ashamed of this low trick."[85] Of course, if Lyons had not himself been so far over on the opposite side he would have been ashamed of his insinuation that Cerf was a Communist. In the polemical war at home antagonists outdid one another in verbal dreadfulness.

After the war Louis Fischer's Russian wife, Markoosha, explained how it was that those fatuous books on the Soviet

Union came to be written. For one thing, most were by a new generation of reporters who had not seen Russia in the thirties, did not know any Russians personally, and were overcome by Russian heroism and sacrifice. They were impressed, too, by the apparent unity of Soviet opinion, not knowing that it was unreal and subject to instant change. Many American correspondents thought of reporting on Russia as war work. The Soviet Foreign Commissariat reacted bitterly to criticism that appeared in America, and correspondents did not wish to provoke it. Back home any reporter who had criticized Russia found he was classed with Bilbo and Gerald L. K. Smith and with the vicious Hearst and McCormick newspapers. As a bonus, praising Russia got you invited to the right cocktail parties in New York and Washington.

Further, the standard arguments used on the Fischers years earlier still worked: criticism plays into the hands of reaction; Russia is fighting imperialism; Stalin is fighting fascism; there is no racial discrimination in Russia. A new one was that criticism might bring a war with Russia nearer. If experienced liberals and leftists were still buying these stale lines, why should inexperienced reporters be any different? she asked. "It is easier to do so because Stalin has supplied the appropriate terminology so that liberals can use the same words while fighting for Soviet totalitarianism that they used when fighting for democracy and freedom."[86]

From the beginning many realized that after victory peace would depend on good relations between the United States and Russia. Fellow travelers and progressives insisted that if things went wrong America would be at fault. Being itself so democratic, and having therefore a democratic foreign policy, Russia was not to be feared. As Freda Kirchwey said, arrangements for peace "will be as evanescent as sky-writing unless they are founded on a system of democratic states in Europe. Russia realizes that and has consistently thrown its support to the active anti-fascist groups in every country," while America followed an opposite course.[87] Even when Russia did traffic with reactionaries that was often good, too. Many progressives were unhappy when Russia accepted the conservative regime of Italy's Marshal Badoglio as a co-belligerent. Not to worry,

Ralph Bates explained. Russia had a secret plan that would set things right. Thanks to socialism, Russia was on the democratic side even when seeming not to be.[88]*

Progressive excuses for Russia drove anti-Stalinists wild. Liston M. Oak of the *New Leader* wrote several articles attacking such double talk, especially that of Bates, whom he had known in Spain. To Oak's knowledge the only time Bates had ever criticized Russia was after the Stalin-Hitler Pact. He had opposed dissolving the Comintern until it was done, after which he praised the decision. When the Allies dealt with reactionary governments Bates complained bitterly. Similar acts by Stalin excited his admiration.

> Any deal that the Joint Advisory Council or other commission may find expedient will be okay by Browder and Bates—by virtue of Russia's participation. In their eyes, Russia "changed the character of the war" from an imperialist to an anti-fascist war, and by the same token if Russian diplomats sign a deal with Darlan, it is only a maneuver to defeat him.[90]

There were times, however, when even progressives had trouble finding the inner reality that appearances belied. When Stalin recognized the Badoglio regime Freda Kirchwey was shocked at first. This was not what she expected from the best friend of European democracy. Why had he done it? If it was to gain a larger role in Italian affairs, this was "irresponsible" and even "a kind of treason." She hoped against hope that in some unknown way recognizing Badoglio was a subtle effort to undermine him. Yet there was the dread possibility that Stalin was trading Western Europe for the East. Kirchwey waxed in-

---

* The rule which held that a bad act by Stalin was not what it seemed worked in reverse for other governments. Fritz Sternberg, a progressive economist, took note that Britain's rulers were conducting the war in an egalitarian spirit. The upper classes were being taxed much more heavily than the lower. Capital investment abroad was drained to meet war costs. Consumption was strictly regulated. Appearances notwithstanding, this showed the Tory mind at its most cunning. Conservatives were making heavy sacrifices "in order to create stable conditions at home and to raise as little opposition as possible to the conduct of an imperialist foreign policy after the war." Perfidious Albion indeed![89]

dignant at the thought. "If this is the price he had to pay for acceptance of his claims in the Balkans, one can only say that inflation in Italy has reached a new high."[91] But this was a momentary lapse. In general Kirchwey agreed with Bates that "while Stalin formally acquiesces in the status quo, he is helping to prepare the way for its ultimate collapse."[92]

During the war conservatives, progressives and fellow travelers vied with one another in presenting a false picture of Soviet government and society. Of those quoted here, the least misleading was Rickenbacker, who believed in management's right to exploit labor and was pleased to see that Soviet executives did, too, and had even a freer hand than American bosses. For the most part, wartime writing on the Soviets, in the first years especially, bore little relation to fact. There was disagreement over the extent to which Russia approached perfection. Some held that Russia had already obtained democracy, others that while the Soviets were certainly democratic at heart, as shown by the Stalin constitution (which had not been and never would be activated), practice lagged behind theory. Some believed that Russia had abandoned revolution and therefore any interest in exporting it, while others held that Russia was still in the vanguard of the world revolution, but that this need not trouble Americans, who should support united fronts, anyway. Most agreed in retrospect that what had hitherto been regarded as the crimes of Stalin had been misunderstood and could now be seen as necessary preparations for war. When, in the interest of credibility, it was desirable to acknowledge Soviet abuses of human rights, these were held not to matter, as also their victims. What counted were Soviet power and Soviet success, which to most American commentators excused everything.

III

The Revival
of Anti-Stalinism

ANTI-STALINISTS had never stopped complaining of the double
talk and double standard of morality employed by progressives
and fellow travelers, but it was not until 1943 that they found a
good opportunity to strike back. This was provided by the release of a pro-Soviet film, *Mission to Moscow,* based on a 1941
best-seller by former Ambassador Joseph P. Davies. He was
one of those wealthy businessmen who were second only to
progressive intellectuals in susceptibility to Russian charm.
Judging by his book, Davies was naïve beyond the Kremlin's
wildest dreams. At one point he is found lecturing Maxim
Litvinov on America's natural resources and physical isolation,
which left it independent of the rest of the world and therefore
in no need of diplomacy in the usual sense—or of diplomats,
one imagines, hence his ambassadorship. Davies found Stalin to
be a "clean-living, modest, retiring, single-purposed man" who
was an "easy boss" of all the Russias. Far from being Communist, Davies discovered a Russia that was only barely socialist.
The heart of Davies' book, and what most infuriated anti-
Stalinists, was his whitewash of the purge trials. All the victims
were guilty, as practically everyone in the diplomatic corps
knew, he explained. He only regretted, Davies wrote in 1941,
that he had not realized at the time that Stalin with admirable
foresight was eliminating the fifth column.[1]

This foolish book was a great success on account of timing. It
came out just when Americans, reeling from early defeats, were
particularly grateful to Russia for holding on. An exception
was Margaret Marshall, anti-Stalinist literary editor of *The
Nation*, who said that Davies' "general provincial wonder at

the 'Soviet experiment' will endear him to those who have taken up the ridiculous line that Stalin, having come over to the Allied side, now stands exonerated of all his crimes; and that the Red Army would not be fighting the way it is if the GPU had not conducted one of the cruelist manhunts in history."[2] Even so, the book, aided by its author's conservative qualifications, appealed to many who were not progressive. That was partly why it became a movie, since Hollywood moguls were not interested in pro-Soviet propaganda as such. Warner Brothers made the film for profit, though also, some held, because of government encouragement. Whatever the reason, it was a mistake. Davies' silliness had been mitigated in the book by sensible observations. In the movie one had to take it straight.

Anti-Stalinists had plenty of time to prepare for *Mission to Moscow*. Long before it came out, gossip columnists were reporting that the film would justify the Moscow purge trials.[3] The *New Leader* disclosed that a former employee of Moscow's International Bureau of Revolutionary Literature had been hired as a technical adviser on the film. High officials of the State Department were said to be unhappy about this, but could do nothing for fear of the "second-front press," which would revile any government critic as an "appeaser-mad-dog."[4]

Trotskyists and their sympathizers were furious because the film, which followed the book closely, was going to show that the exiled leader had been organizing a fifth column in Russia. Albert Goldman of the Socialist Workers Party wrote to Dwight Macdonald as early as January 1943 urging the formation of a protest committee.[5] Anti-Stalinist writers met on April 6, 1943, and again on April 16 to draw up a manifesto attacking the film. The cover letter was dated May 12. It declared that *Mission to Moscow* brought "to the American scene the kind of historical falsifications which have hitherto been characteristic of totalitarian propaganda." It was signed by Max Eastman, James T. Farrell, Sidney Hook, Alfred Kazin, A. Philip Randolph, Norman Thomas, Edmund Wilson and others. Replies were to be sent to Macdonald. Despite the moral and intellectual distinction of its sponsors, many who were asked refused to sign the statement, usually because they thought it too long and specific. James Loeb, Jr., did not want to be committed to the Dewey Commission's analysis of the purge trials, though it was in the main correct. Roger Baldwin said the film was not worth the trouble they were taking over it. James Burnham did sign, but held that the statement put too much emphasis on events in the thirties as against those of the present day.[6]

The manifesto was circulated as a pamphlet by the *New Leader,* which added to it hostile reviews of the film, press statements issued at the time of the purge trials, negative statements by Davies not used in the movie, and the like.[7] John Dewey and Suzanne La Follette, who had been secretary to the Dewey Commission, wrote their own long denunciation to *The New York Times.* They described the picture as anti-British, anti-Congress, anti-democratic, and anti-truth. "It deepens that crisis in morals which is the fundamental issue in the modern world."[8]

The *New Leader* review was predictably scathing. It indicted the film as worse than the book, for though Davies had accepted the Soviet court's verdict of guilty, he had criticized the trial procedures.[9] Reviewers for the progressive weeklies went both ways, sometimes at once. Manny Farber wrote in the *New Republic* that to a "democratic intelligence" the movie was "repulsive and insulting."[10] James Agee, *The Nation*'s distinguished film critic, wrote that *Mission to Moscow* was almost the first Soviet production to come from a major studio. It seemed to him a mixture of Stalinism, New Dealism, Hollywoodism, journalism, opportunism, mesmerism and onanism. On the other hand, he was glad that Russia was given credit for its long record of antifascism. He declared himself neutral on the Moscow purge trials.[11]

Dwight Macdonald was outraged by what he called Agee's "doubletalk." To him it seemed that Agee approved of the film's aim but not its method. Yet the method reflected the aim, which was to do a dirty job. "How can Agee be so agonizingly indecisive about the trials and so blatantly, unqualifiedly cocksure about the even more complex questions of the Soviet Union and war, fascism, and appeasement?" If Munich was appeasement, what about the pact? If conservatives were partly to blame for the war, what about Moscow?[12] Agee defended himself by saying he was politically ignorant—which did not, of course, keep him from making political statements. What he found rotten in the film was a result not of propaganda but of

Hollywood. On the matter of appeasement he declared both kinds discussed by Macdonald to be shameful, but Russia's less so because it was "intelligent." Then Agee trailed off incoherently, saying he was in favor of clarity but against "false clarity," whatever that meant.[13]

Arthur Upham Pope wrote that *Mission to Moscow* aroused a "mad hurricane of protest from reactionaries and revolutionaries alike, of such virulent hostility and utter extravagance of denunciation that it was obviously a release for emotions that had been pent up by America's widespread and enthusiastic appreciation of what Russia was doing in the war."[14] This was probably right. Few anti-Stalinists had changed their politics because the Red Army was fighting well, but so long as it was the main obstacle to Germany they were unwilling to say so. The great Russian victory at Stalingrad in January 1943, a turning point in the war, made it easier to speak up, as the war's outcome was no longer in doubt. *Mission to Moscow* was an ideal vehicle for protest. It was a bad and blatantly propagandistic film, hence a legitimate target. And it dealt with the thirties, allowing critics to get around Russia's present valor and rake up its horrifying past. In a way Roger Baldwin was correct to make light of the movie, which was soon forgotten. But it had opened up a door that was never again to close. Without meaning to, Warner Brothers had benefited democracy after all.

In 1942 Bennett Cerf, founder of the extremely successful publishing firm of Random House, had proposed that the industry withdraw from sale all books critical of Russia.[15] This drastic idea failed, but most publishers lost interest in such books, and hardly any new ones appeared for several years. The first important break was the issuance in 1944 of David J. Dallin's *The Real Soviet Russia* by Yale University Press, which took the lead from commercial publishers who were worried about a possible boycott. Dallin, the *New Leader*'s expert on Soviet affairs, was the author of many well-documented books. He was a Russian social democrat and had been exiled both before and after the Bolshevik Revolution. *The Real Soviet Russia*—as well as its companion, *Russia and Postwar Europe,* published the same year—was written specifically as an antidote to the flood of books praising Russia and Stalin, generally written by reporters who knew little about either. Every journalist, it seemed to Dallin, was privy to Stalin's innermost thoughts. "The Moscow leader always thinks and always decides as he should, for 'Stalin is a realist.' And being a realist his ideas naturally run in a proper, decent, friendly, peaceful direction. How could it be otherwise with a respectable premier of a respectable and religious state?"[16] Dallin rejected the Thermidor concept advanced by progressives, who argued that Russia's revolution was far behind it. Russia had changed superficially, Dallin wrote, but Stalin had "failed to alter either the principles of Soviet foreign policy or the economic regime of the country."[17]

Dallin scoffed at claims that the Stalin-Hitler Pact was justified because it gave Russia time to prepare defenses. The pact cost Russia a possible French alliance and gave Hitler time to overrun much of Europe. Westerners kept pointing to the absence of a fifth column as evidence of Stalin's success, but in Russia all setbacks were blamed on this supposedly nonexistent force. Dallin knew even at the time that there had been a great deal of collaboration with the Germans in occupied Russia. He believed also that the propaganda about Russia's benevolent postwar ambitions was just that. Stalinism had not become something else, as progressives liked to think. The new face was only the old one made up differently.

This excellent book, which was full of information about the bureaucratic state and the instruments of oppression sustaining it, made little impression. Progressives greeted it with the usual closed minds. Ralph Bates was impressed despite himself with Dallin's knowledge and authority. Dallin was wrong all the same, he insisted. Russia was not expansionist and no longer believed in the world revolution. Stalin's only mistake had been his slow response to Nazism in the early thirties.[18] The brush-off was to be expected. So also was the dim reception given Dallin's *Russia and Postwar Europe,* which arrived at dour and broadly accurate conclusions.

All the same, liberal and left critics of Stalinism gained courage and became more outspoken.[19] They acquired a sharp new voice in 1944 with the founding of Dwight Macdonald's magazine *Politics.* After graduating from Yale Macdonald had worked on Henry Luce's *Fortune* before joining *Partisan Review* in the late thirties. At the time its Trotskyist orientation suited him. But by 1943 he had lost interest in Trotskyism, while *Partisan Review* was losing interest in politics. Differences with fellow editors led to his resignation. The next year, aided by his first wife, Nancy, he established his own brilliantly edited journal. Though a very personal organ, *Politics* attracted high-quality writers and reviewers from the start, including historians Frank Freidel, Kenneth Stampp, and William B. Hesseltine and anti-Stalinist intellectuals on the order of Daniel Bell, Victor Serge, C. Wright Mills and George Orwell, whose political feelings, if not his actual ideas, were closest to Macdonald's.

Macdonald was equally against the pessimism of the right and the optimism of the Popular Front left. He disagreed with Arthur Koestler, for example, who maintained that the war was only a matter of national survival. Holding it to be not quite a people's war, Macdonald still saw in it revolutionary possibilities that intellectuals should try to explore.[20] On the other hand, it was definitely not a just war and he refused to support it, even critically, as did some independent radicals. Macdonald called himself a socialist, but without quite realizing it he was already changing. At a time when most democratic socialists admired Soviet collectivism, although not the means used to achieve it, Macdonald rejected both. "Bureaucratic collectivism, not capitalism, is the most dangerous future enemy of socialism," he wrote.[21] A noncollective socialism, which Macdonald appeared to want, left everyone speechless. He was gradually moving toward anarchism, which made more sense than trying to reconcile opposites.

Having exotic political views did not keep Macdonald from being a superb critic. No one wrote better about the follies of war. A classic example appeared in the June 1944 issue of *Politic*s. It was inspired by a recent speech of Churchill, who said that the war had become less ideological and that afterward the world would be run by the great powers along practical lines. Liberals, and even *The New York Times,* were upset by this cancellation of the people's war. Edward R. Murrow, the broadcaster, said of Churchill's speech that for the first time since 1940 national unity in Great Britain had been impaired. On learning of this, Macdonald envisioned

a huge glittering mechanism, the Murrow-meter, testing
a specimen block of national unity, clicking away at its
task month after month, the needle wavering between 260
and 357 degrees (the "Intact" zone), and then suddenly
after Churchill's speech, the needle moves to 358, and
with a great grinding of gears, frantic ringing of bells
and flashing of red lights the Murrow-meter records the
fatal tidings: IMPAIRED.[22]

Nor did progressive journalists escape Macdonald's notice. The
editors of the *New Republic* had attacked Churchill for his
cynical prophecy. "Well," said Macdonald, "he can't say he
hasn't been warned."[23]

Anti-Stalinist intellectuals in the United States now felt free
to lash out at pro-Soviet books, but their English counterparts
were still inhibited. One offensive work was Harold Laski's
Faith, Reason, and Civilization (1944). Forgotten today, Laski
was then a famous progressive. The child of an Orthodox Jewish
family in Manchester, he was such a prodigy that, in an age
when they were rare, he won a scholarship to Oxford University. He graduated with highest honors (a first) in history. After
teaching at McGill and Harvard, he ended up in the right place,
the London School of Economics, which had been founded by
Fabian Socialists. He wrote many books and was a Marxist of
sorts, but did not become a Communist owing to his excitement
over the New Deal. He was also active in the Labour Party,
winning election to its National Executive.

Though intelligent and broadly read, Laski was an exceed-
ingly careless writer, which accounts for the great volume of
his writings and their deserved neglect today. *Faith, Reason,
and Civilization* showed Laski at his worst. Even to his sympathetic biographer it "contained the nearest approach Laski ever
made to an undiluted eulogy of the Soviet Union."[24] This was
very close indeed, anti-Stalinists felt. George Orwell wrote
Macdonald that he had done a review of it for the evening
edition of the *Manchester Guardian,* "generally looked upon as
the only truthful paper in England," which the editor refused to
print.

If you look through it you will see that I have gone about
as far as was consistent with ordinary honesty *not* to say

what pernicious tripe the book is, and yet my remarks were too strong even for the *Manchester Evening News*. This will give you an idea of the kind of thing you can't print in England nowadays. Yet this isn't due to the Stalinists, who aren't much regarded nowadays. Editors will print nothing anti-Russian because of the supposed Russomania of the general public and also because of the complaints which the Soviet government is constantly raising about the British press.[25]

The enclosed review was mild enough. In it Orwell reproached Laski for sliding back from his position of only a year before that Soviet authoritarianism was worrisome. Now Laski was shutting his eyes again to Soviet villainy. Doing so was wrong in principle. It was also to lose the meaning of Russia's experience. Orwell understood this to be that "despotism based on power instead of money is the inherent danger of Socialism."[26] Orwell's own position, expressed in another letter to Macdonald, was as follows.

I think that if the USSR were conquered by some foreign country the working class everywhere would lose heart, for the time being at least, and the ordinary stupid capitalists who have never lost their suspicion of Russia would be encouraged. I think the fact that the Germans have failed to conquer Russia has given prestige to the idea of Socialism. For that reason I wouldn't want to see the USSR destroyed and think it ought to be defended if necessary. But I want people to become disillusioned about it and to realize that they must build their own Socialist movement without Russian interference, and I want the existence of democratic Socialism in the West to exert a regenerative influence upon Russia.[27]

In America's freer air anti-Stalinists could get published, if only by little magazines. In *Common Sense* Louis Fischer attacked Laski's book for urging the world to adopt Soviet values now that they had been vindicated by the Red Army. Indeed, Laski thought the common man already had done so to a large degree. This was nonsense, said Fischer. Russia was not fighting a people's war but carving out a sphere of influence in Eastern Europe. It cared nothing for self-determination or the Atlantic

Charter, and showed no desire for an international solution to the problems of peace. Russia's foreign policy was opportunistic. The Soviet values Laski admired were mere propaganda. The truth was:

> Reactionary social legislation, a foreign policy based on crude power politics and spheres of influence, the decay of even the forms of Soviet democracy, economic hardships, rigorous dictatorship and cruel cynical terror to maintain the counter-revolution—all these explain the Kremlin's crude attempt to concoct a new synthetic faith consisting of Czarist history, irrational Slavism, nationalism and church religion.[28]

Fischer expanded this review several years later. As he saw it, there were two Harold Laskis. "The perceiving Laski sees what is; the believing Laski, in scintillating debate, persuades the perceiving Laski that what he sees isn't so."[29] Laski was urging people to take up values Russia had long since abandoned. Because getting arrested in the Soviet Union was largely a matter of luck, there was an increase in fear of the law but not of respect for it. Fischer had been slow to realize that "dictatorship kills idealism." But he had come to think that, especially for younger Russians, "the effect of Soviet life is to center attention on physical goods." His conclusion, less elegantly put, was much the same as Orwell's.

> It ought to be obvious by this time that the end of the private business man and of the private market in Russia has not brought the millennium. To dethrone the capitalist and enthrone a tyrant who holds the power of the totalitarian state machine plus all the power of all the capitalists is not progress toward decency, plenty, or peace. There must be another way.[30]

Laski's book was widely but unfavorably reviewed in the United States, a sign of things to come. Only the *Survey Graphic*, a magazine devoted to social work and reform, praised *Faith, Reason, and Civilization*. And in England also, despite Orwell's fears, the book got a mixed reception. Kingsley Martin, Laski's future biographer, had good things to say about it, but

The Times Literary Supplement, most prestigious of English book reviews, stepped firmly on the book.[31] A further sign was the lessening of progressive innocence. Dwight Macdonald was surprised to learn in his first year as a publisher that nothing irritated readers more than attacks on Stalinism. As a veteran of the left's war of words, he had assumed that everyone knew the worst and only needed reminding. He was dismayed to learn that knowledge seemed to make no difference. People kept writing to him in protest, not denying the facts about Russia as of old, but admitting them while expressing hope anyway.[32] Read one way, this looked like cynicism. Though not yet evident, it was also a stage in the movement of progressives away from Stalinism. Support for Russia always depended in some measure on denial of the truth. Once faced, the crimes of Stalin became a heavy burden for Russophiles that few managed to carry for long.

As the war ended, anti-Stalinists became more numerous and vocal. In April 1945 Varian Fry resigned as a contributing editor of the *New Republic*, citing the magazine's apologies for Soviet misdeeds. Self-righteous as always, the editors disagreed. They were not afraid to criticize Russia, they said, which was true. But it was true also that they were still printing pro-Soviet propaganda as a matter of course. They accused Fry of being the sort of liberal who wanted Russia painted black, despite all those redeeming Soviet virtues so apparent to the *New Republic*. Anyway, criticizing Russia was practically treason. Attacks such as Fry's "are immediately and gleefully broadcast by the enemy radio"; accordingly "such influence as he has is therefore exerted on behalf of the wishes of the enemy, not his own country."[33] But instead of sending Fry to prison the editors allowed him a rejoinder. In it he denied being anti-Russian. He was only against the Soviet dictatorship and the *New Republic* policy of having one standard for Russia and another for the rest of the world. The editors denied having a double standard. It was simply that Russia had not interfered in any country, except maybe Poland, to impede democracy, whereas Britain and even the United States frequently did so. When Russia meddled, it was almost always on the side of democratic forces.[34]

Anti-Stalinists were less and less willing to allow this kind of thing to go by. Reinhold Niebuhr was becoming critical of *The Nation*'s identification with Russia, though so far only in general terms.[35] Louis Fischer was completely fed up. In May 1945 he sent Freda Kirchwey his resignation as associate editor, saying the magazine now had a "line" he did not agree with. Their editorial relations had always been difficult, even when they agreed politically.[36] But, though he did not say so directly, he was quitting over Russia. Kirchwey met him head on, reviewing *The Nation*'s reasons for favoring Russia. American hostility to Russia endangered the peace. Russia was only safeguarding its security in Europe. Russia was more antifascist than Britain or the United States. Despite errors, Russia was still the progressive power.[37]

In response Fischer acknowledged that it was *The Nation*'s stand on Russia that led him to resign. "You condone and apologize for what Russia does. When you do hint ever so lightly that Moscow may have made a mistake you immediately point to grave capitalist sins. You discriminate; you therefore distort."[38] Fischer did not agree that Russia's acts were purely defensive. All expanding powers, including Germany and Japan, claimed that national security was their aim. Nor did he accept the argument that Russia was more antifascist than its allies. Annexing Eastern Europe was not antifascist, nor was retaining pro-Nazi generals in the governments of Hungary and Bulgaria. *The Nation* printed many letters, mostly hostile to him, that it had received about Fischer. Britain, the Vatican, and U.S. capitalists were plotting to start World War III, was a frequent theme.

Granville Hicks joined the fight, writing that the country needed a "critical liberalism" very different from what one found in *PM* and the *New Republic*.[39] The *New Republic* was indignant, defending *PM* as well. Hicks wanted *PM* to be objective. This was contrary to the purpose for which it had been founded, that being to side with the "victims of oppression," as it still did. Nor was the *New Republic* guilty of covering up Russian sins, as Hicks charged. Besides, if everyone had taken Hicks's view of the function of liberal journalism the Nazis would have conquered the world. It was on account of passionate democrats willing to fight and die—including, obviously, the *New Republic*—"that Mr. Hicks can afford the luxuries of peace and freedom." Hicks was a typical ex-Communist, according to the editors, still possessing the qualities that made him a red in the first place. These were

> a combination of utopianism and a sort of fundamental irresponsibility about the present and the near future. To such a mentality thinking straight, keeping your record clear, expressing your (perhaps recently acquired) indignation about Russia's violations of civil liberties, will always seem more important than tackling the immediate problem and doing the best you can with it, even if you employ the aid of dubious allies, even if the crystal outlines of Truth are somewhat dimmed here and there by the rising dust of battle.[40]

On this note of heroic pragmatism the editors rested their case, having established that clarity, morality and truth were obstacles to good relations with the Soviet Union.

Kenneth G. Crawford, formerly the *New Republic*'s columnist TRB, was also turning around. In *Common Sense* he attacked the progressives' false ideas about Europe, from which he had just returned. Did they really believe, he asked, that there were going to be free elections in Eastern Europe? Did they doubt for a minute that free elections would be held in France and Italy? "Most Americans seem to understand the prime consequence of this war—the simple truth that we have beaten down one expanding totalitarian power and raised up another in the process—much better than do the heavy thinkers."[41]

Max Lerner was getting sick of this and attacked the anti-Stalinist "irresponsibles" in *PM*. He charged them with encouraging a "Soviet war in the name of socialist democracy. This is a more treacherous courtship than the Communists ever pursued, and more lethal both to American progressive thought and the world's hopes." Lerner had in mind Norman Thomas and contributors to the *New Leader,* the *Progressive,* an anti-Stalinist monthly, and *Common Sense*. These people kept saying that Soviet Russia was now the world's main threat, and that American foreign policy was appeasing it. There was only one conclusion to this line of thought, which they shrank from drawing, and that was the necessity of war with Russia. "It is their job to bring the country's mood up to the brink of the precipice while it is the job of the fascists to push us over."[42]

This was a great deal to lay on three small magazines, whose combined circulation was less than the *New Republic*'s, and a false charge in any case, as some readers pointed out. Norman Thomas wrote to say he was against war with Russia now or ever, but against appeasing Russia also. Others said there was no reason why the United States could not criticize Soviet imperialism, as it did British imperialism, while working for peace with both nations.[43] In reply Lerner backed down. He had not meant to say that you must either like Russia or fight it, he explained, though that was certainly how his column appeared to read. "The crucial question is whether your criticisms of Russia inherently deny that it can be a peaceful member of the world community."[44] As few anti-Stalinists thought that war with Russia was inevitable, this seemed to take them off the hook, for the moment anyway.

Kenneth Crawford believed that Lerner had been reduced to grasping at straws. In a recent editorial Lerner had written that Churchill was speaking out against Russia's emerging satellites because he was afraid of social democracy. "That's what's eating the old Tory," Crawford remarked, "he's afraid of those social democracies that are spreading by popular demand through Hungary, Bulgaria, Yugoslavia, Poland, Czechoslovakia."[45] Crawford believed that the progressive line was almost played out. Soon the conspiracy of silence about Russia would be over. What would Lerner do then? He would have to depend on short memories and hope that Russia's expansion was so successful as to wash out the knowledge of how it was done, Crawford speculated. As it turned out, short memories were quite enough.[46]

Recent events, the editors of *Common Sense* wrote in 1945, had shown the bankruptcy of progressive realism. For several years the "realists" had been saying that only agreement among the Big Three could win the war and preserve the peace, and therefore considerations of international morality had to take second place. What resulted was the division of Europe into spheres of influence, and American consent to purges, annexations and the forcible alteration of boundaries. In the name of realism a right of veto was written into the UN Charter. The fruits of this were seen in the London conference of foreign ministers.

> The policy of discarding principles in the interest of agreement has led, inevitably, to the loss of any real foundation for agreement. When interests have clashed, there has been no common ground on which they could be resolved. Those who abrogated to themselves the posts of arbiters for the world have found that they have neither arbiters nor law for the settlement of their own disputes.[47]

Some "who have demanded the sacrifice of justice to agreement" were now appalled and favored throwing "interests after principles in the desperate effort to avoid another war." They were wrong. The right course was to build a world order based on law and justice, which was only "superficially" the more difficult way.

It is hard to know if many people agreed. Support for the UN, despite the veto, which was seen as a weakness imposed on it by Russia, remained high. But feelings about the Soviets were beginning to change. The polls showed a ten percent drop in confidence in Russia during the early months of 1945. In January a plurality had regarded Britain as most to blame for Allied difficulties. By May a majority had come to think that Russia was more at fault. For progressives it was to be all downhill from there.[48]

Even before this, traditional anti-Communists had begun to go on the offensive again, to the distress of progressives and fellow travelers, who properly regarded them as more dangerous than charges made in little magazines. The September 4, 1944, issue of *Life* carried a long article by William C. Bullitt critical of Soviet Russia. Bullitt was not a very nice man, and he was out of power, having been expelled from Roosevelt's sight forever on account of having circulated rumors about Sumner Welles.[49] Just the same, Bullitt had been the first American ambassador to the Soviet Union and was no fool. Moreover, his article was part of a new campaign being launched by Henry Luce. Henceforth Luce's magazines, which faithfully reflected his personal opinions, would lash out at Russia frequently.

Progressives were very upset by Bullitt's article, "The World from Rome," as by the implication, probably justified, that he was speaking for the Vatican.[50] The *New Republic* said that Luce was trying to split the Allies "and thus help the Nazis to escape retribution."[51] Gaetano Salvemini, its regular commentator on Italian affairs, attacked Bullitt's Roman informants for saying that Russia meant to dominate Finland and all of Eastern Europe. He made again the progressive charge that America was to blame for trying to save rotten old regimes. Bullitt had said that Romans believed it was a mistake for America not to have committed Stalin to a postwar settlement in 1941 when he needed help the most. To the contrary, said Salvemini, the mistake was not to give Stalin what he asked for in 1943 (the second front), which would have made him less demanding now.[52]

The *New Republic* was restraint itself compared with *PM*, which threw Max Lerner once more unto the breach. It was with a heavy heart, or stomach, that Lerner undertook "the slightly nauseating job of dissecting the rotten cadaver of Bullitt's piece." Lerner did so because Bullitt's essay marked the first time "outside of the pages of the lunatic fascist press, or the Hearst press, or the McCormick-Patterson axis, that the slimy whispered agitation for a split between America and its Russian partner" had found expression. *Pravda* had already exposed thirty lies in this article, saving Lerner the trouble. Anyway, Lerner was more concerned with Bullitt's intent. To Lerner's mind Bullitt was trying to drive a wedge between the Polish underground and the Red Army; inciting the Finns not to surrender to Russia; pressing Rumania to stay at war with Russia or lose its independence; fomenting civil war in Yugoslavia; and dividing the Allies over Germany. Bullitt was trying to accomplish all these vile things for personal reasons. Being anti-Soviet had led Bullitt to make mistake after mistake. He had been wrong about Russia and wrong in his efforts to shape France's foreign policy before its defeat. He had wrongly tried to change the priority in American military strategy from Europe to the Pacific. He had opposed the spirit of Teheran. Now he was seeking to reverse American foreign policy to show "that he was, after all, right."[53]

This was a generous reading of Bullitt's motives, according to

George Seldes of *In Fact,* who called Bullitt "a fascist agent" and "the foremost helper of the Hitler plot in Europe." "He was always a spy," wrote Seldes, quoting *Pravda* to nail down the point. Bullitt's thirty lies, Seldes calculated, amounted to "one lie in every five lines," which was apparently a record.[54]

The *New Leader* rejoiced, even though disagreeing with Bullitt on particulars. "But whatever our differences, the *New Leader* has been almost alone among American publications in presenting this picture of the very real menace of Stalinist totalitarianism—including the danger that it may be the cause of World War III."[55] And it was delighted with Lerner's attack on Bullitt, which betrayed the weakness of *PM*'s case. Lerner

> can only "answer" Bullitt by following the Stalinist method of name-calling and by ascribing to his opponent vicious intentions. Bullitt's political analysis aids the Nazis, he says, sedulously echoing *Pravda*. Bullitt wants a negotiated peace; Bullitt wants a bloc of nations against Russia; Bullitt wants war; Bullitt is a discredited anti-Soviet conspirator; Bullitt was one of the grave-diggers of France; Bullitt is opposed to Allied unity created at Teheran; Bullitt has always been wrong.[56]

This was the measure of Lerner's desperation.

Six months later a book by William L. White ended the moratorium of commercial publishers on works hostile to Russia. His *Report on Russia* had flaws, as Louis Fischer, who reviewed it favorably, admitted in private,[57] but it was important just the same, and opened the way for stronger books to come. White was a journalist who had visited Russia only briefly, like the many who wrote books praising the Soviet Union. But in his six weeks there White had seen enough to make him uneasy. Americans flying regularly between Iran and Russia told him they were afraid to date Soviet girls, who had a way of disappearing afterward. There was never enough to eat. Even correspondents who received special rations and could buy more at the U. S. embassy's commissary lost weight. Yet White grew sick of rich food and drink because he traveled with Eric Johnston, head of the U.S. Chamber of Commerce, who was feted everywhere. White's effort to explain the Soviet system began thusly: "Suppose you had been born and spent all your life in a moderately well-run penitentiary, which kept you working hard and provided a bunk to sleep in, three daily meals, and enough clothes to keep you warm."[58] There followed a long comparison of Russia with a state prison in Kansas. This was not how progressives were used to hearing the Soviet Union described.

Worse was to come. White did not accept the Soviet view, endorsed by progressives, that Germany had slaughtered the ten thousand Polish officers whose bodies were discovered in the Katyn Forest. White wrote about the forced labor camps, another taboo. It had been explained to him that they were products of the science of social engineering. "The science of social engineering cannot be deflected by personal tragedies, since its objectives are the building of a strong, loyal state. And it should be said in defense of the Soviet government that under similar circumstances it has treated its own people as it did the Poles."[59] This was not much of a defense, since White believed that one and half million Poles had been swallowed up in labor camps. He agreed with William Henry Chamberlin, who had been caught in Bordeaux when France fell and made this remark to another correspondent: "You know, it takes a great upheaval, a catastrophic defeat in war and a national convulsion to reduce a nation to that state of affairs which is normal, everyday life in the Soviet Union."

White's was the most controversial book about Russia since *Mission to Moscow,* though for opposite reasons. Fellow travelers and progressive journalists signed a statement attacking White for warmongering.* John Chamberlain heard that only one newsman of those asked failed to add his name.[60] Except for Edmund Wilson almost every major reviewer criticized the book, even those who agreed with White politically. (Of twenty-nine reviews listed in *Book Review Digest 1945,* only three were entirely favorable.) White was said to be one-sided and unfair. For example, he attributed Russia's success in the war partly to the several hundred thousand military vehicles sent to

---

* They included John Hersey, Quentin Reynolds, Richard Lauterbach, Edgar Snow, Raymond Arthur Davies, Jerome Davis, John Fisher, Alexander Kendrick, Alexander Werth and Ella Winter.

it by America. He exaggerated the number of people in labor camps. He showed no regard for Russian feelings, and so on. White's real sin was prematurity. His book was remarkably accurate, considering his short visit and lack of special knowledge. But White's truths were something that few liberals and fewer progressives wished to hear. They suggested what was actually the case, that Stalin's Russia would not be easy to get along with after the war.

Between the pro-Soviet and anti-Soviet camps there was a middle ground that few intellectuals chose to occupy. Even so, it was more popular than a reading of journals of opinion might lead one to believe. The best evidence for this was the success of Walter Lippmann's *United States Foreign Policy: Shield of the Republic* (1943). Though short, it was a very important, or potentially important, work that was adopted by the Book-of-the-Month Club and sold to hundreds of thousands of readers. After writing about foreign affairs for thirty years Lippmann had come to realize that he was frequently criticizing past decisions that he had approved at the time, and views he had once shared. The reason was that too often he had not been thinking of foreign policy in terms of the national interest. Lippmann was not contemptuous of morality and ideology. It was simply that he no longer believed them to be reliable guides either to the behavior of other nations or to decision-making by the United States. American policy toward Japan was, he argued, a classic example of how a nation should not act. The United States had provoked Japan while at the same time it failed to strengthen its bases in the Pacific. The delusion that you could have a policy while lacking the means to implement it reached a pinnacle of sorts in the summer of 1939, when the Senate Foreign Relations Committee did two things: it advised the State Department to launch a program of economic warfare against Japan, and at the same time it refused to lift the arms embargo which kept Britain and France from buying weapons to resist Japan's German ally. For the sake of what were always called "ideals," in this case peace and disarmament, the nation worked at cross purposes.

What did experience suggest was the right line to take after the war? The alliance with Britain should continue. Russia was problematical. On the one hand, although Russia and America always had antagonistic political ideologies and were always suspicious of each other, in the past each had wished the other to be strong. "They have never had a collision which made them enemies. Each has regarded the other as a potential friend in the rear of its potential enemies."[61] But this historic principle no longer held. After the war there would remain only two great powers, Russia and the United States. Instead of being a potential friend behind potential enemies Russia would become the threat behind our friends in both Europe and Asia. Neither Britain nor the United States would be able to influence the nations of Central and Eastern Europe. Russia was going to occupy them, and the best to be hoped for was that it would allow them to remain neutral. Any effort to make these states outposts of the West was doomed to fail, and would actually guarantee their domination by Russia. In Asia the situation was less clear owing to the weakness of China. Lippmann believed that regional power blocs were going to form. No League of Nations could be expected to keep peace among them. That would depend on continuing present ties. "The will of the most powerful states to remain allied is the only possible creator of a general international order."[62]

As did most people, Lippmann underestimated the strength of both Communism and nationalism in Asia. But he had grasped the central points. The destruction of German and Japanese power was creating vacuums that someone would fill, and a situation in which the interests of Russia and the United States might, for the first time, be in conflict. This was too much realism so far as progressives were concerned, though some attempted to have it both ways. Max Lerner praised Lippmann's book for its enlightened nationalism and common sense, but thought it too conservative. He preferred Wendell Willkie's *One World* (1943), a typical outburst of progressive wishful thinking that to Lerner was more "humanist." Lippmann's hope for the future rested on America's role as a co-belligerent of what in the future would be the main powers—Great Britain, Russia, and possibly China.

Lerner put his faith not in present ties but in what he still thought of as shared beliefs held by "the progressive and anti-fascist powers of the world." Lippmann was preoccupied with tangible things about the Allies to the neglect of "their creative place in the world." Lerner did not mind hearing about the national interest, but beyond it the United States

> has values to defend as well as land. And those values of a feeling [sic] for ordinary people everywhere, a desire to fight along with them for a better world, higher living standards, a freer moral atmosphere, a richer world culture. What allies you will choose in this fight must be determined by the things you and they care for.[63]

So it was back to the people's war again and the "creative place" of nations, as against unpleasant facts, the contemplation of which led only to a "morass," Lerner wrote.

Alfred Bingham of *Common Sense* was disgusted with Lippmann's "thoroughly reactionary book," so foreign to the spirit in which Bingham was waging war. "The ordering of the world by preponderant force, in accordance 'with vital national interests,' is what many people have thought we were fighting against." Nor did Lippmann take account of such vital matters as "social revolution, communism, imperialism, racial consciousness, and the incalculable forces that are rousing Asia to action."[64] This was true, actually, a blind spot Lippmann shared with most nonprogressives. As shall be seen, the progressive canon, even though spelled out unthinkingly, was not entirely wrong. The problem always was that the answers came out automatically regardless of circumstances. Those outside the fold knew this, so even when progressives were right, as to a considerable degree they were about Asia, few were persuaded owning to the cant regarding Soviet democracy and the people's war.

British progressives, though often wittier than the American variety, generally ended up in the same place. Thus, Kingsley Martin compared Lippmann to Machiavelli. "In exactly the same way Mr. Lippmann, avoiding every idealistic phrase and accepting international gangsterism as the norm of behaviour, explains to Americans how they should behave if they are not again to risk losing their share of the loot." Martin was unjust and meant to be. He was annoyed with Lippmann for writing such a successful book without reference to progressive cliches.

The very excellence of Mr. Lippmann's picture as a simple account of "the behaviour of States only serves to heighten the unrealistic character of any account of world politics today which omits the economic and ideological causes of war, and which attempts to found peace on the supposed interests of Governments to the exclusion of the common sympathies and interests of people."[65] In a less dimwitted and obvious fashion than *PM,* Martin had traveled a similar route. It was a long way from Machiavelli to the people's war, but he got there just the same.

Lippmann's book, despite its large sale, had no visible effect upon the progressive mind. This was too bad, not because Lippmann was always right on the issues, but because he was thinking in the right way, trying hard to judge issues on their merits rather than out of established prejudice. In a few years progressives would be agreeing with Lippmann without having learned anything from him. Lippmann's view of Russia, so conservative in light of the people's war, would become more appealing to progressives as the Cold War deepened. They would, however, continue to misunderstand the reasoning behind it.

The noted historian Carl Becker took an approach similar to Lippmann's. His shrewd little book *How New Will the Better World Be?* (1944) showed that common sense and a general knowledge of history (he was not writing as an expert) could take one far, even in a time of high feelings. Becker held that war psychology was deluding people into thinking that this awesome experience had generated the wisdom to make a better world. Progressives had gone overboard, he wrote, in assuming that nationalism and the sovereign state could be drastically limited. He reviewed Western history to demonstrate that nationalism was "the principal political force of our time; and the historically created nation-state is the form which political power takes in the modern world."[66] Nor was this necessarily evil, since it was nationalism that was saving America in the world crisis.

"Can We Abolish Power Politics and End Imperialism?" he asked rhetorically. All politics involved power, and so diatribes against power politics made no sense. People who talked about ending imperialism seemed to have only the British Empire in mind. They forgot that the United States and Russia, and China too, had incorporated alien parts and were empires also, though the parts were consolidated and not spread all over as were Britain's. A narrow anti-imperialism obscured the vital fact that America had more in common with Britain and the English-speaking dominions than with other nations. Our future was tied to theirs. And, as empires went, Britain's was a good one. Let us leave to the British the job of setting their house in order, Becker urged.

Progressives were trying to have their cake and eat it too, he believed. On the one hand, the white powers must get out of Asia. On the other, they must help China keep the peace. In the same vein, progressives were calling on the great powers to design a lasting peace, while also insisting on the right of all peoples to self-determination. Yet one could not ask the white powers to fight desperately to stay in the Far East if immediately afterward they had to get out. And one could not demand a great-power settlement that also involved the right of all nations to choose their own governments. Whatever the terms for peace might be in Eastern Europe, many peoples would remain dissatisfied.

Becker chopped through thickets of progressive rhetoric to arrive at essential facts. Contrary to liberal opinion, most Americans were not fighting for the freedom of mankind but to preserve American life, hardly a shameful thing since that life was beneficial even if imperfect. He hoped that in the future there would be more social democracy and national planning, though not at the expense of private profit or individual liberty. Internationally he thought that a Federation of Europe similar to the United States of America was impossible. A new League of Nations, with or without a police force, seemed to him, as to Lippmann, unlikely to keep the peace. That would require continued agreement among Britain, Russia and America. This should be possible, Becker argued, because the different security requirements were compatible. Britain and America saw control of the Atlantic as vital; Russia was mainly concerned with Eastern Europe. So there was no great conflict of interest among the great powers.

Becker did not touch all bases. He overestimated the force of reason in human affairs, perhaps deliberately. It was an emotional time when coolness and common sense were in short supply. He underestimated, like nearly everyone, the strength of nationalism in Africa and Asia. The book was important anyway, or would have been if progressives had taken it seriously.* In their eagerness to have a better world, progressives were, as Becker said, making things worse. Despite lack of evidence, they declared the world conflict to be a people's war. They attributed virtues to Russia that the Soviets did not possess. They were unable to distinguish between morality and self-interest, or between what was and what they knew in their hearts ought to be. Thoroughly confused themselves, they misled as well everyone who looked to them for guidance. Little wonder that books such as those by Becker and Lippmann had no effect. Progressives were going to have to learn their lesson the hard way.

---

* Becker's book was praised, even if not heeded, by most reviewers. An exception was Malcolm Cowley, who attacked Becker for believing in the permanence of nation-states and the national interest, though he added kindly that elsewhere Becker's work was "not so utterly hopeless."[67]

IV

The "People's War" Falters: 1943–1945

THE REVIVAL OF anti-Communist sentiment in the last years of the war made life difficult for progressives, but the actions of Soviet Russia were more troublesome still. At first progressives had only to deal with the negative image of Russia built up by decades of anti-Soviet propaganda. From 1943 on they were faced with a bad press arising from Soviet misconduct in the liberated territories of Eastern Europe. One tactic was to make light of Communist offenses. Thus, early in 1943 when two Polish (and Jewish) democratic leaders were executed by the Soviets, Max Lerner rebuked them while also insisting that small mistakes like this were no obstacle to good relations.[1] The *New Republic* took a harder line. Yes, Ehrlich and Alter were innocent and the Soviets ought not to have killed them. On the other hand, the Allies did not have clean hands themselves. What about British outrages in India? What about Sacco and Vanzetti?[2] The reasoning seemed to be that as the Allied nations had committed evils in the past, fresh ones by Russia made no difference.

When they could, progressives liked to deny Soviet wrongdoing entirely, as in the Katyn Forest. During 1943 Germany revealed the burial site of thousands of Polish officers captured and executed by Russia after it occupied eastern Poland in 1939. Though the German charge was true, Max Lerner recognized it instantly as a Nazi lie, owing to his profound knowledge of Soviet psychology. "The Russians can be hard and cruel when there is a political point to it. But when they are, they make no pretense of concealing what they have done."[3] Too bad the Polish government was taken in by this German trick and suspended relations with the Soviet Union, Lerner continued. He knew that Polish folly was a function of Polish reaction. "We must find a Polish government that can lead the Polish people to a new Europe," wrote Lerner, as if Russia had not already done so.

Though he still contributed to the *New Republic,* Lerner now worked for *PM,* the progressive daily newspaper in New York. Its most distinctive feature was that at first it accepted no advertising, on the theory that a press could not be truly free that had to satisfy commercial interests. Having little money, it printed little news, making up the difference with editorials and personal columns. As newspaper readers wanted ads and news, few subscribed to *PM* except those who agreed with its politics. This was fine with Lerner, who told his old friend Associate Justice Felix Frankfurter of the Supreme Court that writing editorials for it was "more rewarding work than any I have thus far done."[4] In his editorials and frequent columns Lerner wrote about everything, bringing to each subject the insights he enjoyed by virtue, as he told Frankfurter, of belonging to the tradition of Jefferson, Henry Demarest Lloyd, Debs, Veblen and other great American radicals.

The *New Republic* too was disgusted with the reactionary Polish government-in-exile for using Katyn as a pretext not to discuss boundary questions with Russia. "Even its opposition to Hitler was nationalist rather than anti-fascist," the editors wrote of Poland's government, establishing a test of fitness that Russia could not have passed either. Still, it was healthy to get this conflict out into the open, they said. Everyone could see how bad many of the governments-in-exile were. The task now was to get behind the democratic and progressive Polish leaders (most of them Communists), so as to head off problems after the war.[5]

The Nation also despised the Polish government-in-exile, which was solely to blame for its troubles with Russia. It persisted in the foolish hope that Poland could become independent again. It refused to sign away former Polish territories demanded by Russia, even though they were inhabited mostly by Ukrainians and White Russians. The government-in-exile was wrong in practice, since defying Stalin would only make him more greedy, and wrong in principle too for not acknowledging the right of self-determination. The exiles were out of touch with the Polish masses, who would have the last word. "At the moment of victory they will perceive the paths open to them and make their choice. This choice will decide the future of Poland."[6] Of course the Poles were not going to decide their fate, as *The Nation* in saner moments knew. But progressive journals were always trying to square circles. They wanted to believe that what Russia did out of self-interest was morally right, and that the most brutal war in history was a people's struggle in which all things tended toward ultimate good.

After the Red Army crossed into Poland, Max Lerner counseled *PM* readers once more to ignore the Polish government. Poland would have to shed its old ruling class in order to get along with Russia. This should not be difficult, the long tradition of rancor between Poland and Russia notwithstanding, on account of the Poles themselves—whose collective heart Lerner had plumbed as deeply as he had the Russians'. Thus he could say that "the mass of the Polish people are more concerned about peace and economic reconstruction than they are in the question of territorial irredentism."[7] Anyway, they had to know that only in alignment with Russia could they move toward economic and social democracy. This movement did not, however, include plebiscites or any of the self-determinative apparatus of the old League of Nations. The principles of Versailles were dead. The future world order was to be a "Great Powers world federation," in which, naturally, great powers like Russia must feel secure. For the sake of the right kind of democracy the wrong kind, which allowed people to make their own choices, must be put aside.

In 1944 the Warsaw underground revolted. It took German forces sixty-two days to suppress the uprising, during most of which time Stalin would not allow his allies the use of Russian bases to airlift supplies to Warsaw. Nor did Russia try very hard to reach the city in time. Warsaw was therefore destroyed in a way that did not seem quite consistent with the idea of a people's war. *The Nation* was upset, but stopped short of blaming Russia.[8] The *New Republic* went further, charging Russia with acting in a "dictatorial" manner.[9] This was a change from the week before, when an American fellow traveler had assured readers that the Soviet Union was so far removed from any wish to dominate that it "would even prefer not to have communist governments in border states."[10] Its betrayal of the Warsaw uprising threw cold water, if only briefly, on such fantasies. Some two dozen books dealing with Russian-Polish relations came out in 1943–44, all of them asserting Russia's willingness to see a strong and independent Poland emerge from the war. After Warsaw this argument could not honestly be maintained. In Poland, according to the historian of American opinion, Russia lost the goodwill earned by its resistance to Hitler.[11]

Having nothing else, progressives clung to their faith just the same. On May 6, 1945, Max Lerner gave a radio talk, which ran in *PM* the next day, on sixteen Polish underground leaders who were in a Soviet jail. They were linked with the Polish government-in-exile and had been lured into Russia by promises of immunity, supposedly to discuss the future of Poland, actually to be seized on charges of killing Russian soldiers. On the face of it, Lerner admitted, this seemed hard to justify. Having been invited to Moscow the Poles ought to have enjoyed something like diplomatic immunity. But maybe the Soviets had a good reason. None had yet been given, so Lerner thought up a few. These made him feel better. It remained an apparent fact that the Yalta Agreement, which called for the inclusion of non-Communists in the new Polish government, had been used to entrap the sixteen.

There was some ground for bitterness in London and Washington, Lerner admitted. But the big picture had to be kept in mind. The Russians were tough and cynical. Still, if "they had been a different sort of nation, they would never have held out against almost the full force of Hitler's strength for four years."[12] Then, too, the United States had been cynical also, over getting Argentina into the UN and by attempting to isolate Russia diplomatically. Lerner forthrightly condemned Russia's methods in Poland, concluding, however, that these must not be allowed to hurt Russo-American relations or compromise the more important negotiations over Germany to come. And we would need Russian help against Japan, or else the war might go on for six more months and cost another half-million lives.

So much for the sixteen Poles, who had gotten lost in a tangle of larger considerations.

Yet this was not the end. There was a trial, and, as Soviet trials had a way of doing, it resolved Lerner's doubts. Evidence was brought forward to prove that the sixteen had committed anti-Soviet acts. The defendants confessed. Who could ask for more? Certainly not Lerner, who declared the Poles to be guilty not just in a Moscow court of law "but in the court of world opinion," over which he seemed to preside.[13] The Polish government, which had insisted on their innocence, was finished, Lerner happily reported. It turned out that even the claim that the Poles had been duped into going to Moscow was false, as they themselves admitted. This settled matters for Lerner, who found nothing so reliable as the word of a prisoner of the NKVD. Russia was being generous, in any case. Though the Poles had confessed to acts of terrorism and other crimes, the Soviet court gave them mild sentences.* This proved to Lerner that the Russians were sensitive to "liberal world opinion." It made British and American diplomats look foolish for having tried to depict the Soviets as barbaric and ruthless. Now the way was clear to build in Poland "far greater security, a far less feudal economy, a far juster social system than Poland has had." Lucky Poland to have such protectors, and fortunate America to have a Lerner to make things plain.

Fellow travelers were even more shameless. I. F. Stone told *Nation* readers almost immediately after the Poles were arrested that he knew enough "to advise American progressives to keep their shirts on." Stone had obtained the truth from Moscow radio, which was that the sixteen "had been arrested for the installation and maintenance of illegal transmitters in the rear of Soviet troops and for acts which had cost the lives of more than one hundred Red Army officers and men."[15] Secretary of State Stettinius had released a false story about the Poles as part of an anti-Soviet conspiracy. The entrapment of the Poles was, to

---

* Even this was deceitful. Stalin promised Harry Hopkins, who was putting pressure on him, that the sixteen Poles would receive light sentences. But as it happened, "many of them died in prison. Of the six or so released, some were rearrested in Poland, some fled to the West."[14]

Stone, a mere legalism. The key point was that the Poles were not democrats as Stettinius claimed. At least two were anti-Semites and fascists. Stone had this straight from an agent of the (Communist) Lublin government, an even better source than Moscow radio.

During the war progressives generally held that the main barrier to a lasting peace was not Russia but the United States. In their gloomiest moments it seemed to them that just as the excellence of Soviet foreign policy was a function of the health of Soviet society, American failures abroad resulted from sickness at home. In 1943, noting the end of domestic reform and the replacement of New Dealers by conservatives, Malcolm Cowley wrote that "it is possible that a fascist state could be instituted here without many changes in government personnel, and some of those changes have been made already."[16]

As usual, Max Lerner took a cheerier view. When Arthur Koestler, a former Comintern agent, wrote a grim article on the world situation in *The New York Times Magazine,* Lerner had a perky rejoinder. Given that most people are inherently conservative, what amazed Lerner was not the defeats but the victories of liberalism. The antifascist coalition was not a defeat, nor were trade unionism, collective bargaining, the minimum wage and other reforms. This was a revolutionary era full of exciting changes. Beyond the New Deal there was the greatest fact, unmentioned by Koestler, the Soviet Union. "Russia has broken what used to be the last bastion of the primitives—the myth that socialism is against human nature and that no collectivist society will work."[17]

Lerner had no peer when it came to knowing less and writing more about the Soviets. Early in his tenure with *PM* he did six editorials under the heading "Russia and America," based, he said, on the premise that these were "the creative and powerful nations of the future."[18] In them he gave voice to the usual progressive clichés. Russia was led by realists interested mainly in security. Neighbors had nothing to fear from this state, because Russia's aims were nationalistic, not imperialistic. The postwar situation depended chiefly on America. "What it all amounts to is that, in default of a line of action on our part to help build a genuine structure of European security on progressive principles, Stalin intends to seek Russian security in Europe itself." But if the United States gave up dealing with European reactionaries "we can build a structure of security together."[19] Lerner anticipated the stand taken later by revisionist historians, who would blame the United States for its poor relations with Russia.

Before an important meeting of foreign ministers in Moscow the *New Republic* assigned Heinz H. F. Eulau, who had a doctorate in political science and once worked in the Justice Department, to explain how far America lagged behind the Soviets. Readers learned once again that the USSR was chiefly interested in security, which had been its motive for the Stalin-Hitler Pact. At the same time Moscow saw the inevitability of revolution in Europe and aimed to ride with it. While Britain and the United States backed reactionaries, "Stalin is busy winning the friendship of Europe's revolutionary masses." Yet hope remained. Launching a second front would show that Anglo-Americans sincerely wished to help Russia. The dissolution of the Comintern was "an invitation to unity of all progressive forces outside of the Soviet Union." While Russia's formation of its own Polish government-in-exile showed that it would not tolerate reaction in Eastern Europe, its mutual-assistance treaty with the Czech exiles "suggests that the Soviet Union is ready to support such governments as are deemed genuinely democratic." Russia had a better German policy too, offering a free Germany peace and prosperity instead of unconditional surrender. Thus, Russia had a "positive" foreign policy, in contrast to the "unimaginative wait-and-see policy of Washington and London." Russia was "stealing the show in Europe" on account of being in tune with the people's war and the century of the common man.[20]

The success, as progressives thought it to be, of the Moscow Conference inspired jubilation. I. F. Stone wrote that Roosevelt had led America out of isolation, brought about an "entente between capitalist America and Communist Russia," and taken "the first step toward preventing World War III."[21] This justified everything Roosevelt had done that Stone disapproved of, which was plenty, including most recently the forcing out of Undersecretary of State Sumner Welles, a favorite of progressives. The *New Republic* cheered also. For their work in Moscow the Big Four powers had

> earned the gratitude of the free people of the world. But it is clear that if primacy in this gratitude belongs to anyone, it is to President Roosevelt. His was the shaping conception, his the initiative that brought the men together, his the genius for compromise that kept them in the channel of the main chance while avoiding the shoals and rocks of their differences.[22]

To the *New Leader* their joy was further evidence of the progressives' double standard. William Henry Chamberlin pointed out that the *New Republic* had said of the Moscow Agreement that Secretary Hull "wisely" accepted Russia's absorption of the Baltic States as a fait accompli. But the magazine never accepted Japanese absorption of Manchuria on that basis, though it was equally an accomplished fact. The *New Republic* had said of the agreement that "the only losers are the enemies of humanity." Chamberlin asked what the Poles, the Finns, the Letts, the Estonians and the Lithuanians had done that made them enemies of mankind. Max Lerner had written in *PM* that nothing in the agreement suggested that the Atlantic Charter would be betrayed. This was sophistry to Chamberlin, who observed that nothing guaranteed that Russia's neighbors would regain self-determination and their old borders as the Charter stipulated. Chamberlin saw that there was no practical alternative to accepting what could not be denied Stalin, but that was no reason to crow. "When an injustice has been acquiesced in, it is far more sensible and realistic to acknowledge the fact than to commit the hypocrisy of representing an unscrupulous piece of power politics as an expression of the highest ideals of freedom and self-determination."[23]

Progressives welcomed 1944. "Throughout the world the swing is not to the Right, but toward the democratic left," announced the *New Republic*.[24] Even Malcolm Cowley was less glum than usual. He attacked the false optimism of the Communist *New Masses,* while admitting there were signs of hope. "The forces on our side are more powerful in the end, being the kindness and devotion and good sense of ordinary people in all nations, including our own."[25] Unfortunately, the United States was still failing to prove itself a worthy ally of Russia. The task at hand, according to *New Republic* editors, was to establish "genuine political cooperation of a sort that would convince Russia she can safely entrust her future to collective security underwritten by the two great Western powers."[26] Further impediments to peace and freedom were the anti-Stalinists at home, called the "Hang-Back Boys" by Bruce Bliven in one editorial.[27] They seemed to him less interested in winning the war than in scoring points against Stalin.

Bliven had in mind particularly the *New Leader*, which was locally famous for hanging back. It answered him with a sharp article by Daniel Bell. Bliven had praised the "democratic leadership" of Stalin, adding that people in Eastern Europe who didn't like the new territorial arrangements should be allowed to emigrate. Bell wondered if this meant Polish reservations similar to those for American Indians. Here was another example, Bell said, of the "totalitarian liberalism" practiced by the *New Republic*.[28] It seemed a popular line nonetheless, for the *New Republic* was enjoying record sales. Its circulation in the first half of 1944 was forty-two percent greater than the year before, an all-time high.[29]

Progressive spirits rose again after the Big Three conference at Teheran, where a meeting of minds between Roosevelt and Stalin was said to have taken place. The normally restrained *Atlantic* magazine reported that the Americans had returned "with the impression that Stalin is both a military genius and a man of his word.[30] *The Atlantic* believed American suspicion of Russia to have been a result of Soviet secrecy, which was now, it hoped, at an end. Heinz Eulau took a sterner view. Revolutionary partisans who meant to keep the old regimes out of Eastern Europe had to be supported. "Frank recognition of the preponderance of Soviet interest in this area is clearly the most promising feature of Russo-Anglo-American political collaboration." Soviet dominance was not imperialistic but derived from the "tremendous popularity which the USSR enjoys among large sections of the Balkan peoples, especially peasants and workers."[31] This arose, Eulau explained with habitual progressive confidence, from admiration for the Red Army, racial affinity, and Soviet leadership in "the liquidation of the old ruling classes and the federal solution of the nationality problem." East Europeans would be happy to take a leaf from Russia's book. "Those who raise the cry of 'Soviet Imperialism' fail to understand that the overwhelming majority of the common people in the Balkans do not fear Soviet influence," wrote Eulau from the safety of America.[32]

Anna Louise Strong was even more reassuring. So far were the Russians from wanting to impose their will that any non-fascist system was fine with them. She knew this from talking with a Russian newspaper editor as follows: "I asked, 'Would the Soviet Union and the Red Army support the extension of the American form of capitalist democracy in Europe for a long period?' He nodded, 'If this is the form the people in Europe choose, then Europe would be better than before.' "[33] That was on a par with Max Lerner's discovery of the lesson of Russia's military victories. In a column giving thanks for them he recalled a drive through rural Wisconsin. Seeing the prosperous farms, he was struck by "the sharp contrast between a people who organize the use of their rich resources by greed and haphazard planning, and people who had learned to plan production for the use of the whole people." It was thus that "I learned something about the meaning of Russian victories."[34] As luck would have it, Wisconsin farmers, not previously known for their avarice, seldom read *PM*.

The *New Republic* remained complacent for a time. In June 1944 it remembered with satisfaction how people used to say that we need not concern ourselves with Europe's future, because the Soviet Union would decide things. "According to one version she would revert to Tzarist imperialism, absorbing everything in sight. At the very least she would demand Finland, the Baltic States, and Poland, thus making a mockery of conscientious war aims." These and other fears had been laid to rest by the recent Anglo-Soviet treaty. The *New Republic* understood that some Communists would not easily give up their hopes for world revolution. Not to worry. "If the British and Americans believe that with their principles a new order for the common man can be created, they need not fear that Communist hope of revolution will ever be realized. After all, neither Moscow nor London but man himself, will in the end everywhere decide what sort of regime he will live in."[35] As outside of Britain and the neutral states Europeans did not have the slightest say in how they were governed, this showed a marvelous faith.

The Nation too was optimistic, especially J. Alvarez del Vayo. He was a journalist and politician who had been the Spanish Republic's ambassador to Mexico, representative to the League of Nations and, during most of the Spanish Civil War, foreign minister. After the republic's fall he made his livelihood by writing and lecturing, serving also as an editor of *The Nation*. Freda Kirchwey supported him loyally despite repeated charges, which were true, that he fellow-traveled. Vayo would admit that Soviet Russia sometimes made errors. These were never serious enough to shake his confidence.[36] His specialty was combining soft soap with radical enthusiasm. Thus he often wrote that Russia had said goodbye to revolution, so there was no cause for alarm. On the other hand, Europe was going to move left anyhow, thanks to Russia's example.

Capitalists liked to distinguish between the Soviet state and the Russian people, giving all credit to the latter. But the "common man, whose century Henry Wallace has announced," knew that Russian victories were a function of the Soviet state. "To the peoples of Europe, that Socialist Russia which has so ably organized production, which has created the best army in the world, which has drawn its factory foremen, its engineers, its generals, from the working class, remains an inspiration."[37] The common man might not want the proletarian dictatorship, Vayo conceded, but he was positive that because of Russia the masses yearned for socialism. Soon the war had to end and British and American troops would depart, leaving "the settlement of European problems to the European peoples."[38] Backward capitalists would naturally attempt to block the spread of socialism, but in vain. "Not even war weariness or disillusionment can head off a change which is part of the whole historical process of our time." He did not mention the Red Army, which was, of course, no barrier to the self-determination of European peoples, being itself part of the historical process.

A chief obstacle to Europe's glorious future, progressives were beginning sorrowfully to think, was President Roosevelt himself. When making concessions to Russia FDR was reassuring, but too often he seemed on the wrong side. In 1944 Max Lerner asked how were we to reconcile Roosevelt's "greatness of spirit and proven liberalism" with the blind and illiberal policy he had been pursuing in North Africa, France, Spain, and seemed bent on continuing? Lerner thought it was partly a question of style. Roosevelt liked to play off parties against each other, a game he enjoyed and was good at. Thus, in France Roosevelt was balancing de Gaulle's Free French against the collaborators. FDR's foreign policy was not a grand design but arose from habit, a desire to avoid political fuss, an unwillingness to offend Catholic voters, a liking for power politics, and similar practical concerns. This was not good enough, Lerner declared sternly, in a time demanding "social clarity and forthrightness."[39]

Lerner had gushed over Roosevelt before and would do so again, but, like many other progressives, on a daily basis he had come to prefer Henry Wallace. The most encouraging thing about FDR was that he had made Wallace his Vice-President, and, Lerner had been told by "insiders," Roosevelt meant to keep Wallace on for another term despite the opposition of urban leaders and conservative Southerners—the alliance of boss and Bourbon that was actually to prevent Wallace's renomination in 1944. Wallace's strength, Lerner explained, came from his willingness to fight for the people against the interests. Other New Dealers when under fire had the habit of running for cover, and got picked off anyway. Wallace had never done this and was now the only high official believed in by the masses. He was the enemy of wealth, monopoly, and fascism at home, "the people's spokesman" and even "a sort of latter-day Lincoln." He thought in global terms and was trusted by Latin Americans, Russians and other aspiring peoples. Wallace was "a symbol for the progressive democracies that are emerging in Europe," Lerner wrote, having in mind Russia's future satellites.[40]*

---

* He forgot about this afterward. In a television interview years later Max Lerner said of Harry Truman, "I did everything possible to have him made Vice-President because we knew, many of us knew during Roosevelt's last term, that he was not long for this world, and that he would probably die in office, and that became a very crucial vice-

It was a black day for progressives when, after sending out signals in both directions as usual, FDR dropped Wallace and took Harry S. Truman as his running mate. Bruce Bliven urged them not to lose heart. Liberals had put up a good fight on Wallace's behalf at the Chicago convention. Truman was a New Dealer. Roosevelt was still better than Dewey and would certainly win again. Liberals should take strength from the gains made during the previous twelve years and keep fighting for a bigger and better New Deal after the war.[42] Having no other choice, progressives supported Roosevelt, sometimes with enthusiasm. George Seldes defined the alternative in his understated way with this headline: "Dewey's Backers: Duponts, Dulles, Merchants of Death; Hoover and Hitler; GOP-Nazi Cartel Plot in America."[43]

Though progressives voted for Roosevelt in 1944, doubts remained. Some feared he would never rise up to Stalin's level of vision, others that he could not cope with Stalin's increasing greed. The *New Republic* welcomed 1945 with little of the pleasure displayed a year earlier. Readers were warned not to expect much from the peace. America could not force Britain or Russia to follow its enlightened lead. The task was to work for a good settlement, while remembering that utopia was impossible and that the main goal still was to win the war.[44] In this spirit it received news of the Yalta Agreement. "On the whole, the results at Yalta represent a substantial victory for Stalin," the editors wrote, showing none of the joy similar events had aroused previously. Their hopes for a just and lasting peace were now more and more focused on the planned United Nations Organization.[45]

Conservative attacks on Yalta, which would go on for years, prompted a weary gesture of support. "If for nothing else, one would be pre-disposed toward the conference for the enemies it has made."[46] True, Stalin had obtained most of what he wanted. But his puppet government of Poland was to be broadened and free elections held. This was important to the *New Republic*, which still expected obvious wrongs to be put right by

---

presidential choice." Readers of his column in 1944 would have been very surprised to hear that Lerner favored Truman.[41]

popular votes in all the occupied countries. The editors shared the common belief that America would leave Europe after the war, as it had last time. And they were still worried about British ambitions, as also now about Russia's. They hoped that America, the most disinterested of the great powers, would act as a watchdog. Yalta was not a bad agreement, they maintained, and if the United Nations worked out, its errors could be corrected.

Conversely, *The Nation,* ever faithful to the people's war, was delighted by Yalta. I. F. Stone, who didn't like the Roosevelt Administration, wrote that Yalta vindicated it. "This Is What We Voted For" was the title of his story.[47] But in reviewing the press response *Common Sense* found that many disagreed. The *Christian Century* said that there was no excuse for the praise Yalta had received. It was just a matter of Britain and the United States paying Stalin's price for joining the United Nations. G. A. Borgese, an Italian antifascist now an American citizen, was more severe. He attacked the notion that Yalta conformed to the Atlantic Charter. "There can be no justice if America, simply because she could not obtain what is right, condones what is wrong."[48]

Reinhold Niebuhr was less despairing. He believed that liberals were right to support Yalta and the Dumbarton Oaks Conference (which laid the basis for the United Nations Organization), even though they were great-power agreements in which most of the world had no say, and despite the fact that Russia seemed bent on controlling Eastern Europe.

> Dumbarton Oaks is different from Munich because Russia is different from Germany. Russia is not driven by the mania of world conquest, though it obviously has residual fears of the Western world. Shall we seek to quiet those fears by efforts to achieve a mutual-security system, or shall we play upon those fears and make another war inevitable?[49]

This was the *New Republic*'s view also. It was unhappy that Dumbarton Oaks retained the odious doctrine of national sovereignty. But had it not done so there would be no United Nations.[50] It was further encouraged by the United Nations conference at San Francisco, which seemed to justify earlier hopes. The big powers did not split up. The little powers had their say. Russia had been splendid.

> We believe that Russia came out the unquestioned winner in terms of moral prestige. She knew from the very beginning what she wanted, worked hard for it and gave ungrudgingly at the end when it proved necessary. The country which suffered most in loss of moral stature was the United States, which engineered the entrance of Argentina, showed hostility to the USSR and haggled over the questions of full employment and independence for colonial peoples. Americans can feel little pride in the role we played at San Francisco.[51]

The Potsdam Agreement raised the *New Republic*'s morale higher. Germany would not suffer a punitive peace. Reparations would be limited and confined to goods. The Polish solution was excellent. "Free democratic elections, with the participation of all anti-Fascist parties, are assured. Freedom of the press and opportunity for foreign correspondents to observe and report are guaranteed."[52] The rest of Eastern Europe would benefit similarly. All in all, the *New Republic* believed, it was a great improvement over the Versailles Treaty that in ending the previous war had sown the seeds of another. When Russia signed a peace treaty with China, this was further evidence to the *New Republic* that all worries were over. "There remains no danger of a clash of American or British interest with Russian 'imperialism' in the Far East. So another hobgoblin is banished."[53]

But soon the *New Republic* was depressed again by a meeting of foreign ministers. Both Russia and America were at fault. Russia had failed to relax censorship in Eastern Europe and was acting unilaterally. It made unreasonable demands, as for a trusteeship over Libya and Eritrea. It was behaving more like a stock market speculator than a planner. America was refusing to share its atomic secrets with Russia and had canceled Lend-Lease aid to Britain. The *New Republic* called for a practical "engineering" approach to peacemaking. The United States had done this in Italy, waiving reparations because Italy could not pay them, making Trieste a free port, and adjusting the Italian–Yugoslavian border. Such pragmatic methods should be applied to other issues.[54]

Anti-Stalinists were disgusted by all the great-power agreements. As Bertram Wolfe put it, at "Teheran secretly, at Yalta openly, Europe is divided into spheres of power and the three biggest states decide the fate of the lesser ones without the lesser powers being represented."[55] To him, as to many others, Poland was becoming "the test for a moral and enduring peace." And, Anna Louise Strong to the contrary, things were not going well. Yalta raised the question in Wolfe's mind as to whether there was to be an independent Poland at all. Dumbarton Oaks was equally distressing. Louis Fischer said it showed that in international relations and among the Big Three there "is only a new immorality which defends the old cynicism."[56] He could not understand why these callous deals won the favor of so many Americans who claimed to be democratic.

Most in their camp had long since given up hope that peace would bring anything more than the end of fascism. But *Common Sense* had desperately wanted to believe that the war was making things better. Though anti-Stalinist, it was at the same time semiprogressive, a believer in the people's war and a democratic peace. Yet as early as 1943 *Common Sense* had feared that the one might not lead to the other. "Our diplomats are trying to create a post-war bloc of states—democratic, perhaps, in formal structure but reactionary in content—that will frustrate the revolutionary aspirations of Europe's millions and that will, above all, isolate the dreaded Russian influence behind a wall of steel."[57] In doing so the United States was bringing about the very thing that it feared most. *Common Sense* worried that in recognizing the Italian government of Marshal Badoglio America had scuttled the people's war.[58] The editors wrote in 1944 that liberals "must ask themselves whether they can seriously expect this administration to unleash revolution abroad."[59] *Common Sense* had never mistaken FDR for Leon Trotsky. But it had hoped for a more radical and democratic outcome than anyone, most especially a liberal capitalist, could or would deliver, and it was, accordingly, shattered by the actual results.

For *Common Sense,* disillusionment with the war set in even before it was over, unlike last time, when enthusiasm lasted until the armistice.

> But in this war the emptiness of victory was unrolling before the eyes of men who still were dying to achieve it. Franklin D. Roosevelt had promised less than Woodrow Wilson; but even the half loaf that had been offered was vanishing before men could touch it. In Greece, Poland, Belgium and Bulgaria, Britain and Russia were underlining in blood the terms of the secret treaties without waiting for the collapse of the German armies.[60]

Britain was struggling to save its empire, Russia to seize all the territory it could. No one spoke any longer of the people's war.

Yalta was the last straw. "The Crimea declaration is bad not only because it is the product of cynical power politics but because it pretends to be a victory for international collaboration and democratic self-determination. In order to sustain this pretense a network of lies, half-truths, and self-deceptions must be constructed." *Common Sense* believed that the division of Europe was a victory for American and Russian imperialism alike. America's chance to become the moral leader of the world was gone. Millions had "hoped we would release and support constructive, progressive, democratic forces in Europe. We've kicked these millions of desperate men and women in the face. We have abandoned them, not simply physically, but spiritually. This is the most real reality of Crimea."[61]

And so it was. The Yalta compromises, though not necessarily bad and perhaps even as good as could be obtained under the circumstances, exposed the hollowness of Allied claims to be waging war for freedom and democracy. It was, as should have been expected, a great-power settlement that paid only lip service to the rights and needs of suffering humanity. Roosevelt did not surrender to Stalin at Yalta, as conservatives have always maintained.[62] Yalta was a turning point just the same. It destroyed all serious attempts to represent the world struggle as a people's war leading to a people's peace.

.   .   .

By 1945 the American honeymoon with Russia was over. The Cold War was still only a gleam in Harry Truman's eye. Many, perhaps most, Americans still hoped that difficulties with the Soviet Union could be smoothed over. A few people, such as Walter Lippmann and Carl Becker, were trying to find a middle ground between faith in and fear of Russia. But traditional anti-Communism had revived, and anti-Stalinism, scorned by liberals after the German invasion of Russia, was rising with it. Soviet misconduct more than *Politics* or the *New Leader* accounted for the change. They were proving to be right even so. For progressives it was the beginning of the end.

V

In the Postwar

THOUGH SOME GOT OFF the bandwagon after Yalta, most progressives had too much invested in the cause to give up so easily. Yet the old certainties had been shaken, and the *New Republic,* for one, found itself on a roller coaster, its hopes for peace rising and falling with each new development. At the end of 1945 things looked bad, but another meeting of foreign ministers raised the editors up again.[1] When Soviet spies were arrested in Canada and charged with stealing nuclear secrets the magazine was unhappy. It rallied to the old flag even so, calling for international control of atomic energy to lessen Soviet fears and the need for Soviet espionage.[2] Story after story explained that things were going well in Poland. Russian troops were leaving. The morale of organized labor was high and workers were animated by the "feeling of social revolution." If there was little democracy now, there would be more after reconstruction.[3] The main danger in Poland was not Stalinism but discontented reactionaries. "Already the choice is between either the new Poland or a fascist Poland."[4]

More and more, *New Republic* editors looked to the United Nations as "The Greatest of All Our Hopes."[5] If only the rivalry between Britain and Russia did not destroy the UN it might still save the world. The *New Republic* worried about America's growing hostility to Russia, as also sometimes the Soviet actions that fed it.[6] But the *New Republic*'s usual response to Soviet belligerence, as in February 1946 when Stalin harshly attacked the West, was to call for more concessions. America should make a loan to Russia so that its standard of living would rise and its disposition improve. A loan would show good faith and promote trade and cultural relations, always seen by progressives as helpful to peace. And there should be more social reforms at home, as they too, in some mysterious way, strengthened peace.[7]

At critical moments the *New Republic*'s instinct still was to side with Russia. In 1946, under heavy pressure from the United States, Russia withdrew its troops from northern Iran. The Shah then liquidated puppet governments Russia had left behind. Iran was one of the first clear-cut victories for the West in its struggle with Russia, but alarming to the *New Republic*. This was partly because the Shah was reactionary, mostly because victory had been gained in the wrong way, by threatening Russia instead of waiting patiently for Stalin to cooperate. Taking a hard line showed the bankruptcy of American foreign policy. It was all done for oil, of course, and would prove self-defeating. "By denying to Russia what we claim for ourselves, we have encouraged the Russians to obtain in their own way what we would not grant them."[8] Other articles defended Soviet objectives in Iran and contrasted high living standards in the Soviet Azerbaijan Republic with poverty in Iranian Azerbaijan, implying that the Soviets should annex it.[9] At the very least Iran would be well advised to model itself on Soviet Azerbaijan, as against the backward colonies of Britain and America.[10]

The *New Republic* continued to print little fables about the wonder of Polish socialism. An interview with Stalin by Harold Laski showed him not to be a dictator after all but a team leader, captain of the Soviet varsity.[11] Even so, the editors kept agonizing over how to deal with Russia, which, in saner moments, they were beginning to have doubts about. Before 1946 the realistic course, in their view, was to give Stalin what he wanted. Now they were less sure. In September, for the first time in years, they ran a genuinely critical essay. The columnists Joseph and Stewart Alsop began by saying that the "liberal movement" (meaning actually the progressive wing) was ignoring Soviet imperialism. Liberals must press for bold American action to end misery, famine, feudalism and other breeding grounds of Communism. A worldwide program of relief and rehabilitation was in order. Liberals must support the United Nations, but must also recognize that Russia was keeping it from being effective. For too long liberals had viewed Russia in terms of its admirable goals rather than the ugly realities. There was much agreement among liberals on ends—a strong UN, reconstruction, weapons control and the like. "The liberals will destroy themselves, however, if they think these ends can be gained except by a realistic political approach. And in destroying themselves they will destroy our world."[12]

Max Lerner answered for the *New Republic*. He felt the Alsops were really asking progressives to abandon Henry Wallace and support the "Truman-Byrnes, Dulles-Connally-Vandenberg policies," which involved backing reactionary governments and programs. An American diplomacy based on fear of Russia would in the end be guided by nothing else, he predicted. Lerner favored resistance to both Western and Soviet imperialism, conceding the obvious at last. But it was foolish to imagine that alliances with right-wing regimes would result in liberalism and social reconstruction. He called on readers to oppose both Communism and anti-Communism on behalf of democratic and socialist movements everywhere.[13]

These two articles pointed up the dilemma. The Alsops were right. Progressives had been deluding themselves for a long time about the Soviet Union and would be ruined if they did not wake up. But Lerner, who in the past had been as self-deceived as anyone, was right, too. Anti-Communism did mean getting into bed with Franco and Chiang Kai-shek and sacrificing, except in Japan and Western Europe, liberalism and reform to military needs. Liberals, and progressives even more, had hoped that they could have it both ways. They wanted security for America and its allies, social progress for the underdeveloped world. At first history seemed on their side. The New Deal, the defeat of fascism, the collapse of colonialism, even the growth of Soviet power, all pointed in the right direction. But Soviet-American harmony was a key ingredient in the better world that progressives dreamed of, and it was in question. Progressives knew there were obstacles to the friendship with Russia—Western imperialists, monopoly capitalism, William Randolph Hearst. They had refused to believe that the other side would present even greater ones. Now the facts of life were being forced upon them.

The *New Republic* did not surrender easily. At the end of 1946 it began another series of articles on how to get along with

Russia. Entitled "A New Deal with Russia," they began in the same old way. Russia had suffered great losses in the war. American Lend-Lease aid to it was only a third of what the British Empire received. A loan to Russia would be nice. No one should complain of Soviet expansion, as the territory taken was only what Russia had lost in the First World War, and not all of it at that.[14] The habit of apologizing for Stalinism was hard to break, and the *New Republic* would go on doing so for a while yet, though with diminishing conviction.

At the end of 1946 the magazine underwent a facelift. Henry Wallace, who was at liberty, having been fired from the Cabinet by President Truman, became editor. The format was altered. Michael Straight of the owning family became publisher. George Soule resigned. Stories aimed at the common man increased. Reporting on foreign affairs and culture declined. These changes were more apparent than real. Straight wanted to make the *New Republic* a liberal version of *Time* but failed. Apart from writing editorials, Wallace did not add much. Bruce Bliven remained, with Straight, the guiding spirit. Though not so progressive as during the war, the *New Republic* sounded much the same.

An effective United Nations remained its best hope.[15] It continued to view events in Eastern Europe benevolently. When a Polish election resulted in eighty-five percent of the vote going to the pro-Soviet government, a CBS correspondent explained this was not fraud, only a response to good administration plus fears that America was building up Germany.[16] Everything was fine in Czechoslovakia too, the only European nation that had Communists in its government, close relations with Russia, and internal democracy. In one of the worst guesses of 1947 Owen Lattimore wrote that perhaps "the Czechoslovak Communists, heartily backed by the Soviet Communists, are giving a thorough trial run to a policy of suggesting, to the nation's neighbors, that socialism and eventual communism can be reached by an easy transition, with prosperity all along the way and without massacre or coercion."[17] Czech democracy had, at that point, fewer than six months to live.

When President Truman, who did not share this sunny view of coexistence, announced a program of military aid to endangered nations, beginning with Greece and Turkey, the *New*

Republic was naturally alarmed. The Truman Doctrine meant, wrote Henry Wallace, that there "is no regime too reactionary for us, provided it stands in Russia's path."[18] Wallace favored a massive program of economic rather than military aid to wipe out poverty and misery, which were said to be the ground in which Communism flourished. The intent of the Truman Doctrine, another writer believed, was to turn Europe over to Wall Street. The financiers around Secretary of State George C. Marshall—Robert Lovett, James Forrestal, Averell Harriman—and the employment by Marshall of "Russophobes," such as Charles Bohlen and George Kennan, were evidence of this.[19] When a program of economic aid to Europe was proposed, as Wallace had been urging, the *New Republic* hoped that Russia would participate so that the Marshall Plan would "not become simply a new guise for an old bugaboo—a Western European bloc under US financial sponsorship."[20] But Russia did refuse to cooperate in the European Recovery Program, which immediately lost its progressive character. Wallace now thought that the Marshall Plan would fail. "The workers will hate us because they think we are trying to maintain or install reactionary governments and influence the economic system of Western Europe to the benefit of Wall Street."[21]

While still insisting that Russia wanted peace, the *New Republic* found less and less to admire in the Soviet system, apart from economics. Alexander Kendrick, its Moscow correspondent, noted that prewar levels of consumption had almost been reached. If the trend continued, "then the years directly ahead are going to make even the golden days of 1935–38 seem pale by comparison," he wrote, taking a remarkably narrow view of the era of Stalin's great terror.[22] In an appeal to greed, the *New Republic* wrote about a Philadelphia man who traded with the Soviets. He found them to be as efficient as Americans and completely absorbed with reconstruction. They were easy to deal with, he said reassuringly, having lived a charmed life. There were fewer soldiers on the streets of Moscow than New York, proof positive of Soviet amiability. We should set aside the Truman Doctrine and make money out of Russia, he advised.[23]

In darker moments, though, *New Republic* editors were coming to feel that both sides shared responsibility for the developing Cold War. And both sides were making false charges. The Soviets were wrong to say there was no democracy in the United States, but "in turn we wrongly equate civil liberty and democracy." Civil liberties were an outgrowth of capitalist democracy, but there were other kinds. "In many Eastern European countries whose peoples are moving directly from feudalism to socialism, majority rule exists and makes its claim to democracy."[24] But except for the rising tide of self-government in Eastern Europe Michael Straight found little to cheer about. The "doctrine of peaceful coexistence" between Russia and the United States had broken down. All countries were being herded into one bloc or another. Great-power rivalry was crushing hopes for freedom and democracy on both sides of the Iron Curtain. "In a universal vacuum of political morality neither Russia nor America makes any claim to leadership."[25] The foreign policies of both countries were bankrupt. Only getting back to the Four Freedoms could save us, he maintained, reverting nostalgically to wartime cant.

While united on the Four Freedoms, *New Republic* writers could not agree on the question of Cold War guilt. It was still easier for many to blame what they disliked in the East on actions by the West. Thus, when the Warsaw Pact was announced Kendrick wrote that "it is one of the ironies of the present anti-Communist crusade that, as always happens, it has merely strengthened forces it seeks to destroy."[26] Straight disagreed. The Warsaw Manifesto was "the exact counterpart of the Truman Doctrine, just as false and destructive of the hopes for peace."[27] Harold Laski absolved Russia of blame, chiding people for getting too excited about the Warsaw Manifesto. "Everyone knows that Russia does not want war and cannot afford war." It was just that America was pushing Russia in a direction it did not want to go.

Every sin with which the US charges Russia can fairly be charged against itself. War talk, expansion, bases, satellites, economic predomination, communism as a threat to world peace, encouragement of the most reactionary groups in Europe, and even in China, reduction of Japan to a position of US vassal, witch-hunting crusades in the

United States itself—all of this is grimly reminiscent of the period when the nascent Russian state was not only treated as a pariah but had good reason to fear intervention.[28]

Laski advised the West to forget about Russia and look to its own economy, which was on the verge of collapse.

The Nation clung to its line more determinedly, grinding out apologies for Stalinism as before. To J. Alvarez del Vayo the main danger still was covert fascism in the West.[29] At the end of 1946 Alexander Werth announced that all was well in Russia, except for artists, who apparently were going to have to wear uniforms again, another purge having begun.[30] Walter Duranty explained that even it was nothing to worry about. In Russian, "purge" meant to cleanse, and that was all Stalin intended. He had launched "a general cleaning out of the cobwebs and mess which accumulate in any house when its occupants are so deeply preoccupied with something else that they have no time to keep it in order."[31] It was nothing like the terror of the 1930s, though even that had a good side, he recalled. Duranty's homely metaphor was comforting, unless one remembered that he had said the same thing in the thirties. Stalin's bloody broom was in fact sweeping additional millions into the Gulag Archipelago, where many would perish. Only a Duranty could liken this to good housekeeping.

Reinhold Niebuhr, *The Nation*'s chief claim to liberalism, was less cynical and did not insult the intelligence of readers. But he too favored giving Russia the benefit of every doubt. After a meeting in England of the World Council of Churches he returned to say that Europeans were more interested in peace than were Americans. An example of this was the Council's rejection of a motion saying that Communism and Nazism were identical. Many delegates, including Niebuhr, it seems, "insisted that communism possessed creative aspects and not purely nihilistic ones like nazism."[32]

Max Lerner continued to be easily mollified. In the fall of 1946 Stalin answered a newsman's questions soothingly. Lerner claimed that this showed *PM* to have been right all along. War hysteria was unjustified. The Henry Wallace position that there could be peace without appeasement was vindicated. Some people were saying that Stalin's mildness resulted from the tougher line taken by Secretary of State Byrnes. Lerner was willing to concede them something. Stalin, he admitted, had been testing the United States a little. Limits needed to be set. The Russians now understood this, and the way was open for a peaceful competition between Communism and capitalism, as Stalin had remarked.[33]

The Nation went on believing that however deplorable Soviet foreign policy might be, America's was worse. In lectures Freda Kirchwey was saying that U.S. demands for free elections in Eastern Europe and the withholding of loans and food supplies from Russia's satellites was either bullying or the product of ignorance and complacency. It was "childish" to ignore the history "and the terrible, the shattering experiences that made revolutions in those countries inevitable and democratic methods impossible to expect and foolish to demand." The answer to what we didn't like in Eastern Europe was to assist the new dictatorships to raise their standards of living. And how could Americans criticize Russia when "it is not the United States but the Soviet Union that has been leading the fight for a democratic Spain . . . and for the right of Europe to go socialist if it needs and wants to . . . and for the feeding of starving peoples."[34] But of course it was not foolish to maintain that Russia acted appropriately by demanding democracy in Spain, where it had no power, while withholding it from the nations under Soviet control.

Vayo remained optimistic. He kept repeating that there would be no war in Europe, not, as Harold Laski said, because Russia was weak, rather because Russia was strong. Whereas the West could expect only depression and decay, the Soviet system was bouncing back. And the economic reforms Russia had imposed on Eastern Europe were far more meaningful than the cries of Westerners for free elections. Despite the presence of fascists in the Popular Front governments of the East, a new and better life and possibly a new and better democracy, "mass democracy," was developing there.[35]

The Nation believed that only reactionary warmongers wished to stay the progress of revolution in Europe. The Truman Doctrine was, predictably, just such an effort. Kirchwey said that President Truman's message to Congress requesting aid for Greece and Turkey was "a plain declaration of political war against Russia."[36] It was based on a false reading of the situation in Greece, whose left-wing insurgents had majority support. Truman was wrong about Eastern Europe as a whole, where there was "no practical alternative to revolution." Instead of trying to prevent social change, the United States should, in some unspecified way, "take the revolution away from Russia."[37] The Marshall Plan was a little better than the Truman Doctrine. Kirchwey supported aid to Europe tepidly, fearing that it would be used to restrain Communism and the social revolution.[38]

Harold Laski thought Europe would be better off with no aid at all rather than a plan which seemed designed to strengthen capitalism. I. F. Stone said it would fail anyway because not enough money would be appropriated by Congress, and Eastern Europe was being left out.[39] Kirchwey appeared to feel that the trouble with American policy was that it aimed to strengthen the nation's friends instead of its enemies. "By a paradox that seems to me a simple fact, peace and prosperity will be more secure in America if we accept the process of revolution in Europe and the East instead of subsidizing resistance to it."[40] In her view this was not appeasement, only common sense. She could not understand why some liberals kept objecting to the spread of Communism, since the alternatives to it were obviously worse.[41]

The ugly sight of liberals disagreeing at home compared unfavorably with the progress of revolutions abroad, though not always. When the elected government of Hungary was overthrown Kirchwey had misgivings. As usual when there was bad news from the East, Kirchwey wanted liberals to suspend judgment. For *The Nation* itself, as during the purge trials of the thirties, rationalizations were in order. Kirchwey attacked Americans for saying the change in Hungary amounted to a Soviet coup or a Communist putsch. Russia merely intervened helpfully. The Soviets had not, as charged, fabricated a plot to justify ousting the Smallholders Party. It was a nest of traitors, as proved by court trials whose reliability could not be doubted. It was, unfortunately, true that Russia controlled Hungary "in all essentials," but Westerners complained of this only because Russia got there first, not out of any real interest in Hungarian freedom. "The Truman Doctrine undoubtedly stimulated Russia to counter-moves," she wrote, stopping short of saying Hungary was one of them, as this would have undercut her argument that a Smallholder plot was the real reason. Soviet meddling in Hungary was sometimes regrettable, but were it not for Russia there would be no chance of a "decent order" in Hungary. Anyway, Western nations had no right to complain, because twenty-eight years earlier they "betrayed their promise of help to a Social Democratic regime in Budapest and deliberately permitted the dictator Horthy to seize power."[42] *The Nation* was always most illogical when a country was being Stalinized. Communism meant having a social revolution, which was clearly a good thing. It purged reactionaries, which was also good, strengthening as it did the revolution and removing barriers to democracy. But Stalinization always involved purging democrats too. This was not so good, though perhaps necessary and in any case the West's fault, if not now, then in the distant past.

Once Stalinization was complete, however, *The Nation* rested easier. Visiting Poland, Alexander Werth found signs of progress on every hand. Recovery was well advanced. "The loss of the non-Polish territories in the east is not greatly regretted." Everyone loved the new boundary in the west, where Poland had been compensated for land lost to Russia with land taken from Germany. The government, though disliked by many, commanded "very great respect" on account of its organizing skills and "clearness of vision." "Of course the Polish Government is not strictly democratic according to Western standards," and had fixed the last election.[43] This was necessary to avoid chaos and reoccupation of the country by Russia. Once East European democrats were all silenced or in jail, it was clear to *The Nation* that everything had been for the best.

Books praising and defending Russia continued to appear for a time. Little, Brown, an old and distinguished Boston firm, had become the leading published of pro-Soviet propaganda. An egregious volume issued by it, called *The Great Conspiracy*, portrayed Russia as a peace-loving, united, harmonious, just society that was constantly being aggressed, spied upon, subverted and maligned. Thanks to Stalin, the plotters always got their just deserts.[44] The equally distinguished house of Knopf enabled Frederick Schuman, all doubts now behind him, to bring forth *Soviet Politics,* his definitive work on the benefits of Stalinism. The purge victims were once again defamed and Stalin glorified. The end justified the means repeatedly. Too bad about the lack of democracy, but if outsiders would leave the Soviets alone they would acquire it. Schuman rejoiced that the blessings of Stalinism were descending upon Eastern Europe. It too would now enjoy scientific knowledge employed for "social betterment."

Schuman believed the Soviets had accomplished two things that excused all the blundering and brutality.

> One is the cure of the mass neuroses of our time through the reintegration of personality around community values and purposes which afford escape from loneliness and, ultimately, from the class snobberies and mass envies characteristic of deeply divided societies. The other is the cure of economic paralysis and stagnation . . . the building of an institutional framework wherein all who are able and willing to work may find productive employment in a constantly expanding economy.[45]

Nor did Schuman shrink from embracing what even many progressives found distasteful. "The dictatorship of the Communist Party, moreover, is not an accidental feature of socialism in the USSR but a pre-condition of its success." He tortured the meaning of democracy as usual. Admittedly there were no free elections in Russia, but instead freedom from poverty, exploitation, illiteracy, prejudice, together with a great increase in human dignity and self-respect. "These purposes are of the essence of the democratic dream." In this sense the Soviet Union was "a democratic polity—in its ends and in its achievement, if not always in its means."[46]

This was not meant to be taken very seriously. Schuman knew of evils in Russia and dismissed them. Freedom was good for Westerners, but in the East it was not much needed, and probably got in the way of progress. Stalin was cruel in order to be kind. Oppression brought forth constantly rising levels of human dignity. This was the central contradiction in progressive thought, which, as it could not be resolved, was invariably passed over. To apologists for Stalinism there was no Gulag

Archipelago, only unpleasant and possibly harsh measures, mostly in the past, which were, in any case, justified by Soviet gains.

Heinz Eulau said Schuman's book corrected the ignorance and misrepresentations of Soviet Russia that were still all too common. He was full of praise for all Schuman's opinions, even his vision of the future when the West would be socialized and the East democraticized, leading to global synthesis, peace, and the world state.[47] Just as predictably, William Henry Chamberlin was disgusted. It was bad enough that Schuman did not know any Russian, worse still that he justified all of Stalin's works. There was only one good thing about the book. It was more restrained than an article Schuman had recently contributed to *Soviet Russia Today,* the magazine of fellow travelers and simpletons, according to Chamberlin. The theme of Schuman's book, fairly summarized by Chamberlin, "is that any attempt by England or America to check Soviet aggression is a form of warmongering, while Soviet aggression is a high form of devotion to peace."[48]

Richard Lauterbach, who had written a fatuous account of his stay in Russia during the war, produced another book in 1947 that was not so much optimistic as wistful about the prospect of better relations with the Soviets. He had recently traveled through Russia from east to west, discovering that Russians were no longer forthcoming as they had been during the war. Even though they would not talk with him, Lauterbach was still certain that the "people of the Soviet Union, and most of their responsible leaders, sincerely desire peace."[49]

Edgar Snow too wrote about another book about Russia, which was also more restrained than his previous one. It consisted of three articles, first published in *The Saturday Evening Post,* attacking the sources of Soviet–American misunderstanding. These seemed to be largely a matter of ignorance compounded by the different meanings applied by the two peoples to words like "fascism" and "democracy." Snow ransacked the messages of Stalin in search of enlightenment. He evoked Russian suffering to excuse Soviet paranoia once again. He described the Cold War as seen through Soviet eyes. Snow did not defend everything Russia had done, but argued, as revisionist historians would later, that since America was more powerful than Russia it had a greater responsibility. He suggested that the United States might "offer major economic help in exchange for irrevocable steps toward world peace."[50] Whether from expediency or conviction, this was a better book than Snow's previous effort, *The Pattern of Soviet Power*. He did not glorify Stalin as before (though he kept insisting that Stalin was not a despot but "titular" leader of the Politburo). He did not put forward Soviet opinions as being revealed truth. Snow's book was a rearguard action just the same. The progressive interpretation of recent history was losing ground, in the mass media particularly. He would not write for *The Saturday Evening Post* in this vein again.

As American foreign policy stiffened, progressives and fellow travelers had to work harder to rationalize events and keep their spirits up. The correspondence of Raymond Robins reflects this. Senator Claude Pepper of Florida, one of two progressive U.S. senators (Glenn Taylor of Idaho being the other), was a friend of Robins, who supported Pepper in local politics. When the Truman Doctrine was first announced, Pepper believed it could be defeated. He testified before the Foreign Relations Committee and received what he considered "a splendid hearing."[51] To Robins this was a "battle for the RIGHTS of the group of Toil in our America—CONGRATULATIONS!" President Truman, "the ignorant, lying, cowardly little Goodfellow of the penitentiary crook BOSS Pendergast's *political servants*," was betraying Roosevelt's heritage. Robins urged Pepper to keep reading *The Nation* and the *New Republic*, and *PM*, especially Max Lerner's editorials. Contrary to appearances, things were going well, he assured Pepper. "Jefferson's POLITICAL FREEDOM and Promise of EQUALITY: has met LENIN'S ECONOMIC FREEDOM AND FULFILLED EQUALITY—and the *new wine* of LIBERTY in old bottles has begun to ferment, and elemental forces are surging in the minds and hearts of mankind even in the quietism and mysticism of the ANCIENT EAST."[52]

This faith sustained Robins, isolated in his Florida estate, but was not so useful to Pepper, who had to live in the real world. In May 1947 he told Robins that the last few weeks had been among his worst as a senator. He was being harassed at home and throughout the country for his stand on foreign policy. Truman was following the "McKinley line" of promoting imperialism. Before Truman announced his Doctrine, Pepper, Taylor, Helen Gahagan Douglas and a few other congressional progressives opposed to it tried to meet with him. Truman refused, fobbing them off instead on Undersecretary of State Dean Acheson, who gave them a bloodcurdling talk on the need to stop Communism everywhere. Pepper, who had planned to support aid to Greece for the sake of his political future, ended up voting against it. He agreed with Robins that Truman had become "the mouthpiece and a tool of the militarists, the reactionaries, the monopolists and cartelists, all those who want this nation to forsake its true role in the world."[53]

Robins was close to Pepper, but the Senator's foreign policy was not based on love of Soviet Russia like his own. Robins was more comfortable with fellow travelers such as Agnes Smedley. She supported Russian but especially Chinese Communism, being one of the best-known Western apologists for it. When Robins was curious about a border incident between Nationalist China and Mongolia he naturally turned to her. She was able to supply the facts, having learned them from a Mongolian spokesman in London. As she had suspected, the incident was "a vicious gangster action of Chinese Fascism" intended to extract more aid for Chiang Kai-shek from the United States. Luckily, intrepid Mongolian troops and the Mongolian Air Force had thwarted his evil design.[54]

In turn Robins tried to keep her spirits up, sending her small checks and letters of praise and encouragement. Smedley had much to be depressed about. She suffered from ulcers and was penniless. Never had the future looked so dark. "The great banks, corporations, and their warlord henchmen who control our government are so vicious that they are capable of 'pulling a Pearl Harbor' on Russia any moment."[55] Still, Henry Wallace was fighting heroically to prevent this, as were the workers of France and Italy and other progressive forces. And most of all she looked to the Chinese Communists. At the end of 1947 they were not doing so well militarily as she and Robins hoped. The good work went forward, anyway. "The Communists do not merely make raids—they dig deep, uprooting feudalism completely, planting democracy. But this means endless labor and much time."[56] Too much time in her case. Smedley died before democracy came to China, as perhaps we all shall.

Except for Anna Louise Strong, Robins did not personally know the left-wing journalists he corresponded with. But he had friendships among progressive and fellow-traveling ministers, dating back in some cases to his own career as a lay evangelist. One of these ministers was Sherwood Eddy, whose faith in Russia was waning, Robins had heard. He wrote Eddy about this, daring him to read Schuman's new book on Russia. Eddy assured Robins that his concern was misplaced. Eddy had read *Soviet Politics at Home and Abroad* and agreed with it completely. The great issue today was friendship with Russia. God intended America to spread the demand for liberty and vital religion throughout the world, and Russia to promote economic justice and racial equality. Eddy said he wanted to "read anything and everything in the future in favor of Russia."[57] Alas for the cause, those who detected signs of weakness in Eddy were not mistaken. A year and a half later, Jerome Davis, a fellow-traveling minister, gave Robins the bad news. Eddy had launched a "hate campaign" against Russia and was saying there were fifteen million people in Soviet labor camps.[58]

Though Robins liked all the pro-Soviet writers, Schuman was his favorite. "Red Fred," as he was sometimes called by students at Williams College, specialized in giving to propaganda the appearance of scholarship. But what Robins most enjoyed were Schuman's extravagant attacks on American policymakers. Robins was thrilled by an article of his in *Soviet Russia Today* indicting Secretary of State Byrnes, who had just written a book—*Speaking Frankly* (1947)—that Schuman called "the most baffling, incredible and terrifying document to come from the pen of a responsible American official in many years."[59] This was because Byrnes supported the Truman Doctrine and the Marshall Plan, which were inspired by the Devil. Schuman personally was unafraid. The Soviet Union would not "abandon" Eastern Europe. The Russian people would not be blackmailed. "To the last man, woman, and child they will all face death again before they yield to such demands as Byrnes proposes." If America did not back down there would be nuclear war. "Only this is clear: if the American people lack the wit and will to recapture the vision of Franklin D. Roosevelt and Wendell Willkie, and to give new life to such hopes as are voiced by Henry A. Wallace, Glen [sic] Taylor, Claude Pepper and

Wayne Morse, they will have made a covenant with hell and a pact with death."[60]

A mark of the fellow travelers, and many progressives too, was that they did not realize how demented this kind of rhetoric seemed to others. Robins loved Schuman's denunciations of American policy and blanket defense of Russia, sending him the customary check and letter of appreciation.[61] Pepper wrote that Schuman's diatribe was "magnificent."[62] Robins also sent a check and letter to Jessica Smith, the editor of *Soviet Russia Today*. Schuman in his zeal wanted a copy of his article sent to every U.S. senator, and Smith asked Robins if he would underwrite the cost and put his name to the venture.[63] Robins, who had a keen instinct for survival, gave her money but would not lend his name. Caution won out over passion, and not for the first time. In this only did he differ from his friends.[64]

As a propagandist Schuman failed on account of intemperance and blindness to the feelings of nonbelievers. He had been taken seriously in the 1930s, but little attention was paid to him in the postwar years. More skillful writers were harder to deal with. In 1947 the *New Leader* attacked the Foreign Policy Association and its best-known staff member, Vera M. Dean. According to Fred Porter, the FPA was regarded as nonpartisan and reliable, partly because of its eminent sponsors, who included Senator Warren Austin, James Byrnes, John Foster Dulles, Herbert H. Lehman and other establishment figures. This was a misconception, as the FPA had been subtly pro-Soviet for years, Mrs. Dean most of all, Porter maintained.[65] Frederick Lewis Allen, a popular historian and editor of *Harper's* magazine, rejected the charge. FPA officers were all "anti-communist liberals," he explained, Dean too. She did seem to favor the USSR at times, but only out of an understandable eagerness to have Americans "understand the Russia in which she was born."[66] Allen did not mean to admit what he was denying, though that was the result. The confusion arose because, while Dean allowed Russia the benefit of every doubt, she did not usually give offense, except to militant anti-Stalinists.

Dean was born in Russia, moving to America with her family in 1919, and was educated at Radcliffe, Yale, and Harvard, from which she received her Ph.D. in 1928. She was then employed by the Foreign Policy Association, remaining there until

1966. During most of this period Dean was the only Russian scholar writing for a general audience. Her view of Russia changed very little during the 1930s and '40s despite the rush of events. In a 1933 pamphlet for the FPA she described the Soviet Union as a force for peace. She minimized but did not deny Soviet evils. Nor did she represent Soviet claims to be the literal truth. The result was both flattering to Russia and comforting to Americans.[67]

Her last major effort along these lines, *The United States and Russia* (1947), was much the same. She still found a great deal in the Soviet Union to admire. Of course, Russians had no political rights, but "if the term democracy includes active participation by citizens in the economic and social development of the community—subject to drastic limitations on political activities—then it could be said without disingenuousness that democracy in that sense exists in Russia."[68] Too bad about the lack of liberty, she wrote, as in her earlier pamphlet, but since the Russians had never known freedom it was not greatly missed. Dean rejected the argument that abrupt changes in foreign policy showed the Soviets to be hypocritical and unreliable.

> It is difficult to escape the conclusion, however, that Russia was correct in its appraisal of the international situation when it pointed out the danger of Nazi and Fascist activities in Spain, and expressed fear that the Western powers might be willing to let Germany expand eastward provided it left them untouched, especially if this expansion were to weaken the position of Russia and of Communism. If Russia—and the Third International—seemed subject to sudden conversions, the Western powers, too, were not always consistent when they first "appeased" Germany and then, once Hitler, as a result of their concessions in the east, had girded Germany for expansion to the west, belatedly sought Russia's aid against the Nazis in 1939.[69]

Insofar as this passage makes any sense it says that if Russia was opportunistic in the thirties, so were Britain and France. She put Allied waffling and muddle on a par with Stalin's betrayal of antifascism and his swallowing up of the Baltic States plus areas of Poland and Finland. Dean failed to note that it was Russia, not the Allies, that secured Germany's eastern frontier, enabling it to go to war, and that it was the Allies, not Russia, that fought Hitler in 1939 and '40. Making a case for Russia always called for evasion and omission. The lack of freedom had to be balanced by false claims for economic virtue. These were never examined. Nor was the boast that the Soviets had abolished racism, and for the same reason. The Gulag Archipelago had to be played down. Communism was made to seem progressive and even democratic in its way. Dean differed from most pro-Soviet writers in several respects, however. She favored social democracy and argued that there was a common ground where East and West could meet without great sacrifice of principle. Her intent was to portray the Soviet Union as a country that Western civilization could get along with. There was something to be said for this, as for her lack of anti-American polemics. These qualities made her work more attractive than Schuman's, and certainly more admired. Chester Bowles thought her book was excellent, and it received generally favorable reviews.[70]

Such books were part of a thinning stream. To the *New Masses* it seemed as if anti-Soviet works were pouring off the presses. Even when a "good" book on Russia, for example *The Great Conspiracy,* was issued, the publisher did not get behind it.[71] Anti-Stalinists were now in full cry. During the summer of 1946, *Partisan Review* fired its strongest blast at what it called the " 'Liberal' Fifth Column." Though it still had only about six thousand subscribers, *Partisan Review* was firmly established as the nation's foremost literary magazine. It no longer paid much attention to politics, but it was increasingly annoyed by the refusal of progressives to face facts. Its editorial began by quoting the *New Republic*, which had written that "nothing is gained for us vis-à-vis Russia by 'getting tough.' " With statements like this the *New Republic* editors were "actually helping to herd Social Democrats into concentration camps in Germany, helping to shoot democrats of every shade and color, in Germany, Poland, Rumania, Bulgaria, Hungary, Austria."[72]

A long indictment followed. During the Iranian crisis *PM* had leaped to defend the "Socialist Fatherland." Doing so was part of the double standard according to which the atomic bomb in

American hands was a threat to peace but if owned by Russia would secure it. Progressives favored democracy everywhere but in the Soviet Union. They were always claiming that war was imminent because of American policies. *Partisan Review* saw the problem differently. Though it had been against American entry into World War II, minds had changed since then. "If war between Russia and the United States is not inevitable, then perhaps the only way to avoid it is to stop licking Stalin's boots. After the disastrous record of a whole decade's appeasement of Hitler, surely it is the depth of folly and self-degradation to cast sheep's eyes at appeasement as the way out of war."[73]

Many readers complained of this harsh attack. Heinz Eulau, who wrote of the progressives as if he were not one, said that where they erred it was not out of disloyalty but rather a disillusionment with the postwar world. *Partisan Review* divided these replies into several categories. One was composed of Trotskyists, or Third Camp Socialists, as the editors had once been. These were held to be still reciting the ritual phrases of 1917. Another group were political dropouts, such as Dwight Macdonald. He accused the editors of "Stalinophobia," a label they rejected. As Stalinism was the main threat to socialism and democracy, the healthy course was to resist it. They scorned Macdonald's position as defeatist, a matter of saying "the answer to Stalinism is moral uplift."[74] The editors were unfair to Macdonald, who was much more political than they. But he was now a pactifist, and the editors were annoyed with him over this and other matters of doctrine.

The trouble with *Partisan Review,* Mark Schorer believed, was that it did not bring the same quality of mind to politics as to literature. Schorer, then beginning his distinguished career as a literary scholar, was not a progressive even though writing in the *New Republic*. It had assigned him to review an anthology drawn from *Partisan Review*'s first decade. Schorer agreed with Lionel Trilling's introduction to the volume, in which he had called the journal an "ambiguous monument." It was a monument because of having lasted; ambiguous because so few subscribed. Ambiguous, too, Schorer added, because of the political distance between writers and editors. Its own politics were as dreary and boring as the Stalinism it attacked. *Partisan*

Review had published the very best living writers. "But as the editors should by now have learned from their writers, one cannot be serious and great and at the same time, all the time, churlish and self-righteous and nail-biting."[75] Schorer preferred Macdonald's *Politics,* and with good reason.

Macdonald's own politics were in a state of flux. He had given up Marxism, but for what was unclear. Kenneth Rexroth, the poet, warned him that Trotskyism was creeping into the magazine, a danger inasmuch as Trotskyists were too neurotic even for the Communist Party. Irving Howe, on the other hand, condemned *Politics* from a Trotskyist point of view.[76] Amid such confusion little wonder that the subscription list, small to begin with, was dwindling. At the end of 1946 Macdonald reported to George Orwell that, having lost five hundred subscribers since the spring, his list was down to five thousand.[77] This did not result from a fall in quality. The magazine remained as brilliant as ever, but the times were against it, as also Macdonald's uncertain philosophy.

Life was simpler for the *New Leader,* still the most obsessive of anti-Stalinist publications. Though narrow and intolerant, it provided readers with great amounts of useful information on the work of Stalinists and fellow travelers. In one issue it exposed *The Protestant,* a magazine which believed that Soviet civilization was based upon the teachings of Christ.[78] As new Communist fronts were established the *New Leader* exposed them too.[79] In the fall of 1946 it published a special supplement by Norbert Muhlen entitled "Submission to Moscow: A Fellow-Travelog in the Empire of the Mind." This was an exceptionally thorough review of Communist and fellow-traveling activity in the United States that, while overstating the problem as usual, indicated why the *New Leader* was still anxious. Although the CP had only seventy thousand members, public-opinion polls showed that about seven percent of adult Americans sided with Russia in all its disputes with the United States. For every Communist, then, there were scores of progressives; more affluent and better educated than the average American, they were concentrated especially in the universities and the media. Through them the CP controlled seventy national organizations and committees and scores of publications.[80] Taken by themselves *The Nation* and the *New Republic,* and even *PM* with its substantial circulation, did not pose much of a threat to liberty. But seen as only the tip of an iceberg of potential disloyalty, they took on a more sinister aspect.

Though not unwarranted, the fears of the *New Leader* were unnecessary. Time was running out for pro-Soviet leftists, not on account of yellow journalism and mass hysteria, as they liked to think, but because the facts of Russian behavior in Eastern Europe were so damning. No book showed this more clearly than *Russia's Europe* (1947), by Hal Lehrman. He was a progressive journalist who went to Europe in 1945 to cover the outbreak of peace. Lehrman expected to find problems resulting from America's misguided foreign policy. It wrongly supported conservative governments in Italy and Greece. As chief of the Office of War Information branch in Turkey he had been dismayed by Washington's support of its autocratic and Russia-hating government. Though Lehrman went to Europe as a free lance, he could count on progressive outlets—*PM, The Nation* and in Britain *The New Statesman and Nation*—to run his stories.

Lehrman was jolted even before he reached the Continent. At Port Said he encountered a shipload of American and British troops who had been freed from POW camps by the Red Army. Instead of being grateful they were militantly anti-Russian, having been mistreated and accused of cowardice by their liberators. Shocked though Lehrman was by this, it remained his clear duty to put the best possible face on things. Though not allowed to interview American or British soldiers, he found two Canadian ex-POWs who had no complaints. He wrote them up for the *Toronto Star,* which headlined his story "Canadians Saved, Fed by Russians."

Greece was more reassuring. Allied policy was as bad as he had believed it to be, the royalist government as brutal and incompetent, and the insurgents, if not so pure as he hoped, still on the side of right. He left Greece certain that whatever he found in Soviet-occupied Europe had to be an improvement. Lehrman was wrong. Conditions were bad in Yugoslavia, worse in Hungary and Rumania. Soviet garrison troops had run wild for up to a year, he learned, murdering and looting with impunity. The Russians had set up memorials to their war dead throughout the region. These were known locally as monuments to "the Unknown Watch-Stealer." And the Russians he encountered, despite their victory, were frightened, not only of their Western allies, but of one another too. A paralyzing fear of error led to prolonged delays as officials stalled or passed the buck. "This fear had crucial significance for a liberal. It traced back to the core of the Soviet system. To see this fear was to know, once and for all time, that such a system could hardly exert beneficial influence on any decent society of the future to which the liberal might aspire."[81]

When Lehrman's stories began to reflect these discoveries progressive editors dropped him. Lehrman was not surprised. He had lost faith in Russia only because of personal experience and would not, he thought, have changed his mind had he stayed in America. To make certain of his facts he revisited parts of the Balkans. It was still the same everywhere. The Russians had looted Eastern Europe more thoroughly than the Nazis. Communist governments were more brutal than the fascist regimes preceding them. The Balkan peoples hated Russia and would never ally with it voluntarily, he was certain. And he believed also that Russian misbehavior foreshadowed further expansion to the west. Czechoslovakia would be the next to fall, he predicted accurately. By 1947 Lehrman was ready to accept the Truman Doctrine, though as a liberal he hoped it would not become a prop for reaction. Despite the risks, firmness was necessary.

Lehrman had no illusions that progressives would give up their belief that because the Allies did not always behave well they were no better than the Russians, and possibly not as good. He predicted accurately that his finding would make little impression. Though it was the most revealing book on Soviet policy in the Balkans to have yet appeared, only seven reviews of it were listed in *Book Review Digest* (as against thirteen for Edgar Snow's little tract *Stalin Must Have Peace*), most of them critical. *Russia's Europe* was too choppy and episodic, poorly organized and lacking in sophistication, it was said, defects that never seemed to matter in books by progressive journalists. Only *The Saturday Review of Literature* grasped the book's significance.[82] It was a portent of things to come even so.

The surest sign of change was the formation of Americans for Democratic Action in 1947. It grew out of a tiny liberal organization, the Union for Democratic Action, headed by Reinhold Niebuhr. The UDA had been founded in 1941 by Socialists opposed to the isolationism of party leader Norman Thomas. It was unique among liberal organizations in excluding Communists from membership. This put it ahead of even the ACLU, which, while not allowing Communists to be officers, tolerated them as members. The UDA's anti-Communism made it unpopular so long as America and Russia were allies. Afterward the wisdom of its decision became more apparent. Consequently over four hundred liberals met in Washington on January 3, 1947, in response to a call from James Loeb, executive secretary of the UDA. Chester Bowles called upon them to organize a "progressive front" free of Communist influence. The next day liberal leaders, including Walter Reuther of the United Auto Workers, Eleanor Roosevelt, Joseph Rauh, Marquis Childs the columnist, and the anti-Stalinist union head David Dubinsky, met to establish such an organization. Leon Henderson, former chief of the Office of Price Administration, and Wilson Wyatt, another New Dealer, became co-chairmen of the organizing committee. Loeb was named secretary-treasurer.[83]

The threat to progressivism was obvious. Max Lerner wasted no time accusing Americans for Democratic Action of giving in to red-baiters, and he was echoed by the *New Republic*.[84] Eleanor Roosevelt disagreed with Lerner, telling him that if ADA prospered liberals would benefit: "The American communists seem to have succeeded very well in jeopardizing whatever the liberals work for. Therefore, to keep them out of the policy making and staff positions in an organization, seems to be very essential even at the price of being called red-baiters, which I hope no member of this new group will really be."[85]

As so often before, Lerner backed down. He agreed that any liberal movement must be independent and could not have Communists in key positions. Indeed, he had criticized the newly established Progressive Citizens of America on that account. But it was wrong of ADA to lump Communists and fascists together. Attempts to impose a liberal orthodoxy would lead to narrowness. "To my mind the danger of provincialism in any liberal organization is greater than the danger of Communist infiltration—great as that is." The liberal movement needed creativity, which could come "only from the honest scrutiny of divergent opinions, and cannot come from excluding brands of non-Communist opinion which one may not happen to like."[86] Since progressives were hardly fountains of original thought, this argument was not very convincing. Nor was there much to Lerner's claim that progressives were "genuine liberals." It was true that progressives favored liberty at home. The reason why ADA had come into being was precisely that to progressives the demand for freedom stopped this side of the Iron Curtain.[87]

Freda Kirchwey agreed with Lerner. There was no need for two liberal organizations. Only extremists cared about the Communist question, she editorialized.[88] Kirchwey, Lerner, Roosevelt and other liberals held a private meeting at which it became evident that the issue of Communist participation was far from trivial. ADA leaders were not interested in unity with the Progressive Citizens of America, though hoping to win over its rank and file. Progressives could not unite with ADA, Kirchwey was certain, so long as it was tainted with (Louis) "Fischerism" and (David) "Dubinskyism."[89] Kirchwey practiced what she preached. A *Nation* supporter in California wrote to Kirchwey that she was very distressed about the Communist presence in liberal organizations and *The Nation*'s lack of concern. Recently she had been visited by Lillie Schultz of The Nation Associates, which raised funds to meet the annual deficit. The correspondent asked Schultz point-blank if she believed Poland was an independent country. "Yes, without a doubt," was the answer. This was the Communist position, and it alarmed one reader if not Kirchwey herself.[90]

James Wechsler believed that more divided ADA from progressives than the Communist question. The trouble with progressivism, he argued in *Commentary*, the new magazine of liberal Jewish opinion, was that it never had any ideas of its own but only devotion to President Roosevelt. No wonder liberalism had been in retreat since 1937. In point of fact *The Nation* and the *New Republic* had not canonized Roosevelt until after his death. When he was alive their pattern was to complain of the lack of progress in Washington for most of each presidential term, rallying to FDR as the hope of liberalism just before each election. In optimistic moods they claimed as evidence that history was on their side New Deal measures—none, as Wechsler made mention, enacted later than 1937—plus the rise of Soviet power and left-wing liberation movements. Wechsler argued that in attacking Truman's foreign policy progressives were missing the point. It was not Truman's policy abroad that was defective but his approach to domestic problems, inherited, of course, from Roosevelt. Throughout the entire Roosevelt-Truman era there had been no genuinely liberal movement in America, only under FDR the illusion of it. If liberals were to get anywhere they had to break their links with totalitarianism, but equally they had to come up with a realistic program of reform. This was the mission of ADA which Wechsler endorsed.[91]

At first it did not seem as if ADA had much of a chance, its distinguished sponsors notwithstanding. At the end of their first year of rivalry PCA had fifty thousand dues-paying members in twenty-five states, while ADA was half that size. PCA had glamor, money and Henry Wallace, who increasingly seemed to be both the peace candidate and Roosevelt's heir. Yet there were small signs, seldom noticed except by the *New Leader,* pointing the other way. *The Atlantic* was now firmly pro-containment and anti-Wallace.[92] It still hoped for peace, not as progressives did but on the basis of Walter Lippmann's conservative theory of great-power relations.[93] Stalinism itself was declining. Pro-Soviet radio commentators were going off the air, despite well-organized campaigns in Los Angeles and New York to save them. The *New Leader* recognized that low ratings rather than ideology was at work. It was encouraging all the same.[94] So also was the annual meeting of the American Unitarian Association in 1947. By a margin of three to one it sustained the removal of Stephen H. Fritchman as editor of the association's magazine. After years of fellow-traveling he had gone too far, condemning American imperialism while upholding Russia's claim to military bases in the Dardanelles.[95] In the same year the New York chapter of the American Newspaper Guild, a chapter long run by Communists, elected an anti-

Stalinist late of officers. And Little, Brown apologized to the anti-Stalinist author Jan Valtin, who, it admitted, had been slandered by Michael Sayers and Albert Kahn in *The Great Conspiracy*.[96] These were small changes, to be sure, important only in retrospect. They were little trickles that came before the flood.

VI

The Rise and Fall
of Henry Wallace

WALLACE HAD BEEN the favorite of progressives ever since 1942, when, as Vice-President, he spoke at a Soviet Friendship rally in Madison Square Garden. He said then that Russia and America had much in common, especially as both favored the common man. They differed mainly over democracy, the United States having perhaps too much political democracy and the Soviets too much economic democracy. But there had to be a golden mean in each case toward which, Wallace never doubted, both countries were moving. There was no such thing as too much "ethnic democracy," which the Russians had already achieved, nor too much "educational democracy" either. "It is because Stalin pushed educational democracy with all the power he could command that Russia today is able to resist Germany," Wallace announced. Given all this communality the American and Russian peoples "can and will throw their influence on the side of building a new democracy which will be the hope of all the world."[1] Though inconsistent on particulars, Wallace would hew to this line throughout the forties, speaking again and again of the "people's revolution" and the "century of the common man."

Wallace won further esteem among progressives with another speech in Madison Square Garden after the war calling for a soft line toward Russia. "The tougher we get, the tougher the Russians will get," he maintained.[2] The *New Republic*, thrilled by Wallace's call for peaceful relations, endorsed his theory that the two countries were converging as Russia became more democratic and America more concerned with social justice. "We live in a progressive world. We would be a lonely, an isolated weak nation under President [Robert] Taft and Secretary [Arthur] Krock. We lead the world as progressives or not at all. In voicing our progressive spirit, Wallace stands as a world leader."[3]

This was not President Truman's view. Though he had approved the text of Wallace's speech in advance, hostile reactions to it persuaded Truman that he was a liability. Accordingly the President removed him as Secretary of Commerce. In response the *New Republic* called all progressives to his side, as Wallace had shown there was an alternative to the "defeatism" of Secretary of State Byrnes.[4] Wallace soon became titular head of the *New Republic,* in whose pages his changing ideas on world order found expression. Sometimes, as in the speech that cost him his job, Wallace seemed to want a policy of friendly spheres of influence. Other times he wanted common men everywhere to form one happy family. But he was always for giving in to Russia, the number-one aim of progressives.

They had been thinking of him as a presidential candidate even before he was dropped from the ticket by President Roosevelt in 1944. After the election Freda Kirchwey wrote that what the country needed was a new united front headed by Wallace. Perhaps, she speculated, the National Citizens Political Action Committee, an offshoot of the CIO's Political Action Committee, would be the nucleus for it.[5] The PAC was then the only national political organization with real local strength, having roots in the precinct level wherever the CIO was active. It was also the means by which Sidney Hillman regained power. The leader of a garment union, he had once been close to FDR but was out of favor. When appointed by Philip Murray to head the CIO-PAC, he saw the possibilities. Hillman now had the same need as John L. Lewis a decade earlier when he was building the CIO. The historian of Communism in the labor movement put it this way:

> For a spectacular effort, he had to have the self-sacrifice and fervor of a sizable inner group, one that could bring into the enterprise the fresh capital of prominent figures, middle-class left-liberals, philanthropists, and the like. Not only did he make the same kind of decision that Lewis had made, and for the same reason, but, like Lewis, he

was also completely confident that he was the hunter and would get the bird.[6]

Accordingly, Hillman turned to the Communist Party. John Abt, a Communist lawyer, became the PAC's attorney and Hillman's assistant. Lee Pressman, another veteran Communist, was made co-counsel. "C. B. (Beanie) Baldwin, a resourceful executive and reliable party-liner, who had served under Wallace in the Department of Agriculture, became assistant chairman."[7] Baldwin was the PAC's operating manager, as of 1943, with a staff of 135 full-time workers in national and regional offices.

The next year Hillman created the National Citizens Political Action Committee. One purpose was to get around the law prohibiting labor organizations from contributing to federal election campaigns. A larger reason was to move beyond labor and make the PAC attractive to middle-class people. In theory independent, the NCPAC was chaired by Hillman and run by people such as Baldwin from the CIO-PAC. Besides Communists the NCPAC included well-known liberals such as Senator George W. Norris, James Patton, Freda Kirchwey, Gifford Pinchot and Max Lerner, plus assorted businessmen, bankers and labor leaders. Though administered by Communists, it was not an organ of the Party. It was, in fact, a popular front as in the thirties, but with the red influence played down. Hillman, an old hand at this, salted the NCPAC with followers from his union, the Amalgamated Clothing Workers, to ensure that he remained the hunter, not the bird.

The Communist Party found it necessary, therefore, to set up its own front, the Independent Voters Committee of the Arts and Sciences, nominally linked with the NCPAC but in practice separate. It was chaired by Jo Davidson the sculptor and directed by Hannah Dorner, a New York theatrical agent and Party-line organizer. The IVCAS, renamed the Independent Citizens Committee of the Arts, Sciences and Professions, enjoyed great success. Its directors included Eddie Cantor, Bette Davis, Lillian Hellman, Albert Einstein and Harlow Shapley, a scientist. The war had aroused strong feelings even in Hollywood, which the ICCASP was able to exploit. In consequence it attracted famous entertainers, and through them more attention, perhaps, than any earlier front.

Thus, when Wallace became interested in running for President the basis for his campaign already existed. The Progressive Citizens of America resulted from a merger of the ICCASP with the NCPAC, leaderless since the death of Sidney Hillman in 1946. As Wallace was the only major political figure urging concessions to Russia, the PCA had nowhere else to turn, and, indeed, no desire to. Wallace's position appeared to have wide support. A Wallace rally in Los Angeles on May 19, 1947, was the biggest political event there in years. Twenty-eight thousand people paid admission to it, donating $32,000 to the PCA besides.[8] Progressives hoped Wallace might capture the Democratic nomination, but even when the chance of this faded polls indicated he might get ten percent of the vote as an independent.

Anti-Stalinists despised Wallace without regarding his candidacy as alarming at first. David T. Bazelon, writing in *Commentary* well before the fact, said that the Wallace role in a "progressive upsurge" would not be hard to predict: "As long as it is more Stalinist than socialist, and more religious than militant, he might well be at the head of it. But he would serve as the speechifying symbol of such a movement, rather than its actual leader. So far he has shown no talent as a practical politician."[9] James Wechsler also thought a progressive third party would not get far. It "would be a creaky bandwagon, rattling loudly toward nowhere and creating confusion along every mile of the road."[10] Wallace would cause trouble all the same, benefiting the Communists and, in reaction, the isolationists, and forcing liberals to show more enthusiasm for the Truman Doctrine than they actually felt. It would be harder than ever to draw a line between the "Wallace wonderland and simpleminded Trumanism." John Dewey went the other way, arguing that liberals might gain from a Wallace campaign, as it would show the Democratic Party to be anti-Communist and thus attract enough new voters to offset those lost to Wallace. In this he was quite correct.[11] And there would be local gains also, the *New Leader* speculated. The Communist-controlled American Labor Party in New York was already being hurt. One faction wanted to support Wallace, while another, led by the Amalgamated Clothing Workers, was pledged to Truman. It would not survive the election, the *New Leader* predicted.[12]

In the January 5, 1948, issue of the *New Republic* Wallace announced his candidacy and resigned as editor. In the next issue Wallace described his alternative to the Marshall Plan: a UN reconstruction fund similar to UNRRA that would give economic aid to any needy nation on a no-strings basis.[13] This was one of his decisions that hurt Wallace most. Aid through the UN meant that American money would go to Communist states, an unpopular idea by this time. Moreover, there was no chance of getting it through Congress, where many were still opposed even to the Marshall Plan. Few people in authority were willing to sacrifice West European recovery to Wallace's impossible dream. The *New Republic* itself disagreed with Wallace, regarding half a loaf as better than none.[14]

Wallace was further damaged by the Communist takeover in Czechoslovakia on February 25, 1948. Progressives had thought of Czechoslovakia as the ideal European state because it retained democratic freedoms while cooperating with Russia and sharing power with local Communists. When the Communist minority took control anyway it put an end to hopes that Communists and democrats could work together. And it strengthened fears that Russia meant to seize the rest of Europe. Of the responses available to him Wallace picked the worst, rationalizing the coup. It was inevitable, he said two days later, and no different from what America was doing in France and Italy. Czechoslovakia proved that "a 'get tough' policy only provokes a 'get tougher' policy."[15] In light of the Truman Doctrine, Russian leaders "would, from their viewpoint, be utter morons if they failed to respond with acts of pro-Russian consolidation."[16] On March 16 in an interview with Albert J. Fitzgerald, co-chairman of the Wallace for President Committee, he went further, saying that the Communist coup had been made in anticipation of an uprising by Czech reactionaries. The American ambassador was also to blame for encouraging this in some way. Wallace was echoing the Communist line, giving evidence that his critics were right, Wallaceism did mean yielding to Soviet aggression.

Historians have since defended Wallace by charging that liberals red-baited him in 1948.[17] Truman Democrats and the ADA did hit Wallace hard on the Communist issue, accusing him of appeasement, of being the Communist candidate for President, and even of having tolerated "the grossest kind of racial segregation in the Census Bureau" when he was Secretary of Commerce—a dirty trick inasmuch as Wallace was the boldest enemy of racism among the major candidates.[18] But nothing liberals did hurt Wallace more than his own statements, plus his blind eye to Communists in the Progressive movement. Later Wallace would play dumb, saying he had never met a Communist and did not know of any in his organization. This seems unlikely on the face of it, and in at least one case Wallace was refuted by himself.

Lee Pressman, who had been general counsel of the CIO for twelve years, resigned his office and joined the Wallace campaign at a high level in 1948. He had been a Communist for a long time and was known to anti-Stalinists as such. The *New Leader* even ran a story to that effect when he joined the Wallaceites, pointing out that though Pressman always said he would sue anyone who called him a Party member he had failed to do so recently when identified as one by the *New York World-Telegram*.[19] Nor could Wallace convincingly deny knowledge of Pressman's record. Wallace had fired him, along with other leftists, from the Agriculture Department in the thirties. Further, Wallace's published diary contains this entry for October 1, 1942: "Gallarz wanted to let me know that his friend Jim Carey who is secretary of the CIO is being kicked around in the CIO by the communist group, including Lee Pressman, which is still very strong."[20]

Communists were the backbone of the Progressive movement, as even friendly historians admit, and provided the most funds and manpower of any group. The Progressive Party was not itself a Communist front. Wallace determined policy, not the Communists, who were a minority in his "Gideon's Army." To Progressives this has always meant that labeling them Communist stooges was red-baiting, especially when done by liberals who should have known better. But it was certainly not red-baiting to say that Wallace wished to appease Russia, since he did. And it was not red-baiting to say that Communists were active in his campaign. Wallace disliked Communist support.

He said repeatedly that Communists cost him more votes than they brought in. Others thought so too. At one point Lillian Hellman, who was in charge of Women for Wallace and had good connections with Communist leaders, begged them fruitlessly to ease off.*[21] It is not clear why they refused. Wallace was valuable to Russia only to the degree he was trusted by Americans. The presence of substantial numbers of Communists in his entourage undermined that trust and, in the end, helped destroy his usefulness.

Joseph Starobin, who was then a Party member, later made a penetrating analysis of Communist reasoning. Party leaders wanted to organize a broad antimonopoly coalition led by themselves. In theory this would break the straitjacket of the two-party system, give the CP a public forum, and, presumably, "legitimatize the political activity of the hitherto-concealed Party influentials," that is, secret Communists who worked in aid of the Party from high positions outside it. But everything went wrong. No major labor leader or prominent black organization and hardly any New Dealers joined the Progressives. Among the few sympathetic groups were business and professional people who agreed with Wallace on foreign policy. They were the first to leave on account of the Progressive Party's decision to call for nationalized basic industries. This plank had been advanced by Paul Sweezy and Leo Huberman, Marxist economists, who then "largely abstained from the party's campaign on the ground that it was insufficiently socialist in character."[22]

Another and worse mistake was the Progressive Party's failure to pass a mildly worded resolution saying that it would give no blanket endorsement to the foreign policy of any nation. But Progressives believed that all blame for the Cold War lay at America's doorstep and thus did agree entirely with the Soviets. Accordingly, the timid "Vermont Resolution" was shouted

---

* She relates this story in *Scoundrel Time* (1976). During the campaign Hellman was more disingenuous. She told Women for Wallace that the CP did not control the Progressive Party and that if it, or any other body, tried to take over she would resign. Though the Progressive line was handed down by Wallace, Communists did run the party organization. This made criticism of it more valid than expedience allowed her to admit. No doubt the end was still justifying the means.

down. Hugh De Lacey, a fiery Popular Front congressman from Washington State, denounced it.

> If there is any virtue in this platform which we are about to adopt, and I believe there are many virtues in it, it is its chief virtue to come out fighting for a sound, solid basis for friendship between the United States and the Soviet Union. [Applause] And that friendship will not be established under the present bi-partisan and controlled government, unless we are willing to take a position and fight for it and hold it and not back up with some kind of phoney declaration that doesn't mean anything. [Applause]

James Hayford, who sponsored the amendment, insisted that as it stood the platform was going to be interpreted by everyone as a statement "that we endorse Soviet foreign policy one hundred percent."[23] Rexford Tugwell and Lee Pressman claimed there was no need of any amendment because the point was already in the platform. To show this, Pressman read a bland section that said that avoiding war was a joint responsibility of Russia and the United States.

Communists were not to blame for the Progressive campaign's one-sidedness. The candidates themselves made the biggest blunders, as when Wallace defended the Czech coup and Senator Glenn Taylor, his running mate, said that "Nazis" were in charge of "our government, so why should Russia make peace with them?"[24] It was Wallace himself who watered down a plank that Frederick Schuman had written condemning totalitarianism of the right and the left. Wallace thought this was too much like red-baiting and amended it to abjure fascism only. The Progressive Party's main flaw was not its Communists, though they made it vulnerable, but the kind of thinking Wallace so perfectly embodied.

Dwight Macdonald had noted this a year earlier in articles which became a book-length attack on Wallace and Progressivism. Macdonald held that Wallace lacked character, then tried to show why he appealed so much to certain liberals anyway. Congenial habits of thought was the answer, Macdonald argued, describing them as follows. "Wallaceland is the mental habitat of Henry Wallace plus a few hundred thousand regular readers of the *New Republic,* the *Nation,* and *PM.* It is a region of perpetual fogs, caused by the warm winds of the liberal Gulf Stream coming in contact with the Soviet glacier. Its natives speak 'Wallese,' a debased provincial dialect." Macdonald had fun with progressive jargon. "Wallese is always employed to Unite rather than to Divide (hence the fog), and to Further Positive, Constructive Aims, rather than Merely to Engage in Irresponsible and Destructive Criticism."[25] Wallese employed terms as loosely as possible, so as to avoid antagonizing anyone. A phrase like "the general welfare" was prized because it meant all things to all men. "It is understandable that Henry Wallace would not want to endanger such a concept by defining it."[26]

Macdonald reviewed Wallace's career as Secretary of Agriculture, when he allegedly sold out to agribusiness, and as Vice-President, when, after 1941, "he took the whole world for his benevolent province, losing whatever contact with reality he had had up to then and becoming more and more an oratorical gasbag, a great wind of rhetoric blowing along the prevailing trade routes of Stalinoid liberalism."[27] Wallace's moral and intellectual low point as Vice-President came in 1944, when, on a goodwill tour of Siberia and China, he told "the forced-labor deportees of Soviet Asia how inspiring it was to look into the open faces of free pioneers."[28]

This was literally true. In his book *Soviet Asia Mission* (1946) Wallace quoted himself as saying even before he left America that he expected in Siberia "I shall feel the grandeur that comes when men wisely work with nature."[29] Accompanied by Owen Lattimore, he found what he was looking for. The Siberians turned out to be "not unlike our farming people in the United States," and when they were suspicious, this was merely "the natural cautiousness of farm-bred people." That these were survivors of Stalin's Great Terror presumably had nothing to do with it. The Wallace party was guarded by elements of the dreaded political police, whom Wallace described as " 'old soldiers' with blue tops on their caps. Everybody treated them with great respect. They are members of the *Nkvd,* which means the People's Commissariat of Internal Affairs." Like Stalin they had a great sense of humor. Their detachment's leader had accompanied Wendell Willkie earlier and told his guests that if he were to write about that tour it would be called

"Vodka, Vodka, Vodka." His hypothetical book on the Wallace visit would, however, be called "Kipicheonia, Kipicheonia," which was translated as "boiled water," a tribute to Wallace's famed austerity.[30] Collective farming did not escape unpraised, nor any sign of industrial advance. The whole thing was certainly an eye-opener, Wallace told the much put-upon inhabitants in one speech. Siberia used to mean to Americans "frightful suffering and sorrow, convict chains and exile," but he was glad to see that that was no longer the case.

Siberia, in point of fact, had no shortage of brutalized victims at the time. As everyone but progressives knew, its economic growth was based upon forced labor. Eleanor Lipper was a prisoner of the infamous Kolyma gold-mining district when Wallace visited it. The prisoners hoped his coming would lead to some kind of improvement. Instead he was given the Potemkin Village treatment, the historic Russian method by which foreigners were made to see what did not exist. The access roads to Lipper's camp had been lined with wooden watchtowers. "In honor of Wallace these towers were razed in a single night."[31] The starving prisoners were kept out of Wallace's sight. When he visited a model farm the swineherd girls Wallace saw were office workers assigned to play the part. The stores were laden with goods no one had seen before or would see again. Lipper was bitter about this, as about Wallace's description in *Soviet Asia Mission* of the Kolyma prisoners as volunteers. She was even angrier with Owen Lattimore, who in an article for *National Geographic* reported seeing the prospecting shafts around Kolyma from the air, while making no mention of palisades and watchtowers that must have been equally visible. He described the local administrator as a cultivated man. What, Lipper asked, would Lattimore think of someone who had visited the Nazi camps of Dachau and Auschwitz, only to report that the SS commander had "a sensitive interest in art and music?"[32] Of course, Lipper took a narrow view, having little knowledge, it seems, of the people's war and the century of the common man.

As Lipper was still a prisoner when she wrote her book, Macdonald did not have the use of her experience. His attack on Wallace was devastating even so, a slashing, biting, witty exposé that though sometimes unfair was never dull and remains a model of its kind. However, it did not sell. Attacks on Wallace still bothered many liberals. Even anti-Wallaceites were put off by Macdonald's ad-hominem attack and lapses of taste. Macdonald kept attacking just the same. He went on tour, speaking against Wallace to any who would listen. Americans for Democratic Action, later to be accused of meanness to Wallace, offered no help. Macdonald asked ADA to sponsor his talks on college campuses in vain. James Loeb told Macdonald that as *Politics* and ADA were so far apart on other issues, "our only common ground would be negative." Macdonald was incensed that ADA was allowing petty scruples to get in the way of business. "If I were *for* Wallace, I'm sure the C.P. boys would not hesitate to get up some meetings for me, despite other disagreements. That's because they are serious about their politics, and thus show a lively aggressive, imaginative approach which ADA, so far, I'm afraid, has failed to show." Macdonald thought the attitude of Mayor Hubert Humphrey, who came to one of his talks, was "much more sensible than that of the ADA central office. But of course in Minneapolis they have a real fight on with the Commies, and consequently want to get the knife into Wallace even at the risk of being 'completely negative.'" There was nothing personal in this, Macdonald assured Loeb, only bad feelings arising from "my disgust at the way the Commies are outplaying 'my' side, which is also ADA's side."[33]

Macdonald's fears were exaggerated. Years of Wallace-watching and immersion in the progressive press led him to give the third-party movement more credit than it deserved. Anti-Stalinists had been isolated for so long it was hard for them to appreciate the turn in public sentiment. The *New Leader* resembled Macdonald in this. It attacked Wallace repeatedly, ending with a harsh indictment by John Dewey just before the election. In his view the Wallaceites had decided "against human freedom, against democracy, against civil rights for all. Their support for Wallace is consistent with what they seek—an expansion of Soviet influence and the destruction of the democratic forces in Europe, the debilitation of the Marshall Plan." A genuinely new party would be democratic and "would believe it morally reprehensible to explain away the excesses of a police state." The Progressives were appeasers and wished America to become isolationist so that the Communists might have a free hand in Europe. If Wallace had his way all of Europe would succumb to "Soviet totalitarianism."[34]

A more thoughtful critique of Wallace that year was made by Gardner Jackson, an old New Dealer, in *The Atlantic*. He had known Wallace a long time and believed that the Progressive campaign was not a Communist operation, despite the Party members and fellow travelers who were running it. Rather it was a "Wallace-seeking-his-destiny campaign." Years of acclaim from progressives had gone to Wallace's head, leading him to sacrifice principle to expediency, as when he endorsed "the unbelievable Johannes Steel," a fellow-traveling radio commentator, for Congress in 1946, and praised Vito Marcantonio, a Party-liner, as having "the best voting record in the House." There were signs of rot as early as 1942, when Wallace had announced a loss of faith in "Bill of Rights democracy" as against Soviet "economic democracy." Indeed, Gardner thought, "the key to his whole New Party campaign is to be found here." Some liberal senators who knew Wallace when he was Vice-President felt that Wallace had come to believe that collectivism was inevitable everywhere and that he personally was destined to ride this "wave of the future." As Jackson read the situation, Wallace really believed that the Democrats were the war party, keeping up war production so as to fatten corporate profits. Thus, even if the GOP won, that would be good for peace.[35]

C. B. Baldwin, Wallace's campaign manager, replied to Jackson's charges. Anti-Stalinists believed that Baldwin was a Communist and, through Lee Pressman, the Party's link to Wallace. James Wechsler had told Macdonald, "I do not know of course whether Baldwin has signed his [Communist] party card, but I am pretty certain that he no longer pretends to be innocent."[36] Baldwin did nothing to support a contrary opinion. There was good reason, he insisted, for Wallace's faith in the Soviets. "The treatment accorded Wallace's Open Letter to Stalin certainly bears out his contention. Although the Russian press criticized many of its provisions Stalin considered it a reasonable basis for discussion. This is, I feel, evidence of the Russian's sincere desire for peace." Further, "the silence in Washington tends to confirm Wallace's contention that the cold war is really directed not at Russia, but at democracy—at home and abroad."[37] Without, one supposes, meaning to, Baldwin showed that the critics of progressivism were right.

Macdonald hated Wallace most for embodying the totalitarian liberalism of progressive journalists. Surprisingly enough, however, they refused to support Wallace's campaign. The *New Republic* did back Wallace at first. Even the Czech coup, of which it disapproved, failed to make a difference. As late as May the editors seemed on the verge of an endorsement. Truman was unfit to be President, they believed. "As a candidate, he will leave in the wake of his defeat a split-up labor movement, a broken party, a great body of liberals and independents divided, embittered and disillusioned with politics. American liberalism deserves better than this and it will do better. Nineteen-forty-eight can still be a year of hope."[38]

But as the Wallace campaign faltered doubt crept in. A third-party effort could only divide liberals. The Progressives' reliance on Communist help was alarming, and so was Russian behavior. Stalin gave the Democrats a hand by shutting off access to partitioned Berlin, which the U.S. Air Force and the Royal Air Force then supplied by air. The *New Republic* regretted all those Western errors that led up to this, but supported the airlift, since "to abandon Berlin at this moment would be to accept finally the division of Europe and of the world." It would also mean abandoning other outposts like Vienna, accepting the partition of Germany for good, the continued occupation of Europe by Western and Eastern troops, and maybe war. For the first time the *New Republic* got behind American policy, calling for military as well as economic aid to Europe.[39]

It had hoped until the last minute that Democrats would stop short of renominating Truman, favoring Wallace for a time and then Senator Paul Douglas. While remaining cool to Truman, the editors were agreeably surprised by the Democratic convention, where a strong civil-rights plank was pushed through by ADA liberals, forcing Southern racists to walk out. Liberalism might still win out.[40] In September the *New Republic* limply endorsed Truman. "If liberals and labor work together to sustain all that has been and still is good in the Democratic Party, 1948 will be a new beginning."[41]

TRB, the magazine's Washington correspondent, blew hot and cold on Truman all year. At first he was certain Truman would lose, but in June he saw signs supporting "the President's bull-headed notion that he knows more about the political situation than all his advisors combined."[42] A month later TRB was again certain of Truman's downfall. Just before the election he wrote a valedictory for Truman, but afterward TRB laughed at all those pundits, including himself, who helped Dewey lose by making him overconfident. The magazine too was jubilant. In a cocky editorial it announced that ten years of liberal inaction were over. The people had spoken. It was time now for a new Hundred Days, as when the New Deal began.[43]

The Nation followed a similar course. By 1948 it had largely given up apologizing for Russia, which it now admitted was a danger to Western Europe. But it still favored revolution, arguing that Western Europe must choose socialism and unity in order to save itself. "The only way to head off revolution by force throughout Europe is to organize revolution by consent."[44] Even I. F. Stone was losing faith in Soviet benevolence. When the State Department began publishing captured German documents relating to the Stalin-Hitler Pact, Stone was highly indignant. It was a Cold War maneuver designed to increase fear and hatred of the Soviets, he insisted. The documents indicated that Russia had made the first overtures to Germany with one hand, while deceiving Western powers with the other. This was difficult for Stone to believe, as it was holy writ among progressives that Stalin had turned to Hitler only because of continued Western appeasement. Maybe evidence would turn up, Stone vainly hoped, showing Western perfidy and justifying Russia.

The important aspect of Stone's essay, however, was not the old yearning to deny Russian cynicism but a new awareness of it. When the full story was told, Stone wrote, it would show that Stalin acted as any Russian ruler would have under the same circumstances. This was not to condone "much that was morally reprehensible in Moscow's dealings, but to be on our guard against a propaganda campaign designed to drag us closer to a third world war."[45] Here was progress indeed. Stone's argument did not actually hold water. A decade earlier he and other progressives had not let fear of war keep them from attacking Nazi Germany. It was still a matter of whose ox was being gored. But recognition of Soviet failings, however reluctant and incomplete, was a step forward just the same.

The destruction of Czech liberty prompted another hesitant advance. Kirchwey's first reaction was to blame the West as usual. America had refused to grant Prague loans and credits, treating it as a Soviet puppet before it was one. Now American officials were dropping "crocodile tears on the tomb of 'Czech democracy'!" "Is this to be the American role wherever the great issue is joined—to weaken or openly fight the democratic forces in each country and so help prepare the way for dictatorship?"[46] Two weeks later she wrote that Czechoslovakia was only further evidence of the need for socialism and unity in Western Europe. The death of Jan Masaryk, who may have committed suicide shortly after the coup, was not America's fault, but "it would be unfair to ignore his profound bitterness over the refusal of the Western powers to lend their strength to the support of freedom in Europe."[47] Kirchwey was writing from force of habit. American aid could not have saved Czechoslovakia, and would no doubt only have hastened its fall. On some level Kirchwey knew this. At the year's end she visited Prague, writing a sad article on its loss of freedom, which she failed to attribute to the United States.[48]

The Berlin Blockade had no effect on *The Nation,* unlike the Wallace convention. Kirchwey had wanted Wallace to disown Communist support, and by refusing to do so he alienated *The Nation.* Kirchwey said that no one was going to be fooled by its name into thinking that this Progressive Party in any way resembled those of Theodore Roosevelt and Robert La Follette. "The new party's platform and the speeches of Mr. Wallace and Senator Taylor echoed the party line closely enough to dispel any idea that a break with the Communists is likely." Independents were certain to be estranged by a platform that did not qualify its critique of American foreign policy with any reference to Russian actions, and that failed to find any virtue in the European Recovery Program. "Only a handful will accept the thesis that it [the ERP] is nothing more than a 'capitalist conspiracy' to enslave the world and force it to buy American goods."[49] Hewing to the Communist line was going to cost Progressives the large protest vote that otherwise would have been theirs. Truman's victory surprised the magazine without cheering it up. Even Robert Bendiner, an ADA liberal and the *Nation* staffer most interested in the election, did not expect another Hundred Days.[50]

Max Lerner, and *PM* also, dropped Wallace early on. That summer Dwight Macdonald would savage Lerner and Kirchwey for rejecting Wallace not because he was cowardly, dishonest and a front for the reds, but for the only good thing about his campaign, its challenge to the major parties.[51] This was unfair. Progressive journalists were against the third-party strategy from its inception, fearing that it would guarantee a Republican victory. But they had, finally, lost confidence in the united front as well and opposed Wallace for promoting it. Lerner's thought for New Year's Day 1948 was that liberals who wanted peace with Russia could not afford to entertain illusions about Communism. The new liberalism "must reject Russian totalitarianism without rejecting Russian friendship or world peace. It must reject the Communist philosophy without depriving Communists of their rights and protections under the law."[52] But, while defending the rights of Communists, liberals could not work with them. This was the lesson of Czechoslovakia, which "demonstrated for all except the willfully blind that the Communists use a Popular Front only as long as it is useful to them and smash it at their first chance to capture power."[53]

Lerner still admired Wallace. He was "a great political figure of our time and a profoundly moving democrat with a small *d*." But Wallace was wrong about the Soviets and wrong about American Communism. Consequently, "his campaign will be a futile insurgent gesture, with the main organizational strength provided by the Communists, whose prize victim and trophy Wallace has become. And the movement he leads will go down in history as a valiant but mistaken fringe movement, instead of part of the central current of American liberalism."[54] The Progressive convention made him all the surer. Lerner had been calling for a progressive third party for years, but this was not it. A real progressive party would not be dominated by Communists and would be "less confused on the issue of an unequivocal democratic liberalism whose passion for liberalism does not stop at the borders of America."[55] In the fall Lerner would cast a reluctant vote for Norman Thomas.

Lerner was right, erring only on the side of charity. Wallace's campaign was at once the high point and the death rattle of the old progressivism. Some have tried to put responsibility for this on others, usually Truman Democrats and the ADA, which misses the point. Progressivism fell of its own weight, borne down by the Soviet connection. Many liberals had reservations about American policy and thought the Truman Doctrine went too far. But they could not go along with what Macdonald said amounted to this: "the most militarist, imperialist, anti-democratic and reactionary nation in the world [Russia] is precisely the one on which millions of Americans and Europeans have fixed their aspirations for world peace, national independence, democracy, and human progress."[56] If Wallace had been less dim and reckless, and if Progressives had not insisted on working with Communists and attributing all virtue to the Soviets, things might have gone differently. The whole problem, however, was that his movement was not a reasoned political body but an emotional outburst. Thus it required a leader such as Wallace who could be counted on to muddle every issue. As Macdonald said, Wallace did not analyze a problem, "he barges around inside it throwing out vague exhortations." A movement that aimed to square democracy at home with tyranny abroad demanded such a figurehead and got, accordingly, just what it deserved.

The Wallace debacle (he received only a million votes, half of them in New York) had the short-term results critics expected. Groups aligned with progressivism were ruined if not destroyed. In New York City, American Labor Party candidates were crushed by Democrats and Liberals, a defeat from which the ALP never recovered.[57] The Southern Conference for Human Welfare, an expression of Popular Front liberalism, collapsed also. It had always been in trouble for allowing Communists to be members. Endorsing Wallace sealed its fate. Liberal unions stopped financing it. Loyal Democrats dropped out. It was dissolved two weeks after the election.[58]

The Communist Party suffered, too, as the Trotskyist *New International* had predicted. Its issue of February 1948 carried an article saying that a Wallace third party supported by Communists would drive away "captive liberals," wreck the ALP, encourage a purge of Communists from the CIO, and, in the end, would cost the Party much influence regardless of how many votes Wallace gained.[59] This was exactly what happened. Moreover, even those who believed on principle in working with Communists could not avoid seeing the actual consequences of doing so. Thereafter only fools and fellow travelers remained in the Stalinist orbit.

The Progressives never understood why most prospective allies failed to rally round them. Wallace himself once composed a verse, set to the music of his favorite folk song, "Passing Through," showing the lack of comprehension.

> *When the phony liberals leave,*
> *Let no Progressive grieve. One new party*
> *must be made of two.*
> *When the Marshall Plan is dead,*
> *And One World is just ahead,*
> *We'll all be brothers*
> *And no longer passing through.*[60]

But the events of 1948 showed that brotherhood, still less peace, was not to be had by appeasing Russia. This was clear even to Harold Laski, Britain's archprogressive. He announced after the election that Europeans welcomed Truman's victory. They were glad Wallace did badly, as it was a defeat for Communism. A good showing by Wallace had not been wanted, especially as it would have strengthened the forces inside Russia who opposed better relations with the West.[61] Laski did not explain this cryptic remark, perhaps out of embarrassment. Over the years no "democrat" had stood up for Russia more frequently. But after Czechoslovakia and Berlin even his desire to placate was wearing thin. Edgar Snow also was reversing himself. In discussing Tito's break with Stalin he hailed Yugoslavia for limiting Russian expansion. Snow declared the very virtues he had once found in the Soviets to be myths. The neighboring Communist governments Snow used to claim were grateful to Moscow for guidance and deliverance were now, it turned out, eager to escape "Russian dictatorship."[62]

Although few knew it yet, the struggle among intellectuals

over the nature of Soviet Russia and the proper response to it, which had been going on since the early thirties—and in some cases since 1918—was nearly over. No doubt the quarrel would have ended soon anyway, Stalin was seeing to that. But the Wallace movement pushed matters forward by exposing the bankruptcy of pro-Soviet reasoning, as also of the Popular Front. It was a service, even if unintentional, the Progressive Party's only accomplishment.

2

Under Freda Kirchwey (1) *The Nation* became America's most consistently pro-Soviet journal of opinion. Admired by progressives, it was
anathema to anti-Stalinist intellectuals, many of whom, like Edmund
Wilson (3), were former Marxists. Other notable additions to the
democratic left were Philip Rahv (4), co-founder of *Partisan Review*,
and Dwight Macdonald (2), who in 1943 established his own magazine,
the legendary *Politics*.

4

5

6

7

9

10

In the war years progressives had things much their own way. I. F. Stone (7) in *The Nation* and Max Lerner (8) in *PM* were two of many who defended Soviet policies. So also did Harold Laski (5), an English intellectual who often wrote for American magazines. Henry Wallace (10) was their favorite politician. At Yalta the Big Three (9) signed an agreement that progressives regarded as nearly perfect. Among the independent leftists dissenting was George Orwell (6), soon to be famous as the author of *1984*.

11

After 1945 the tide turned. Anti-Stalinist intellectuals such as Arthur Schlesinger, Jr. (14), Sidney Hook (13) and Reinhold Niebuhr (12) demolished pro-Soviet arguments. Right wing anti-Communists led by Senator Joseph McCarthy (15 rt.) persecuted Owen Lattimore (l.) and other eminent progressives. Most were silenced for a time, and some, notably Harvard professor F. O. Matthiessen (11) who committed suicide, permanently.

FIVE PHOTOS: UPI

15

16

17   18

The entertainment industry was a special object of attention during the postwar red scare. A few actors, including Robert Montgomery, George Murphy, and Ronald Reagan (16), welcomed it. Montgomery became President Eisenhower's media adviser, Murphy a U.S. senator. Reagan too did well for himself. Adolphe Menjou remained in show business (20). The Hollywood Ten (shown here with attorneys) (19) went to prison for refusing to testify about their work as members of the Communist Party. They were blacklisted too, as were other activists such as Edward G. Robinson (18), but not José Ferrer (17), who barely escaped.

21

22

The struggle continues. Political enemies in the thirties and forties, these writers are still in conflict. Mary McCarthy (21) and Diana Trilling (23) criticized Lillian Hellman (22) at their peril.

THREE PHOTOS: UPI

23

VII

The Eclipse of Progressivism

NINETEEN FORTY-EIGHT marked the end of progressivism as a force in American life. The Wallace debacle showed it had no real political strength. *The Nation* and the *New Republic* lost many subscribers. *PM* collapsed, as did two short-lived successors. Progressivism declined intellectually as well. Norman Podhoretz, as a student at Columbia College in the late forties, was excited by the rise of anti-Stalinist vitality. "Whereas the anti-Communist liberals were full of the dynamism, élan and passion that so often accompany a newly discovered way of looking at things, the fellow travelers could marshal nothing but boring clichés and tired arguments."[1] What Podhoretz thought of as "fellow-traveling liberalism" and Dwight Macdonald had been attacking as "totalitarian liberalism" was becoming the wave of the past. "The new, revisionist liberalism of the fifties" would find expression in new magazines, notably *The Reporter* and *Commentary*. The old liberalism of the old magazines faded.

The Nation conceded less to changing times than the *New Republic,* which endorsed NATO and stopped printing the work of fellow travelers. *Nation* readers still had the benefit of Vayo's pro-Soviet columns, though they were more guarded than before. And Alexander Werth was still peddling good news from the East, as when he reported that while the Czechs were sorry to have lost their liberty, Communism had nonetheless "stirred the imagination of the young." Unpleasant thoughts of executions and labor camps were banished by the knowledge that "80,000 Prague schoolchildren are to have a week's winter holiday in the mountains free of charge." This led Diana Trilling to ask the editors how much evidence of dictatorship and oppression Werth needed "before he can feel some degree of revulsion."[2] Quite a lot, time was to show.

Both magazines suffered from loss of direction. Henry Wallace no longer inspired them, but no one could take his place. Russia had let them down. The fall of Chiang Kai-shek was clearly a good thing, but progressive journalists never were able to develop the same enthusiasm for Chairman Mao that they had earlier for Stalin. As revolutions multiplied around the world Freda Kirchwey's appetite for them seemed to wane. The forward march of history with which progressives had identified was becoming less agreeable, or at any rate more complex and contradictory, than before. It had all been so simple in the old days. Then the liberty-loving and potentially democratic peoples of the world were rising to smash tyranny and enthrone the Four Freedoms. Chiang was an honorary democrat for a time, and Stalin even more so on account of his splendid constitution and all those kinds of democracy—racial, educational, social and especially economic—that flourished in Russia. The omission of political democracy was a small thing soon to be repaired. The Soviets were leading people to a better way through the perfection of their domestic institutions and instinctive support of the democratic side everywhere. All that progressives had to worry about in those days was that American fascists and monopolists, probably in combination with British imperialism, might delay the brave new world's arrival.

Even before the Korean War this vision was fading. Wallace demonstrated that the Popular Front was intensely unpopular. Stalin proved that the spread of Russian power meant the extinction not only of old ruling classes and unjust economic arrangements but of freedom and human dignity too. And it was becoming harder to deny that progress in Russia itself had been gained at a frightful cost. Many would not believe that millions had died in the purges and the forced labor camps until Khrushchev said so. But after World War II there was enough evidence for David Dallin and Boris Nicolaevsky to publish a book, *Forced Labor in Russia* (1947), that presented a broadly accurate picture of what Solzhenitsyn would later call the Gulag Archipelago. Fellow travelers sought to discredit *Forced Labor in Russia* by ridiculing its figures. On the basis of the 1939

Russian census, which listed labor camps under the heading of urbanization, Dallin and Nicolaevsky estimated that at any given time there had to be between six and fifteen million inmates. As there were some twenty million adult males in the Soviet armed forces during the war, this meant that forced labor had to have been used in industry and perhaps even the army. Alexander Werth heaped scorn on this estimate in a letter to *The New Statesman and Nation,* in whose pages a controversy had arisen. "So it was really the half-dead chain gangs of the slave camps who helped to win the battle of Stalingrad, just as, according to Dallin, it was they who built the Stalingrad factories during the first Five Year Plan."[3] Though denied by Werth, this was indeed the case. Even in 1947 most American reviewers accepted the work as basically on target. Progressives had stretched their principles beyond the breaking point often enough in the past to condone or rationalize Stalinism. But for many it was becoming impossible to admire a system that condemned millions of its own citizens to slavery and death, as now increasingly had to be admitted.

Other cherished progressive beliefs were being compromised by experience also. In 1950 Reinhold Niebuhr challenged liberal doctrine on the future of democracy in underdeveloped countries. "Official liberals" were always calling on the United States to support democratic and popular leaders in the third world. But the odds against them seemed astronomical in places where there was no democracy to begin with. Could a democratic force have been built up in China? he asked rhetorically. Even in the Philippines, which America had controlled for many years, democracy was not working. The hard truth to Niebuhr was that "our living standards, which, in our opinion, recommend our form of society to the world, actually make our political ideals appear almost irrelevant from the standpoint of Asia and Africa."[4] American disadvantages in dealing with the third world were enormous, and not to be overcome by liberal insistence on the need to support democratic forces that scarcely existed.

The low state to which progressives had been reduced was illustrated by the "Cultural and Scientific Conference for World Peace," held at the Waldorf Hotel on March 25–27, 1949, organized and sponsored by numerous celebrities.* Their aim was to have American fellow travelers meet with their opposite numbers from Western Europe, plus an assortment of Eastern Communists.[5] Popular Front leftists still believed, even after the Wallace campaign, that it was good publicity and a blow for peace to have famous people get together and praise Russia. The idea, never too sound, made little sense after the Cold War began. An early sign of the times was that the State Department denied visas to many European fellow travelers, and to conference delegates from several Communist states. The conference therefore consisted largely of talks by American fellow travelers and Eastern-bloc Communists. It was picketed by conservative anti-Communists, and penetrated by anti-Stalinist intellectuals, who had been organized at the last minute by Sidney Hook. Calling themselves American Intellectuals for Freedom, they included Dwight Macdonald, Robert Lowell, Mary McCarthy, Bertram Wolfe, A. J. Muste, Max Eastman and Arthur Schlesinger, Jr., a remarkably diverse group who agreed only that pro-Soviet propaganda could not be allowed to go unanswered. They attended several sessions, asking embarrassing questions from the floor, and held a separate public meeting of their own.

Frederick Schuman tried to give the conference a less partisan cast by saying in his speech that there were elements in both Russia and the United States favoring war. A. A. Fadayev, head of the Soviet delegation, took issue, explaining that no one in Russia wanted war. Schuman thereupon recanted, admitting that only Americans desired it. This was the mood of the session on writing and publishing as well, in which the anti-Stalinist writers naturally took a special interest. The official American participants in this session were Agnes Smedley, W. E. B. Du Bois, a famous black intellectual who would soon join the Communist Party, Howard Fast, a Communist novelist, Norman Mailer, who had been active in the Wallace campaign,

---

* Sponsors included Leonard Bernstein, Aaron Copeland, Lillian Hellman, Canada Lee, Norman Mailer, Budd Schulberg, Angus Cameron, Langston Hughes, Matthew Josephson, Rexford G. Tugwell, Paul Robeson, Norman Corwin and Agnes Smedley, as well as Clifford Odets, Arthur Miller, Albert E. Kahn, Dashiell Hammett and Thomas Mann. They were all familiar names to progressives.

and F. O. Matthiessen, a distinguished literary scholar and well-known fellow traveler.

Macdonald described the session in *Politics,* but his notes taken at the time offer even more information.[6] Professor Matthiessen, who looked unhappy and did not speak well, read a "deplorable" speech that "presented Thoreau, Emerson, Whitman, and Melville as spokesmen for human rights and the underdog who were predecessors of CP and Soviet Russia today." Macdonald spoke from the floor, challenging Fadayev to reveal the truth about missing Russian writers, Max Eastman having assembled a list of thirty-three who were unaccounted for and presumed dead. Fadayev responded with various lies which Macdonald wanted to expose but could not, as session chairman Louis Untermeyer's "liberalism was not fanatical enough to allow this." But Untermeyer was fair, generally, Macdonald believed, and gave the anti-Stalinists opportunities to speak. Mary McCarthy asked Matthiessen if he thought Emerson and the rest would be able to live and work in Russia today. No, Matthiessen conceded; on the other hand, Lenin would not be able to live in the United States today, either. There was a good deal of this sort of thing. Macdonald felt that the effort was worthwhile anyway. The anti-Communist side had been heard, for a change. And he was happy with the young novelist Norman Mailer, who surprised everyone by denouncing Russia as well as the United States.

The Waldorf conference received much publicity, first because it seemed outrageous to hold a pro-Soviet meeting at this point in the Cold War, and then because of the lively anti-Stalinist presence at it.[7] The effects lasted quite a while. Freda Kirchwey thought it was of "dubious value" because both sides were so partisan. The State Department behaved badly by keeping so many delegates out of the country. The mostly Roman Catholic pickets were "a choice sample of the Christian Front Lumpenproletariat."[8] Sidney Hook's AIF group behaved correctly, she admitted, but their aim was to show that freedom of expression did not exist in Communist countries, which everyone already knew. Anyway, if the anti-Stalinists were to organize a peace conference would they allow pro-Communists to speak? Kirchwey still believed that to achieve peace "we" had to deal with Communists and speak to them and try to work something out, though, she confessed, there were problems. She had attended a Communist-sponsored peace congress in Poland the year before which accomplished nothing because all the Communist delegates spoke as one. *The Nation*'s position now was that while Communism was bad, anti-Communism was, too. The right thing was for liberals to sit down and have a dialogue with Communists, even though this was impossible.

The Nation's confusion was more evident still in its longest story on the subject, which was not about the Waldorf conference but on press coverage of the event. Except for *The New York Times,* press reporting was said to be scandalous, an outburst of yellow journalism at its lowest, according to Tom O'Connor. The real story was that peace-loving radicals had invited like-minded people from other countries to discuss common problems. The State Department had responded by denying visas to the representatives of Hungary and Rumania and to all who applied from Western Europe save one Englishman. (Hook and the AIF had in fact protested this, thinking theirs was the better way to deal with Communism.) But did the press report these simple facts? No, instead it showered the public with hysterical misinformation. The moral was equally simple. In order to avoid war and make the right decisions people had to have accurate information. "Soviet journalists sneer at our vaunted freedom of the press, and say we mean by it freedom to print lies and distortions, to misinform and mislead the people. Surely it is depressing to reflect how much we have done to prove them right."[9]

The Nation's story was angrily refuted. Dwight Macdonald wrote in to say that O'Connor was wrong on certain particulars and misrepresented the conference by describing it as a matter of "left-of-center intellectuals" contacting their opposite numbers abroad. The conference was pro-Soviet propaganda masquerading as intellectual inquiry. It was this blatant rigging that inspired anti-Stalinists to act as they did.[10] Hook was even more severe. The AIF did not, as Kirchwey claimed, reject every attempt to talk to Russians or Communists. Its objection to the Waldorf conference was precisely that no discussion was going to take place, as only Communists and pro-Soviets, except for Norman Cousins of *The Saturday Review of Literature,* were invited to speak. It was to protest this intellectual fraud and discuss the need for intellectual and artistic freedom everywhere that the AIF staged its own rally, at which "more differences on foreign policy were expressed than have ever been voiced at the dinner forums of the *Nation* since the days of Oswald G. Villard." Her misrepresentations were typical of Kirchwey, whose record of "totalitarian liberalism" and "intellectual and moral double-dealing" had been spread over the pages of *The Nation* for ten years.[11]

Kirchwey denied everything, reviewing her own record and finding it to be spotless. Hook was particularly mistaken when he charged *The Nation* with no longer reflecting liberal opinion. In the past ten years it had published items by twenty-five members of the AIF and fifty other well-known anti-Communists, including thirteen by Hook. This was true but not her doing. One *Nation* tradition that Kirchwey had not yet broken was that culture and politics were separate. The editorial staff had no control over the "back of the book," which was run by the anti-Stalinist Margaret Marshall. Thus for years book reviewers had been expressing opinions contrary to those of Kirchwey and her staff. Kirchwey was not really happy about this, though it was convenient for purposes of answering Hook, and in a few more years she would achieve unity by forcing Marshall out.

Not surprisingly, Marshall's good-natured account of the Waldorf conference differed from Kirchwey's. It was the sponsors' own fault that it took such an unexpected turn. By making it so one-sided they dramatized the issue of freedom of expression. By presenting themselves as representatives of American artists, scientists and writers (the conference was sponsored by the Wallaceite National Council for the Arts, Sciences and Professions) they had made the AIF response both inevitable and necessary. It was provocative to invite the distinguished composer Shostakovich, who had been publicly humbled in Russia and forced to confess his political sins, and worse still to bring over Fadeyev, who was famous for his attacks on America and American writers, whom he had called hyenas. The organizers "were surely inviting the attention of the curious on the one hand, and the furious on the other." She drew her own moral from the experience.

The Soviet Union suffers today from the great delusion that repression has a future. Yet it is surely clear by now that repression, no less than imperialism and racism, leads to stultification at home and conflict abroad. Friends of the Soviet Union should be the first—should have been all along—to say so. As long as they continue, instead, out of ignorance or misguided "revolutionary" zeal to support and encourage that delusion, they are not diminishing but increasing the tensions and fears that divide the East and the West; and what is much worse to my way of thinking, they are performing the function of a fifth column not against capitalism and imperialism but against the freedom of the mind and all its fruits.[12]

The point had seldom been made so well. Fellow travelers imagined that by siding with Russia on everything, they were fighting for peace and progress. But, as Marshall said, they were deceived. Pro-Soviet intellectuals had no effect whatever on the policies of either Russia or the West. President Truman did not care what the National Council for the Arts, Sciences and Professions thought; neither did Marshal Stalin. On the other hand, it was wrong of *Partisan Review* to have said, as it did a few years earlier, that by defending Stalinism certain journalists were "helping to shoot democrats of every shade and color, in Germany, Poland, Rumania, Bulgaria, Hungary, Austria."[13] That was a delusion, too. It was hard for intellectuals, feeling strongly as they did and being so articulate, to accept their relative powerlessness. Progressive journalists always wrote as if government were hanging on their every word. They enjoyed publishing open letters to heads of state. Anti-Stalinists, who had few illusions about their own potency in the thirties and forties, were sometimes caught up in the fantasy also, crediting progressives with an influence they did not have.

What was really at stake, as Margaret Marshall recognized, was the integrity of intellectual life. Nothing said at the Waldorf would affect foreign policy. But it might conceivably nudge the thinking of liberal, educated people one way or another. Although in the minority, they were not an insignificant fraction of the polity. They determined what was taught in universities and, to a degree, what appeared in the media. How they thought bore some relation to public support for one policy or another. In the end, the politics of intellectuals and liberal-left journalists did matter, not, as they often seemed to feel, because they molded opinion and swayed government directly, but because they helped erect the intellectual scaffolding of their time. The debate over foreign affairs recorded here was about specifics, to be sure. The immediate struggle had to do with what kind of state the Soviet Union was and what should be done about it. The larger meaning of this experience, however, given its marginal relation to policy-making, was the quality and character of American thought—"freedom of the mind and all its fruits," as Margaret Marshall said.

Dwight Macdonald recognized this, and in the forties he devoted much time and effort to meeting the dual challenge raised by pro-Soviet intellectuals. The immediate problem of their mistaken beliefs led to direct attacks, as in his campaigns against *Mission to Moscow* and the Waldorf conference. More often he sought to expose the false assumptions upon which pro-Soviet propaganda rested, and the corrupting means used to advance it. This was the special function of his magazine *Politics*. The journal and Macdonald had other interests—German war guilt, popular culture, European social thought being only a few. But nothing became *Politics* more than its treatment of Stalinism at home and abroad. It ran many penetrating analyses of Soviet life, culminating in the Spring 1948 issue, which was entirely about Russia. Its fullest exposé of American apologists for Stalinism was Macdonald's attack on Henry Wallace and his masterful summary "The Wallace Campaign: An Autopsy."[14]

Philip Rahv of *Partisan Review,* a somewhat unfriendly ally of *Politics,* said Macdonald's position was: "Everything has failed us, liberalism, Social Democracy, Bolshevism, and the working class too—therefore let us go forward to the earthly paradise."[15] This was not quite fair, and, in any case, *Politics* embraced many points of view. Despite their differences, most contributors were independent radicals, antagonistic to the official pieties of both capitalism and Communism.* *Politics* had

---

* They included James Agee, Daniel Bell, Bruno Bettelheim, Nicola Chiaromonte, Paul Goodman, Irving Howe, C. Wright Mills, Peter Meyer, George Orwell, Victor Serge, Simone Weil (posthumously) and George Woodcock.

not supported the war effort, had not believed it was meant to realize the Four Freedoms, and had not thought it was leading to the century of the common man. Accordingly, it was not surprised that the peace was so hollow, since a bad war could scarcely have produced any other result. *Politics* was a magazine of criticism, out of necessity if nothing else. Contributors agreed by and large on what they were against, but, being independent, could not get together programatically. Apart from shared dislikes they were sustained by one interest, opposition to all the great powers. By 1949, however, this was weakening. As the Communist threat grew it became harder to criticize both sides of the Cold War equally. Macdonald himself came to believe that the East was a greater danger and so, reluctantly, chose the West. But though the logic of events, as he saw it, forced this choice, Macdonald could not be made to like it. He lost interest in politics and in *Politics* too, which he folded up at the year's end.

The Cold War did not produce so rapid a change in Max Lerner. Nineteen forty-eight had marked his turn away from Stalin and Henry Wallace. He remained faithful to his other beliefs. Liberalism to him still meant opposing American intervention abroad. He still felt U.S. foreign policy involved too many confrontations with Russia and a lack of scrupulousness in choosing allies. He continued to oppose German rearmament. Yet Lerner also greatly admired Adlai Stevenson, despite the mildness of his liberalism, and was critical of Alger Hiss, whom progressives were supposed to rally behind.[16] Lerner was now, for the most part, in the mainstream of liberal opinion, where he would remain, moving only from left to right by a few degrees.

This did not keep him from being red-baited, for postwar anti-Communism was indiscriminate. At a time when the hawkish Secretary of State Dean Acheson was being accused of softness toward Communism, Lerner, even though no longer pro-Soviet, would not go unscathed. As early as 1947 he was being included in lists of fellow travelers compiled by witch-hunters. In 1951 such attacks had become so common that timid sponsors were canceling his lectures.[17] Lerner survived the McCarthy era nonetheless. He defended himself vigorously against all charges. He could produce columns critical of the American Communist Party dating back to the late thirties as proof of his independence. He had not been pro-Stalin or pro-Soviet since 1948. His column had been moved to the liberal *New York Post*. And he was working on a book, *America as a Civilization* (1957), that would bring him a renown far greater than anything he had known earlier as the favorite journalist of progressives.

In his drift toward liberalism Lerner resembled many other progressive journalists. Yet in other respects Lerner was anything but typical. As the chief spokesman for *PM,* with its hundreds of thousands of readers, and as a syndicated columnist besides, Lerner had reached a greater audience than most of his peers. This made Lerner a special target of the anti-Stalinist intellectuals, who unmasked him repeatedly to no effect during the years of Popular Front liberalism. All the same, two attacks have worn particularly well. Both were made in 1945, when Lerner was riding the progressive wave. Dwight Macdonald was moved by Lerner's entry into Germany behind the Ninth Army to write one of his most inspired polemics. Lerner had become a war correspondent just in time for the war's end. Crossing the border in his jeep, he encountered a group of German refugees. As he explained it in *PM* these consisted of older people, a few children, and one baby, whose homes had been destroyed by American artillery. Lerner dismounted to ask if they were guilty of Nazism and World War II. He was appalled to discover that they all denied their war guilt, claiming as Roman Catholics to have been against Hitler. Macdonald summarized Lerner's response:

> "I came away heartsick and discouraged," writes Lerner. "The crime of these people was cowardice and moral callousness rather than active criminality. . . . Nowhere did I find the moral strength to face the fact of guilt. Only protests that they were not responsible for what had happened." Even the baby apparently lacked a sense of responsibility for Hitler, which shows how deeply ingrained this moral callousness is in the German national character.[18]

Lerner also reported a happier encounter when two Soviet major generals visited the Ninth Army. They were better dressed than the German peasants, and more important. "Finally," wrote Macdonald,

> they were Soviet generals, people's generals, democratic
> generals, very inspiring generals altogether, generals on the
> Right Side, the People's Side, the Yalta Side. Yes, they
> were clearly Max Lerner's kind of people—the progressive,
> democratic and victorious people, not like those wretched
> German farmers with their shabby clothes and shell-
> wrecked homes and hungry faces and their callous and
> cowardly refusal to lick the boots of an accredited *PM* war
> correspondent.[19]

This was typical of progressives, for whom all virtue resided in one's friends and all evil in one's enemies. It was the double standard of morals, enriched by sentimentality and emotionalism. Progressives were uplifted by thoughts of Soviet gains and the glorious Red Army, but shed no tears for the victims of Stalinism, still less for innocent German refugees. Indeed, to Lerner, as Macdonald said, there were no innocent Germans. Every last one of them was responsible for Nazism and the war and deserved worse than they got.

Another corrupting aspect of progressive thought, also embodied by Lerner, was an obsession with ends at the expense of means. Granville Hicks spoke to this in an acute review of *Public Journal* (1945), which contained one hundred editorials and columns (out of a total of four hundred) written by Lerner for *PM* over a two-year period. "The preoccupation with the effect rather than the truth of an argument has become increasingly common in liberal circles, and Lerner displays it in many forms. If Protestant clergymen object to the indiscriminate bombing of German cities, he suggests that they are helping Hitler."[20] All criticism of Russia was handled the same way. Though he did not single it out, Hicks could have cited Lerner's treatment of the Katyn Forest massacre. As we saw, Lerner first tried to suggest that the Soviets had not murdered thousands of Polish officers, then raised the inevitable point that in any case dwelling on it weakened Allied unity and benefited Hitler. The appeal to unity, as after 1945 to peace, was a way of excusing mass murder—made easier because those slain were the wrong kind of people who had missed the train of history.

On April 1, 1950, F. O. Matthiessen, a professor of literature at Harvard, jumped to his death from the twelfth floor of a seedy Boston hotel. He left behind a note written out of deep depression. To it he added a postscript: "How much the state of the world has to do with my state of mind I do not know. But as a Christian and a socialist believing in international peace, I find myself terribly oppressed by the present tensions."[21] At the time of his death Matthiessen was the most intellectually distinguished fellow traveler in America.

Matthiessen graduated from Yale in 1923 after a brilliant career during which he had served as editor of the *Yale Daily News* and the *Yale Literary Magazine,* been named class orator and class deacon, elected to Phi Beta Kappa, and given a Rhodes scholarship, among other awards. He received a B.Litt. from Oxford in 1925 and in two more years earned an M.A. and a Ph.D. from Harvard. He joined the Harvard faculty in 1929, remaining on it until his death. Matthiessen wrote many books of literary scholarship, the best known being *American Renaissance: Art and Expression in the Age of Emerson and Whitman* (1941). It was the most important study of American literature to that date, helped launch the new field of American studies, and remains a landmark work to this day.

Sensitive and deeply felt, *American Renaissance* was notable also for its skillful eclecticism. According to one scholar, "Matthiessen was more methodologically aware than any critic of his time," drawing upon current approaches—the New Criticism, Marxism, the New Humanism, Freudianism—as they served his purpose. In *American Renaissance* Matthiessen set out deliberately to show the importance of literature to life, not out of a cheery optimism, but with a sense both of the tragic character of human destiny and of the importance of democratic egalitarianism. The result, as Henry Nash Smith put it, was not a system of ideas but

the remarkable deepening of literary study consequent upon his determination to subject the writers he examined to ultimate tests of their value, by relating them at once to the long cultural past of western Europe, to the tensions of American society in the mid-twentieth century, and to his urgent personal need for integration. It was a gigantic task, perhaps an impossible one. But his commitment to it was heroic, and it gave to his scholarship an intensity and dignity that are unique in our contemporary cultural life.[22]

Matthiessen excelled as a teacher also. He was not a good lecturer. Leo Marx described him as small and nearly bald, "his voice impersonal and a little metallic," but he was very effective in small groups and with individuals.[23] In the thirties Matthiessen attracted followers who would themselves become major scholars. He was a generous teacher and friend, hospitable, a faithful correspondent, especially during the war years when former students were spread around the world. And, despite personal oddities, he seemed to combine scholarship of the highest order with an unsparing dedication to political and social change. This made him a compelling figure to gifted young men.

Matthiessen's political life was varied and full, astonishingly so for one who socialized frequently and was a productive scholar. He was a founder and later the president of the Harvard Teachers Union, an active member of the Massachusetts branch of the ACLU, and belonged to at least twenty-eight fellow-traveling and Communist-front organizations. He was heavily engaged in the Wallace movement, gave a seconding speech for Wallace at the Progressive convention, and campaigned actively for him. Matthiessen did not limit himself to giving speeches, joining organizations and signing manifestos, all of which he did with great frequency. He also labored on the precinct level, watching polls and canvassing voters, something he was said to enjoy.[24]

This mixture of scholarship and activism inspired radical young intellectuals at the time, and in some cases afterward. George Abbot White was a graduate student and new leftist in the 1960s looking for a way to integrate literature and politics. He was thrilled to discover Matthiessen. "Why had this man's achievement and his history been withheld?" he asked, an inevitable question at a time when conspiracy theories abounded. His answer was more surprising. White held that Matthiessen's memory had been obscured by the New Critics, who dominated literary scholarship in the fifties and rejected politics and everything else except textual analysis as corrupting influences. Further, Matthiessen had made enemies because history and literature, the field of concentration at Harvard led by him and Perry Miller, the great intellectual historian, admitted only fifty students a year, presumably alienating the rest. White decided to right this wrong. He wished also to emulate the master, which he did with little success, so far as scholarship was concerned, judging by his essay on Matthiessen.[25]

The problem that Matthiessen poses for anyone seeking to enshrine him as a scholar-activist is that his politics do not bear inspection. White handled this by ignoring the substance of Matthiessen's political life, finding its mere existence to be enough for purposes of celebration. Though it was an easy out, taking it buried the point of Matthiessen's experience. His politics turned on his belief that the Soviet Union and, less perfectly, the American Communist Party, represented the left and were always to be defended. He arrived at this conviction perhaps as early as his Oxford days, when he began calling himself a socialist, and clung to it all his life. As a result his politics were the opposite of his scholarship, being immature, sentimental, partisan, mindless and wrong.

These qualities were not so apparent in the thirties, when many academic people defined the left as Matthiessen did. Popular Front liberalism flourished at Harvard, as at most better colleges and universities. There was even a Communist cell made up of a handful of graduate students and instructors, which after its demise was ruthlessly investigated by the House Committee on Un-American Activities. In the main, though, leftism at Harvard was progressive rather than Communistic. It was centered in the Harvard Teachers Union, where the great issues of the day took precedence over collective bargaining. And it embraced the usual Popular Front activities—petitions and rallies on behalf of the Spanish Loyalists and other approved causes, folk singing, and performances of left-wing plays and musicals. More is known about the Popular Front at Harvard than elsewhere because so many Harvard progressives and leftists wrote about it, because of the HUAC investigation, and thanks especially to a symposium held at Hobart and William

Smith Colleges in 1975 attended by many veterans of the Harvard Front.

Though it was a nostalgic occasion, some participants indicated that leftism at Harvard had been a function of the unexamined life, a matter of everyone being thoughtlessly progressive together. Rufus Mathewson, a student at Harvard in the thirties who went on to study and teach at Columbia, compared the two campuses. Leftism at Harvard was genteel, he recalled.

> Columbia, on the other hand, was much closer to the grimy center of things. . . . One could drift out of the Harvard left unstained, undamaged, without trauma, and keep a good memory of it. I think most of the present company is no exception. New York's intellectuals had a much clearer view of the ugly side of the Soviet experience as I later came to know it—"trials," spies, prisons and the offhand murder of millions, which we at Harvard were likely to dismiss as the slanderous fantasies of the class enemy.[26]

Matthiessen thrived in Harvard's atmosphere of uncritical progressivism. Whether he pulled his students to the left or they him, as Harry Levin argued, the man seemed well suited to the hour.

> It was his exceptionally sensitive conscience, the intuitive warmth of his democratic sympathies, his ever-increasing determination to take seriously the ideals of Emerson and the manifestoes of Whitman, which drew him along in the direction his favorite students were taking. To them, in turn, he imparted a deeper realization of what was meant by social responsibility.[27]

Edward Whiting Fox, then a Harvard student and later a professor of history at Cornell, said that in those days Matthiessen "was in one way or another the hero of everyone" present at the symposium.[28]

It might seem odd today that pursuing the ideals of Emerson could lead one to Stalin, but reconciling opposites was the touchstone of Popular Front liberalism. The Nazi-Soviet Pact made this more difficult at Harvard, as almost everywhere. The Harvard Teachers Union divided over whether the war in Europe was imperialist or not. The union was never as strong again, the agreement of intellectuals never as complete—despite the appearance of unity when America went to war.

Those who knew Matthiessen in the thirties felt that life afterward disappointed him. The best and brightest students went away to war or enrolled in training programs. The postwar generation of students, most of them veterans, were not much interested in politics. Leo Marx said that "there was none of that somewhat innocent and cavalier headiness of Popular Front days."[29] Though still considered one of Harvard's best teachers, Matthiessen was not the cult figure he had once been. Matthiessen remained pro-Soviet into the Cold War, which estranged him further from many of his colleagues.

Matthiessen had one last great moment as a teacher, which would result, ironically, in his worst book and contribute to his death. In the summer of 1947 he was the star of a seminar on American civilization held in Salzburg, Austria. Matthiessen was buoyed up by teaching a select group of students from all over Europe, calling it later the finest teaching experience he had known. Kenneth Lynn, one of his Harvard students who was there, agreed, saying it was the high point in Matthiessen's teaching career. He opened the seminar by speaking in the garden of the *Schloss* where classes were held, using as his text T. S. Eliot's poem *The Wasteland*. That was Lynn's best memory of Matthiessen, "talking out of his American heart in the heart of Europe."[30]

Alfred Kazin, who also taught the seminar, remembered Matthiessen differently. Though he would write affectionately of Matthiessen in the memorial volume assembled by the editors of *Monthly Review,* Kazin had been disturbed by Salzburg. He found Matthiessen to be "amazing in his sudden vehemence, his intellectual rages in front of his audience, all mixed into a deadly brew with literary and political pieties." Matthiessen's power over students, Kazin thought, resulted not from his ideas about literature, which were conventional, but rather "the lonely passion of the man. They were not familiar with the many volcanoes seething in the United States. A secretary innocently coming up to Matthiessen with a telephone message—he was lecturing—made him scream with anger." In the end, Matthiessen's effect was almost sinister. "I have never known another teacher whose influence on students had so many harsh personal and political consequences. His suicide in 1950 was to magnify this."[31] Kazin's testimony runs counter to that of almost everyone else. It is not to be discounted all the same, for Kazin seems to be the only person to write about him who was not Matthiessen's follower, student or obligated friend.

From Salzburg Matthiessen went on to lecture at Charles University in Prague. This was uplifting also. Students there were responsive to him. The Czech attempt at cooperation between Communists and democrats seemed to be working. He left the doomed republic in high spirits as shown by his travel diary, published the next year as *From the Heart of Europe* (1948). Personal experiences and thoughts on literature excepted, it was a work of staggering banality, a monument of sorts to the shallowness and bad taste of his politics. Like most fellow travelers he was addicted to the false analogy, as when comparing censorship in Russia with American popular culture. "Both are committed to official versions of life, and must, therefore, be resisted at every point by anyone concerned with breaking through the official to the real."[32] In the same vein he compared William Z. Foster, an old Stalinist hack, with Eugene Debs, and Henry Wallace with Jefferson. A quick tour of Central Europe had not shaken his belief that Communism was progressive. The rise of Communists to power in Hungary and elsewhere had nothing to do with terrorism and the Red Army but was solely a result of their popularity. Economic democracy was on the march throughout Communist-dominated Europe, he was happy to report. Slight reservations notwithstanding, the book was a mind-numbing exercise in propaganda.

One aspect of *From the Heart of Europe* disturbed anti-Stalinists particularly. This was his treatment of Czechoslovakia. His tributes to Czech democracy had not even gone to press when Czechoslovakia was deprived of it by the Communist takeover. Instead of revising or modifying his text, Matthiessen added footnotes justifying the coup. Czech friends had told him "that the new government possesses the confidence of the mass of the people." One had explained to him that the loss of liberty was democratically arrived at. "We preferred to give up a part of our individual freedom to save the economic freedom for the whole nation."[33] Matthiessen even repeated the Communist slander that Jan Masaryk, a Czech national hero, had committed suicide on account of reproaches from his Western friends, though everyone knew that the great patriot, if indeed he had not been murdered, died from grief.

Owing to the survival of progressive illusions, *From the Heart of Europe* received better reviews than its intellectual and moral dreadfulness would lead one to expect. The *Christian Science Monitor* and *The New York Times* were complimentary. Professor Robert Lynd had kind words for it in the *New Republic,* as did Malcolm Cowley in the *New York Herald Tribune.*[34] But it was too late in the day for such a book to escape unmarked. *Partisan Review* asked Dwight Macdonald to give it "the works." Matthiessen, William Phillips believed, had been "getting away with his politics because most people still think he's just a literary man—a little dopey but just a literary man."[35] Macdonald hesitated, so the job went to Irving Howe, who put his finger on the most distressing aspect of Matthiessen's politics. Fellow travelers in the thirties, Howe pointed out, naïvely believed there was democracy in the Soviet Union and would have been "horrified at the accusations against Russia which Matthiessen blandly accepts as true." In the old days, consequently, if you could persuade fellow travelers that Russia was dictatorial, corrupt and brutal you might win them over. This was not true of Matthiessen. He did not care at all about the evils of Stalinism, displaying instead "an advanced case of a calloused moral indignation."[36]

The curious thing about Matthiessen was the manner in which his politics were a betrayal of everything he stood for otherwise. *The Nation*'s reviewer explained it this way:

> Obviously his political actions are less governed by those truths he has found for himself than by those noble feelings and immature longings which are exploited by demagogues everywhere. There is small hope for the genuine American Labor Party for which Professor Matthiessen pleads as long as eloquent dilettantes continue to confuse the issues. The difference between socialism and Stalinism is not one of mere method. The first builds on the foundations of the Bill of Rights, the latter destroys them. The ideal of socialism is the free moral personality, the ideal of Stalinism, the well-fed robot. Perhaps mankind on its tortuous

way will have to pass through another period of slavery but no admirer of Shakespeare and Melville ought to help us into it, however innocently.[37]

Though encouraged by friends, Matthiessen was upset by the hostile reviews, which he could not understand.[38] In most cases he wrote letters to the magazines defending himself, and in the case of *Time* directly to the publisher, having known Henry Luce since they were students at Yale.[39] Protesting did Matthiessen no good, nor did the news from Czechoslovakia. Joseph Alsop told Matthiessen that "a sufficient number of your former colleagues at Charles University have now felt its [repression's] effects, so that I imagine you would not find the old complacency if you now returned again."[40] Matthiessen did not return, no doubt because he already knew what he would find. John Finch, who directed the Salzburg seminar in 1949, informed him that only four students from Czechoslovakia managed to reach it, three of them having obtained passports by lying about their destination. Finch was especially bothered by the plight of one girl, who represented for him "the whole desperation of the young Czech intellectuals." Of his own visit to Czechoslovakia he said only that "as a political experience, the whole trip was [as] jarring and disturbing as anything I've ever lived through."[41] A student who had been in Matthiessen's class at Charles University was more specific. A member of the English department had committed suicide. None of the students who applied to study in the United States had been allowed to go. He and a friend would soon receive their Ph.D.s in American literature, after which no more were to be given.[42]

Pete Steffens, the son of Lincoln Steffens and Ella Winter, was reassuring. He had visited Prague and talked to students who made only minor complaints.[43] His mother was less naïve, even though her heart went out to Czech Communists. "They really did awfully want and hope to be able to carry through a 'bloodless revolution'—they really mind not being able to. I honestly believe they would have if we had let them. Someday maybe a 'middle road' will be built?"[44] Anyway, as she remarked to Matthiessen in another letter, there was a war on and casualties had to be expected. "But I suppose in any army (as we all more or less are) one cannot pause long enough before action to get the niceties adjusted. That's the hard part for intellectuals."[45] This was of a piece with Matthiessen's explanation of the Czech coup, expressed privately, that you could not make an omelet without breaking eggs.[46] Statements such as these led anti-Stalinist intellectuals to feel that Communist brutality was not an obstacle to fellow traveling but one of the benefits. As a soldier in the army of Stalin's foreign friends Ella Winter could enjoy the thrill of violence without having to commit it.

Matthiessen conceded nothing as the oppression of Czechoslovakia wore on, dying, so far as is known, with the faith he had lived by. Some of his friends believed all the same that events had dealt him a mortal blow.

> It would be difficult to estimate the effect on Matty of the putsch in Czechoslovakia of February, 1948, and the subsequent tragic end of Masaryk. I always regarded his failure to change the conclusion in his book on Czechoslovakia—and that possibility was available to him after the events of the Communist seizure of power in February —as a psychic symbol of defeat. It was not merely the gesture of a tired man, but of one who wished to cling to a last illusion that had seemed the only way out of an aching ideological impasse.[47]

According to this reasoning a truth about Communism had been revealed at last to Matthiessen and he could not live with it. This remains speculation. What seems most plausible is that Matthiessen took his life while in a state of deep depression brought on by more than one cause. He had known mental illness before, having suffered a nervous breakdown after the publication of *American Renaissance*. Further, Matthiessen was homosexual and tormented by it. All his friends knew this, but it could not be discussed. Worse still, Matthiessen's companion of twenty years died in 1945, opening a wound that never healed.[48] Political setbacks contributed to but were hardly the whole reason for his morbid frame of mind.

The testimony of his friends shows Matthiessen to have been a complex and difficult man. Though warm and sociable, he had a quick temper and caustic tongue. A generous friend, he was demanding too, giving and expecting more than was usual in such relations. Matthiessen was always looking for fellowship, even among working people, about whom he was inclined to be sentimental. The emotional basis of his socialism was his experience as a college student tutoring Hungarian workers. He gained from them, as he said in *From the Heart of Europe,* "a kind of comradeship I never wanted to lose." Students meant a great deal to him in somewhat the same way, too much so, probably. The shrinking of his student cult after the war contributed to Matthiessen's depression, some friends believed. It was no accident, in their view, that he killed himself while on leave from teaching.

This is the picture drawn of Matthiessen by his friends in their memorial volume to him, and in May Sarton's novel *Faithful Are the Wounds* (1955) based on his life. Both books ignore his homosexuality, unmentionable still in the 1950s, but are full of information otherwise. Sarton in particular wrote vividly of Matthiessen's brilliance, intensity and lack of defenses, what a friend called his "unshielded sensibility," that made students uncomfortable even as they looked up to him.[49] She was convincing on the effects upon Matthiessen (Edward Cavan is his fictional name) of the Czech coup. After it his insomnia grew worse and personality changes occurred. And she explained, more concisely than anyone, why so many of Matthiessen's friends who disagreed with his politics respected him just the same. A character in the novel puts it this way: "Because of the reasons for what he believed. The reasons, you see, were generous, deeply human reasons, even if the conclusions, as far as we can see, were unworthy."[50]

This was a widely shared opinion. Almost no one tried to defend the content of Matthiessen's political thought—except Paul Sweezy, who agreed with most of it.[51] By 1950 Matthiessen's continued faith in the Soviets not only was unpopular and embarrassing, but showed a remarkable unwillingness to learn anything from history. Unattractive in its own right, Matthiessen's dogmatism led to petty acts, as when he tried to stop Philip Rahv from teaching at the Kenyon College summer school out of hatred for Rahv's anti-Stalinism.[52]

One can see why friends reached for excuses to resolve the paradox of a highly ethical person condoning government by terror.* Most fellow travelers shared the same contradiction, though few to such a pathological extreme as Matthiessen. Because he was so deeply disturbed, many contributors to the *Collective Portrait* explained both his politics and his suicide in clinical terms. But though hardly any fellow travelers took their own lives—Matthiessen may have been the only one not blacklisted to do so—he was typical of many in that his politics seemed not so much to flow out of his central beliefs as to go against them.

It has been observed, most eloquently in Richard Crossman's *The God That Failed* (1949), a book of essays by prominent former Communists, that the appeal of Stalinism was religious. So it appears to have been for Matthiessen. He often said that as a Christian he could not join the Communist Party (though if French he would have anyway for unexplained reasons). Yet it is evident that Christ was not enough for him; he needed Lenin and Stalin too. Matthiessen and his kind were very different from the first generation of intellectuals who admired Communism. Max Eastman, John Reed and Lincoln Steffens, to name a few, were drawn to Communism not out of blind faith but because as secular persons in a rational age they believed it to be scientific, the next step forward in mankind's progress toward an intelligent social order. They often spoke of Soviet Russia as an experiment, implying that if it did not work out useful knowledge would be gained even so. Unlike them, Matthiessen approached the Soviets on his knees. His faith was absolute and unrelated to performance. It was not the actual working out of the idea but the idea itself that attracted. Matthiessen could not be swayed by reason or history because his politics had never been based upon them.

This was true also of Raymond Robins, who was not only a Christian but a Republican, and armored against bloody collectivist revolution on both counts, it might be supposed. To the

---

* His latter-day acolytes, in contrast, pay no heed to this. One of them seems about to when he raises the question as to whether Matthiessen was not "guilty of certain lapses in moral vision." But what the author, Giles B. Gunn, has in mind was Matthiessen's admiration for T. S. Eliot.[53]

contrary, his experience in revolutionary Russia, as was true of other Westerners, had been decisive. Skeptical at first about aspects of Soviet policy, he slid gradually into Lenin worship until by the end of his life Russia could do no wrong. A true believer, Robins never doubted that history would turn out as Lenin had predicted, no matter how bad things got. In one of the prayerful statements he liked to compose Robins assured himself that even if war broke out between East and West Russia would survive and become the world's foremost power, able at last to fully realize Lenin's dream.[54]

Robins needed all the faith he could muster in his last years. The Cold War made the lives of fellow travelers darker and more narrow, and as the pressure mounted defections increased. No loss hurt Robins more than the abandonment of progressivism by Claude Pepper. The events of 1948 had obliged Pepper to back away from his earlier position that Russia could be trusted. In 1949 he endorsed the North Atlantic Treaty, saying in a radio speech that it was needed to prevent another world war through miscalculation. He sent Robins a transcript, along with a covering letter expressing private reservations. He feared that the treaty might create "a new system of regional rivalries to take the place of the national rivalries."[55] He opposed the arms buildup that the pact seemed to call for. Still, the Russians appeared to be showing more goodwill now, and as the international situation improved so too would his chances for reelection in 1950.

In another letter Pepper reminded Robins that anyone going against the forces making American foreign policy would be destroyed as Wallace had been. The Soviets were not helping matters with their "provocative acts" and failure to see the Western point of view. People were genuinely frightened, "however unfounded in fact such fright may be." He himself was scared by the new Secretary of State, Dean Acheson, who was a real fire-eater. Acheson took such a tough line when testifying before the Foreign Relations Committee that Senator Vandenberg had been moved to ask "if there was not a little sugar which could be put upon these pills we're asking the Soviet Union to take." Acheson made it clear that he was not interested in Soviet taste buds. His aim was to reach agreement, if possible, with Russia in a manner requiring the least cooperation possible. "He said the kind of agreement we were interested in from the Soviet Union was one where the obligation on their part was negative or where performance was as near as possible automatic, or the agreement was self-executed." Yet Pepper remained hopeful. Truman wanted peace, he was sure. So did the American people, militarists and "State Department imperialists" notwithstanding. Although nothing in America's foreign policy was going the way Pepper wanted, he believed that he would survive politically and that "if war or depression does not come we should be able to get by, and at the same time stand up for decent principles."[56]

Robins answered that they were going to have to part company on this issue, as Robins was doing all he could to prevent ratification of the North Atlantic Treaty. But he assured Pepper that keeping the Senator in office remained his "first political objective."[57] Pepper's optimism had little basis in fact. Florida was not the state to keep a progressive senator in office. Though Pepper had backed down in foreign policy, his record before 1949 was against him, as also his support of liberal causes. George Smathers, his exact opposite, defeated Pepper on May 2, 1950. The next day Robins, who had been completely immersed in the campaign, wrote to his sister-in-law that Pepper had been beaten by "DOLLARS—LIES—RACE HATRED—SOCIALIZED MEDICINE—FEAR OF RUSSIA" and yellow journalism.[58] His defeat was a blow to Robins on two counts. Pepper had been, after Ickes left office, his only personal friend of importance in Washington. And Pepper was the guardian of Robins' special arrangement with the federal government by which it took over his estate as a wildlife sanctuary, relieving him of costs and taxes, while allowing him to go on living there as before and to have a strong voice in its management.

Even more wounding than his defeat was Pepper's change of heart. Soon after the Democratic primary in Florida, North Korea invaded the south. Robins automatically sided with the Communists, while Pepper supported the decision to aid South Korea. In response to a warm letter from Pepper, Robins ended their friendship, suggesting—not very seriously, in view of his poor health—that they meet again in ten years to see if relations could be started up again. He also cut Pepper out of his will.[59] Mary Dreier, Robins' sister-in-law, who shared his beliefs completely, may have expressed Robins' own opinion when she wondered if, having given up progressivism in foreign affairs, Pepper might now also "betray the negroes and change his mind about the Health Insurance bill too."[60] She was wrong. Pepper later won election to the House of Representatives, where he still serves faithfully and with distinction as a liberal member.

It was hard for a fellow traveler to remain optimistic in 1949 and '50, especially if in bad health. Robins managed the feat, but one of his correspondents, Agnes Smedley, did not. Little remembered today, in her time Smedley was one of the leading apologists for Chinese Communism. Born to rural poverty, described in her autobiographical novel *Daughter of Earth* (1935), Smedley made her way to Germany and then in 1928 to China, where she found her calling as a revolutionary journalist. Freda Utley, who met her there a decade later, has left a vivid portrait of Smedley, who was then in her forties. "She was one of the few people of whom one can truly say that her character had given beauty to her face, which was both boyish and feminine, rugged and yet attractive." Utley considered her to be one of "the few spiritually great people I have met."[61]

Smedley was not one of those radicals who loved the masses but ignored suffering individuals. Though devoted to Chinese Communism, she was always helping people in need, notably wounded Nationalist soldiers who during their war with Japan received virtually no medical care. It was thanks to her, Utley believed, that in 1939 the International Red Cross finally began helping the Chinese Red Cross. She seemed to Utley "a heroic and tragic figure, doomed to destruction by her virtues, her courage, her compassion for human suffering, her integrity, and her romanticism."[62] Smedley wrote many articles and five books promoting the Chinese Revolution, *Battle Hymn of China* (1943) being the best known. She was the only left-wing journalist Utley met in China whom this fiercely intolerant, red-baiting fanatic did not come to hate.

Utley believed that her friend was on the skids as early as 1943, when they last met. Though only a little over fifty, she seemed to have aged greatly and exhibited personality changes. Perhaps also Smedley was losing faith in Communism. Utley, owing to her political extremism, is not a reliable source. Certainly there is no trace in Smedley's correspondence with Robins of any change politically. But by 1949 she was physically unwell and deeply depressed over the Cold War. Consequently she was in no shape to withstand attacks on her reputation, especially the issuance of a report, based on Japanese police files, by General MacArthur's office in Tokyo naming her as a Soviet agent.[63] Smedley leaped to her own defense, retaining a progressive attorney, O. John Rogge, and sending an open letter to President Truman asking him to clear her name. In the manner of progressive journalists, certain of their importance, she declared that in slandering her MacArthur's aide General Willoughby had "brought shame on the American people" and "dealt a deadly blow to American prestige among the people of Asia."[64]

She also wrote a long letter to at least one newspaper, and probably others, accusing her critics of being part of a "war conspiracy" to rearm Japan with the aim of crushing the "new China." She wound up by saying, "I consider all Americans who support Japanese war criminals or such treacherous and vicious warlords as Chiang Kai-shek to be enemies of the American people."[65] This was in the best tradition of fellow traveling, according to which one was always the voice and embodiment of the people and one's enemies were invariably fascists and warmongers. But privately Smedley was less assured. She wrote Robins about all that she was doing to win her fight but said the struggle had exhausted her; she could not sleep without drugs and felt ten years older. "Ho, my friend, why didn't I go to China and become a Chinese citizen months ago? I could have worked in peace there. But this country is no place for anyone who loves liberty. A general can simply say 'A.S. is a spy and agent of the Soviet govt.' because she defends China."[66] Smedley regarded herself as "a bad revolutionary" for feeling so tired and discouraged. She thought of the heroic past of the People's Liberation Army of China, whose soldiers gave their lives, and kept telling herself, "Be worthy of them, be worthy!"[67] Even after the Army retracted its charge, which it soon did as there was no good evidence showing her to have been a secret agent, Smedley remained depressed. Her heart ailment had returned on account of the strain, she told Robins.[68]

As he had so many others, Robins invited Smedley to visit

him and live on his property, where she could finish her book (a biography of the Communist hero Chu Teh, published post-humously) in ease and tranquility. She was in desperate shape, ill and unable to gain work. Because of the spy charge she could not obtain lecture engagements or place an article in any commercial publication. But she decided instead of Florida to go to England, where there was no blacklist.[69] Practical matters aside, America was no place for someone like herself.

> Another thing that causes me to wish to go abroad is the reactionary atmosphere in this country. It is more than paralyzing to any creative writer or worker generally. A cloud forever hangs over my head—it is a dark cloud indeed. I am never free from it, night or day. It is the same as in Germany when the Nazis were coming to power. I no longer feel that I am a citizen of this country.[70]

Spiritually she had not been a citizen of this country since the thirties when she gave her heart to Communist China. She would have gone there, no doubt, had it been possible in 1949. Or maybe not. On the eve of her death she wrote Robins to say that her ulcers had worsened and that the next day two thirds of her stomach, her duodenum, and her gall bladder were to be removed. Perhaps she would survive the operation, but she had no desire to do so. "American fascism, and what in reality is my exile, has caused this serious situation. I see no hope in sight for myself or for the U.S.A."[71] She expired following the operation on May 6, 1950. Robins deduced from her last letter to him that she had died at least partly from the Cold War. This was not the same as Matthiessen's suicide, yet bad enough. There was little that fellow travelers and progressives could do to put a cheerful face on the event. Mary Dreier attended a memorial service for Smedley in New York which she found depressing. Harold Ickes wrote that his wife, Jane, "was glad that she had died in hospitable England instead of inhumane America."[72] Cold comfort indeed for those who had thought they were helping make a better world.

Anna Louise Strong was different. A pro-Communist writer like Smedley, she was exactly what her name suggested. By 1949 she was in a much more trying position than Smedley, having been expelled from Russia despite years of loyal service as a non-Party propagandist for the Soviet Union. Although Stalin never needed a reason for such acts, the most likely of several possibilities was official displeasure with Strong for praising Mao Tse-tung as an original thinker and stressing the nationalistic features of Chinese Communism.[73] Stalin was determined to remain the sole leader of world Communism, as he had already shown by breaking with Tito, and relations between Soviet and Chinese Communists were cooler even this early than the world believed. Strong added to her sins by writing in the American press afterward of her ill-treatment. Consequently she was ostracized by American Communists and many fellow travelers.

Robins, who had known her a long time—she had stayed in the guest house on his estate ten years earlier—remained friendly, for which, in her isolation, she was very grateful. In consequence she told him more about her situation than he probably wanted to know. Most fellow travelers seem to have sided with Jerome Davis, who asked Robins to pass on to Strong his belief that peace was more important than individual problems such as her deportation from Russia. "What we must all strive to do is prevent such things from being used for war and war propaganda."[74] But, though capable of taking the long view when others suffered, Strong was not so willing to put politics ahead of her own misfortune. She was bitter that progressives and fellow travelers like Davis failed to defend her, and she had already transferred her loyalties from Russia to China.[75]

In principle Strong agreed with the line taken by Davis. Soon after returning to the United States she indicated to Robins that though chilled by her expulsion she was still trying to keep her perspective. Russia was not our "second fatherland," she wrote.

It's a hard, tough state, and its got to be. We, progressives of other lands owe it neither allegiance, nor praise, nor even understanding, for we shall not honestly be able to give these things at all periods. We owe one thing only: to keep the peace. . . . So that they—and we—may build what we have it in us to build. And we owe this not to them alone, but to ourselves. . . . For our allegiance is to the American people, and through them, to all the people of today's and tomorrow's world.[76]

In practice, however, it was hard to be philosophical. Strong wrote several critical articles on her expulsion for the *New York Herald Tribune* which gave additional offense to Stalinists. After spending a month with Robins she went north again, to find herself still under assault. A friend had been told by someone at the Russian Embassy that her recent writings had shown her to be a "traitor" to the Soviet Union. And *Soviet Russia Today* published an attack on Strong that made her blood boil. She thought it arose partly from malice, as, she claimed, Jessica Smith of *SRT* had been jealous of her for twenty years. Even so, she found herself reacting badly.

> What most disturbs me is the change that I detect in myself,—a gradual hardening against things that so far I have loved beyond my own life. . . . I am enough of a psychologist, even if not enough of a Marxist, to know that one cannot be repeatedly kicked in the face without eventually disliking the source of the kicks . . . My love and admiration for the USSR was not upset by my arrest; I think no rancor appeared in even my Tribune stories . . . In these, I even made up the best case I could against myself, in order to make the USSR seem rational to myself and to others . . . But now I'm sorry I gave that handle to people to hit me with, as Jessica is doing . . . I wish I had just said: "They called me a spy but never said what I had done and never gave me a chance to reply . . . I don't know of anything I ever did against that country and I don't know why they called me that." . . . That would have been true also, and better for me.[77]

Strong found defending herself to be a strain, but though she was sixty-three at the time of her expulsion from Russia she was remarkably durable. With the publication of the State Department's white paper on China later that year she gained a new lease on what would prove to be a very long life. In an excited letter to Robins she said the report "convinces me of my own propaganda." More than that, "nothing I ever claimed for the Chinese Communists surpasses what those State Department records—*received in 1943 and 1944,* disclose." Further, the State Department documents, together with her own experiences in China and Russia, pointed to the following conclusion.

> I think that within the rising Communist world there threatens the same kind of split that took place in the early Christian church, and that Mao intends to avoid it if possible and at any rate to postpone it as long as possible, because this is in the interests of the whole world and specifically of China.[78]

This in turn revealed her new mission, "to follow Mao's lead." More particularly, "I must NOT attack either side, for this weakens the anti-imperialist front, but I must energetically spread—and tactfully—all data as to Mao's new contributions to thought . . ."[79] The last third of her life would, in fact, be spent promoting Communist China, as the previous third had been given over to advancing Russian interests. And most of it would be spent in China, where she was already determined to go. In the meantime she was working through her local Progressive Party chapter in California, where she had settled, to get back into the good graces of Communists and fellow travelers. Progressive leaders in Santa Clara County, she informed Robins, were "sold on the idea."

Rehabilitation was not to be so easy as Strong hoped. In another letter to Robins she said that the boycott was still effective. The Communists "split every local organization that tries to listen to me," including the Progressive Party.[80] And her new book, *The Chinese Conquer China* (1949), was selling poorly for the same reason. Communists had prevented "progressive bookstores" from selling it, which hurt because there were twenty such in California alone. The same obstacle kept her from lecturing. Cedric Belfrage of the fellow-traveling *National Guardian* wanted to publish her articles, but could not as it was Party members who kept his paper afloat. It was ironic, Strong said, that the fight against her was being led by the Committee for a Democratic Far Eastern Policy. The irony, she did not need to tell Robins, arose because by "Democratic" the committee meant a pro–Chinese Communist policy, which no one desired more than Strong.[81]

Strong pressed on regardless, making a lecture tour in the spring of 1950 sponsored by the "young Progressives." This was going well, according to a letter she circulated to friends, making her think that the fight for American friendship with Russia and China was far from hopeless. Talk that the United States was drifting inevitably into fascism and was was "criminal trash," to her mind. She was also trying to get her expulsion from Russia cleared up, as it interfered with her profession of "explaining revolutions."[82] Corliss Lamont tried also, soliciting Robins and other fellow travelers to join him in asking the Soviet ambassador to Washington for a review of her case.[83] These efforts were fruitless. Strong was not cleared by Moscow until 1955.

Failure did not paralyze Strong. She had joined a progressive Unitarian church in Southern California which gave her moral support. And the outbreak of war advanced her fortunes because she was one of the few Americans who knew anything about North Korea, having visited it in 1947. Pamphlets she had written earlier were now in demand. A new one, "Inside North Korea," sold out its first printing of five thousand copies almost at once. Reuters, the British news service, was interested in having her write about Korea. She had a series running in the *Compass,* a successor to *PM,* and was being published elsewhere too. She was still on the Communist enemies list, but interest in the war was so great as to partly offset this.[84]

For some reason modest success put Strong in a reflective mood. In the fall of 1950 she sent Robins a long confessional letter about her life as a flack for Stalinism. She had been aware of evils in the Soviet Union for fifteen years but had never known how to deal with them. It was the same problem that split organizations like the National Council of Soviet-American Friendship, she said. Some of its board members agreed with Corliss Lamont that it was more honest and also better propaganda to admit that the Soviets were human and made mistakes. But Communist members would not allow any criticism of Russia. Communists always won, because they would destroy an organization rather than yield the point, and fellow travelers, knowing this, usually gave in. Or else, as Lamont did when the board of the NCASF refused to support his effort to get Strong cleared by Moscow, they resigned.

For me it has been a personal problem for many years. Especially since the purges of 1936–38. I did not turn against the USSR because of them, as most "liberal" correspondents did. But neither would I go to the meetings of Moscow News trade union which "gave thanks" to the Soviet Power for removing the "wreckers" from Moscow News staff, when I knew that these same "wreckers" had been until yesterday considered our hardest working, most devoted people, and that nobody would tell us WHY they were "wreckers" now. I saw so many good persons of my acquaintance who had been killing themselves with devotion to building the country, and who suddenly disappeared into Siberia, or what not. Some later came back, not all. I was willing to think that I myself might be mistaken in many of the cases, but it was impossible for a person of American background to think that it was right that no "civil Liberties" organization to investigate and defend such persons should exist . . .

She resorted to "evasion," going to Spain, to China, to Soviet-occupied Poland, so as to find subjects she could write about with conviction. Strong was still able to "grow truly lyric" over construction and reclamation projects inside Russia.

But she found it harder and harder to write about the USSR, because her audiences would not accept what she saw as a balanced picture. One side would not admit any virtues, the other denied all flaws.

The people I really cared for, on whose side I felt myself to be fighting,—they winced so if a single human weakness in the USSR were noticed . . . So I let my audiences pressure me into giving what I knew was a partial picture. I told no lies, but I didn't tell all the truth . . . And I still think this may be the correct procedure.[85]

Doubts remained, even so. In recent years she had tried to avoid the issue by speaking and writing only about Chinese Communism. Strong asked Robins to pass judgment on her conduct. Though Robins was the wrong person for this, having closed his mind to uncertainties about Russia long before, Strong was less anguished than her letter suggested. She met disillusionment with one idol by erecting another. Her last communication to Robins, a four-page newsletter, was straight Communist propaganda.[86] In spite of what she knew about police states Strong did make her way later to China, where she survived all the bloody turns of Mao's reign by applauding them.

Robins' political correspondence during the final years of his life was mostly with progressives and fellow travelers, falling largely into three categories. Some letters asked for money, others provided information, and the rest were meant to be uplifting. Financial appeals were common, as Robins was a frequent and generous contributor to organizations and individuals—readier with cash than with endorsements by this time. Thus Leo Huberman of *Monthly Review* wrote to Robins after the death of F. O. Matthiessen saying that the magazine had been founded on a pledge of five thousand dollars a year for three years made by an anonymous donor. That person was Matthiessen, who had left them only five thousand dollars in his will, which was being contested.[87] Conversely, Louis Adamic, a fellow-traveling writer whom Robins had helped before, wrote an understanding letter after Yugoslavia broke with Russia. Adamic was on Tito's side and knew this meant no more help from Robins on account of his deep feelings "about Stalin and the USSR."[88]

Informational letters usually brought bad news, though often presented optimistically. A friend who had been at the ill-fated Waldorf peace conference announced its success. "The peace conference was really thrilling. I think its importance can be measured in part at least by the opposition it aroused and the attention it attracted in other parts of the country and the world."[89] This was the official line. Hannah Dorner, executive director of the NCASP, explained to the executive committee that only fourteen sponsors out of 566 had resigned because of the bad publicity, a signal achievement.[90] John A. Kingsbury, an old friend and chair of the National Council of Soviet-American Friendship, assured him that the council would survive—which it didn't—despite being red-baited and having to cut staff salaries.[91] A fellow-traveling minister who circulated a newsletter, *United Front,* told Robins that he was being forced to leave Saskatchewan after ten years on account of red-baiting. This seemed to him unfair inasmuch as the local

Communists hated him, even though he sang their songs, talked their language and tried hard to work with them. "Communism is a grand thing," he concluded, "but only for grand men."[92] Willard Uphaus, another minister who believed in peace as defined by Communists, was surprised that working in their movement made him unpopular. The board of the Religion and Labor Foundation "got hysterical over my having been to the Warsaw Peace Congress and fired me. It seems unbelievable. The labor members of the Board were especially persistent in getting me out. One of the tragedies today is that labor leaders are so caught in the war economy." Still and all, "the Warsaw Congress was a moving demonstration of the demand for peace."[93]

Robins had willed himself to be optimistic all his life, but ill health and anti-Communism were wearing him down. America had become, he told Freda Kirchwey, "the Land of the Frightened and the Home of the Slave."[94] Consequently a man who had for years written encouraging letters to others now needed them himself. Scott Nearing complimented Robins on the bravery with which he had endured life as a paraplegic, reminding him that they had both been privileged "to see the dawn of a new day," especially in Europe and Asia.[95] Albert E. Kahn, co-author of *The Great Conspiracy,* a Stalinist interpretation of modern history, reminded Robins of how much he had done for Soviet-American friendship and other causes and how much he was admired. Kahn had recently mentioned Robins at a mass meeting in Madison Square Garden, "and the ovation your name received was an indication of what the progressive people think of you."[96] Jerome Davis went even further: "I proposed your name as a candidate for the Stalin Peace Prize award. There is no one in America that deserves it as much."[97] This was a kindly exaggeration inasmuch as many Americans had done more for Stalin than he.

Yet it seems fair to say that no one exceeded Robins in zeal, as can be gathered from his correspondence with Mary Dreier. His health permitting, Robins wrote to her almost daily, as also she to him, and in the most unguarded way. Their letters expose the fellow-traveling mentality at its simplest and most intense. They were always denouncing President Truman and Secretary Acheson and other warmongers. They needed no time for reflection before passing judgment on every event. All accused of spying for Russia were innocent, of course. American businessmen were rotten to the core and inclined toward fascism. When Russia developed its atomic bomb Robins was overjoyed. It would enable Russia to go on benefiting mankind. International peace was certain to result.[98] They were always thanking God for Russia's leadership. "What a blessing Stalin is and how courageous," Dreier liked to say.[99] She and Robins kept the faith, even after Korea when many progressives and fellow travelers lost it.

When North Korea invaded the south most Americans were caught off guard. Not so *Nation* readers, who had the benefit of Andrew Roth's outstanding reports on Asia. Almost a year before, he had outlined the situation brilliantly, drawing on his knowledge of China, where he had been calling the turns. Korea was highly unstable, he pointed out. South Korean leaders were asking for U.S. military aid that would enable them to forcibly reunite the country, it having been divided into Russian and American occupation zones. North Korea was infiltrating agents into the south and organizing local rebellions. Skirmishing had taken place along the 38th parallel, which divided the two Koreas. The last remaining American combat units had been withdrawn in July 1949, leaving behind only a five-hundred-man training mission. This had worsened matters, because American troops had been not only a deterrent against aggression from North Korea but a check against South Korean adventurism.

America's withdrawal resulted from a promise given to the UN that had to be made good once Soviet troops left North Korea the previous December. Supposedly South Korea could defend itself, because it was supplied with enough weapons to equip a regular army of 100,000 plus 200,000 reserves. Roth, on the other hand, thought that if it came to war the Republic of Korea would lose. To him Korea in 1949 looked very much as China had earlier. The government of "Free" Korea was despotic and corrupt, that of North Korea was as red as China's, and in the same way. Three of its top five leaders were products of Yenan, wartime capital of Communist China. Allied policy had created a rightist police state in the south and a leftist police state in the north. Roth doubted that even with U.S.

aid there would be much recovery, because, "as in Kuomintang China, South Korea's corrupt clique-ridden government is more interested in fighting communism militarily than competing with it economically."[100]

The explosion Roth predicted took place in June 1950, when North Korean troops poured over the 38th parallel, brushing aside the ROK's feeble defense. President Truman ordered American naval and air forces into battle. When they failed to stem the attack, ground forces were introduced. These managed to hang on to Pusan after the rest of South Korea was overrun. Because Russia was then boycotting Security Council meetings Truman obtained UN support for his actions. It was as a UN force that Americans landed at Inchon in September and routed North Korea's armies. General Douglas MacArthur, supreme commander in the Far East, conceived the attack and pushed it through despite fears that a landing could not be made at Inchon. This offensive was the most inspired of his long career, and a triumph for the United States, which destroyed a powerful invading force with the relatively small peacetime military establishment that existed in 1950.

Opposition to American intervention in Korea was confined at home to Communists and their allies, a small group by now, aided by the much larger body of conservative isolationists who were still against fighting foreign wars. Both the Communist *Daily Worker* and the reactionary *Chicago Tribune* assailed Truman for dragging the country into war illegally—though they would not have been any happier if Congress had issued a formal declaration. Liberal anti-Stalinists rejoiced. The *New Leader*'s David Dallin wrote that for Korea the "hour of liberation and unification has struck."[101] Dallin was premature but read the cards correctly. Washington could not resist the temptation presented to it in Korea. Once North Korea was beaten, the UN forces advanced toward Korea's border with China, in disregard of warnings from Peking. China struck back across the Yalu River, driving the UN forces, still mainly American, back into South Korea. Seoul, the capital of South Korea, was taken by the Communists again, and then retaken by the UN, after which the battlefront stabilized along a line corresponding roughly to the 38th parallel. Though the *New Leader* insisted that there was no going back to the status quo ante, and called for the reunification of Korea even after China came in, this was not to be.[102] After several years of inconclusive fighting and negotiations a truce was established by the Eisenhower Administration that left things much as they were.

The *New Republic*, like the *New Leader*, supported American policies throughout the war. It accepted the common view that Stalin was responsible for the North Korean attack. It endorsed Truman's decision to strengthen the Nationalist Chinese garrison on Formosa, and embraced also the theory that by going to war in Korea the UN was avoiding the mistake of its predecessor, the League of Nations, which had doomed itself and brought on another world war by allowing Italy to conquer Ethiopia.[103] TRB praised Truman for not backing down and offering Korea "all aid short of help," as many in Washington had expected. And he wrote with satisfaction that the United States now "finds itself automatically playing the role of world policeman and will probably keep on doing it for good."[104] Fletcher Pratt criticized the CIA for not giving advance notice of the invasion and the Defense Department for being underarmed and unready for combat.[105] Harold Ickes was scathingly critical of American policy in Korea, writing that it was wrong to have supported the "corrupt police state of South Korea," but wrong also to have pulled out before the ROK Army was strong enough to resist aggression.[106]

After MacArthur's great victory the editors called for the reunification of Korea by force, noting, but not taking seriously, warnings that if unfriendly troops neared her border China would enter the war.[107] In a long review of the Cold War, *New Republic* editors backed all major foreign-policy decisions taken by the Truman Administration, including those it had disliked at the time. Republicans had issued a white paper blaming all of America's troubles abroad on the Democrats, but it was they themselves who were at fault, according to the *New Republic*. "They have weakened the faith of Americans in their government, undermined the US abroad, served the interests of Soviet Russia at a critical time, and so brought us closer to war."[108] Even more than its support for American intervention in Korea this blanket endorsement showed the distance traveled by the *New Republic* in just a few years. Formerly a magazine vaguely of the left, it was now an organ of liberal Democrats. Accordingly, where before it had seen Western Europe as setting a good example in the Cold War, it now took the opposite view. Except for Great Britain the *New Republic* was struck "by the mounting fear and confusion, the apathy and cynicism, the hopelessness and opportunism which characterized the already low state of European morale even before Korea." There was a general failure of nerve leading to an "almost pathological" demand for "appeasement of the aggressors, for a 'deal' with Russia," on the part of both left and right.[109] The Continent needed moral support from America even more than material aid.

Nothing showed more clearly how far the *New Republic* had come than its stand on Indochina. Though progressives had been wrong about Europe, equating Russia's policy of imposing socialism by force with revolution, they were right about Asia, where genuine revolutions had broken out. Apart from China, nowhere was this more evident than in Indochina. Progressives were certain that the French effort to hang on there would come to grief, and the United States also if it became involved. Even before Korea the *New Republic* had backed away from this position. It was still saying that the day of old-fashioned imperialism was over, while at the same time endorsing limited aid to the French military.[110] After fighting began in Korea, the *New Republic* dropped its reservations. It now favored backing the French, while also calling for reforms, an end to the puppet government of Emperor Bao Dai, and the promise of free elections once victory was achieved. It asked, that is to say, for the policy that failed in China to be pursued in Indochina.[111] When they abandoned progressivism the editors gave up much of what was true in it as well as what was not.

It is unclear to what extent the *New Republic* shared the thoughts of other ex-progressives. There was no necessary reason why becoming anti-Soviet should have led them to change their minds about Asia too, as Max Lerner demonstrated. He had consistently opposed the American policy of supporting Chiang Kai-shek and Bao Dai.[112] Aid to losing causes only drove Oriental Communists closer to Russia, Lerner maintained, when it was in the American interest to see them become as independent as possible. He backed American intervention in Korea, feeling that Truman had little choice. But he was against giving more help to other Asian despots.[113] After the Inchon landing he warned against becoming carried away with success. "If we move beyond the 38th parallel, and try to take North Korea as well, we will inevitably run into trouble with the Chinese Communists," he wrote, going against MacArthur, who advised Truman that China would not come into the war, or at least not effectively.[114]

After the decision was made to cross into North Korea, Lerner warned that there would be a price to pay even if China did not intervene. "What we may accomplish by our plunge across the border is not only to reunite the two parts of Korea but also to alienate the whole of China and throw it permanently into the Russian camp."[115] And when China did attack, though critical of it for doing so, Lerner insisted that China should be admitted to the UN even so, as nothing was gained by not speaking to it. He called America's defeat in North Korea the "Great Chastening," and blamed it on the "Great Fear" at home inspired by reactionary anti-Communists, the "legion of political terror," who prevented Washington from behaving responsibly.[116] McCarthyism at home led straight to the debacle in Korea, he argued with considerable force.

Unlike World War II, which he had thoroughly enjoyed, Lerner found Korea trying. He remained upbeat just the same. Two years after the war began he went over recent events, finding much that was positive. Although the Korean War was unpopular, Truman and Acheson had done the right thing. Lerner only wished that they had made clearer in advance how the United States would respond, as that might have deterred aggression. The Kremlin had erred in failing to see that Korea would lead to massive American rearmament and an intensified arms race. Korea had been a test of collective security and given new life to the UN. Though the truce talks had stalled, it was a plus to have decided that Communist prisoners should be allowed to decide if they wished repatriation. That more than half of those captured by the UN forces did not want to return home ought to discourage Communist wars of aggression in the future. There was still reason to believe that peace could be won not just in Korea but generally.[117]

This was Lerner's high point as a columnist. He had been most acclaimed during World War II when he was turning out leftist platitudes about the people's war and gushing over Russia. He did his best thinking during the Korean years, when it was hard to maintain the progressive view of Asia even though it was right. Owen Lattimore was being ruined for having in the past called for what Lerner still advocated regularly. Yet Lerner not only expressed many of the same ideas as Lattimore, but defended Lattimore himself.[118] Lerner showed courage in those years, and discrimination too, atoning in this way for his shallow past.

The Nation had changed also, though not enough. It supported Truman's decision to fight in Korea, but otherwise the same writers were still saying many of the same things, even if more quietly owing to events and the hostile climate of American opinion. Vayo kept boasting of Russian strength and purposefulness. Thanks to its wonderful economic system it could afford both to finance rearmament and to maintain high living standards, unlike Western Europe, where rearmament would mean risking "economic collapse, social upheaval, and the probable victory of communism."[119]

Alexander Werth had gone from Moscow to Paris without learning anything. The movement for peace in Russia was progressing splendidly. Writers and composers, formerly under a cloud, "have rehabilitated themselves by joining wholeheartedly in the movement." "Around this symbol of peace a kind of national solidarity, remarkably like that which existed during the war years, has crystallized."[120] Reconstruction was proceeding apace, living standards were rising, "and the imagination of the people—especially of the younger generation—is stirred by the gigantic reforestation plan, and by such projects as the newly announced Kuibyshev hydroelectric plant," intended to be the world's largest. To fellow travelers, Soviet public-works projects were still evidence of moral superiority. So also was European support for America's enemies. Werth described the British "Peace with China" movement, quoting, and seeming to agree with, Kingsley Martin, who at a "peace" rally defended China's intervention in Korea on the ground that it had every reason to suspect America of "the most sinister designs."[121]

Edgar Snow explained that Russia did not want war and that Western rearmament was not only unnecessary but dangerous in that it might lead to adventurism, such as attempts to "liberate" countries under Communist rule. Snow no longer assumed Russia's intentions to be benevolent, as before, but continued to insist that nothing need be done about them.[122] This was *The Nation*'s new policy, continued by Carey McWilliams when he took charge in 1955. The magazine had never given up progressivism, only the notion that Russia was the vanguard of world progress. In other respects things remained much the same. It kept on attacking the largest part of American foreign policy and applauding leftist revolutions everywhere. No longer sympathetic to Communism, *The Nation* did not favor containing it either—drawing the line only at outright invasion as in Korea.

To many fellow travelers the change was hard, if not impossible, to make. When fighting broke out in Korea, Mary Dreier recognized it at once as a replay of the American Civil War. "We fought to save the union and free the slaves primarily, that was at the bottom of it; the northern koreans [*sic*] are fighting (if they are) to unite Korea and free the people for a more abundant material life on this earth."[123] She was sustained in her views by the *Compass*, especially its pro-Soviet writers such as Max Werner and Johannes Steel. I. F. Stone was still her favorite, though she worried about him sometimes. Dreier need not have. Stone was unhappy about the Korean War and Russia's role in it, but hoped to prove it was South Korea's fault, the thesis of his *The Hidden History of the Korean War* (1952). Dreier raged against everyone who took America's side. She stopped speaking of the war to Harold Ickes, a very old friend, on account of his treacherous conviction that Russia and North Korea were to blame. Henry Wallace let her down also, proving himself to be one of those "tired radicals" they all knew about. When MacArthur drove the North Koreans out of the south she was "sorry and sad".[124]

Most saddening was the consequence of her position. Even more than Robins, because she only wintered in Florida, Dreier had an active social life among progressives, many of whom she had known since her earliest days as a reformer almost half a century before. Some had gone through the same evolution as she had from the Progressivism of Theodore Roosevelt to that of Henry Wallace. But the Korean War was different. "Nearly all my old friends are on the other side," she told Robins in 1950.[125] Dreier tried to make up for the loss by becoming active, seemingly for the first time, in pro-Soviet organizations —attending meetings of the National Committee for Peaceful Alternatives and the National Council of Soviet-American Friendship. Yet they were unsatisfactory because while all the members knew one another, she herself knew no one.[126] Her correspondence with Robins in the State Historical Society of Wisconsin ends in 1950, though they must have continued writing, since Robins did not die until 1954 (Dreier living on until 1963). But what is there mirrors the experience of countless others.

The Wallace campaign had been a crucial event, but the Korean War was equally so. It drew, finally, a line between fellow travelers and progressives. Before the summer of 1950 they were often difficult to tell apart. Fellow travelers did sometimes criticize Russia. Progressives frequently belonged to Communist fronts. After Korea this seldom happened. Many progressives, it became evident, had genuinely believed that Russia wanted peace above all, and consequently that the Communist-led peace movement was the real thing. The invasion of South Korea, supported by Russia, showed the falsity of this. Most progressives either withdrew from active politics or changed sides. Life, accordingly, became more difficult for pro-Communists, now reduced to a small band of zealots.

The fellow-traveling press was hard hit by these developments. In 1951 the *Compass* was the only non-Communist daily still following the Party line. It had a press run of fifty thousand, subscribed to mostly by Communists and fellow travelers. The *Compass* did not, in any case, long survive its financial backer Anita Blair, an eccentric daughter of Cyrus McCormick. More durable was the *National Guardian,* also funded at the outset by Mrs. Blair. The *Guardian* was a weekly paper established during the Wallace campaign by men who believed in collaboration on principle. James Aronson and Cedric Belfrage, who was English, felt that the Communist Party was "the core of the radical movement" but that it had erred by turning away from Popular Front activities after 1945. Although, as they admit in their history of the *Guardian,* they were fellow travelers, they decided, once more on principle, to be dishonest. "With the

Progressive Party we decided against commitment to socialism, for we hoped to win a public beyond the 'converted,' 'starting where they are' and leading them by subversively rational steps to where we were."[127]

Regarding themselves as democratic socialists, they observed a policy of having no enemies on the left—except the real democratic socialists such as Dwight Macdonald, Norman Thomas and Sidney Hook. To the *Guardian,* Soviet Russia, even when wrong, was the hope of the world; anti-Communism, however right, the side of war, capitalism and man's inhumanity to man. The *Guardian* did not believe that Stalin was inhumane, because all who said so were anti-Communists and not to be trusted. After Khrushchev's exposure of the crimes of Stalin the *Guardian* did believe, but also didn't care. Although words like "decency" and "honesty" appear frequently in their history, Aronson and Belfrage offered numerous examples that they did not practice the ethics they claimed to admire.

A typical instance concerned Konni Zilliacus, an English politician and erstwhile fellow traveler, who was falsely accused by the Czech government of espionage during one of the infamous "show trials" of the early fifties. Zilliacus was angry about this for good reasons, as the *Guardian* knew. It did not speak up for him even so. Aronson explained why in a letter to Zilliacus.

> We feel compelled to suppress a moral conviction because we think we'd do more harm to what we most deeply believe in by expressing it. I would be sorry if at least somebody of your stature hadn't taken your position [making criticisms of Soviet misdeeds, his real offense in Communist eyes], but by taking it we would separate ourselves from the movement in this country, poor and weak as it may be. I suppose it's thoroughly jesuitical, but it's the best we can do in a period of many confusions.[128]

Zilliacus understood this, Aronson recalled, having done the same thing himself often enough, no doubt. Anyway, he knew "that at its worst the *Guardian* never approached the daily jesuitry of *The Times* of London or of New York." The main question when it came to jesuitry, one can see, was who benefited from it. Fellow travelers believed, with Communists, not only that the end justified the means, but that lack of scruple on the enemy side excused their own. This was bad ethics and, sometimes, it encourages one to believe, bad politics.

The *Guardian* was a typical fellow-traveling periodical in every respect but one—it survived. The others passed away, victims of the Cold War and internecine warfare on the pro-Communist left. *In Fact,* which had the biggest circulation, failed because George Seldes took Tito's side in the break with Moscow, after which pro-Soviet labor unions canceled the block subscriptions that had been his mainstay. Yet the *Guardian* went on, despite the loss of Mrs. Blair's money and numerous defections from the "movement." The editors were, perhaps, more tenacious than others. Mainly it seems that having no rivals made the *Guardian* indispensable to fellow travelers, who, though fewer than before, were still numerous enough to keep one paper going. Corliss Lamont became its "most consistent financial angel," and Pete Seeger the folk musician was "a major fund-raising magnet for us." *Monthly Review* editors helped out, as did some of the Hollywood Ten. Other supporters included Harry Bridges the union leader, Vincent Hallinan, a leading Progressive and the William Kunstler of his day, and W. E. B. Du Bois. Among those who wrote for it were J. Alvarez del Vayo, I. F. Stone, Harry F. Ward, Mary Van Kleeck and Frederick Schuman.

Like all the faithful, *Guardian* editors saw the Korean War as a product of Western imperialism: "the reality was that the turn from cold war to hot, moving from threat to massacre for the imposition of capitalism, had arrived."[129] It came as a surprise that many progressives did not share the *Guardian* view. A majority of the Progressive Party's national committee went along with the *Guardian*-Communist line, but Henry Wallace defected along with most who had voted for him. The editors attributed this to cowardice, avarice, hysteria, fear of witch-hunters, and similar ignoble motives. In the case of O. John Rogge, who went from being the favorite attorney of Stalinists to becoming a friendly witness for government investigators, "we never had a clue as to what changed him and when." Rogge's change of heart was in fact unusually easy to understand, as he had explained it in *The Saturday Evening Post*. Rogge had spoken up for Tito and so was expelled from his position as vice-president of the Partisans for Peace. This persuaded him at long last that Communists and progressives could not work together.[130] The larger difficulty was that ardent Stalinists, whether in the Party or out, could not understand why changing Communist policies might lead individuals to fall away. Stalinists had signed up for the duration and had little use for anyone who expected Soviet policy to conform to anything except Russian self-interest.

Yet they expected America to conform at all times to the highest principles of law and morality. The three books written by Aronson and Belfrage in justification of themselves are saturated with moral indignation caused by American lapses from ideal standards of conduct. Aronson's *The Press and the Cold War* (1970) indicted the press as a whole and *The New York Times* (once his employer) in particular for their disgraceful failure to express his political opinions. Belfrage's *American Inquisition, 1945–1960* (1973) denounced the mistreatment of political "heretics" like himself. (A British subject, he was deported in 1955.) *Something to Guard* (1978), a joint effort, depicted their heroic devotion to duty in the face of widespread cowardice, warmongering and imperialism. Ronald Radosh, a new-left historian, in a shrewd review of the book, noted both the moral and the strategic defects of this approach. On the one hand, Aronson and Belfrage were among those "who smirked at American liberals for referring to Vietnam as an aberration, [but] view the Gulag simply as one of Stalin's errors." And, on the other, they never asked themselves if "perhaps the perpetual defense of Stalinism helped destroy the possibility of a genuine socialist movement in America."[131]

If the *National Guardian* was the popular press of non-Party Stalinism, *Monthly Review* was its intellectual expression. The founders were Paul M. Sweezy, an economist who had taught at Harvard, and Leo Huberman, formerly labor editor of *PM* and the educational director of the National Maritime Union in its Stalinist days. With Matthiessen's money they established what its cover described as an "Independent Socialist Magazine." The *New Leader* sneered at this claim, saying it meant only that the editors hailed the Soviet system as socialistic rather than communistic. To democrats *Monthly Review* seemed devoted to praising socialism in theory and apologizing for socialism as it was actually practiced in Eastern Europe.[132] This was pretty much the case, though by doing so in its own way *Monthly Review* offended Communists too, who did not welcome variations on the Party line.[133]

Monthly Review was most blatant when siding directly with Communist governments. The first issue editorialized against the North Atlantic Treaty and in favor of Chinese Communism. The Soviet atomic bomb was welcomed later as a "powerful force for peace."[134] When North Korea invaded the south the editors did not deny this fact but approved of it. An American victory in Korea would accomplish nothing, they reasoned, whereas a Communist victory would solve most problems. A year later the only change was that the editors had discovered the war to be a capitalist plot after all. President Rhee of South Korea, egged on by Chiang Kai-shek, Dean Acheson and John Foster Dulles, provoked North Korea, which, by launching its invasion, "fell neatly into the trap."[135] The obvious objection was that if South Korea wanted the attack, why did North Korea come within a hair of overrunning it? The editors passed over this awkward fact to get to the crucial one. General Mac-Arthur's counterinvasion of North Korea proved that he had started the war in order to make this possible and planned, further, to take on China as well. This was much the same as arguing that in 1939 Britain provoked Germany so as to have an excuse for landing in France.

Another example of the remarkable leaps which such reasoning entailed was "Freedom under Socialism," by Howard Kaminsky, a graduate student in history, one regrets to say. He had been troubled, Kaminsky explained, like many thoughtful socialists by the seeming paradox that in America you can oppose the government but in socialist countries you cannot. To resolve this problem he spent a year in Czechoslovakia as a student at Charles University. There he learned to square the circle. Almost every Czech was benefiting in a practical way from socialism, he observed. Even anti-Communist peasant women used the village washing machines provided by the government. And the anti-Communist worker took advantage of wage increases and free vacations. The discipline of socialism was forced upon people, but they enjoyed the advantages voluntarily. It followed from this that "every day, individuals are recognizing the relation between the benefits and the discipline, and *by this act of recognition* are emerging into the realm of freedom."[136] This was to say that freedom did not consist of the right to make one's own choices, as in the decadent West, but arose from the perception that one was being ordered around for one's own good. Freedom was benevolent slavery, he announced, and *Monthly Review* agreed. The editors balked only at his contention that regardless of what kind of socialism "we" want, Stalinism is what "we" are going to get. Though they were always excusing tyranny, the editors continued to hope that it might not always be inevitable.[137]

This issue, which troubled fellow travelers more than any other, could not be disposed of so easily. One reader disagreed with Kaminsky, asserting that civil liberties as practiced in America would go on under socialism, though perhaps after an interval.[138] John A. Bachrach, an economist at the University of Pittsburgh, refused to dissemble. He had read George Orwell and was reminded by Kaminsky's piece of what in *Nineteen Eighty-Four* were called "Newspeak" and "Newthink." That there was no liberty in Russia or the East had to be admitted. Bachrach rejected out of hand "the dialectic which miraculously transforms a one-party open ballot into a 'new' democracy, or compulsion and restraint into a 'new' freedom."[139] This was too much honesty for Arthur K. Davis, a sociologist. He defined freedom to mean efficiency, claiming that every working social system possessed it. "In this sense 'freedom' is to any social order as 'health' is to any biological organism." Or, more plainly, freedom was "a subjective feeling of well-being caused by living in any relatively well-integrated society."[140] Davis did not shrink from the obvious implication. If freedom meant a justifiable sense of well-being experienced by a majority, was not Germany under Hitler, for example, free? "Within limits, yes" was his answer. The weakness of fascist freedom, as against Socialist freedom, was that it did not last.

Monthly Review was written mostly by intellectuals, which accounts for these painful torturings of fact and reason. Unlike the *National Guardian,* the left equivalent of yellow journalism, *Monthly Review* subscribers were literate. Sermons by Anna Louise Strong on the happy peasants of this or that police state did not satisfy them. They knew there was something rotten in the Communist East, but wanted to be persuaded that they should support it even so. *Monthly Review* accomplished this in two ways. One was to redefine basic ideas such as freedom and democracy so as to reconcile opposites, enabling one to be at the same time a Stalinist and a democrat, for example. Another was to show how obvious horrors were not so bad as they seemed, and the West's fault in any case. Thus, an astonishingly candid study of anti-Semitism in Russia concluded that it was growing, but was not an official policy of the government (though it was) and consequently things might change.[141]

Even more dismal was the editorial treatment of yet another wave of purges in 1953. These, *Monthly Review* explained soberly, resulted from the Dulles doctrine of liberation for Eastern Europe and should surprise no one, as regimes when attacked are in the habit of retaliating. Anti-Zionism, similarly, was a result of Israel's de-facto alliance with the United States. The editors did admit to seeing signs of anti-Semitism in Russia and Eastern Europe. While this was certainly unfortunate, it was too early to pass judgment, and in any case there was reason to hope that the "healthy instincts of the working class" would put an end to Jew-baiting.

After these ritual assertions *Monthly Review* got down to business. The editors had been worrying about purges and trials since the great terror of the 1930s. The Soviet position that every so often leading Communists committed acts of treason, sabotage and the like did not wash, because it required one to believe "too much that is simply incredible."[142] A likelier explanation was that from time to time there was a struggle over basic policy. The losing side, feeling the issue to be crucial, would then ally itself with enemies of the regime, not to abolish socialism, as the Soviets claimed, but with the idea of saving it. The winning side would see this as a conspiracy and put the dissidents on trial. At this point they would regain their senses and see that they had indeed been used by enemies of the regime and, as true revolutionaries, would admit their guilt. Why, then, the editors asked, were the accused shot even though repentant? Because they remained security risks. Potential Quislings had to be destroyed.

The editors did not endorse the practice. "We certainly would not deny that the trials give evidence of a systematic practice of deceit and violence, not only by the opponents of the regimes but also by the regimes themselves."[143] But was this reason enough to condemn the trials and executions? Of course not. All regimes were based on deceit and violence. Think of the British Empire and American imperialism. A socialist had to discriminate. One distinction would be the amount of violence. By this standard, Soviet-bloc countries "would come off pretty well" in comparison with the West—certainly one of their more breathtaking computations. An even better question was "whether violence is used to perpetuate a state of affairs in which violence is inevitable, or whether it is used in the interests of creating a truly human society from which it will be possible at long last to banish violence altogether."[144] This, naturally, was the crucial point. Western violence perpetuated injustice. Socialist violence was building a just social order and was, therefore, a higher and better and altogether finer kind of violence. And, anyway, it was the West's fault for being so anti-Communist. Socialist regimes do make mistakes, the editors concluded, and these should be pointed out. What was wrong was to use them for antisocialist purposes.

The above was a typical *Monthly Review* exercise. First it involved, for the sake of appearing honest and independent, recognition of a Stalinist evil. Then an elaborate theory, based on no evidence whatsoever, was developed to make the wicked thing seem rational and necessary. Finally, it was justified in the interest of building socialism, a stand that had nothing to do with what went before and could be taken as easily—was frequently taken—by people who did not deny the crimes of Stalin at all.

Such thinking was the despair of democratic socialists. Lewis Coser and Irving Howe, in their new magazine *Dissent,* attacked *Monthly Review* for having distorted the very meaning of socialism. To Sweezy and his friends socialism was the absence of private ownership, nothing more. And its success was reckoned entirely in material terms. *Dissent* believed that Marx's great achievement had been to show that economics could not be understood except in the context of social relations. He had rejected the fetish of the commodity, to which the "left authoritarians" like Sweezy had reverted. The only difference was that they substituted the fetishism of the plan for the fetishism of the commodity. Unlike fellow travelers of old, they knew the worst about Russia and didn't mind. They justified atrocities in the name of industrialization, or historic necessity, or the glorious future.

> At the same time, however, "left authoritarianism" preserves and enlarges a cynical element of the traditional fellow-traveling outlook by connecting it with the most up-to-date and sophisticated theories of managerial and bureaucratic society: let the eggs be broken as they will, the omelette will still be made. It permits them to be indifferent to human values while retaining their faith in Dnieperstroy. It thus has become the perfect philosophy for those who have lost faith in both capitalism and socialism.[145]

It was true that—verbal trickery, evasions, false analogies, blindness, lack of evidence, and want of logic aside—what sustained *Monthly Review*'s faith was that its socialism had been reduced to practically nothing. No crime of Stalin's was so great that it could not be excused by state ownership of the means of production. This was not socialism as it had been understood before 1917, but it was good enough for *Monthly Review*, which only paid lip service to the liberties and moral values it was once thought socialism would promote. As Irving Howe said after *Monthly Review* sanctioned the repression of a workers' protest in the Soviet bloc, Sweezy and his group upheld "the radicalism of the blackjack."[146]

Fellow traveling reached its lowest point in the middle fifties, intellectually, morally, politically, and numerically too. The *Guardian* soldiered on because the "movement" was just large enough to support one paper and *Monthly Review* because it was cheap to produce. But the dream of building a just society through Stalinism was over all the same, and well before Khrushchev exposed the crimes of Stalin so persuasively that even Sweezy and Huberman had to face them.*

---

* For this and other reasons they subsequently decided that China, not Russia, was the hope of the world.

VIII

The Blacklist

IN 1941 LEO ROSTEN, a social scientist funded by the Rocke-feller and Carnegie Foundations, published an exhaustive study of the movie industry during the years of its greatest success. Motion pictures were then earning 67.4 cents of every dollar spent on commercial entertainment in America. Ninety percent of all films made in America were shot in Hollywood, and sixty-five percent of all films made in the world. It had the largest press corps of any American city, New York and Washington excepted. Some four hundred columnists and reporters labored to satisfy the appetite of fans for gossip about movie stars, turning out more journalistic swill than anywhere else in the free world. Power in Hollywood was highly centralized. Eight studios generated ninety-five percent of all film rentals, the most important being Metro-Goldwyn-Mayer (owned by Loew's, Inc.), Twentieth Century–Fox, Radio-Keith-Orpheum, Warner Brothers, and Paramount. Wealth was centralized also. Of some 34,000 people who worked in the industry in 1938, only twelve earned more than $300,000 a year—nine actors and three executives. These were, however, among the best-paid Ameri-cans.[1] In 1940 five out of the fifteen highest salaries were earned by movie people. Yet all this did not keep Hollywood from becoming a center of Stalinist intrigue.

According to Rosten, Hollywood had no politics until 1934, when film executives, like other wealthy Californians, were frightened by the sudden rise of Upton Sinclair, who nearly became governor, running as a Democrat but on a semisocialist platform. Alarmed studio heads raised a half-million dollars to fight Sinclair, mostly by assessing their more affluent employees a day's pay. This forced levy antagonized creative workers, hastening the establishment of the Screen Writers and Screen Actors Guilds. In 1938 Melvyn Douglas the actor helped create the Motion Picture Democratic Committee, which aided candidates for public office. Foremost among other movie political groups was the Hollywood Anti-Nazi League, a Popular Front organization started up in 1936 that claimed five thousand members and raised $90,000 over the next three years. The Popular Front collapsed in Hollywood, as elsewhere, after the Stalin-Hitler Pact. Douglas and other influential members submitted a resolution denouncing the pact to the Motion Picture Democratic Committee. When it was voted down they resigned. This spelled the end of MPDC. The Anti-Nazi League failed also when its leaders, mostly Communists and fellow travelers, hewed to the new Soviet line. Yet the collapse of Hollywood leftism was more apparent than real. American entry into the war would rekindle political feelings among moviemakers. Then, too, the conditions that had radicalized many in the first place still existed.

Writers were the mainstay of Hollywood leftism in the 1930s and '40s. Some had become political in New York earlier. Others were drawn in during the fierce struggle to organize. Most studios fought unionization even after the Screen Writers Guild became a certified bargaining agent, not giving way until forced to by the National Labor Relations Board in 1941. This put an end to many abuses visited upon screenwriters but did not change the hard fact of their lives, lack of creative control. "The motion picture is a great industry as well as a defeated art," Raymond Chandler, a writer of detective stories and screenplays, explained.[2] Hollywood produced up to five hundred films a year, using teams of writers to maintain production. As many as sixteen might work on a single script, which in the end would be written not to their taste but to that of a producer. Although a few writers earned large incomes, most were poorly paid. Of perhaps one thousand screenwriters in 1949 only two hundred made a living from films.

Most writers suffered from insecurity and also lacked respect. Though writing screenplays was a demanding craft, serious writers despised it as piecework done to order. Producers treated writers with contempt, or so it was believed. Dalton

Trumbo, one of the most successful screenwriters in history, said that "the system under which writers work would sap the vitality of a Shakespeare. They are intelligent enough to know that they are writing trash, but they are not intelligent enough to do anything about it."[3] Many held that screenwriters became Communists out of guilt at earning so much money, but a likelier reason was self-hatred arising from the way it was made. Becoming a Communist, and therefore, symbolically at least, a revolutionary allowed one to protest the system and at the same time to profit from it—or, more commonly, to cherish the hope of doing so.

Little wonder, then, that at their high point something like a quarter of the Screen Writers Guild may have been Party members. With the aid of fellow travelers they controlled the SWG for a time, making it perhaps the reddest of all Communist-dominated unions.[4] There were other reasons for becoming a Hollywood Communist. After 1941 patriotism was a factor, as Party members outdid all others in supporting the war effort. But the prominence of writers in Hollywood leftism arose mainly from guilt projected outward as hatred of the system. Producers and sometimes directors controlled the outcome of moviemaking and were seldom radicalized. Even actors, who were more susceptible, retained their pride of craft. They could give an honest performance however bad the movie. Few became Communists, though progressivism was common among them. For writers above all, films were a "defeated art." Of 169 members of the SWG who responded to a question by Rosten concerning movie quality, 133 were entirely negative. No group in Hollywood needed moral support more than screenwriters, or found it in a worse place.

Though Communist writers would become the chief excuse for McCarthyism in Hollywood, most activists in the forties were progressive Democrats. Their organization was the Hollywood Democratic Committee and its heirs. It was formed by people who had campaigned for Governor Culbert Olson in 1938, and again in 1942, when he lost to Earl Warren. In 1943 they established the HDC to retain momentum between elections. The HDC gained favorable publicity by attacking the "zoot suit" rioters who mobbed young Mexican Americans in Los Angeles that year, and it grew rapidly. In 1944 the HDC, with two thousand members, was able to support Democratic candidates in important ways. It spent $135,000 to nominate and elect five local Democrats to Congress and to reelect President Roosevelt, who was wildly popular in Hollywood. The money was used for thousands of spot announcements sent to radio stations all over the country, for two broadcasts on network radio, and to distribute half a million pieces of literature. Many entertainers contributed to this effort and served on the HDC's board, including Olivia De Havilland, Duke Ellington, John Garfield, Ira Gershwin, Rita Hayworth, Walter Huston, Jerome Kern, Edward G. Robinson and Franchot Tone. In 1945 it affiliated with the Independent Citizens Committee of the Arts, Sciences and Professions, becoming the HICCASP. That year it opened a joint office in Washington with the ICCASP, paying half the costs. In 1946 it reached a peak membership of about 3,300, who were served by a staff of eighteen.[5]

Nineteen forty-six was also the best year for the national ICCASP. James Roosevelt, son of the late President, became national director of political organization, and Harold Ickes signed on as executive chairman. *Time* magazine did a cover story on Chairman Jo Davidson, a sculptor well known for his heads of famous people. *Time* called him a "nice old man" but rather naïve, who all the same had become a political leader of stature because of the ICCASP. It was effective primarily because of its New York and Hollywood chapters, which amounted to a who's who of show business.* In addition to campaigning for Democratic candidates, the stars of ICCASP gave numerous speeches against racial, religious and ethnic discrimination. In 1946 these included talks at different functions by Edward G. Robinson, Paul Henreid, Cornel Wilde and Olivia De Havilland.[6]

But even this early the worm was in the bud. *Time*'s story accused the ICCASP of having a "leftist tinge," and when Davidson came to Los Angeles early in 1947 reporters tried repeatedly to make him talk about allegations that his organiza-

---

* They included, besides those mentioned already, Frank Sinatra, Gypsy Rose Lee, Lena Horne, Fredric March, Eddie Cantor, Charles Boyer, Humphrey Bogart, Charles Laughton, Zero Mostel, Arthur Rubenstein and Norman Corwin, plus artists and professors without number.

tion was controlled by Communists.[7] James Roosevelt, in answer to one such inquiry, gave the official position: "I feel very strongly that to adopt a principle barring from membership so-called known communists is a very dangerous and un-democratic procedure."[8] It would weaken them to employ such "fascist methods." The rule of the ICCASP, which Roosevelt supported, was that members need only be citizens of the United States and subscribe to the "progressive principles" embodied in the ICCASP constitution. The HICCASP in particular had not been taken over by Communists, because liberals were in the majority. The ICCASP as whole was too broadly based, Roosevelt said, to fear a Communist takeover.

Four months later he resigned. Roosevelt told Chairman Davidson that his departure was owing to ill health, later giving as another, if contradictory, reason that he had taken the chairmanship of the Democratic State Central Committee of California.[9] In a letter to John Cromwell, chairman of the HICCASP, Roosevelt was more open. Actually, he sent two letters, a long explanation covered by a note telling Cromwell how he wanted it used. Either the letter was to be released in full or, if it was condensed, two paragraphs were to be omitted. They dealt gingerly with the Communist issue, and Roosevelt did not want them published except in the context of his full statement, which affirmed the HICCASP's liberalism and independence. The key paragraph, to be released only as part of the complete text, warned that the committee would not achieve maximum support until it persuaded the general public "that it is willing to take a positive stand in favor of improvements in our economic system within the framework of private property and private enterprise." Many unions had done so by stating their opposition to Communism. "I have felt that you were working toward a solution of this complicated problem and I heartily joined in the effort to accomplish this purpose—without joining in the flood of red-baiting which is hitting the country now, as it did following World War I."[10] According to the testimony of Olivia De Havilland before the House Un-American Activities Committee years later, Roosevelt left the HICCASP after she had failed to get the executive board to pass just such a resolution.[11]

Many others shared Roosevelt's concern and resigned also,

including De Havilland, who had been a mainstay of both the HDC and the HICCASP. The resignations of prominent people continued when the HICCASP merged with the National Citizens Political Action Committee, becoming the Arts, Sciences and Professions Council of the Progressive Citizens of Southern California. The new hybrid was known as the ASP-PCA, but in 1948 it was decided to undo the merger. The ASP became independent again, though only for tactical reasons. The national director of the ASP explained to the Southern California branch that it could promote Henry Wallace's candidacy more effectively on its own than as part of the PCA.[12]

If the ASP hoped to mollify anti-Communists by separating from the PCA, it was mistaken. Nominal independence did not change its policies. It had become a Popular Front organization, confirming its position in 1947 by defending the notorious "Hollywood Ten," some of whom, notably Dalton Trumbo, belonged to the Hollywood chapter. The ASP did work for Wallace in 1948 and organized the Waldorf "peace" conference in 1949. This event was followed by another in Los Angeles organized by the local ASP chapter that had begun life as the Hollywood Democratic Committee. The regional conference was chaired by Linus Pauling. The actual manager was George Pepper, who had been the HDC's senior staff member and held similar positions later with the ICCASP and the ASP.

By 1949 it was not easy to put on such an affair. Threats were made and, while the mayor assured Pepper "that your right of assembly will be protected by the police force of the city of Los Angeles," the conference still had trouble finding a site.[13] It was now also difficult to find sponsors. The famous artists and movie people of yesterday were no longer available for Popular Front activities. This was not only on account of the blacklist, but sometimes for reasons of conscience. Christopher Isherwood the writer sent a long letter detailing his own doubts. He regretted press attacks on the ASP conferences in New York and Los Angeles, and the denial of visas to many foreign delegates, yet as a pacifist and a conscientious objector in World War II he had asked himself if such a meeting as was being organized in Los Angeles would really benefit peace. The call to it he had received seemed to be neither pacifist nor neutral, as it listed the misdeeds of America but not those of Russia. It was self-evident to Isherwood that the Russian guests (including poor Shostakovich again) were there to make propaganda. They were instruments of the Cold War and would be seen as such by most Americans. Consequently he did not think the conference was going to aid peace, and he would not support it.[14]

The conference, held on April 9 and 10, 1949, realized Isherwood's fears. Many papers were read, but they were all by the faithful—J. D. Bernal the English scientist, Aaron Copland the composer, F. O. Matthiessen, Clifford Odets, Frederick Schuman, Harlow Shapley and others less well known. This was the last major production of what, as the HDC, had once been able to attract thousands of members, many of them world famous, and had raised hundreds of thousands of dollars in cash and services. Popular Front liberalism was dead in Hollywood, as elsewhere, thanks to world history and the blacklist.

The blacklist did not arise directly from the great body of Hollywood political activity, which has only been touched on here, though there was a connection. Progressivism in Southern California depended to a large extent upon the movie industry. The region as a whole was conservative and Republican, dominated by the right-wing *Los Angeles Times*. The antiunion tradition was still strong, and the unions themselves, though they had gained from New Deal policies and the growth of defense industries during World War II, were themselves frail and divided over loyalty issues. Hollywood political activity, being mostly liberal and left, annoyed the local power brokers, but also the studio heads, who were resentful at having been forced to recognize the guilds. Conservative craft unionists were upset, too. There was a fierce jurisdictional strike in 1945 between the AFL's craft union, the International Alliance of Theatrical Stage Employees and Moving Picture Machine Operators of the United States and Canada (IATSE), and the left-wing Conference of Studio Unions. After violence broke out, Popular Fronters staged a mass meeting in support of the CSU, sponsored by such left groups as the Citizens Committee for the Motion Picture Strikers, the HICCASP, the NCPCA, the National Lawyers Guild and the Screen Writers Guild.[15] The CSU and its allies were savagely red-baited by the IATSE's international representative, Roy Brewer, who blamed the strike on

"Communist-CIO agents."[16] Though IATSE won, conservative animosities remained that found expression in HUAC's investigations of Hollywood subversion.

The House Committee on Un-American Activities began its attack on Hollywood leftism in May 1947, with hearings in Los Angeles. This was not its first attempt. The Dies Committee, which preceded HUAC (as the HCUA was commonly known), had made a similar investigation in 1940, which failed because most Hollywood political activists had been shocked into neutrality or anti-Communism by the Stalin-Hitler Pact. In 1947 the climate was more favorable to congressional investigators, and the record of Hollywood radicals longer and more exploitable. The Los Angeles hearings were closed, their purpose being to lay the groundwork for open hearings later. Fourteen friendly witnesses told stories, many of them true apparently, to demonstrate how Communism was infiltrating the movie industry. HUAC's first target was Hanns Eisler, a refugee composer whose brother Gerhart was a Communist agent. Hanns, who had a long record of Communist associations, was named by Robert Stripling of the committee's staff as the "Karl Marx of Communism in the musical field."[17]

The main hearings began in Washington on October 20, 1947. Studio heads such as Walt Disney and Jack Warner testified to the prevalence of Communist activity. Disney was very conservative. Warner had been outraged by the jurisdictional strike in 1945, the low point of which was a riot at his studio gates; he is alleged to have declared afterward that he was through making pictures about "the little man."[18] This may be apocryphal but is the sort of thing Warner could have said. He was a typical studio head of the period, crude, arrogant and grasping on the one hand, terrified of bad publicity on the other.

Actors such as Robert Montgomery, George Murphy, Ronald Reagan and Adolphe Menjou described red activities in the Screen Actors Guild. Morrie Ryskind and other writers did likewise for the SWG. This ranged from detailed and specific remarks by Ryskind down to Ayn Rand's charge that the inclusion of smiling Russians in wartime films was Bolshevik propaganda. About a dozen friendly witnesses were members of the Motion Picture Alliance for the Preservation of American Ideals, formed in 1944 to fight Communism in Hollywood. It had not done well then, on account of the Soviet-American alliance. In the *The Saturday Review of Literature* Elmer Rice had accused the MPA of being racist, reactionary and isolationist. Ryskind denied the charges, but Rice insisted that no matter what they said in public many MPA leaders were known to be "anti-Semitic, anti-Negro, anti-alien, and anti-labor: in short, fascists."[19] Years of such abuse made it easy for MPA members to be witnesses for HUAC in 1947, when at last the tide turned in their favor.

Yet after a week of hearings little had been revealed that patriots might find alarming. Communists and fellow travelers possibly controlled the Screen Writers Guild, but no others. Only three films were shown to have reflected the Communist point of view—*Mission to Moscow, Song of Russia* and *North Star.* All were made during the war, and only *Mission to Moscow,* which did not do well critically or at the box office, was blatantly Stalinist. Studio heads wanted to make money, not enemies. Their major offense was against good taste, often unknowingly. The only reason Warner Brothers produced *Mission to Moscow,* it was widely believed, was that people in government had told them it would be appreciated.

The hearings went forward anyway, perhaps because HUAC members hoped to gain politically, maybe out of real concern. Something like a hundred reporters covered these hearings. The hostile witnesses called next gave them plenty to write about. HUAC had originally subpoenaed nineteen unfriendly witnesses. For various reasons this was reduced to a hard core of ten. Most were writers and all Communists except for a director, Edward Dmytryk, who had recently left the Party. Numerous efforts would be made to depict not only the "Hollywood Ten," as they were to be called, but everyone badgered by HUAC as political innocents. This was true in the technical sense that few unfriendly witnesses had committed crimes. But HUAC, if not from principle then out of common sense, seldom called up people who had not been Communists or fellow travelers. It wanted to avoid the embarrassment of making allegations that could not be sustained. Accordingly, while the unfriendly witnesses were legally blameless as a rule, they were not free from compromising political activities or associations. This is not to defend HUAC. It was in the business of punishing people by exposure for having exercised their constitutional rights. But while obviously unjust and immoral, it was not lawless. The courts maintained that the right to investigate was implicit in the right to legislate. Congress had to be able to gather information. If in the process lives and reputations were destroyed, this was too bad, but no reason to limit Congress.

The nineteen, except for Bertolt Brecht, who was leaving the country, had agreed in advance to act together. Two explanations were later given for their decision not to answer political questions. Ring Lardner, Jr., believed they had no choice. Witnesses before HUAC were not allowed to answer selectively. If they testified as to their own politics they were obliged to tell about everyone they had been associated with, or so courts at that time seemed to be ruling. Some of the nineteen wanted to come out publicly, in defiance of the Party policy that called for dissimulation. On the other hand, no one wanted to inform on others. The normal course would have been to invoke the Fifth Amendment, which protected witnesses from self-incrimination. But this meant saying in effect that there was something illegal about being a Communist, which was untrue. Accordingly, they decided not to answer political questions on the basis of the First Amendment, the protector of free speech. Doing so had the further attraction of offering, so they thought, better protection if an industry blacklist was established. And it enabled them to challenge HUAC's right to exist. Some actually believed that this could be a winning strategy. If indicted for contempt of Congress on account of refusing to answer political questions, they would be sustained on appeal and HUAC gravely weakened. As Ring Lardner, Jr., put it:

In a situation, therefore, in which the only safe and acceptable course open to us was to repudiate everything we believed in and prove we meant it by making trouble for other people, we could not be regarded as heroes for choosing a course of decency instead. In fact, we were doubly disqualified from heroic status: We weren't volunteers and we thought we could be winners.

Lester Cole, another of the Ten, remembered things differently. He insisted that they took the First Amendment out of heroic dedication to civil liberty, specifically to "protect it [the First

Amendment] from cold-war annihilation."[20] This was the line they took during the hearings and in their memoir *Hollywood on Trial* (1948). Cole was angry at Lardner for claiming self-interest as a motive. Yet the Ten lived in the predatory world of the movie industry and must have given a thought to it. Nor would this have been the first time when the smart thing to do also seemed to be the right thing.

In the event, they agreed not only to stand on the First Amendment but to represent themselves as simple liberals and patriots rather than as the veteran left wingers that they were. Indeed, they carried this as far, according to Philip Dunne, as to mislead their own attorneys.[21] Some also decided, for reasons never explained, to be not simply unfriendly but openly hostile. John Howard Lawson, the first to be called, refused to answer certain questions, attacked the committee, made speeches, and was finally removed from the witness stand.[22] Dalton Trumbo in his testimony compared HUAC's proceedings to the Reichstag fire that accompanied Nazism's rise to power. Off the stand he shouted out that this was the beginning of "an American concentration camp." Albert Maltz addressed Stripling as "Mr. Quisling" and kept saying that he expected to be asked about his religious beliefs next. In their prepared statements, which they were often not allowed to read, at least in full, they wrapped themselves in red, white and blue. Lawson declared piously that he never agreed to write a picture "unless I am convinced that it serves democracy and the interest of the American people."[23] HUAC's subpoena was an attack on the millions who enjoyed his films and, in fact, on all 130 million Americans—including infants—whom he represented.

Samuel Ornitz compared Congressman John E. Rankin, a racist member of the committee, to Adolf Hitler. Herbert Biberman congratulated himself on his good citizenship and said he had been called up because he loved and respected his fellow Americans and believed "they will constantly achieve a richer social and economic life under the Constitution, which will eliminate prejudice and inequality in spite of the efforts of the Committee to prevent it."[24] Adrian Scott, producer of the film *Crossfire*, which attacked anti-Semitism (Dmytryk directed it), accused HUAC of waging a "cold war" against "the Jewish and Negro people." Lester Cole said HUAC was waging a "cold war against democracy." And so it went. These overstatements, and the belligerence of some of the Ten, suggest that HUAC's historian was right about their motives. He guessed that they welcomed the hearings as a chance to play a public role and express views which Party discipline and movie censorship had prevented them from getting into films.

The Ten were not without considerable support at first. Newspapers generally did not approve of HUAC's investigation. The movie colony rallied round. A Committee for the First Amendment that was established by Philip Dunne and John Huston before the hearings included many film celebrities— Paul Henreid, Danny Kaye, Fredric March, Charles Boyer, John Garfield, Sterling Hayden and Gene Kelly among others. A chartered plane flew movie people to the hearings, where they lent moral support. Two network radio broadcasts were arranged. The usual petitions, meetings and press conferences abounded. The Committee for the First Amendment grew into the Committee of One Thousand, chaired by Harlow Shapley. And the studio heads also seemed willing to stand fast. Eric Johnston, speaking for the Motion Picture Producers Association, criticized HUAC before the hearings and warned against the danger of censorship. Privately he assured the Ten's attorneys that there would be no industry blacklist.

On November 24, 1947, after a conference at the Waldorf-Astoria Hotel, the Motion Picture Producers announced the suspension of the Ten. It was the start of the blacklist, which later spread throughout show business and was extremely effective. Many believed at the time, and some still do, that the producers caved in needlessly. Although the misbehavior of some of the Ten had generated poor publicity and diminished the enthusiasm of the Committee for the First Amendment, newspapers were generally critical of HUAC. A Gallup poll taken in November, after the Ten were indicted for contempt of Congress, showed that public opinion was evenly divided on the propriety of HUAC's investigation.* If the producers had shown courage,

---

* Dore Schary, a studio executive, believed that the Ten were their own worst enemy. Their conduct on the stand alienated the press and cost them most of the support they had at first enjoyed. Schary had advised them not to answer HUAC, but also to call a press conference afterward

or even been content to sacrifice the Ten, HUAC might have been held off and an industry-wide blacklist averted. This was, however, to expect too much of the studio heads and their bankers and owners in New York. Moviemakers had always been sensitive to public opinion, blacklisting stars for moral turpitude and imposing upon themselves an absurdly stringent code of sexual censorship. Having given in previously on the lesser issue of sex, producers were not going to hold fast on the greater one of loyalty.

HUAC returned to Hollywood after a four-year interval, which had bolstered rumors of a deal between the committee and the producers. It was believed that studio heads set up the blacklist in return for an end to HUAC investigations. That the committee held hearings on entertainers almost every year between 1951 and 1958 seems to disprove this. The hearings in 1951, when HUAC went after fellow travelers and progressives and demanded names, were most extensive and left the worst scars. It was at this time that the blacklist went into high gear. By then committee procedure was well established. Unfriendly witnesses were given a Hobson's choice. They could take the Fifth Amendment (not the First, which offered no protection), but as this was understood to be an admission of guilt, doing so made them unemployable. If they did not invoke their constitutional right, witnesses had to name those they had worked with politically, which was also damaging.

People were now going both ways. In the 1951 hearings actors Howard Da Silva, Will Geer and Gale Sondergaard (the wife of the Ten's Howard Biberman) took the Fifth, as did writers Robert Lees, Waldo Salt and Paul Jarrico. Larry Parks, a young actor who had just achieved stardom in *The Jolson Story,* begged to be let off the hook but was ground down mercilessly and forced to give names. HUAC acclaimed his patri-

---

and declare their political affiliations. This would, he thought, have established that they were defying HUAC on principle. But their lawyers opposed this course, and the Ten went along with counsel. "My feelings then and now are that HUAC acted with malice and no evidence of the American values they were supposed to protect; that the Hollywood Ten were badly advised and provided an impetus for what happened following their appearance; that the producers behaved cowardly and cruelly." Dunne and Huston made similar efforts.[25]

otism, but he never starred again. Edward Dmytryk was a friendly witness, having changed sides during his imprisonment. José Ferrer, John Garfield and Edward G. Robinson abased themselves, with varying results. Big stars and small were now all in the same boat. Refusal to testify meant ruin; doing so made them look ridiculous and perhaps even dishonorable.

Writers fared a little better. Most faced the same alternatives but did not always suffer the same fate. Lillian Hellman appeared before HUAC in 1952, gave a defiant statement, and took the Fifth. People remembered the statement and forgot the rest, earning Hellman a reputation for heroism in later years. Arthur Miller the playwright really was brave. He appeared before HUAC in 1956 and neither named names nor invoked the Fifth Amendment. Surprisingly, though he had refused to grovel—the only other way to survive—he was not found to be in contempt of Congress. No doubt the somewhat improved political climate of the midfifties accounts for Miller's escape. He showed courage anyway, and dignity too, which was equally unusual.[26]

At first, congressional hearings yielded up some information. HUAC knew much about the Ten, for example, and when they refused to testify had data on membership in Communist fronts read into the record. But once the basic pattern of Communist activity was established and the main figures were identified, the hearings were clearly punitive. From 1951 on, HUAC turned up virtually nothing new but subjected witnesses to grueling and often humiliating ordeals. These were justified on the ground that only the truly contrite were entitled to absolution. Confession was the proof of this, and was ruthlessly exacted.

Desperate people even asked to be questioned in hopes of getting off the blacklist, though with uneven success. Edward Dmytryk was a notable case in point. He broke with the Ten while still in prison, from which he was released on November 15, 1950. Yet despite this turnaround, Dmytryk, who had earned $2,500 a week before being subpoenaed by HUAC, could not get film work. With the help of the Motion Picture Industry Council, representing management and labor, he was given the standard rehabilitation. Dmytryk asked to testify again before the committee and named names. He gave *Saturday Evening*

Post readers an account of his misspent political life.[27] He was attacked for this by his ex-comrade Albert Maltz, who took out an advertisement in the *Hollywood Reporter* accusing Dmytryk of selling out his principles to get work. "He has lied and befouled others with his lies; he has traduced the good principles for which he once stood; and now he buys his way back into the film industry trampling the careers of thirty others."[28] Maltz exaggerated. It appears that, as was usual by this time, most of the names were already known to HUAC. Nor did Dymtryk fully buy his way back into the industry. MPIC figures, including Ronald Reagan, president of the Screen Actors Guild, and Roy Brewer of IATSE, took out a counteradvertisement explaining how they had helped Dymtryk purge himself.[29] But while Dmytryk did get pictures to direct after this, his career never really recovered.

Sterling Hayden was one who took the point. He had joined the Communist Party out of the customary motives, plus the rare experience of having worked with Tito's partisan forces as a member of the OSS—wartime forerunner of the Central Intelligence Agency. His career had been unremarkable until in 1950 he got his first role in a good film, John Huston's *Asphalt Jungle*. But instead of the numerous offers which he expected, no further parts came his way. Fearing that he had been blacklisted, Hayden wrote to the FBI asking how he could clear himself. He gave it a statement describing his Party activity. In 1951 he was subpoenaed by HUAC. Mindful of what had happened to Larry Parks, who had "consigned himself to oblivion" by pleading with the committee, Hayden did not take chances and told all, writing a forty-page statement in advance. This was a winning strategy. Many starring roles came his way, resulting in the production of many forgettable pictures. Through a clipping service he received two thousand news stories on his testimony, nearly all of them favorable. "Not often does a man find himself eulogized for having behaved in a manner that he himself despises," Hayden wrote in his self-punishing memoirs.[30] Survival had been bought too dearly. Ashamed of what he had done, Hayden drank, spent and quarreled recklessly in the years that followed, suffering almost as much, it appears, as many who were blacklisted.

Edward G. Robinson, one of Hollywood's foremost stars in

the 1930s and '40s, saved himself also, though with greater difficulty. His autobiography contains a richly detailed picture of Hollywood politics. At MGM in the late thirties, he explained, the executives were all antiliberal and ate by themselves. The writers ate at another table, which was a hotbed of progressivism. The few conservative writers lunched with the directors, "whose table was a hotbed of people who longed for the reincarnation of Calvin Coolidge."[31] The intrusion of politics into gastronomy upset Robinson, who took to eating in his dressing room. Digestive problems notwithstanding, Robinson was more active politically and for a longer time than any other star. He belonged to so many groups, including Communist fronts, that he could not remember them all, signing petitions and checks with abandon from the early thirties until 1948 or '49. His identification with left-wing causes had begun to hurt him even before this, Robinson believed. But his downfall resulted from Dalton Trumbo's request for a personal loan. Robinson had worked with Trumbo politically and was an early member of the Committee for the First Amendment, so he naturally sent Mrs. Trumbo a check. Once this became known he was out of work.

Robinson did everything he could to gain reinstatement. He made a list of all the organizations he could remember joining and, with his accountants, of all the checks he had given them. He sent this data and copies of his relevant correspondence to J. Edgar Hoover, who did not answer. When Robinson's passport expired he was denied a new one. HUAC would not call him to testify, as no accusations had been made against him. Through the intervention of Mayor Sam Yorty of Los Angeles, HUAC finally allowed him to appear before it. Yet even this did not result in employment. Robinson believed that the committee would not give him a clean bill of health unless he confessed to being a fool and a dupe of Communism, which as an intelligent, if not very discriminating, person he didn't think himself to be. Finally he gave up trying to protect his honor and got down, as he saw it, in the dirt—though as he was never a Communist, he did not have to name anyone as a Party member. But even naming names was not enough. It was only after Yorty brought him together with Victor Riesel and George Sokolsky, conservative newspaper columnists with much influence in these matters, that his name was cleared and his passport restored. This enabled him to work again, though only in cheap B pictures. Robinson did not climb back into the majors until Cecil B. De Mille gave him a good part in *The Ten Commandments*. Too old for leading roles, Robinson worked steadily as a character actor from that time on.

There was a radio and television blacklist too. It began in 1950 following the publication of a booklet, *Red Channels,* listing 151 persons by name as guilty of subversive associations. Two years later the ACLU decided to make a special study of radio and TV blacklisting, raising a fund for this purpose and assigning the task to board member Merle Miller, a novelist. When published as *The Judges and the Judged* (1952), Miller's report was attacked in the *New Leader* by another board member, Merlyn S. Pitzele, labor editor of the magazine *Business Week*. He accused the Miller book of being prejudiced and one-sided; further, it was poorly researched and did not deal with the blacklisting of anti-Communists.[32] In a statement to the board, Miller defended himself vigorously and asked Pitzele to apologize for implying that he was pro-Communist. He said he felt obliged to preserve the anonymity of informants, which Pitzele had complained about, as they would not have talked otherwise. The blacklist had reduced the income of those named in *Red Channels*, even though, as Pitzele said, most still seemed to be working.[33]

The ACLU appointed a committee headed by Ernest Angell to review Pitzele's criticisms and found some truth to them. There were errors of fact in the book—for example, Miller's claim that a sizable minority of persons named had no Communist or front listings after 1945. Actually, of 151 persons named 74 were listed as recently as 1949. Other Pitzele charges were found to be lacking in substance. The board voted to accept this report but not make it public, allowing the staff to release all or parts of it later if need be.[34] The board also renominated Miller and Pitzele for membership, Miller unanimously and Pitzele by a margin of one vote.

Issuing a brief statement on the report rather than the document itself was a mistake, as soon became evident. In October a newsman, on the basis of a forthcoming article in *Commentary,* accused the ACLU of suppressing the Angell report because it was so damaging.[35] This was untrue, for the report, though conceding errors, had defended Miller's book as a whole against Pitzele's charges. The ACLU received a bad press all the same, and needlessly, as Edward L. Bernays, a public-relations specialist, pointed out. Concealing the report put those who had signed an advertisement for the book, including Bernays, in an awkward position. He had not known of it until called by a reporter when the newspaper story broke. He and the other signers had a right to expect that Miller's book was accurate, and if not, to be informed of developments. "The most puzzling aspect of all this is the idea you expressed to me, that by withholding the complete findings of the Angell Committee, the ACLU would avoid controversy."[36] The controversy already existed. How could an act of "semi-suppression" not fail to increase it? He hoped the ACLU would learn from this to leave such investigations in the future to impartial bodies such as the Social Science Research Council. The ACLU then released the Angell report, too late to make up for the bad publicity.

Bernays was right on both counts. The ACLU should not have hushed up the Angell report, and ought not to have authorized Miller's book in the first place. The ACLU had been led astray by its desire to become active in an area where legal action could not be taken. In later years the ACLU would be criticized for having been too passive in the McCarthy era, but this was not from lack of desire.[37] Board members sometimes chafed at the restrictions imposed by the ACLU's commitment to legal work. But when they went beyond it, as with *The Judges and the Judged,* the results were not always satisfactory. Miller's book was flawed, as Pitzele had said. He was mistaken in one respect, however. Miller had tried to find material supporting the claim that there was a blacklist of anti-Communists. The ACLU made it a policy to track down all such allegations, but never found hard evidence.[38] It did go so far as to include the names of two alleged anti-Communist victims in a brief against blacklisting filed with the Federal Communications Commission. This outraged one of them, Ralph De Toledano, a right-wing journalist. In a letter to *The New York Times* he declared that "the A.C.L.U. has used my name to give a spurious cloak of 'impartiality' to its present vociferous campaign to thrust Communists, pro-Communists and fellow-travelers down the throats of broadcasters."[39]

It is not at all clear that there ever was a blacklist of anti-Communists. Morrie Ryskind was convinced that one existed and that he was on it, but also that it could never be proved. Ryskind said that nobody on the liberal side would admit they had a blacklist of their own, offering various excuses to explain why anti-Communists were not working. In Ryskind's own case it was said that he was "all written out." The fact was, Ryskind maintained, that he had all the work he wanted between 1935 and 1947, when he testified against the Hollywood Ten, after which his career as a screenwriter abruptly ended. Now it was claimed there was no reason to hire Ryskind, because he hadn't had a film credit in seven years. Ryskind, who used to be outspoken, would not even give the name of a local ACLU figure he believed to be one of the blacklisters. This was because of a successful suit against the mother of Ginger Rogers a few years earlier.

> When Lela Rogers was to debate Emmet Lavery on Communism in Hollywood, she asked a half-dozen of us to read over her speech and make suggestions. We did—and the next thing I knew Lavery sued for libel and a jury of my peers decided that Lavery's play flopped because Lela mentioned it. And it cost me, what with suits and lawyers, ten grand. I just can't afford this sort of thing much longer. But thanks just the same.[40]

Being out of work was not, of course, proof of a blacklist. Adolphe Menjou, Ronald Reagan and other leading anti-Communists continued to appear in movies despite their anti-Communism. Ryskind explained this by saying that the stars had been kept on because they were money-makers. Yet that had not saved Edward G. Robinson, a far greater box-office attraction, when he was blacklisted by the right. What anti-Communists meant by blacklisting was probably more like discrimination. Emotions were high, and it would be surprising if liberals in a position to pass over enemies failed to do so. But, as Philip Dunne observed, most hiring was done by producers, a highly conservative group unlikely to punish those with whom they agreed.

Though unjustly criticized at points, Miller's book failed—and not simply because of factual errors. Louis Berg, in the *Commentary* article that led to the ACLU's embarrassment, indicted Miller on two main counts. Like Pitzele, Berg was irritated by the use of anonymous informants. Miller had actually used some names, apparently because their cases were already well known. They were, however, not important sources. As Berg put it, "With some exceptions, where there are names, there is no testimony; and where there is testimony, there are no names. It is fair to state that his key witnesses are nameless, which means that their crucial testimony cannot be checked."[41]

Berg saw Miller's refusal to name informants as a "somewhat futile extension of the general hush-hush defense set up in liberal circles when the embarrassing question arises of Communist influence on various movements and causes." This was wrong in principle and practice.

> By now it is amply clear that this defense, whatever the motives behind it, has protected no one from baseless charges, or damage to his reputation and livelihood. It has served only to sabotage all efforts, governmental or private, to elicit the genuine facts, and has maintained and spread the whole atmosphere of suspicion and conspiracy that has bedeviled this problem from the beginning. It has helped make a national figure of the notorious Senator McCarthy. It has duped many respectable and patriotic citizens. It has been used to shield the guilty rather than to protect the innocent. Nor has it, as I have said, diminished by one little whit the voice of wholesale slander.[42]

Berg did not go too far in saying that, for Miller, being named in *Red Channels* was a mark of honor, proof not only of innocence but of character and "superlative talent besides." Miller answered blanket accusation with blanket whitewash. "Prove it, he says, and in the same breath: Don't you dare try."

Berg was brilliant and just, but did not stop here. He went on to say that the panic in the media was sometimes deliberately manipulated by leftists to hide their guilt. In any event, the Miller position that employers had no right to inquire into the politics of employees was faulty and inconsistent with Miller's own record in the American Veterans Committee, where he was a leader in the fight to turn Communists out of office. The ACLU itself kept Communists off its boards. How, then, could the ACLU say that what was proper for it was not for employers? Civil libertarians had done all they could to protect the right of leftists to keep their politics secret, leaving the battle against Communism to be carried on by reactionaries and demagogues. "We of the liberal faith have largely surrendered to them the fight against Communists in this country, which should have been the concern and duty of every person interested in civil liberties."[43] Berg argued that instead of trying to protect everyone accused of bad politics, liberals should support a board of inquiry that would clear the innocent and reformed. Those who were Communist sympathizers could then still be defended by civil-libertarian absolutists such as Miller. Berg thought Hollywood was setting a good example. Of some two hundred named persons, all but twenty had been found innocent by various examining bodies. This showed the value of voluntary action based on free discussion. "Whatever happened to the old liberal conviction that, in the fight for justice, the best weapon is the truth?"[44]

Miller's book and Berg's response to it raised most of the issues that agitated liberals during the McCarthy era. Libertarians generally opposed investigations into Communist influence and economic reprisals occasioned by politics. Nonlibertarian liberals such as Berg favored investigations and sanctions against those found to be still Communists or fellow travelers. As always in times of stress, logic suffered. In attacking Miller and the ACLU for being inconsistent on the Communist issue, Berg missed the point. Political rights meant very little if a person could be denied work or sent to jail for holding unpopular views or belonging to an unpopular organization. At the same time, defending the rights of such people did not bar libertarians from disagreeing with or even campaigning against them, in open, legal, nonpunitive ways. Miller had every reason to oppose blacklisting, which was indeed a threat to political freedom. Yet he was also entitled to campaign against Communist candidates for office in the voluntary organizations to which he belonged.

Moreover, Berg was premature in hailing the methods used by Hollywood. When in full operation, the movie blacklist would deny employment to hundreds. Already, obtaining a clean bill of political health was extraordinarily difficult, even for a great star like Edward G. Robinson. The blacklist penalized individuals for taking part in constitutionally protected activities. It was never a crime to belong to the Communist Party or its fronts, or to try to keep such memberships from being known. Further, the blacklist encouraged deceit and other abuses. To imply, as Berg did, that blacklisting somehow involved the robust exercise of fine old liberal beliefs was silly.

On the other hand, Berg was absolutely right in maintaining that Miller's book met a demagogic half-truth with a liberal half-lie. *The Judges and the Judged,* in common with much libertarian propaganda, represented blacklistees as innocent victims who, solely on account of liberal and even patriotic activities, were being unjustly persecuted. This, not the errors, the careless research or the juggled figures, was the central weakness of Miller's book. Some persons named as Communists or fellow travelers were indeed blameless. In a few cases identities had been confused. But most people cited by congressional committees, and most listed in *Red Channels,* had substantial records.

Official investigators did not usually pick names out of a hat. They were taken from lists of those who had signed petitions, sponsored activities and given money to Communist and front organizations and activities. It greatly confused matters for libertarians to pretend otherwise, and to campaign against blacklisting as if there were no reason for it. Blacklistees had not, as a rule, violated any laws. But they had lent their names and talent in varying degrees to Stalinist enterprises. The issue, then, was not whether mistakes had been made by investigators. It was whether individuals should be denied employment for political reasons. Understandably, many blacklisted persons wanted to invoke flag and country rather than admit to being, or having been, Communists or fellow travelers. Yet it helped no one when liberals went along with this fiction. The air was not cleared or the Bill of Rights fortified when veteran political activists were represented as guileless, if sometimes misguided, advocates of a noble cause.

Miller's book was so inadequate that the Ford Foundation later sponsored another study of the blacklist, in movies this time as well as in radio and television. John Cogley's two-volume *Report on Blacklisting* (1956), while more thorough than Miller's, suffered from comparable defects. Cogley too relied on anonymous informants. He focused especially on the errors of witch-hunters, giving the impression that blacklisting was bad because people were wrongfully accused. He evaded the question of whether anyone should be deprived of work on political grounds. Cogley did show how some blacklisted writers continued to work for television through the use of stand-ins, usually less successful writers who passed off scripts as their own for a share of the fees. And he exposed the activities of leading witch-hunters. Despite its flaws, the Cogley report was annoying enough to have its author subpoenaed by HUAC, which mistreated him in the usual way. He suffered no permanent harm. Neither did the blacklist, which went forward despite the efforts of liberals and the ACLU.

Entertainers suffered most. Pete Seeger, the left-wing folk musician, did not make it back onto television until 1967, and even then his hosts, the Smothers brothers, had their show canceled for this and other small gestures of independence. Will Geer, a blacklisted screen actor, did not appear in films until 1970. He would prosper after this in a television series, *The Waltons,* but his survival was an exception to the rule. A few directors were able to find work in European films. Writers fared best. Some remained in demand under assumed names, and a need for their services, together with inspired leadership by Dalton Trumbo, enabled them to break the blacklist finally.[45]

After the Cold War began, media people developed a habit of making light of their political records. Whether anonymously, as to Miller and Cogley, or before congressional committees, most would testify that in signing petitions, giving money, appearing at rallies, they hardly realized what they were doing. None, it seems, had ever knowingly joined a front or had any serious political ideas beyond wanting to do good for humanity. Even the Hollywood Ten, though boastful of their democratic and egalitarian sympathies, had represented themselves as advancing these principles mainly through films or war work, passing over the numerous Communist or front organizations to which they had actually belonged. In later years Trumbo remained faithful to this tradition. In 1970 he said that he had resigned from the CP in 1948 because he was "far too busy to attend its meetings, which were, in the event, dull beyond description, about as revolutionary in purpose as Wednesday-evening testimonial services in the Christian Science Church." He claimed further that he had never regarded the working class as "anything other than something to get out of."[46] Though obedient to custom, these remarks hardly did justice to his past militancy. He had been a Communist Party activist, not simply a bored participant in devotional exercises. It was because the Ten had been highly political that HUAC subpoenaed them. It went after the real Communists first, saving the hangers-on for later.

Unlike the other nine, as he jokingly observed, Trumbo had actually risen from the proletariat. He was a self-taught writer, having only a year of college when his father's death obliged him to seek employment with a commercial bakery. He published his first short story while working for it. Trumbo free-lanced briefly and in 1934 was hired as a reader, the lowest form of creative life in Hollywood. He soon became a screen-writer and a member of the infant Screen Writers Guild, whose first president was John Howard Lawson, most prominent of the Hollywood Communists. Trumbo became editor of the SWG's magazine and was active during the difficult early days when studio reprisals, including Trumbo's own firing by Warner Brothers, drove SWG membership down from two hundred to fifty. During this period Trumbo joined or supported numerous front organizations. He was particularly active during and after the war in the Hollywood Writers Mobilization, the Hollywood Democratic Committee, the HICCASP and the turbulent 1945 strike against the IATSE, during which he gave a major speech. He also found time to write four novels, the most successful being his antiwar classic *Johnny Got His Gun* (1939).[47]

In 1946 Trumbo signed a contract with MGM that was the envy of his profession, giving him a maximum of money and independence. He was earning as much as $95,000 a year at this time, while also writing for magazines ranging from the *New Masses* to *The Saturday Evening Post*. Trumbo had joined the Communist Party in 1943, long after he was a Communist in all but name. Though his politics were boringly Stalinoid, he himself was the opposite, a flamboyant individual who relished ease and comfort. When called before HUAC, Trumbo was, after Lawson, the most boisterous of the Ten, welcoming, so it seems, the chance to live in public the role he had been playing under wraps for years. Like the others he suffered from over-confidence, arising from years of unpunished left-wing activities and the initial outpouring of support received from movie peo-ple. They had expected to be indicted for contempt of Congress but to win on appeal, as later happened to Arthur Miller. But the Ten went to prison, most, including Trumbo, for a little less than one year. The blacklist, which at first did not seem too bad, also proved worse than expected. For a time Trumbo con-tinued to make money. He sold four scripts at good prices, under the names of writer friends to whom he gave a third of his fees. Trumbo also sold a number of stories, which were not actual scripts but rather proposals outlining how such scripts might be written. This was a degraded art form peculiar to Hollywood, as Trumbo explained in a letter to Nelson Algren, whose name he wished to use. "I am obliged to warn you in advance that an original story, designed for sale on the local market, involves a combination of prose and construction and sentimentality and vulgarity that appalls even me, who am used to it, and would appall you even more."[48] But it paid well and was read only in Hollywood. Trumbo could do one in two weeks at the outside, and had sold $126,000 worth of such stories in 1948 and '49.

After this came hard times. The major studios stopped buy-ing on the black market, and prices for pseudonymous work fell. Trumbo moved to Mexico with other blacklistees, but could not control the sale and handling of his material from there and was often cheated. By the midfifties he was back in California with what appears to have been a well-thought-out scheme to break the blacklist. Trumbo gave up other writing (he had a play fail on Broadway in 1949) and was soon receiv-ing more assignments than he could handle despite his amazing productivity. The fees were low by past standards, as indepen-dent producers could not pay much. Trumbo was grateful all the same and tried to give them good feelings as well as good scripts. In a letter to the journalist Murray Kempton, whose book *Part of Our Time* (1955) had a harsh chapter on the Ten, he described his procedure. Buyers who dealt with him were given code names, picked up their scripts personally, and were heartened by all the confidence-inspiring security devices he could think of. Trumbo surrounded himself with "legally phony bank accounts, mysterious rituals, and awesome oaths."

> Only the boundless courage of cupidity enables them to survive such an ordeal. Once they emerge from it, clutching a script as good or as bad as their taste, I crown them with the accolade Great and Dauntless Enemy of the Blacklist. They stagger off in a glow of moral grandeur, better, sounder-sleeping men for my ministration.[49]

In this fashion Trumbo wrote a number of successful pictures, including *The Brave One,* for which he won an Academy Award in 1957 under the name Robert Rich. His real identity became known, strengthening Trumbo's hand. He was already farming out assignments to other blacklistees. Now he had even more work. Trumbo made it a practice never to admit having written any script, with the result that all popular films of uncertain origin were attributed to him. This gave him a bigger underground reputation and additional leverage. He knew that the blacklist would have to be nibbled away at rather than defied openly. In 1958 he explained the situation to Alvah Bessie of the Ten.

Bessie was a writer whose talent seems to have vanished with his youth. His first novel, *Dwell in the Wilderness* (1935), was also his best, according to one literary scholar.[50] His next, *Men in Battle* (1939), based on his experience with Loyalist units in Spain, was much admired by critics. W. H. Auden said that Bessie showed signs in it of becoming an outstanding American writer.[51] That was not to be. Somewhere along the line Bessie lost his gift, perhaps during the four years he spent as a staff writer for the *New Masses,* maybe in Hollywood, where he had gone to work for Warner Brothers in 1943. He never mastered the film writer's craft and was the least important professionally of the Ten. Having earned a bare living previously, he could not survive under the exacting conditions of the blacklist. His later books failed, too, deservedly, it seems. By the late fifties he was working for a San Francisco nightclub and trying wrongheadedly to end the blacklist. Bessie had asked Trumbo to speak against it at a meeting sponsored by the Communist *People's World*. Trumbo in a kindly letter tried to tell Bessie why this would not work. Open attacks on the blacklist, including no fewer than sixteen court actions, had all failed. It would be broken by getting a good press reassuring to moviemakers, not through bad publicity such as would result from Communist-sponsored activities.

Though Bessie did not take his point, Trumbo moved steadily forward, building up not only his own reputation but that of others too, reasoning that producers would be more willing to hire them openly if the pool of talent was large. Some black-listees were gaining stature on their own. Carl Foreman and Michael Wilson wrote the highly successful *Bridge on the River Kwai*. Wilson was a particular embarrassment to blacklisters, having won an Oscar in 1952 for *A Place in the Sun,* written before he was banned. He was nominated again for *Friendly Persuasion,* prompting the Motion Picture Academy to announce that a secret resolution made blacklistees ineligible for awards. Trumbo won the Oscar in 1957 only because the real identity of Robert Rich was a secret. Two years later the black-listee Nedrick Young was nominated for *The Defiant Ones,* which he had written with Harold J. Smith, who was not on the list but would suffer anyway if the film was rejected. At this point the Academy governors gave up, announcing that henceforth Oscars would be awarded on merit only.

This paved the way for Trumbo's coup. In 1958 he was hired by Kirk Douglas to write *Spartacus* and by Otto Preminger to do the script for *Exodus*. Both were expensive productions, and Trumbo, whose reputation was now without peer, had been obtained to safeguard large investments. It made sense to hire the best, and also to reassure investors by saying so. Preminger was first to go public, disclosing in 1960 that Trumbo was working for him. Douglas followed suit. There were scattered protests, but both films were hits, earning as much money as could be done in those days—somewhere between forty and fifty million dollars each. It was the end of the blacklist for screenwriters, the culmination of years of patient planning and labor by Trumbo, who had done much to make it easy for the producers. Ring Lardner, Jr., acknowledged this with a graceful tribute the next year, saying the hole in the blacklist had "been effected almost singlehandedly by the fertile talent, capacity for hard work, imaginative flair for publicity, and unswerving devotion to a high living standard, of a writer named Dalton Trumbo."[52] This article, which appeared in *The Saturday Evening Post,* was the first Lardner had written under his own name in fourteen years.

Courage, talent and luck saw a small number of writers through this dark time. Performers, like Pete Seeger, who could give concerts survived, as did a few with ties to Broadway, where there was no blacklist. Some found work abroad. But most seem to have been driven to the margin of the entertainment industry or, more often, beyond. No one knows the exact number of people involved, but the figures most often used are that some three hundred were blacklisted in Hollywood and between one hundred fifty and two hundred in radio and television. Some of these were cleared in various ways, so the total of ruined careers has to be less than the sum of both lists, though still considerable. Alvah Bessie, who can be relied on to omit no case however doubtful, gave the names of eleven persons said to have committed suicide on account of the blacklist.[53] Many who escaped it suffered, too, even if not so much. No one can know how many were hurt by the need to betray, as some thought themselves to have done, friends, associations and ideas, or how much it cost to enforce or merely abide by sanctions that few seem to have believed in. Sterling Hayden's memoirs must be only the visible tip of an iceberg of self-contempt.

In the darkest days one could suffer humiliation from the slightest pressure. On December 27, 1952, the American Legion announced that it disapproved of a new film, *Moulin Rouge,* starring José Ferrer, who used to be no more progressive than hundreds of other actors and had already been grilled by HUAC. The picture itself was based on the life of Toulouse-Lautrec and was totally apolitical. Nine members of the Legion had picketed it anyway, giving rise to the controversy. By this time people were not taking any chances. Ferrer immediately wired the Legion's national commander that he would be glad to join the veterans in their "fight against communism." A few days later Ferrer denounced Paul Robeson for accepting the Stalin Peace Prize. On January 2 Leonard Lyons, a columnist,

wrote that in consequence the Legion opposed any further pick-
eting of *Moulin Rouge.* Victor Lasky, another red-baiting
journalist, was said to have withdrawn an article on Ferrer he
had written for the Legion's magazine. On the sixteenth, Lyons
reported that Ferrer had ironed out all his problems with Legion
officials over lunch.[54]

The alternative, as Charlie Chaplin demonstrated, was harmful to the pocketbook. Chaplin was a special target of abuse
because he had left the country to avoid the fate of other witch-
hunt victims. Accordingly his movie *Limelight* failed at the box
office. Chaplin put a bold face on matters, saying that Hollywood had "succumbed to thought control and the illegal methods of high-pressure groups, which means the end of the
American motion picture industry and its world influence."[55]
Chaplin was mistaken, as were also the anonymous screenwriters who had said in *The Nation* that blacklisting was turning
Hollywood over to the red-baiters. "After that there can only be
darkness and television," they warned mordantly.[56] But the
movie industry survived nonetheless, while those who defied the
witch-hunters, for the most part, did not. Even Charlie Chaplin,
probably the world's most famous entertainer, was not safe. He
was too rich to ruin, but his career as a filmmaker never recovered from the boycott.

Though the blacklist is long gone, and many of the blacklistees also, the meaning of it is still debated. In 1976 Hilton
Kramer, art critic for *The New York Times,* wrote an essay
inspired by three creations: a movie, *The Front,* dealing with
the television blacklist; Lillian Hellman's book *Scoundrel Time,*
a blacklistee's memoir; and a documentary film, *Hollywood on
Trial,* about the movie blacklist. Kramer denounced all three
works for giving a false picture of the era, observing that people
on the lists had not been innocent. They were Communists and
fellow travelers, apologists for Stalin's crimes, conspirators who
tried to keep anti-Communists from working. He quoted Alistair Cooke, who in *A Generation on Trial* (1950) had written
that the Hollywood Ten were as guilty as HUAC of turning the
hearings into "a squalid and rowdy parody of a court of law."[57]
Stalinists in their day had viciously attacked anti-Communists
for telling undesired truths.

Kramer's essay inspired a flood of mail. Arthur Schlesinger,

Jr., wrote that the article should be made required reading for everyone born since 1940. Alfred Kazin endorsed Kramer's view of *Scoundrel Time*. Other correspondents disagreed. That the sins of the blacklistees amounted to very little compared with those of the witch-hunters was a common view. "Revisionist" historians supported Hellman's charge that liberal anti-Communism led straight to Vietnam and Watergate. Hellman was right also, they argued, in pointing to the close relationship between McCarthyism and the Cold War, and in wishing to call off the latter. It was this, the historians speculated, that had offended Kramer. He, in response, put up a spirited defense, identifying himself with those liberals in the fifties who were against both Stalinism and the blacklist, the conduct of HUAC and the values of the Communist Party. None of his critics had mentioned the crimes of Stalin or the apologies for them of American Stalinists, nor did the contemporary glorifiers of blacklist victims, who had made Kramer angry in the first place.[58] Neither side of this exchange went beyond what had been said in the forties and fifties, though one might suppose that the wisdom of hindsight ought by now to have shed new light.

Time has in fact made some things clearer than before. To start, there is no evidence, and few have even claimed, that Hollywood Communists were able to exploit films as propaganda. Roy Brewer made a feeble attempt during the 1951 HUAC investigation of Hollywood, saying that Communist writers had generated propaganda through the back door by playing up violence, sex, divorce, prostitution and miscegenation. "The underlying theme of all these motion pictures was that America was a nation of 'decadent bourgeoisie.' "[59] The truth was both different and more complicated than this. Communists did not like sex and violence as movie subjects. It was the desire of capitalists to make money that brought them into films. When given their choice Hollywood leftists went the other way. They loved Frank Capra's pictures in which the virtuous little man triumphed over evil. In their own films they attacked obvious wrongs, racism and anti-Semitism especially, while promoting tolerance and the like. In one of his letters Trumbo said that thanks to the Screen Writers Guild there had been a decline "in the use of reactionary themes, in the slander of minority groups and in general vilification of organized labor."[60] This was a justifiable boast. Progressives were far more likely to emphasize social justice than others in the industry. One frequently cited estimate was that the Ten had used such themes in thirty percent of their films, compared with an industry average of ten percent.[61]

The fruits of this laudable effort were more ambiguous than might be supposed, especially during the war years when government interested itself in getting its message across. The Office of War Information established an office in Hollywood staffed by dedicated New Deal liberals. President Roosevelt and Elmer Davis, head of OWI, believed that films were important, and the industry received preferential treatment. During the war Hollywood continued to make five hundred films a year, which were seen by upward of eighty million people a week—more than ever before. OWI was unhappy at first, however, because though many were war films, they had nothing in particular to say. To correct this deplorable lack of substance Hollywood's OWI branch wrote a "Manual for the Motion Picture Industry" in 1942 as a guide to filmmakers. It explained that the war was not just a struggle for survival but, inevitably, a "people's war" between fascism and democracy. The United States sought to make a democratic world based on the Four Freedoms. Victory would mean a New Deal for all, universal participation in government, an end to colonialism, and other blessings. Prejudice, intolerance and bigotry were fascistic and to be exposed as such. "There can be no peace until militarism and fascism are completely wiped out . . ."[62]

The OWI's Hollywood bureau soon realized that to influence movies it must be heard at the beginning, so it asked studios to submit scripts for approval. The bureau's historians describe its aim as follows. "In the Bureau's ideal combat movie an ethnically and geographically diverse group of Americans would articulate what they were fighting for, pay due regard to the role of the Allies, and battle an enemy who was formidable but not a superman."[63] The bureau also worked to tone down violence in war films, as the "OWI liked reality but not too much of it." The bureau tried to get the censor, whom it did not control, to bar from export movies that depicted the United States unflatteringly—gangster pictures, for example.

The censor, who was at first more open-minded than Hollywood progressives, seldom cooperated until mid-1943, when the OWI was shaken up and new policies were adopted. Many films were denied export licenses after this, and studios began submitting them to the Bureau of Motion Pictures for cutting in advance. From this point until the war's end the "OWI exerted an influence over an American mass medium never equaled before or since by a government agency." The result, according to its historians, was a great many weak films inspired even more than usual by hopes of gain. The memorable war pictures of the forties were, with a few exceptions, made in peacetime when controls had lapsed. Hollywood progressives were, it goes without saying, proud of their mediocre war pictures, which were meant to promote democracy, brotherhood and other worthwhile values. This was especially true of those that Communists had worked on, such as Maltz's *The Pride of the Marines* and *Destination Tokyo,* Trumbo's *Thirty Seconds Over Tokyo* and Bessie's *Objective Burma.* Whatever the defects of these movies, it was not a lack of Americanism.

To the contrary, a more serious charge laid against the war films of Hollywood Communists and progressives was that they were the opposite of subversive. Reviewing *Hollywood on Trial,* the Ten's apologia, a Trotskyist condemned their pictures for containing

> a ton of chauvinism, jingoism, hate incitement, anti-inter-nationalism and flag-waving imperialist propaganda—prop-aganda of a kind without which the Thomas Committee [HUAC] itself could not exist. If there is today a spiritual climate of intolerance, suspicion and hatred, are not these writers themselves partly responsible?[64]

Without accepting the Trotskyist view that whatever furthered American interests abroad was imperialistic, one may still take the point. War films, on which Hollywood Communists labored enthusiastically, did foster chauvinism and hatred of national enemies. One could say, then, that by encouraging patriotism the Communists had contributed unwittingly to their own later downfall. Even so, this was more a matter of symbolic irony than anything else. If there had been no Communists in Hollywood, war pictures would have been made in much the same way, because they were what was wanted.

The actual consequence of Hollywood radicalism was two-fold. As private citizens rather than moviemakers, Hollywood leftists made substantial donations of time and money to Communist-supported causes. But in the end these causes failed, so while it could be argued that such radicals tried to change things, in fact they didn't. The Screen Writers Guild and maybe the Radio Writers Guild were run by Communists for a while. A few progressives were elected to Congress who might not otherwise have gotten there. In the end leftists had little but memories to show for all the time and money invested in politics.

But Communists and their allies did permanently influence movies for the worse, according to Pauline Kael the film critic. She has argued that screenwriting never recovered from "the phony, excessive, duplicit use of patriotism by the rich, guilty liberals of Hollywood in the war years."[65] Hollywood Stalinism arose, she too believes, from feelings of self-betrayal on the part of writers who were paid well but treated badly.

> The lost-in-Hollywood generation of writers, trying to clean themselves of guilt for their wasted years and their irresponsibility as *writers*, became political in the worst way—became a special breed of anti-Fascists. The talented writers, the major ones as well as the lightweight yet entertaining ones, went down the same drain as the clods—drawn into it, often by bored wives, less successful brothers. They became naïvely, hysterically pro-Soviet; they ignored Stalin's actual policies, because they so badly needed to believe in something. They had been so smart, so gifted, and yet they hadn't been able to beat Hollywood's contempt for the writer.[66]

In Kael's view, war gave writers the illusion that they could regain self-respect through politics. The result was "calamitous to talent." In the thirties writers had told lies but didn't believe them. In the forties they did. Even comedy writers who used to laugh at cant began to write it. At conferences held by the Screen Writers Guild and the Hollywood Writers Mobilization, "responsible writers" brought the irresponsible into line. "Show-business people are both giddy and desperately, sincerely intense. When Stalinism was fashionable, movie people became

Stalinists, the way they later became witches and warlocks."
When the Cold War left them stranded, some turned coat, not
out of conviction but opportunistically, she believes.

> The shame of McCarthyism was not only the "shame of
> America" but the shame of a bunch of newly rich people
> who were eager to advise the world on moral and political
> matters and who, faced with a test, informed on their
> friends—and, as Orson Welles put it, not even to save
> their lives but to save their swimming pools.[67]

With loss of ethics went loss of talent. Films were corrupted by
Hollywood Communists, Kael suggests, and though the Communists are gone the rot lingers on. "Show-business Stalinism is
basically not political but psychological; it's a fashionable form
of hysteria and guilt that is by now not so much pro-Soviet as
just abusively anti-American."[68]

The charge is that Hollywood Stalinism was evil, and remains
so, in two ways: morally wrong because based on lies about
Soviet Communism, and aesthetically wrong because bad politics led to bad writing. Another critic has said much the same
about Popular Front music. In 1976 a new recording of Marc
Blitzstein's *The Airborne Symphony* was issued with Leonard
Bernstein conducting the New York Philharmonic and Orson
Welles narrating—the same roles they had when it premiered in
1946. Blitzstein was a favorite of the Popular Front, and his
symphony touched familiar bases, applauding Russia and the
bombing of Germany. Blitzstein served with the Army Air
Force, which commissioned his piece, but enthusiasm for strategic bombing was widespread among progressives, as also the
desire, expressed here by the chorus, to "Open up that second
front! Open up that second front! We will bomb a tyrant's
smile, and from his throat his insane Heil! . . . We will bomb
him, bomb him from the earth."[69]

Dated and banal, the symphony was typical of much art of
the period, or so says Donal Henahan.

> Along with many others of the Blitzstein generation,
> Leonard Bernstein might be cited as an example of a
> composer whose music had never lost a 40s flavor. It

vacillates between orotund platitudes and Stage Door
Canteen breeziness. Even 20-odd years later in his Mass,
a brave attempt to come to terms with another time and
esthetic, he cannot resist getting down on all fours to sing
propagandistic babytalk to his audience . . .

The "Bernstein/Blitzstein rhetoric, with its stress on readily absorbed messages" was characteristic of their entire generation of
composers. Only a few escaped, mostly by chance, argues
Henahan. "Every composer has at least one 'Airborne' or 'Battle' symphony in him, if he looks shallowly enough."[70]
Without any doubt there was a distinct progressive culture in
the forties that expressed itself in virtually every medium. It
idealized the common people, democracy, brotherhood and
Russia, while taking a bloodthirsty view of the enemy—"this
machine kills fascists," Woody Guthrie had written on his
guitar. In addition to shared themes there were shared methods.
Sentimentality was universal, followed by condescension. In John
Howard Lawson's *Action in the North Atlantic* a Liberty ship
docks in Murmansk, where among the joyful Russians is a
beautiful woman who calls out, *"Tovarich! Tovarich!"* An
American sailor thereupon tells his friend, "That means
'comrade'—that's good."[71] This was a low point in the history
of progressive culture, which even at its best was not very good.

The critics who attack progressive or Popular Front culture
for its debased aesthetics are correct. But it has to be said in
defense that progressive culture was bad in the same way and
for the same reasons as popular culture. It was actually a seg-
ment of popular culture, using, with the larger world of show
business, stereotypes, clichés, stock characters and cheap emotional appeals. As with popular culture, drama turned into
melodrama, sentiment to sentimentality. Progressive culture
differed from the mainstream in having political content, but
that only of the simplest kind. Partly this was a matter of con-
straint, but mainly, it seems, of conviction. The makers of progressive culture were often accomplished. What they suffered
from was lack of judgment and taste. And, of course, they
meant well, believing themselves to be in the forefront of worthwhile social and political change.

If Communists did not inject much propaganda into their films, and if they and their allies in show business practiced an aesthetic that was no worse than, and little different from, popular culture's as a whole, and if they promoted certain desirable values, why the old campaigns against them and the bitterness that still persists? Apart from obvious political motives, there seem to be two reasons for attacking media Stalinists. One has to do with personal experiences. It was unpleasant to be an anti-Communist in Hollywood during the war, when progressivism was at its flood and all things Soviet were admired. And while there is no evidence supporting the theory that Stalinists had their own blacklist, all things being equal Communists and progressives liked to hire each other. There was a degree of what John Cogley called backscratching, sometimes no doubt at the expense of anti-Communists—who, however, usually continued to find work, unlike the blacklistees of the fifties.

More annoying and perhaps more important were the union struggles. Communists and their allies worked and voted together in the Screen Writers Guild, and in other media unions where they were at least an irritating presence. Personal hatreds arose from these quarrels, and found expression when the witch-hunting era began. Adolphe Menjou's dislike of Communists and progressives, for example, was extraordinarily personal. He often wrote to Ralph De Toledano, an anti-Communist journalist, crying out for blood. It was terrible, he asserted, when *Newsweek* magazine ran a story on the Weavers, a folk-singing troupe, as they were all reds. He was even angrier on learning that HUAC in its 1951 round of hearings was not going after the big stars on Menjou's hate list—Gene Kelly, Burt Lancaster, Danny Kaye, Gregory Peck, John Huston—but only provable Party members. And Menjou could not understand why Edward G. Robinson was cleared. It was due to the power of Robinson's representative, the William Morris Agency, he speculated. Menjou rejoiced when HUAC went after Howard Da Silva and Gale Sondergaard. He fiercely reviled José Ferrer, who, to Menjou's regret, escaped.[72] It must have taken more than a few harsh encounters with Hollywood leftism to generate such venom.

One can understand why participants in struggles for local power might go to extremes, but this does not explain why

Hollywood Communists are still being criticized long after their downfall, and by people who had no personal stake, such as the Englishman David Caute in his *The Great Fear* (1978). One reason, not excused by their ultimate failure, is that Hollywood leftists were guilty of crimes against morality and, secondarily, against good taste. This was not the same thing as breaking a civil or criminal law, and it in no way justified the imprisonment of the Ten or the blacklist. Even so, they were Stalinists in the literal sense of defending the Stalin regime. And they were Stalinist also in their thinking.

The most famous example of this took place in 1946 when Albert Maltz wrote an article for the *New Masses,* requesting more artistic freedom on the left, that scandalized Hollywood radicals. A meeting was held at which Lawson and Trumbo and others berated Maltz for heresy, forcing him to publish a humiliating retraction. In it he apologized to his comrades, regretting that he had given the *New Leader* and other enemies "fresh proof of the old lie that the Left puts artists in uniform."[73] Maltz confessed to being guilty of a "one-sided, non-dialectical approach" and of having "severed the organic connection between art and ideology." And he was guilty, too, of praising the work of James T. Farrell, an anti-Stalinist hated by the faithful. Maltz should have said, he now realized, that Farrell was an example of how "a poisoned ideology and increasingly sick soul can sap the talent and wreck the living fibre of man's work." Further, Maltz pleaded guilty to the charge of revisionism, explaining helpfully that this was "distorted Marxism, turning half-truths into total untruths, splitting ideology from its class base, denying the existence of class struggles in society, converting Marxism from a science of society and struggle into apologetics for monopoly capitalism."[74] Maltz agreed completely with Samuel Sillen, who had attacked him in the *Daily Worker* on this point.

Here was Stalinism in action, not the real Stalinism of the blackjack and the labor camp, but the ersatz cultural Stalinism of America. It was the substitution of jargon for thought, the transformation of a modest appeal for freedom into "apologetics for monopoly capitalism," the mindless embrace of alien doctrine and, to a small degree, practice. It was this, together with the defense of all Russian acts, that made Hollywood Communists and their allies baneful, and the Ten ridiculous when they portrayed themselves before HUAC as champions of Americanism and free speech. Stalinism was the initial corruption, and it led in turn to others.

It was Stalinism that inspired HUAC to subpoena the Ten, and it was as Stalinists that they refused to testify. It was because of Stalinism that the blacklist was created, and it was Stalinism, or flirtations with it, that made possible all the hearings and investigations that followed. This does not excuse HUAC, or California's own little HUAC, the committee of State Senator Jack B. Tenney, or vindictive individuals who promoted the blacklist.[75] It was un-American, as victims always said, for legislators to conduct punitive investigations of what were perfectly lawful activities, however odious, and to deny people employment because of them. But the one gave rise to the other, corrupt causes leading to corrupt effects. Former Stalinists often pointed out that they had injured no one to the extent they themselves were injured, which was often true. The most damaging thing they did was to recruit naïve persons into activities and associations that turned out to be, though few suspected it at the time, extremely dangerous. The human and constitutional costs of blacklisting were far greater than what they were directed against. Stalinism was an evil all the same, and the occasion for what followed.

Failure to see this is still troublesome. Later experience, and the full disclosure of Stalin's infamy, made participants eager to minimize their political pasts. Hence Trumbo's likening of Communist Party meetings to boring religious events, hence also the astonishing loss of memory that befell so many witnesses. Remarkable also was the ignorance they claimed to have had of the Communist presence in Hollywood. Never, one gathers from testimony before HUAC and from letters and depositions given to studio heads, had so many been so active politically with so little knowledge of what was going on.[76] There was certainly a degree of unawareness. The actor Charles Laughton was close to Hanns Eisler, yet on being told that Eisler had Communist sympathies he exclaimed, "But that's ridiculous: his music is just like Mozart."[77] On the other hand, it is difficult to believe Edward G. Robinson, who was more active in left-wing causes than any other star, when he defended his invincible ignorance before HUAC.

> The revelations that persons whom [sic] I thought were sincere liberals were, in fact, Communists, has shocked me more than I can tell you. That they persuaded me by lies and concealment of their real purposes to them to use my name for what I believed to be a worthy cause is now obvious. . . . Not one of the Communists who sought my help or requested permission to use my name ever told me that he or she was a member of the Communist Party.[78]

Charity might lead one to accept that Robinson could not tell a Communist when he saw one. A member of HUAC said to Robinson that they never thought of him as anything but a sucker. And many witnesses, including anti-Communists, told stories of how they had been misled into sponsoring events that seemed innocent and yet were not. Still, at a time when so many film people, including many of the most political, belonged to the Communist Party in varying degrees of openness, it is unlikely that intelligent people could have no sense of this. Perhaps some were blind and deaf, but the eagerness later of Hollywood progressives to be seen as foolish innocents aroused suspicion. This was an important reason why HUAC made them name each other. It was the surest way of pinning down evasive witnesses, of identifying their present politics as well as their elusive past.

The committee hearings established a crucial difference between movie Stalinists and the much larger crowd of hangers-on. Stalinists took their politics seriously, worked hard at it, and never doubted that it was important. Progressives tended to be dilettantes, party-goers rather than Party members, thoughtless, moved by tides of fashion and friendship. Most seemed surprised to learn that flirting with Communism entailed risk. The punishment dealt to Stalinists was, if un-American, not entirely undeserved, a compliment of a sort to their sense of duty. Progressives were not really entitled to such attention, having done little to merit it. The storm that broke over them was out of proportion, falling as it did upon progressive lambs as well as Stalinist lions. Not all suffered equally. Whereas most Stalinists were expelled from movies, progressives stood a good chance of surviving, though only after much aggravation and humiliating scenes of penitence and denial. This resembled justice. For lesser offenders there was a lesser punishment.

The story of media radicalism combines elements of both tragedy and farce. But it is not a morality play, as often held to be, or at least not as usually construed.[79] That they were penalized unfairly does not absolve show-business Stalinists of political sin. Nor does the failure of their politics make them less bad. Media Stalinists, like other Party members, had put the interests of Russia ahead of their own country's, and had defended or rationalized policies that caused the death of millions and the loss of liberty to many more. And those who cooperated with them overlooked this or held that it didn't matter. The conventional judgment on blacklisting is that it ought to be remembered so as to prevent such a thing from happening again. But the causes of blacklisting should not be forgotten either, and for the same reason.

IX

China:
Progressive Paradox

IN MARCH 1950 Senator Joseph McCarthy accused Owen Latti-more, foremost American authority on Soviet Asia, of being also Russia's top secret agent in the United States. News of this took time to reach Lattimore, who was then in Afghani-stan, but on hearing of it he returned immediately to defend himself. Thus began a sorry chapter in recent American history, the effort to destroy all those held responsible by conservative anti-Communists for the fall of China. There was heavy irony in this, for the progressive role in Chinese-American relations was different from that pursued on behalf of Russia. Progressives, sometimes even the same ones, who were mistaken about the Soviets viewed events in China rightly. But, far from benefiting them, it only compounded their original sin of having been wrong about Russia.

Progressives used much the same language in describing both Europe and Asia, so it might be argued that they got things right in China only by accident. This was true of some, notably the editors of progressive magazines whose lavish generaliza-tions about the common man could not always be in vain. There had to be at least one country where the people's war led di-rectly to a popular revolution. Another reason was that pro-gressives did not have the same emotional investment in China as in Russia and therefore saw it more clearly. Further, the Chinese revolutionary tradition was divided. The Nationalist forces led by Chiang Kai-shek were seen as having a claim on it equal to the Communists'. Progressive thought on China was not partisan from the start, but evolutionary and tied to specific developments. At first progressives supported Franklin Roosevelt's policy of building up Nationalist China and treating it as a great power, despite its modest contribution to the war effort. Progressives did come to see that China was doing little to defeat Japan, but believed even so that it could do more if the differences between Chiang's Kuomintang party (KMT) and the Communists were resolved. This too was Administration policy. Estimates were that half a million of Chiang's best troops were deployed against the Communist Eighth Route Army in north China. This did not leave either side with much to throw against Japan.

Progressives disagreed over who was most at fault. *The Atlantic*'s excellent feature "The Pacific War" blamed the Communists initially, asserting that they "had done almost as much as the Japanese to weaken China."[1] The progressive weeklies thought otherwise. They were increasingly critical of the KMT, some of whose leaders were practically fascists, according to the *New Republic*.[2] But they still saw Chiang as the only truly national leader and the key to China's future. Thus when Chiang announced that there would be constitutional government in China within a year of Japan's defeat the *New Republic* cheered. It asked that no one cast doubt upon the sincerity of "Chiang Kai-shek and his party. This is a time not only for great deeds in China but also for great faith in China."[3] *The Nation,* though its views were much the same otherwise, did not agree. Chiang's speech left things exactly as they were. What China needed to break the stalemate was enough military aid to resume fighting. "Once the whole of China is again united in active warfare, many of its most perplexing problems will disappear. Unity will be forged by a common effort that cannot fail to give the Chinese people a new sense of their powers as well as of their essential democratic rights."[4] As always with China, progressives would be disappointed.

While the war lasted, both magazines toyed with the fiction that the Red Chinese were not actually Communists. In an editorial *The Nation* said that it was wrong to think of them as "Marxian proletarians. They are essentially agrarian radicals whose domestic policies are characterized chiefly by attempts to introduce democratic practices and a program of land reform."[5] Stewart Maxwell, *The Nation*'s staff authority on China, echoed this. In 1943 he took note of a controversy aroused by T. A.

Bisson, who, writing in *Far Eastern Survey,* a publication of the Institute for Pacific Relations, had suggested that the two parts of China instead of being called Nationalist and Communist should be referred to as "feudal China" and "democratic China." Stewart concurred, explaining that, as the only opposition to KMT tyranny, the CP had "attracted a large measure of support from democratic progressive groups, who have little interest in Marxian dogma." This was also a result of the Communists being, in the words of liberal news commentator Raymond Gram Swing, "agrarian radicals trying to establish democratic practices."[6]

The *New Republic* went further still. In 1944 Heinz Eulau, a propagandist for European Communism, turned his attention to China. It was clear to Eulau that Chiang opposed democracy because the practice of it would destroy him. He had avoided total mobilization for war because the outcome would be "irresistible demands for a popular government by the fundamentally democratic Chinese people, which must be avoided at any price."[7] Being democratic, the Chinese masses naturally favored Communism. "Communist China is the closest approach to social and economic, as well as political, democracy that China has ever known." The CP had abandoned socialism and collectivism. It stood now for "agrarian reform, good government, and democratic institutions." In its zone all political parties except the KMT were allowed to run candidates for office. "There is freedom of assembly and freedom of speech." The Communists wanted to extend these blessings to all China, and would do so were it not for Chiang. "China is truly at the crossroads of democracy through civil war or democracy through peaceful constitutional reform."[8] Eulau wanted to show that the CP was not Marxist but populist, seeking only to obtain scientific agriculture and the secret ballot for Chinese sodbusters. Thus it made little sense to call the party Communist. Richard Watts thought so, too. "Since it happens that their current aims and tendencies are in the direction of agrarian democracy rather than collectivization," why don't the Communists change their name to something Americans find less threatening? he asked.[9]

Though useful later to the China Lobby, such Communist-inspired foolishness was not typical of progressive thought. In a general way progressive magazines went from enthusiasm for Chiang to believing that the Communists represented a better, if not ideal, solution to China's worst problems, and were destined to win anyway. Representing Communists as democratic reformers was a phase in this progression, and a short-lived one, ending at the latest in 1946. The change began in 1944, when a Japanese offensive threw the Nationalist armies into desperate retreat. Even *The Atlantic* began to lose faith in Chiang Kai-shek after this. In a long, gloomy survey it embraced the opinion that power in the KMT had fallen into the hands of its most reactionary elements.[10] *The Atlantic* now felt that Chiang was saving his troops for use against the Communists, with whom it was starting to sympathize.[11]

In 1944 also the Nationalists gave in to Roosevelt's pressure and permitted a handful of Americans to enter Communist north China for the first time. They were impressed by the good organization and morale of the Red Army, and the relative prosperity of the region, all in contrast to the wretchedness of Nationalist China.[12] Though dispatches were censored, this became known eventually, to the considerable benefit of Communist China's reputation. While Richard Watts was prejudiced in their favor, he probably spoke the truth when he wrote early in 1945 that most Western reporters

> are convinced that the Communists really are fighting the Japs, that they represent a fresh, constructive and progressive force which has the popular support of the people, that they have brought progressive and forward-looking government to the districts which they control, that they are sincerely interested in a unified, democratic China and that they are by no means tools in the hands of Moscow.[13]

Watts was responding to Lin Yutang, who had just published a book, *The Vigil of a Nation* (1945), attacking Chinese Communism. Edgar Snow took the same line, writing in *The Nation* that he was sorry to have to offend a person he had long known and admired. But Lin was wrong in thus libeling a party that had created a government "more nearly democratic than any China has yet known."[14] Lin Yutang responded sharply. "I was fully aware of the sanctity of America's sacred cow, the

Chinese Communists, and I knew that to suggest that the sacred cow was in fact a red bull in a china shop would arouse the ire of the cow-worshippers."[15] He repeated his view that Chinese Communists were totalitarian like the Soviets, and were using the war to set up their own state and army. By employing CP publications he showed that the Communists had followed Stalin in foreign affairs religiously and that their idea of good government did not include civil liberties, which was chiefly why Lin opposed them. In answer Snow admitted that the Communists meant to establish socialism in China, that they had used the war to their own advantage—as the KMT had also— and that they followed the Kremlin lead in foreign affairs. Just the same, they were working out on their own a system adapted to Chinese needs. Lin's "anxiety and fears on this subject are somewhat neurotic," and unworthy of so distinguished a philosopher.[16]

It was a measure of China's complexity that both were right so far as they went. Chinese Communism was different from that of Russia. For various reasons—the long years of insurgency and isolation, the necessity of winning over a largely rural population—a better way had been found in China. The approximately fifty million people in Red China as of 1945 enjoyed not only more prosperity than those in Nationalist China, but more efficient, juster and even more humane government as well. Most journalists who knew both the old China and the new were favorably impressed by Communist rule. And those few who were able to compare Russian Communism with Chinese Communism mostly preferred the latter.

Lin Yutang did not know Red China at first hand, and so his attacks on it were to a degree unwarranted. But he had studied Communist literature and took it seriously. By their own admission the Communists were then tolerating things—private ownership of property, non-Communist political groups—which they believed to be incompatible with Marxist socialism. Sympathizers played down Communist ideology, pointing out the extent to which actual practice differed from it. Lin Yutang went the other way, arguing that in the long run ideology was a better guide than temporary compromises. When all China was Communist the government would be as despotic as Russia's, he believed. In this Lin was on the mark. Where he erred was in supposing that the KMT offered a real alternative. Lin was not blind to its faults, but held that there was a future for National-ist China even so. His delusion was shared by many Americans, especially in Washington, until it was too late.

At the time of this exchange Edgar Snow's influence was great. He was an editor of *The Saturday Evening Post* and still admired for his classic *Red Star Over China* (1938). Snow had been the first to explain Chinese Communism to Ameri-cans, and was as busy as ever justifying Mao's ways to man in articles and book reviews for *The New York Times* and pro-gressive magazines. He had private meetings with Franklin Roosevelt, being one of those whose brains Roosevelt liked to pick. Snow believed that the President agreed with him and would have cooperated with Red China had he lived. This means nothing. FDR gave practically everyone he talked to the impression of support, which explains why so many who knew him were certain that if he had not died the policies they be-lieved in would have flourished.

Snow had become a China hand by accident. As a young man he embarked on a trip around the world. In 1928, at the age of twenty-two, he found himself in Shanghai working for the *China Weekly Review*. Within a year it sent him to the northwest, where a famine was raging, as happened too frequently in old China. The human condition there was poor enough under the best of circumstances. When famine struck, conditions became appalling. Nothing he saw in all his travels, except the Nazi death camps, disturbed Snow more than what he witnessed in the starving northwest. That experience made him ready to sup-port any political movement that could feed the Chinese people. It appeared to him that the KMT had failed in this while the Communists, whose territory he entered in 1936, were suc-ceeding.

He was impressed by Mao and Chou En-lai not only for creating effective government, but for having vision. They had predicted the future accurately when he visited them, saying there would be war with Japan, leading to a popular front with the KMT, the defeat of Japan, civil war, and their own inevita-ble victory. Snow, an ex-Catholic, also had spiritual needs to which Communism appealed. Writing of himself years later, Snow said that the "yearning to believe in an external and personal savior, once inculcated in the child, rather than to accept personal responsibility, with its agony mixed with its satisfaction, is not easily put aside."[17] Snow believed he had done so, but his support of Red China all the time and under all circumstances makes this seem unlikely. In the event, once convinced' that Communism offered a way of ending the misery he had seen in China, Snow never looked back. His books and articles on China were widely read because intelligently done and comparatively honest. And China experts, for the same reason, valued him highly. As one writer put it, "never has a fellow-travelling reporter been taken more seriously in academic circles, or deserved to be."[18]

Owen Lattimore had much the same views as Snow, who praised his book *Solution in Asia* (1945) extravagantly.[19] Lattimore, though not read by as many people, had an equal or greater authority owing to his numerous writings on Asia, his credentials as a staff member of the respected Institute of Pacific Affairs, and as a faculty member and administrator at The Johns Hopkins University. Communists were the most progressive elements in China, he argued during the war, and the most willing to cooperate with liberalism at home and abroad. They were aware of the political energy of the common people of China "and are convinced that it seeks an outlet in democratic activity, and that they are accommodating themselves to this existing and strong demand instead of trying to force on the people theories, ideas, and forms of organization which they do not want."[20] Russia was following a similar course in Asia, he thought, aligning itself with the best movements. He warned that if the United States did not change course "we shall find ourselves in the front rank of imperialism, saluting Colonel Blimp, while the Russians take command of the ranks of moderate, orderly progressive liberalism."[21]

Progressives agreed that while Russia naturally favored the Communists in China, it had not done much for them. During the war with Japan Russia supplied aid to the KMT, but little, if any, to the Communists. By the end of the war it was neutral, halting aid to the KMT but not supporting the CP either.[22] When fighting broke out between them, Russia seemed to undercut the Communists by keeping its armies in Manchuria and demanding special privileges in north China, which baffled progressives.[23] Progressives differed over what part Russia ought to play in China. Some felt that the future of China was for the Chinese to decide. In contrast *The Atlantic* hoped, as late as October 1946, that a great-power settlement might be imposed.[24] They all believed that American aid to Chiang was mistaken and should be ended.

Theodore White was one of many who wanted the United States to keep its hands off China.[25] White was uniquely qualified to give advice. He had majored in Chinese studies at Harvard and was, it appears, the only American journalist in China with academic qualifications. In 1939, his second year there, he joined Time-Life. White, like most reporters, became disgusted with the KMT. But his dispatches had no effect at home because Henry Luce, who had been raised in China, was devoted to Chiang and would allow nothing in his magazines harmful to the Nationalist regime. In 1944 Luce made the anti-Communist Whittaker Chambers foreign editor of *Time* as insurance.

Worsening conditions led John Fairbank, his mentor at Harvard, to send White a letter saying that all his old friends were ashamed of him for not telling the whole truth. White, who was prevented from doing so by Luce and Chambers, resigned from Time-Life with his colleague Annalee Jacoby. They then published *Thunder Out of China* (1946). It was a brilliant indictment of Nationalist failure and mendacity that reached an enormous audience through a Book-of-the-Month Club edition of 400,000 copies, the third-largest sale in BOMC history to that date. It was widely praised by reviewers, including Fairbank, who in *The New York Times* called it a "vivid, bitter, honest book."[26] As might be guessed, it had no effect on Luce. *Time* went on predicting a Nationalist victory until the inevitable defeat.[27]

By the end of 1946 most progressives had given up hope that a coalition government could be formed in China. Most also had shed the illusion that Chinese Communists were only reformers. References to Chinese democracy were now made chiefly by fellow travelers such as Agnes Smedley, who persisted in calling Mao's forces the "democratic movement."[28] The *New Republic* and *The Atlantic* were notably clear about events. In 1946 the latter published a superb analysis by Fairbank, who outlined the cruel facts. Kuomintang China was corrupt and hopeless and sure to fail. The Communists, though authoritarian and undemocratic, had the great advantage of giving the Chinese people what they wanted, land reform in particular. This was a key point stressed over and over by nearly all who wrote about China. The KMT was the party of the landlords, the CP of the peasants. These were won over not by promises to form communes, as later actually happened, but by the giving of land to those who worked it. This had an enormous attraction to China's peasants, as earlier to Russia's. Fairbank pointed out also why the objections raised against Chinese Communism were false or irrelevant. The Red Chinese were not puppets of Moscow. The fear that Communists would erect a police state was beside the point, since the KMT had already done so. If the United States persisted in trying to stop revolutions there, Americans would find themselves expelled from Asia.[29]

This was the *New Republic*'s view also. The next year it worried, and with good reason, that John Carter Vincent and those who served under him in the State Department's Office of Far Eastern Affairs would be attacked for telling Washington truths it did not want to hear. The Communists were winning not because they were more brutal than the KMT, which they weren't, but because, in return for the sacrifices they demanded, the Communists "give control of the land to the people who till it."[30] America's support of Chiang Kai-shek would only drive Chinese Communists more deeply into the Russian camp. The *New Republic* urged a complete withdrawal from China, admitting this was a gamble but one that had to be taken. Later it ran a piece describing in detail Communist rule on the village level. A *New York Post* correspondent told of how land was distributed to the peasantry and honest government established. It was repressive, but less so than the KMT. There was no democracy, though peasants were active in meetings and could express opinions. Resentment against American support of the KMT was growing.[31]

By 1948 progressives were coming to fear that the Communist government would be more Stalinist than they had earlier expected. A *New Republic* article said flatly that China would be run in much the same way as Eastern Europe.[32] *The Nation* also was afraid that owing to bad American policies "the democratic elements in China have been reduced to impotence and the field left to the cohorts of Moscow."[33] A few thought it was not too late for America to salvage something. *The Atlantic* suggested cutting back aid to the Nationalists for failing to make reforms. Lack of outside support might force changes, or enable a more reformist group to seize control. The United States would then be able to back a popular movement instead of Chiang's "disintegrating dictatorship."[34]

Fairbank went beyond this. Progressives had not called for aid to the Communists, a notion repellent to both the American government and public opinion. Fairbank now raised the question. He said again that America had failed to distinguish between the Chinese Communist movement and the Chinese social revolution. It viewed China in terms of Europe, stressing the genuinely Communist nature of the CP's ideology and practice. But Americans in China were impressed by the authenticity of the new social movement and the high morale and idealism of Communists. The CP's great achievement had been not to create the social revolution—meaning especially the breakup of the family system and politicalization of the peasantry—but to gain control of it. Fairbank wanted America to support this revolution, at the risk of running parallel to, or even "getting into bed" with, Chinese Communism. It might turn out to be as bad as in Europe, Fairbank conceded. Yet unlike the Eastern European parties Chinese Communism was indigenous and not something imposed by Moscow. The United States had to take this into account and look beyond ideology.[35] Domestic politics made it impossible to take such a sensible course. The Administration was already accused of being too soft on Communism, the Truman Doctrine and support of despotic regimes notwithstanding. American policy would fail precisely because it was attuned not to Chinese but to American realities.

An *Atlantic* report commented on the self-defeating character of American relations with China in 1949. The Nationalist forces were collapsing as whole divisions went over to the Communists. The China Lobby, not an organization but a coalition of pressure groups and individuals who supported Chiang Kai-shek, had repeatedly assailed Truman for not sending enough arms to Nationalist China. But defeat showed that "what was lacking was not aid, but the ability to use the aid."[36]

In fact it contributed to Chiang's defeat. He was not an absolute dictator but relied on allies who were "at times undependable and at times downright tricky." Every fresh grant showed that the worse the KMT did, the more it would get. Unconditional aid "increased the power over him of those of his followers who were most intransigent and at the same time most incompetent and corrupt."[37] Thus America pushed Chiang further along the road to ruin. In consequence, *The Atlantic* mistakenly believed, the position of career diplomats who warned against such a policy had been strengthened. It was a logical supposition but did not take into account the need for scapegoats. If any group "lost" China, it was the China Lobby with its constant pressure for unqualified assistance to Chiang. Supporters of Nationalist China did not see this. They blamed Washington for failing to back Chiang totally. It was the fault of Communist sympathizers, they insisted, particularly the Foreign Service officers who had been in China. These diplomats were to be held responsible for the failure of a course they had repeatedly warned against.[38]

The assault on all who had criticized the KMT surprised most progressives. Though unable to stop the United States from going down with Chiang, they hoped something might be learned from the affair and a better Asian policy devised. Issuance of the famous State Department white paper on China in 1949 did not change their minds. It was a richly documented thousand-page effort to free the Truman Administration from blame. "As an apologia for American policy it is unconvincing," *The Nation* said, giving the common view of progressives.[39] In his letter of transmittal Secretary of State Acheson had written that Nationalist China fell on account of its reactionary and incompetent leadership, but that, on the other hand, the Chinese Communists were Russian stooges. The one point seemed at war with the other to *The Nation*. All the same, it found in the report evidence supporting its own opinion, that the KMT could have been kept in power only by American military intervention, which was politically impossible. Instead the United States had provided conditional aid that only hastened the inevitable. If Truman had pressed instead for a coalition government, the Communists would still have won out in the end, but more slowly and with less violence. Under such circumstances America might have retained influence in China.

The white paper's logical conclusion, as drawn by *The Nation,* was that America should accept the Communist takeover and try to offset Soviet pressure on China. Dean Acheson thought otherwise, saying that China was now being exploited by Soviet imperialism but would someday "throw off the foreign yoke." The United States should encourage everything tending toward that end. What did this mean? asked *The Nation;* backing warlords, supporting attacks on the mainland from bases in Formosa? These would only delay the creation of a sane China policy. John Fairbank agreed. The white paper was a record of wishful thinking and unrealism. Chiang had been given two billion dollars in aid even though Foreign Service officers were reporting as early as 1943 that the Communists were providing better government and more effective resistance to Japan. They had also predicted there would be a civil war if the KMT did not reform, which the Communists would win. American help only encouraged Nationalist reactionaries and hastened their end. We killed the Kuomintang with kindness, Fairbank said.[40]

Though conceding too much by progressive standards, the white paper failed to calm emotions even so. Instead it provoked fresh outbursts against the government. Acheson's critics charged that the State Department, having failed because of a weak policy in China, was retreating to a feebler one. They meant to establish that State and the President, obsessed with Europe, had let China down. The white paper itself was evidence, said Owen Lattimore,

> of the increasing ruthlessness of political warfare within the United States. To cover what was being made to look like a moral soft spot on the domestic front in American politics, it sets out to show that in the high strategy of politics in Asia the Administration was as relentlessly anti-Russia as the most fire-eating Republican, and that in pursuit of impeccably anti-Russian aims the United States had engaged in as much intervention as the traffic could possibly bear. It is one of the most astonishing documents in diplomatic history.[41]

Progressives wanted the United States to recognize Red China, allow its admission to the UN, and stop supplying the

Nationalists on Formosa. It was past time, the *New Republic* believed, for America to develop a China policy based on American interests rather than domestic political needs.[42] Yet the editors appreciated Truman's problem, for the China Lobby was in full cry. The *New Republic* agreed with Walter Lippmann, who had said that the lobby was trying "to force our country into an undeclared war, waged without allies, without objects and without hope of a decision."[43] Progressives were grateful that Truman was resisting the most extreme demands of Herbert Hoover and other "warmongers," as Harold Ickes called them.[44]

For a while it seemed that good sense might prevail. Dean Acheson gave an important talk to the Washington Press Club in January 1950 that the *New Republic* believed put an end to the misguided Truman Doctrine. Acheson rejected military intervention against Communist China as a "silly adventure." The United States was not going to war in Asia. He told the press club that Asia was in revolt and that the United States could not alter the course of history there. The Communists had not created this revolution, even in China. And Acheson did not think the Soviets would profit greatly from it, since, as an imperialist nation, Russia must come into conflict with the rising tide of Asian nationalism.

> The heart of Acheson's new policy in Asia is its refusal to intervene, its insistence on tolerance, its encouragement of dissent. Its natural result will be to create a Third Force in Asia, of nations not democratic and not dictatorial, not bound to the West and not satellites of Russia. Then, if Russia continues to press outwards while the West refuses to exert pressure, these nations will move to the side of the democracies. The policy succeeds or fails according to the patience and tolerance of the American people.[45]

The Atlantic's Washington report, though also encouraged by Acheson's speech, was less utopian. China and Russia might very well fall out, having different interests. American intervention could only delay such a break. There was nothing the Russians would like more than to see the United States become bogged down in China. American involvement in China had been a mistaken response to Republican pressure on the Truman Administration. Now it was trying to back off and regain the initiative in shaping a new Asian policy.[46] *The Atlantic*'s China report took a gloomier view. Russia and China were in a very strong position. Their recognition of Ho Chi Minh was evidence of the grim possibilities that lay ahead. By supporting Bao Dai the United States had made another big mistake. There was no evidence suggesting that the Russians and the Chinese were bound to break up, after which China would go Titoist. American policy in Asia, based for so long on wishful thinking, still appeared to be.[47]

War in Korea and McCarthyism, itself partly a result of the war, would make it impossible to have a sane Asian policy. Max Lerner had warned even before Korea that fear of McCarthy was making American diplomacy too negative and inelastic.[48] Yet until China intervened progressives did not entirely give up hope. On the eve of Chinese entry into the war John Fairbank issued a final plea. He said again that no amount of aid could have saved Chiang Kai-shek, as the white paper made evident. The Communists had gained power by establishing "greater moral prestige than the Kuomintang" and had worked hard to keep it. Mao's prestige, even among non-Communists, arose not only from success but from what the Chinese saw as his "sincerity" and "purity of intent." This was consistent with the Chinese tradition of ideal government as being founded not on the rule of law but on "the rule of men and virtue." Failure to recognize this was a major reason for America's weakened position. The first step in repairing it must be to recognize the error and appeal to "Chinese moral sentiment." The United States must further distinguish between the Communist reform program and

> the Chinese Communist integration in the Russian system of imperialism, which menaces both world peace and the welfare of the Chinese people. We must abandon any hope of engineering a Chinese Titoism by some tactic of wooing or bargaining; yet we must never forget that China and Russia are two different countries with different ways of life and different group interests, which may not be forever controllable by Stalinist dogma. [49]

Fairbank called for a policy of balance, of, on the one hand, continuing to battle in Korea, "even if China is maneuvered into fighting us there," but also of allowing China into the UN and doing everything possible to avoid giving unnecessary offense to it. The United States ought neither to support Chiang nor appease Mao, steering instead a middle course. He warned that "there is no hope of friendly relations with the Chinese people until we take ourselves out of their purely domestic politics, take China out of American party politics, and concentrate upon the paramount menace of the Russian totalitarian imperialism which we both face."[50]

Alas for the rule of reason, this was not to be. Once China entered the Korean War all prospects of basing American dealings with it upon the national interest disappeared. In the next two decades Washington would keep making the same mistakes as before, aiding Chiang Kai-shek—and all the little Chiangs too, Syngman Rhee in Korea, a string of losers in Indochina, where, *The Atlantic* cautioned prophetically, "we may yet realize that it is easier to get into a situation than to get out of it."[51] For the United States in Asia nothing would succeed like failure. Each disaster would lead not to new policies but to reaffirmations of the old. Ouster from China would lead to stalemate in Korea and then to defeat in Southeast Asia. Not until President Nixon went to Peking was the chain broken. This was ironic, too, for Nixon used to belong to the China Lobby and had feared the Yellow Peril as much as anyone.

For predicting the outcome of American blunders, the Asian experts, like the Foreign Service officers, would have to pay. Owen Lattimore became the chief scapegoat. Though born in America, Lattimore spent his childhood in China and, after attending schools in the West, returned to it in 1919. He became a journalist and then explored Central Asia, winning an award for his efforts from the Royal Geographical Society. In 1928–29 he studied anthropology at Harvard, but did not earn a university degree then or ever. After further experience in Asia he was made editor of *Pacific Affairs* from 1934 to 1941, and director of the Page School of International Relations from 1938 until 1950. He also served as a political adviser to Chiang Kai-shek in 1941–42, was director of Pacific operations for the

Office of War Information in 1943, and accompanied Vice-President Wallace to Siberia and China in 1944. The next year Lattimore was a consultant to the American Reparations Mission in Japan. He was in Afghanistan with a UN technical-aid mission in 1950 when Senator McCarthy accused him of treason. At that time Lattimore had written ten books and more than a hundred articles, receiving for them numerous honors.

McCarthy had called Lattimore the foremost Soviet agent in America and the architect of America's China policy, saying also that his own case against the State Department, which he had accused of employing a large if constantly changing number of Communists, would stand or fall on Lattimore. It appears that McCarthy singled out Lattimore, rather than Edgar Snow or John Fairbank or some other progressive authority on China, because his government service was the most extensive. He was a poor choice all the same. Lattimore had been publishing at a furious rate for twenty years, and his opinions were literally an open book. Further, he was intensely combative and relished the chance to expose McCarthy's fraudulent charges. Lattimore rushed back to testify before the Senate subcommittee, chaired by Tydings of Maryland, that was holding hearings on McCarthy's accusations.

In his testimony, as earlier at a press conference, Lattimore denied being, or having ever been, a Communist. He had little difficulty in disposing of the specific allegations against him. His official relations with the State Department were not extensive. He had been paid by it for three or four months in 1945 while serving on the Reparations Mission. He had given a lecture to the State Department on Japanese problems in 1946 and participated in a two-day seminar on China in 1949. The best evidence of his failure to mold policy was that Washington had not embraced his proposals, much to Lattimore's regret. "I have been convinced, and many people have agreed with me, that if only the State Department had in fact adopted some of my ideas, and adopted them earlier enough, China would not today be in the hands of Communists, and the structure of American policy and American interests all over Asia would not be in such a mess," he told the subcommittee.[52] Lattimore called his book *Solution in Asia* "a crowded catalogue of unaccepted recommendations."[53]

Lattimore testified for five hours and believed that he had not only defended himself successfully but given a good critique of America's mistakes in Asia. The McCarthy forces tried to undercut Lattimore's testimony by bringing witnesses against him. Louis Budenz, an ex-Communist and frequent witness at such hearings, said he had once been told that Lattimore was either a Party member or under Party discipline. Freda Utley testified differently, saying that Lattimore had been more valuable to Russia as a propagandist than as a spy and would not have been wasted in the lesser role. Lattimore's attorneys, who included Abe Fortas, a future Associate Justice of the Supreme Court, had obtained statements refuting Budenz. Bella Dodd, another ex-Communist, who had served with Budenz on the Party's National Council, swore that she had never heard Lattimore identified as a member or follower of the Party. Frederick Vanderbilt Field, who probably still was a Communist, and who had been associated with Lattimore for many years through the Institute of Pacific Relations, seconded Dodd. Republican members of the subcommittee blocked the reading of Dodd's affidavit, which was given out by Lattimore's attorneys anyway.

Both sides were fighting in the press as well as in the committee room, for in the end public opinion would be the real judge and jury. Budenz's testimony was very effective, even though he did not know Lattimore, was unfamiliar with Lattimore's writings and was in the habit of making promiscuous allegations that could not usually be substantiated. He had great credibility all the same, owing to public naïveté and hysteria. Utley, who had known Lattimore well at one time, did him little harm. Under questioning she had not been able to come up with a single example of Lattimore's published work that followed the Communist line. And she did not inspire confidence when she offered as an instance of Lattimore's furthering of Communism his habit of quoting from people such as Wendell Willkie, the Republican candidate for President in 1940.

Time magazine wrote that "McCarthy had promised to stand or fall on his case against Owen Lattimore, and he clearly had little left to stand on."[54] *The Nation*'s reporter thought that Lattimore had won and speculated that it might be a turning point in the fight against McCarthy.[55] But McCarthy had retracted his earlier charge and was now only claiming that Lattimore's views "paralleled" those of the Cominform. In any case, demagogues were not slain so easily, as Lattimore himself remarked. In his rendering of the affair, *Ordeal by Slander* (1950), completed only four weeks after the hearings ended, Lattimore said that McCarthy was not the artless bully the press made him out to be. He was a master of timing, having launched his attack when Lattimore was out of the country and unable to reply. His methods were impossible to counter fully. One speech of his to the Senate contained ninety-six lies and errors of fact, according to Lattimore, so many that they could not be refuted or even run down in the time available. McCarthy's use of guilt by association was difficult to handle also. And often, after Lattimore and his lawyers had gone to much trouble to refute a charge the newspapers would not print their story. McCarthy's charges were more newsworthy than responses to them and invariably got more space. Lattimore was right. His case, even though a technical defeat for McCarthy, was the beginning and not the end of a demogogic career that had four more years to run.

Nor were Lattimore's own troubles over, as he thought when writing *Ordeal by Slander*. Many senators did not accept the Tydings Committee's report, which exonerated the State Department and Lattimore too. The next year, with tempers running higher because of the Korean War, another Senate subcommittee, headed by McCarran of Nevada, launched an investigation of the Institute of Pacific Relations. It was believed by right-wingers to have organized the conspiracy that defeated Chiang Kai-shek. Unlike the Tydings Committee, which meant to refute McCarthy's charge that Communists or their sympathizers in and out of the State Department had lost China, the McCarran Committee aimed to prove it. The hearings dragged on for a year, Lattimore alone being grilled for twelve days. The McCarran report did not claim that the IPR was a red front, but said that it was controlled by individuals who were Communists or favorable to Communism. Lattimore was named as one who helped change American policy in a direction more helpful to Chinese Communism.[56]

Because he had denied being a Communist or a sympathizer Lattimore was indicted by a federal grand jury on December 16, 1952, on seven counts of perjury. The following May a U.S.

district court dismissed four of the counts, including the principal one that Lattimore had lied about being a Communist sympathizer, as vague and therefore violations of Lattimore's right to be informed of the exact charges against him. This dismissal of the key count was sustained on appeal. The Justice Department, in a remarkable display of vindictiveness, then obtained another indictment against Lattimore for having been a "follower of the Communist line" and a "promoter of Communist interests." These too were dismissed by the district court, which was sustained again by the Court of Appeals in June 1955. At this point the Justice Department gave up. But while it failed to imprison Lattimore, his career was blighted, as would have been the health and sanity of anyone less resilient. He had resigned his directorship of the Page School and gone abroad even before the case against him collapsed.[57] Subsequently he fell into obscurity as a professor of Chinese studies at Leeds University in England. The campaign of legal harassment, and ferocious and unceasing attacks on him by the China Lobby, had done their work.

This was not enough for Freda Utley. After the government lost its final appeal Utley wrote an article saying that not only had Lattimore gotten off the hook, but on account of the Eisenhower Administration's cowardly failure to invade China, or to enable Chiang to do so, he was somehow still in power, "able to exert as strong an indirect influence over United States policy as he used to enjoy when he was an advisor of the State Department."[58] This was nonsense, further evidence if it were needed of how divorced from reality the China Lobby was. By her own admission Utley and the Lattimores used to be friends. But when she learned that Lattimore had defended Stalin's Great Terror, in which Utley's Russian husband had perished, she turned savagely against him. Death was none too good for such a villain, is the impression one gains from reading her tirades against Lattimore, particularly the chapter on him in her popular book *The China Story* (1951).

Utley was the China Lobby's best writer, yet her potential was never fully realized, owing to the very intensity of her feelings. She was born to a middle-class English family in 1898 and became a brilliant student, obtaining an M.A., then usually the highest earned degree of British university instructors. But instead of embarking on an academic career she married a Russian, who was expelled from England in 1928. She went to Moscow with him, finding employment with what became the Soviet branch of the Institute of Pacific Relations. That was how she met Lattimore, who as an officer of the IPR visited Russia several times in the thirties. After the arrest of her husband in 1936 (he died not long afterward, though she did not know this for certain until twenty-five years had passed), she returned to England.

In 1938 Utley went to China, where she spent half a year. She was warmly received by leftists on account of her best-selling book *Japan's Feet of Clay* (1937), the result of a year's residence in that country with her husband. Though no longer a Marxist herself, she liked Edgar Snow, Agnes Smedley and other American friends of Chinese Communism whom she met, and the Communists themselves, who received her warmly—unlike Party members elsewhere. Consequently in her next book, *China at War* (1939), she wrote that the Communists had given up on the idea of dictatorship and were working for "social and political reform along capitalist and democratic lines."[59] She explained this lapse of judgment in her memoirs by saying that at the time she was "still infected with the liberal disease of wishful thinking."[60] The book was not a commercial success, nor was its successor, *The Dream We Lost* (1940), an account of the disillusionment of former Marxists.

The book actually did her harm in the United States, where she now lived, because she had also turned her back on antifascism. Utley had come to believe that Soviet Russia was worse than Nazi Germany, seen by her as a bulwark against Communism. She retained this unpopular view even after the United States went to war. In 1946 Utley returned to China briefly as a partisan of Chiang Kai-shek and the sworn enemy of Stalinist and progressive writers. These two relatively short stays in China were the basis of her voluminous later writings defending the KMT and indicting her former friends as Communist tools. Nor was she content with journalism but worked for a while on Senator McCarthy's staff and testified against Lattimore, John Davies and others during their various inquisitions. Yet she was never really happy on the right, believing that it "lacks above all, the comradeship and the loyalty of the 'left,' and is generally too heartless, selfish, or ungenerous."[61] Then, too, right-wingers made the mistake of confusing "the quest for social justice with Communist treason."[62] And she did not like Roy Cohn and David Schine of McCarthy's staff, resigning finally out of disgust at what she considered their unprincipled career-ism.

At the end she saw herself as a liberal in the nineteenth-century sense, out of place in this one. Her autobiography is the record of a talent that never found its place. Hers was a unique career, the closest parallel to it being that of Max Eastman, the American writer who also passed from Marxism to McCarthy-ism to a vague sort of liberalism. But he never was an apologist for Nazi Germany, nor a witch-hunter, nor a prosecutor of former friends. And he left behind books of enduring value, especially his splendid memoirs.[63] One may sympathize with Utley, who never recovered from the death of her husband, without excusing her conduct. It was as bad as anyone's during McCarthy's worst years.

Utley believed that she knew the truth about China precisely because she had not spent much time there. This kept her from being infected by Communism, as happened to those with more experience. A truer reason was given her by Tillman Durdin, an old friend. When she visited Chungking in 1946 he told her that she had missed the desperate years during which many journal-ists came to favor the reds. "You must understand . . . how easy it was to believe in the Communists. It was so utterly hopeless in Free China! Even I felt that it could not be worse, and must be better in Communist China."[64] It was what not only pro-gressives, but nearly everyone in a position to compare the two Chinas during World War II, believed.

China Lobbyists had a different explanation, which was that "Lattimore and his confederates in the IPR and the State De-partment were responsible for our defeat in China and the vic-tory of Russia."[65] This was the judgment of right-wing flack John T. Flynn in his poisonous book *The Lattimore Story* (1953), written, he said, because Senator McCarthy had failed to expose Lattimore. McCarthy "assumed that Americans would believe the criticisms he made because they were reason-able and plausible and because most of the evidence was there," knowing little of the unlimited reserves of smear, abuse and character assassination that Communists were able to draw upon.[66] The real reason why Lattimore made McCarthy look foolish was that McCarthy didn't know what he was talking about. The McCarran Committee did not make that mistake. Its report ran to five thousand pages and was the result of questioning sixty-six witnesses and examining over twenty thousand documents.

Even so, the committee failed to prove that Lattimore and the IPR defeated Chiang Kai-shek. It did establish that the IPR was infiltrated and influenced by Communists, however. Such had not been what the founders had in mind. They were associated with the Hawaiian YMCA movement and gathered in 1925 to create an organization that would promote a better understanding of Asia. The IPR consisted of a permanent secretariat and a group of national councils, each expected to be self-supporting. The governing board was made up of prominent individuals who were always more conservative than the staff. Edward C. Carter was secretary of the American Council, largest of the members, and became secretary general of the IPR, moving its headquarters to New York from Honolulu and establishing its left-wing character. His personality and programs "carried the seeds both of the IPR's fame and of its destruction," said the institute's historian. With foundation support the IPR established *Pacific Affairs,* while the American Council launched *Far Eastern Survey,* both influential journals. Carter recruited an able staff, of which Lattimore was best known and Frederick Vanderbilt Field ultimately the most notorious after him. Field, one of the wealthy Vanderbilts, was a Harvard graduate and secretary of the American Council from 1934 to 1940, during which time he may have been a Communist. By 1935 he was on the editorial board of *China Today,* a Communist-front publication. Whittaker Chambers claimed that Field belonged to the Communist underground as early as 1937. He became more visible in the 1940s as a contributor to the *Daily Worker* and in the fifties was still subsidizing front organizations.

Carter and Lattimore were eager to have a Soviet Council, which did materialize in 1934. But it was never very active and faded away during the Great Terror. While it lasted Lattimore was careful not to offend Russian sensibilities. The McCarran Committee found a letter from him to the Soviet Council indicating that he would not knowingly print material in *Pacific Affairs* distasteful to it. The IPR published few obviously Marxist tracts in the 1930s, showing its sympathies less directly. In 1938 it began a series of books on the Sino–Japanese War, some of which leaned to the left. Lattimore advised Carter, in another letter obtained by the McCarran Committee, as follows.

> For China, my hunch is that it will pay to keep behind the official Chinese Communist position—far enough not to be covered by the same label—but enough ahead of the active Chinese liberals to be noticeable . . . For the U.S.S.R.,—back their international policy in general, but without using their slogans and above all without giving them or anybody else an impression of subservience . . .[67]

This was hardly evidence of conspiracy, and seems, in fact, to establish that Carter and Lattimore were not Communists and did not wish to be linked with them.

The war expanded IPR's influence, as there was a sudden demand for Asian experts and a short supply. The staff's sympathy with Chinese Communism became more visible, especially in *Far Eastern Survey*. It published what seems to have been the first article describing the Communists as "agrarian radicals," the disreputable piece by T. A. Bisson frequently cited later by China Lobbyists.[68] This came at the peak of IPR influence, when its specialists were most sought after and its budget was the largest, amounting to some $300,000 annually. It was then that Alfred Kohlberg, an importer of Chinese goods who knew the country well, decided that the IPR had fallen into the hands of "pro-Communists," a term he favored on account of its ambiguity. Kohlberg launched a personal campaign, writing thousands of letters over the years and generating widespread unfavorable publicity for the IPR. Kohlberg lost the climactic battle in 1947 when the institute board voted to reject his charges. But he won the war, for, more than anyone else, he had made the IPR controversial, breaking ground for McCarthy's attacks and the deadly Senate investigation.

The IPR had already suffered harm owing to the *Amerasia* case. It was a left-wing publication that, when its offices were raided by the FBI in 1945, was found to be in illegal possession of government documents. The editors and several others, including John Service of the State Department, were charged with violations of the espionage law. This was embarrassing to the IPR, as Field and several staff members had helped found *Amerasia,* on whose board Lattimore and Bisson served. Its offices were in the same building as the IPR, which was home also to the Committee for a Democratic Far Eastern Policy, a Communist front supported by Field.

The IPR survived this blow, and McCarthy's charges too for a while. But revenues fell even before the McCarran Committee hearings began in July 1951, five months after institute files stored at Carter's farm in Massachusetts had been seized. These were not too injurious, though they included Lattimore's letter about staying behind the Chinese Communists. Most damaging was the refusal of some past and present IPR officials to deny charges made against them. Besides Field, two former staff members and one former IPR trustee declined to answer questions relating to Communist associations. Lawrence Rosinger, an influential staff member, took the Fifth Amendment. When the McCarran report was issued by its parent body, the Senate Committee on Foreign Relations, a covering letter stated that but for the IPR China would still be free. The report itself did not go so far, charging only that persons associated with the IPR helped shape U.S. Asian policy in ways favorable to Communist objectives.

Even this overstated the case. Stanley Hornbeck, former chief of the State Department's Far Eastern Division, and a critic of Lattimore and the IPR, and of the Foreign Service officers who opposed Chiang as well, told a reporter that IPR influence on foreign policy had been negligible. Harold C. Hinton, an Asian scholar, summed up the matter as follows. Whatever its defects, the IPR was "a unique organization, without which our knowledge of the Far East would be even less substantial than it actually is." On the other hand, many of its publications

reflect an arid leftist outlook and a tendency to present predetermined and highly debatable conclusions as though they were unchallengeable facts. For this the immaturity of American Far Eastern scholarship and of the generation of intellectuals who came of age during the era of

Normalcy and the Depression, rather than any sinister design, is probably to blame in most cases.[69]

The documents seized in Carter's barn showed nothing more than the existence of this leftist attitude. Owen Lattimore was indeed "an outstanding example of the arid leftism to which I have referred." In *Pacific Affairs* he did sometimes print anti-Communist editorials, often followed by his own rebuttals. In a 1938 issue of the journal Lattimore defended the Moscow purge trials as a stroke for democracy and indicated to the Tydings Committee in 1950 "that he still subscribed to this fantastic view."

Hinton believed that the IPR had some effect on foreign policy, but it was only one of many groups to have done so and not the most important. To Hinton the whole investigation was a waste of time because even if the charges against the IPR were true, which he doubted, they would matter only if America's Far Eastern policy was determined by pro-Communists. At a time of war in Korea, and when the United States was shipping arms to Formosa and Indochina, this was plainly not the case. The investigation only proved that some in the IPR entertained "the same sort of deracinated leftism which has afflicted so many American intellectuals during the past generation." This was not a crime, and in any case was a problem for the schools and churches rather than Congress or the courts. Hinton's measured judgment was an exception in the 1950s, when anti-Communist feelings were most intense and hysterical. On account of them McCarran's investigation finished the IPR, though it exhibited faint signs of life for another decade.

Hinton's view of Lattimore was shared by other unprejudiced observers. In 1950 *The Reporter,* a magazine of anti-Communist liberals, had staff members read all of Lattimore's books plus many of his articles. It described *Inner Asian Frontiers of China* (1940) as a solid work of scholarship. Much of his other writing was journalism, not always of the highest quality but hardly subversive. "He presents no body of ideas, which could be, as has been said, 'more dangerous to the nation than a carload of daisies.' Rather, there is a vast volume of useful information, frequently colored by emotion and diluted by repetition."[70] Lattimore was described as a busy and more or less

pompous man who had sometimes swallowed Communist slogans but had, nonetheless, "industriously tried to present the
truth as he saw it."

This, if unkind, was not unfair. Lattimore was hardly a
Communist, still less a Soviet agent, and definitely not the architect of U.S. Asian policy. On the other hand, he was not an
unqualified hack either, which his enemies began to claim after
the first charges were shown to be ridiculous. In 1951 some of
his friends assembled a book of testimonials from leading
Sinologists to refute this latest slander. They were able to get
thirty-seven letters of support, chiefly from academicians. They
all endorsed his scholarship, citing most frequently *Inner Asian
Frontiers of China,* a work broadly admired by professionals—
even some of those hostile to his politics. In the introduction to
Lattimore the Scholar, Gerald W. Johnson underlined the central point about Lattimore's political effect, which was that he
had not had any. Considering his eminence in the fledgling world
of China studies, and his availability, the State Department
made little use of him. Lattimore's jobs as adviser to Chiang
and member of the Reparations Mission were presidential appointments. State seems to have asked his advice only once,
in the 1949 seminar on China, and rejected it, as also his numerous unsolicited opinions. The McCarran hearings did establish that Lattimore and the other scholars, journalists and Foreign Service officers who favored dumping Chiang socialized
with one another, as was to be expected of people having common professional and political interests. The ideas of Vincent,
Service, Davies and the other young men of the Far Eastern
Division had been formed, in any case, not by Lattimore but
through service in the field.

The worst thing to be said about Lattimore was that he took
the progressive view of both Russia and China, and that in
Ordeal by Slander and before the Tydings Committee he was
disingenuous. Lattimore made himself out to be more anti-
Communist than he actually was. He fudged the question of
how *Pacific Affairs* was slanted during his editorship, claiming
that of some two hundred fifty contributions ninety-four were
right of center and one hundred forty-seven neither left nor
right. This did an injustice to its actual coloration. A historian
who reviewed *Pacific Affairs* during the Lattimore era found

that while thirteen contributions were by anti-Communists and eighteen by pro-Communists, the number of pages given to each position amounted to only 146 for anti-Communism and an impressive 729 for the other side. Lattimore alone wrote almost as much as all the anti-Communists combined.[71]

But on the main issues Lattimore was forthright, condemning the American policy of supporting right-wing despots in Asia and warning that Communism would benefit if the United States kept on trying to prevent revolutions. Lattimore had no reason then or later to retract his published opinions, for, though not unique to him, they were remarkably on target. His 1945 book *Solution in Asia* was, as he said, a catalogue of proposals that would have strengthened the American hand. His last effort to influence policy, *The Situation in Asia* (1949), was even more prophetic. Lattimore stressed again the likelihood of Chinese Titoism and the certain increase of revolutionary nationalism in Asia. This, he believed, was creating a "third force" between the Cold War blocs—what would later be called nonalignment. Though satisfied with the Russian position in Europe, he was less pleased with its role in the Far East. Russia's appeal there derived from the great progress made in Soviet Asia between 1924 and 1941. It was accomplished by harsh means, but they were not offensive to Asians who had never known democracy and did not consider the price paid too high for the gain. Even so, Russia had an unfortunate habit of tightening its grip on satellites during times of crisis, which was self-defeating in that it led to a loss of influence outside the sphere. This showed the limits of Soviet power, he maintained.

Lattimore predicted the Western defeat in Indochina, though it took longer than he expected, owing to American intervention. He was most astute in sizing up Korea.

If there is to be a civil war, South Korea would not be able to subdue North Korea without a great deal more American help than is now available. North Korea would be able to overrun South Korea without Russian help, unless stopped by American combat troops. America, which has in China complained of the bad luck of having inherited the Kuomintang through no fault of its own, has in Korea manufactured its own Kuomintang. To support our proclaimed policy of world-wide opposition to police states, we have in South Korea created a weak and unreliable police state of our own.[72]

This was indeed the case, events soon demonstrated.

If the Lattimore-progressive position on Asia was right in the main, as history has shown it to be, why did it not prevail—or at least enjoy greater currency? In the first instance, as we have seen, popular and governmental support bore no necessary relation to the facts, which were subject to manipulation and different readings anyhow. Thus the progressive view of Russia succeeded in the early forties because it suited Americans to have as an ally the Soviet state described by fellow travelers rather than the one that actually existed. And that view was later discarded not because anti-Communists had the better argument, though they did, but because America and Russia fell out over vital issues. Political needs always took first place, regardless of conditions. And as the Cold War worsened, this feature became even more pronounced, so that not only government became locked into a self-defeating Asian policy but liberal anti-Communists as well.

The *New Leader* and *Commentary* made war on the progressive theory, later proven out, that Chinese Communism, being an indigenous movement, would not blindly follow the Russian lead and ought to be treated differently. David Dallin hated this idea. In 1949 he reminded readers that during the war it was always said that Chinese Communists were only agrarian reformers.

> The new idea is that Chinese Communism is a nationalist movement; that its leader Mao Tse-tung is or will become the Tito of China; and that Moscow will not be able to control Chinese affairs, even if Chinese Communism takes over. We are told by the "experts" that a profound divergence—even conflict—has developed between Russia and Chinese Communism. We expect fellow-travelers to invent such theories; after all, that is their job.[73]

But he was incensed that some non-Communists thought so, too. He attacked Lattimore and Edgar Snow for advancing this proposition, calling for a South Korean invasion of the north, greater aid for Nationalist China, and the rearming of Japan.

When the respected columnists Joseph and Stewart Alsop warmed to the theme two and a half years later, Dallin attacked again. "The notion of Chinese Communism as an autonomous movement has played a fatal, ruinous role in American foreign policy. Originating in the wartime U.S. embassy in Chungking, it spread to Washington, gained wide currency among fellow-travellers, and inspired countless articles and books." The truth, said Dallin, was that Chinese independence did not exist. It was a myth fostered by Moscow to lull the West and encourage aid to Mao.[74] Like so many anti-Stalinist intellectuals, Dallin, who was brilliant when talking about Russia, his area of expertise, did not know Asia. He simply projected the European experience on it, often, as here, making grave mistakes.

He compounded them by maligning Henry Wallace. He charged that Wallace had been the carrier of false promises made by Stalin to Chungking in 1944, thereby contributing to the fall of Nationalist China. Though no evidence of this existed, Dallin was sure that when the relevant government documents were released they would sustain him. Dallin was wrong, but Wallace was so stung by the accusation that he replied with a partially fabricated story of his own. Wallace denied having passed on any messages from Stalin, and there is no proof to the contrary. But Wallace also denied having urged Chiang to come to terms with the Communists, which was in fact why Roosevelt had sent him to Chungking and which his own notes, made at the time, show him to have done. It was a sad commentary on the times that Dallin accused him on the basis of hearsay; a worse one that Wallace felt obliged to deny having carried out a legitimate order from his chief.[75]

If Cold War emotions kept anti-Stalinists from thinking clearly about China, it had the same effect on thoughts about Lattimore. The *New Leader* was hostile to Lattimore, as to all progressives. This prompted Elmer Davis the broadcaster to rise to his defense. If liberals could not back Lattimore, who was well known to them, whom could they defend? Damning Lattimore was to say in effect that there was no middle ground between Communism and reaction. Granville Hicks responded that he had not meant to say in a previous article that informed people like Davis should not speak up for Lattimore. What he objected to was the tendency of liberals to say that Lattimore must be innocent because McCarthy said he was guilty. Hicks's position was that one need not defend Lattimore in order to fight McCarthy. The Hiss case had scared a lot of liberals, Hicks said, agreeing with Davis, "but it doesn't seem to have taught them much."[76] Though Hicks was thinking of Davis, he might well have had himself in mind. The difference between Hiss and Lattimore, as Davis said, was that liberals rallied to Hiss even though they could not possibly know the truth because the allegations had to do with secret actions. Lattimore's case was the opposite. Within days of his first appearance before the Tydings Committee, McCarthy dropped the Soviet-agent charge and was only accusing Lattimore of having paralleled the Communist line. Lattimore's views were on record and easily verifiable. Yet though Hicks was the most scrupulous of anti-Stalinists, he remained suspicious of Lattimore, showing how far things had deteriorated.

At the time, however, the most remarkable thing about Hicks was that he entertained doubts at all. Lattimore's friends were insisting that he was a great scholar and a paragon of virtue, the other side that he was a spy or worse. *Time* magazine took the position of Freda Utley and others that Lattimore was more of a menace than McCarthy's original charges had painted him. *Time* did not support McCarthy, who it admitted was probably an "irresponsible demagogue." Instead it compared Lattimore with John Strachey of England and Frédéric Joliot-Curie of France. Strachey was an influential Marxist writer in the thirties who had long since recanted, Joliot-Curie an atomic scientist and open member of the Communist Party. Lattimore was said to belong to this company because of having advocated disastrous ideas. Accordingly, he and the other two were more dangerous than "a carload of spies."[77]

Lattimore, scrappy though he was, could not handle this kind of abuse. Bracketing his name with that of Joliot-Curie was carrying guilt by association to absurd lengths in that he had almost nothing in common with the French scientist (nor for that matter with Strachey, by then a respectable Labour Party politician). What good was it to have written so much if one's ideas could be so distorted? What good was it to have been right about China when the reward for vision was smear and slander?

What could Lattimore do about being blamed for government politics which were contrary to what he had advocated?

In this astonishing way Lattimore and other leading progressives were completely neutralized. The foremost journalists were blacklisted, Theodore White for a decade, Snow for longer. Lawrence Rosinger of the IPR was frozen out of Chinese studies. John Fairbank was protected by Harvard, becoming dean of the American historians of modern China, but he too was blacklisted and did not get published by the national press again until the Vietnam War. He and other progressives who had reviewed eighty percent of the books on China for *The New York Times* and the *Herald Tribune* before 1952 were completely excluded thereafter. The Foreign Service officers who had warned against what came to pass in China were driven from the Far Eastern Division of State, and many from government service altogether. And the nation embraced more tightly than ever the policy that had failed in China. The Department of State was still inveighing against the "Sino-Soviet bloc" in the 1960s long after it disappeared. Things fell out as the progressives had foretold, especially in Indochina. They remained prophets without honor all the same so far as government was concerned. Only one positive thought can be drawn from all this. Fairbank believes that George Marshall, Dean Acheson and their anti-Kuomintang Foreign Service officers kept America from intervening directly in the Chinese civil war.[78] That at least was to the good. Perhaps their sacrifices had not been made in vain.

In only one respect might progressives be said to have merited their ill-treatment, and that was largely a matter of guilt by association with the larger progressive community. The defense of Stalinism ruined it, and justly so. But ruined, too, were the Asian experts, most of whom were not active parties in the debate over Europe. This was wrong though understandable. It would have taken heroic objectivity for any anti-Stalinist who had read Snow on the Soviets to have any faith in Snow on Chinese Communism. Most Asia-oriented progressives were not tainted in the same direct way as Snow, and to a lesser extent Lattimore, but intellectually and rhetorically they were united with the Europeanists and therefore compromised. Explications of China written in progressivese or, worse still, Wallese or, worst of all, Stalinese could only inspire doubt and hostility even when correct. Thus the Asian wing of progressivism paid for the sins of its other half. In this sense only were the wounds suffered by Asian progressives self-inflicted.

Yet in the end they had no choice. There were various schools of thought on Russia to which a liberal might subscribe. But on China there were only two ways to go. One favored either the Nationalists or, if opposed to them, Chinese Communism as the only alternative. Having anti-KMT sentiments aligned one with the progressives regardless of intent. Thus some experts on China became progressives by default. They were conscripted, as it were, unlike those oriented toward Europe, who were volunteers. This makes the reprisals against them seem even more unfair.

X

The Question
of Liberal Guilt

AFTER SOUTH KOREA was invaded, the old quarrels dividing intellectuals faded away and new ones took their place. Few people any longer defended the Soviet Union, fewer still American Communists. The new issues arose from McCarthyism, a term that embraced the entire red scare. One cause for dispute was whether the thing itself existed. In 1947 Arthur Schlesinger, Jr., deplored HUAC and the Truman Administration's loyalty program, but argued that reports of a climate of terror were greatly exaggerated.[1] The *New Leader* regularly scoffed at the fearful, pointing out in 1948 that polls inspired confidence. "The overwhelming majority of Americans are definitely not hysterical: there is no approval of witch-hunting nor war-mongering, there is only a firm will to resist submission to Moscow."[2] It clung to this line throughout, resolutely ignoring the obvious.

Carey McWilliams of *The Nation* in his book *Witch Hunt* (1950) put the blame on Truman's loyalty program. This was a theory that leftist historians would strongly promote in later years.[3] McWilliams said President Truman's loyalty order of March 22, 1947, was an experiment in thought control, claiming that the real issue was not loyalty but adherence to orthodox ideas. The witch-hunters pretended to be concerned with disloyalty, when their real aim was heresy. For McWilliams, as for sympathetic historians later, there was no chance that one might be anti-Communist out of principle. To him it was always a mask for something else, usually the desire to suppress liberal and leftist opinions.

Irving Kristol found McWilliams' book to be flawed by misleading techniques. An example was "the Bland Omission," as when he made no mention of Alger Hiss, Claus Fuchs and other frightening cases. Another was "the Specious Parallel," such as McWilliams' comparison of the American loyalty program with Soviet purges. The book employed faulty assumptions, a major one being that any bad event was not accidental but the result of a plot by Wall Street. A second premise was that anything unpleasant in America was the forerunner of worse to come, whereas evils in the Communist world were beyond judgment at this time. America, on the other hand, "is not only eternally judged but eternally condemned."[4] Kristol's own belief was that civil liberties had never been stronger.

Kristol found it easy to expose McWilliams' partisanship and want of logic. It was not so easy to be impartial and clear-thinking on his own. A year after demolishing *Witch Hunt* Kristol wrote an essay that has been held against him ever since. Kristol was a veteran of the ideological wars at the City College of New York, a hotbed of radicals in the thirties, many of whom became distinguished intellectuals. Kristol had been a Trotskyist, and retained the sect's fondness for intellectual combat and verbal overkill. After World War II he joined the staff of *Commentary,* an anti-Stalinist Jewish monthly devoted to culture and politics. It was as managing editor of it that he wrote his notorious essay " 'Civil Liberties,' 1952—A Study in Confusion." This was inspired specifically by Alan Barth's recent *The Loyalty of Free Men* (1951), which, like so much libertarian propaganda, Kristol argued, rested on the misconception that "because a vulgar demagogue lashes out at both Communism and liberalism as identical, it is necessary to protect Communism in order to defend liberalism."[5]

It was a fatal error, Kristol held, that gave McCarthy his strength. "For there is one thing that the American people know about Senator McCarthy: he, like them, is unequivocally anti-Communist. About the spokesmen for American liberalism they feel they know no such thing. And with some justification."[6] This has been cited as evidence that Kristol endorsed McCarthy. Actually, he was attacking liberals for employing a double standard in defense of Communists and fellow travelers. The offending statement came before pages of examples in which prominent libertarians were shown to have passed over the nature of the Soviet Union and Communism as if they were not at issue. In the matter of Alger Hiss such liberals were found to dislike Chambers, who told the truth, while sympathizing with Hiss, who didn't. Kristol was notably exercised by their portrayal of Owen Lattimore as an innocent dissenter when, in Kristol's view, he followed the Communist line. Kristol went too far here, as anti-Stalinists often did. But Lattimore was largely in favor of Russia's Asian policy, and Kristol had some reason to make the following statement.

> In his denunciation of Lattimore's pro-Communist record and in hurling unsubstantiated charges against him (chief of Soviet espionage, etc.) Senator McCarthy may well have been aiming a blow against independence of mind and nonconformity of spirit. For Messrs. Commager, Barth, and Chafee to defend Lattimore's pro-Communist record in order to defend such independence and nonconformity, is for them to play the Senator's game, on the losing side.[7]

Liberals were reluctant to admit that they had been wrong about Communism and the Soviets in the past. Worse still:

> There is a false pride by which liberals persuade themselves that no matter what association a man has had with a Communist enterprise, he is absolutely guiltless of the crimes that Communism has committed so long as he was moved to this association by a generous idealism.[8]

This was a great mistake, to his mind. The truth was that the generation of reformers who helped make the New Deal had also "lent aid and comfort to Stalinist tyranny." Failure to admit this played into McCarthy's hands. "If American liberalism is not willing to discriminate between its achievements and its sins, it only disarms itself before Senator McCarthy, who is eager to have it appear that its achievements *are* its sins."[9] At the very least, if Communists were to be defended it must be in full awareness that they are the enemies of freedom and very different from ourselves. To the extent that a liberal "insists that they are on our side, that we can defend our liberties only by uncritically defending theirs, he will be taken as speaking as one of them."[10]

Many found this argument reprehensible. Numerous correspondents rightly complained that Kristol imputed views to

Alan Barth that he did not hold and made out the liberal record to be worse than it was.[11] The fullest rejoinder came from Alan Westin, Harvard teacher, lawyer for the Massachusetts ACLU and a frequent writer of articles on civil liberties. Westin claimed that Kristol had made four errors. One was to see McCarthy as the popular ideal of anti-Communism and assert that liberals had to confess to having aided Stalinism before fighting for civil liberties. Another was Kristol's failure to distinguish between the civil freedoms of Communists and the commission by them of criminal or conspiratorial acts. Kristol mixed together the question of procedural fairness for witnesses before congressional committees and the danger Communists might pose to sensitive government agencies. Still another was to misrepresent Barth, Henry Steele Commager and others as believing that Communists were only radical liberals and in any case on our side. Finally, Kristol wrongly implied that liberals need not defend the civil liberties of Communists at all if they didn't want to.

What Kristol had done, Westin argued, was to define civil liberties so as to omit the actual cases Americans were faced with, which often did involve unsavory characters or situations. Westin believed, to the contrary, that it was precisely the worst cases that needed to be fought so as to ward off the possibility of having everyone's liberties violated. In defending the rights of Communists, liberals were, in the end, defending their own. The freedoms of Communists had to be upheld in order to protect the right of dissent and free inquiry. And civil liberties had to be protected so as to retain "our moral leadership in the world as the arsenal of freedom."[12] In response Kristol backed down slightly on the New Deal's complicity in the crimes of Stalin, but stood by his narrow definition of civil rights, allowing only that as Communists did not presently constitute a danger to the state it was all right to extend to them "at this time and in certain areas of our society, a toleration and freedom to which they have no moral or legal right."[13]

Like Westin, Alan Barth took the opposite side of the authentic debate over loyalty—which did not include polemicists such as Carey McWilliams. Neither side included Stalinists, on the one hand, or witch-hunters on the other. Both believed in civil liberties. The differences were striking all the same. Barth held that loyalty was not a big problem in America and that government was going to ominous extremes in defense of what was not endangered. Kristol maintained that disloyalty was a real problem and that government had responded to it sensibly. Despite the excesses of McCarthy and others, liberty was safe. Barth felt that the chief duty of liberals was to protect the Bill of Rights, Kristol that liberals should disown their guilty past and fight Communism.

But though both men were within the realm of legitimate discourse, they were not equally right. Both made partisan misjudgments. Barth praised Harry Dexter White for standing up to HUAC, while ignoring the evidence against him. White was an Assistant Secretary of the Treasury who may well have passed on confidential information to the Soviets, and who seems to have appointed assistants who were Party members.[14] Accordingly, his behavior was more self-serving than Barth wanted to admit. By the same token Kristol was unfair to Lattimore. When it came to quality of argument, however, there were large differences between the two. Kristol believed in the rule of reason but was not always able to practice it. Like many anti-Communists he could not keep the loyalty problem in perspective. By 1952 the government had been ransacked for subversives. Only a handful of disloyal persons had been turned up, and of these only a few were even accused of passing on data harmful to national security. This is not to make light of treason, only to say again that an immense weight of concern rested on a small number of cases.

How people view the Bill of Rights is, to some degree, a matter of opinion, and Kristol was as entitled to his narrow definition as Barth to his broader one. But the extent of the loyalty problem was a matter of record, on the basis of which it is safe to say that Kristol and those who agreed with him, however numerous, were wrong. And Kristol was wrong also in arguing that to be effective liberals had to disassociate themselves from Communism as absolutely as McCarthy had done. This was precisely what the Truman Administration did by establishing a loyalty program so harsh that libertarians saw it as a threat to freedom possibly equal to McCarthyism. Yet this had not saved the Administration from being red-baited. On the loyalty issue it sacrificed principle for political advantage and lost both. The lesson, as after World War I, was that liberals could not defend themselves from right-wingers by embracing their position.

Kristol's argument was not only faulty in the abstract but specifically as it related to Barth's *The Loyalty of Free Men.* While one would not guess this from Kristol's essay, Barth was an anti-Stalinist and in the book criticized Communism and Soviet Russia, though he also explained why both appealed to intellectuals in the thirties. He made Kristol angry by offering good motives as an excuse, but Barth's point was that no disloyalty was involved, only lack of judgment. Accordingly, while he wrote for *The Nation,* there was a great difference between Barth and Carey McWilliams, who denied there was a Communist problem and therefore could not explain the fear of it. Allowing for brevity, which led to oversimplifications in the instances of which Kristol disapproved, Barth's work was exemplary, making a strong case for civil liberties in an emotional time.

It is always difficult to keep one's head in a storm, and never more so than when everyone else seems to be losing theirs. The weakness of anti-Stalinism in the late forties and fifties was that though times had changed, many could not see this. Philip Rahv, a founding editor of *Partisan Review,* pointed out that those who had been anti-Stalinists in the 1930s and early '40s failed to recognize that anti-Communism was now virtually "the official creed of our society." The need was no longer for more about the badness of Stalinism but ideas on how to defeat it. The anti-Stalinists were of little help in this because they no longer could, and in some cases never had been able to, distinguish between Stalinism as a foreign threat, which was grave, and Communism as an internal danger, which was slight. Consequently they had been led into activities that were not their proper business. "Of course, so long as the Soviet power exists its propagandists and spies will circulate among us and it is up to the intelligence agencies of the government to deal with them. It is scarcely the function of politically-minded intellectuals, however, to serve as an adjunct of the F.B.I."[15] An instance showing the danger, not cited by Rahv, was the bizarre Yaddo affair.

. . .

In February 1949 Dwight Macdonald received a letter from Elizabeth Hardwick urging him not to accept an invitation to visit Yaddo, a retreat for artists and writers administered by Elizabeth Ames.[16] Hardwick, her husband, Robert Lowell, and several other guests of Yaddo were organizing a protest arising from the recent charges made against Agnes Smedley by General MacArthur's headquarters. Smedley was a friend of Ames and a frequent guest at Yaddo, as were other pro-Soviet and fellow-traveling writers. FBI agents visited it after the story broke, and Lowell and several others subsequently decided to clean out what they saw as a nest of Communist rats. At a meeting held on March 1 they accused Ames of disloyalty, urging the directors to fire her. After talking with them Macdonald agreed not to visit Yaddo, writing Ames a stiff note of explanation. Yaddo was supposed to be a refuge, "not a center for pro-Soviet propaganda." That Smedley, a lifelong "fulltime journalistic apologist for Communism and the Soviet Union," had been able to make Yaddo her base and "occupy a specially privileged and influential status" there, and that Ames had defended Smedley, all seemed to indicate that Communists had a "strategic behind-the-scenes position at Yaddo." Accordingly, Macdonald was joining the protest.[17]

But there was another side, as Macdonald discovered. Within three weeks he received a long form letter from John Cheever, Eleanor Clark, Alfred Kazin and two others saying that the Yaddo board of directors would meet in New York on March 26 to decide the fate of Mrs. Ames. It summarized the events leading up to this, rejecting the charges made against Ames and pointing out that many anti-Stalinists had been guests at Yaddo, as well as nonpoliticals. No weight was given by Ames's critics to the fact that the Army had withdrawn its accusations against Smedley. Nor did they mention that Ames was on record as disapproving of Smedley's activities and finally had asked Smedley to leave Yaddo on account of them. The whole star-chamber proceeding was

a perfect example of the use of innuendo and personal disparagement in lieu of evidence. Those responsible for it have made it clear, and have stated privately, that they do not care what happens to Yaddo in future. Their sole appetite and concern seems to be to create a tabloid case. We regard their action as a thoroughly foolish and nasty performance, dangerous to the extent that it weakens any sober fight against Communism.[18]

The signers asked recipients to add their names to an enclosed statement to the directors of Yaddo denying the charges against Ames. Alfred Kazin was shocked by the number of writers, artists and composers, former guests of Yaddo, who refused to sign even though knowing the truth. Many had families and jobs and said they could not take the risk. Some were displeased over their treatment at Yaddo or did not like Ames. "The lesser poets were not only the biggest cowards, but impossible to shut up in their boring, whining self-defense. They were concerned with Lowell's power to affect their reputations even when they had no reputations."[19]

Ames and Yaddo were saved, the treason of the clerks notwithstanding. But Malcolm Cowley, a director, was disgusted that it had been necessary to wave the flag to achieve this end. Things had gotten to the point where "in order to gain support for your side you have to prove that it is more patriotic in essence than the other side."[20] Cowley believed the affair resulted from the desire of some "to rule or ruin Yaddo," blaming also the general paranoia and Lowell's illness.[21] But he refused to write publicly about it, saying that Lowell was "a fine poet and normally a fine man too, and I'd hate to tell a story that would reflect on him."[22]

Macdonald later regretted having let himself be talked into joining the protest and apologized. Ames replied graciously that she would have been even more dismayed over the witch-hunt of 1949 if many friends had not rallied to her side. Then, too, "your apology with those of others received from time to time has helped to restore my confidence."[23] It transpired that Lowell was in a manic state during the affair, preceding a spell of insanity, as had happened to him before. The others had no such excuse, except as they were party to the madness of the times.

Anti-Stalinists did not have a monopoly on foolishness. In 1951 *The Nation* filed a suit against the *New Leader* for libel and slander. As the most intransigently anti-Communist liberal publication, the *New Leader* had often savaged *The Nation,* which usually stood above the battle, seldom replying in kind. Thus when Granville Hicks sharply rebuked *The Nation* that same year Freda Kirchwey did not become excited. Hicks criticized *The Nation* for carrying on as always even though Communism had grown more dangerous. He was especially annoyed by the *Nation* issue that celebrated its eighty-fifth anniversary. Kirchwey had said again that Communism was the wave of the future because it satisfied people's needs while the United States had lost its faith in democracy. Vayo had written that South Korea was not worth saving and could not be saved. Isaac Deutscher was still predicting that in a decade or two Russia would be so prosperous that it would no longer need to menace. In Hicks's view, despite some improvement *The Nation* was continuing to explain away or make light of Russian faults while condemning America's. *The Nation* had "preserved what was weakest and blindest in the old liberalism, and has carried over attitudes that once were merely irresponsible but now are dangerous."[24]

Kirchwey defended herself and *The Nation,* saying that it was not pro-Soviet. She invoked the praise given it by distinguished figures in connection with the magazine's anniversary as proof of continued liberalism. Kirchwey dismissed Hicks as just another troublemaking ex-Communist who divided liberals at a time when they most needed to unify.[25] She was unfair to Hicks. He bore no resemblance to people like Louis Budenz, who distressed liberals by behaving as anti-Communists in much the same fashion that they had as Party members.[26] Her call for unity was the demand of an embattled few that the many give in to them. This was characteristic of Kirchwey's *Nation.*

What destroyed her composure and led to untypical actions was a letter from Clement Greenberg. He was an authority on modernism and had served as *The Nation*'s art critic from 1943 to 1949. He was also ardently anti-Stalinist, a good example of *The Nation*'s divided personality during those years when the front of the magazine had one kind of politics and the back another. The *New Leader* issue of March 19, 1951, carried a letter that Greenberg had originally sent to *The Nation,* which refused to print it, attacking J. Alvarez del Vayo. Greenberg said that it was disgraceful for *The Nation* to have as foreign editor and regular columnist a man who was pro-Soviet and, worse still, pretended not to be.[27] Two weeks later the *New Leader* announced that it was being sued by *The Nation*, to which it had sent proofs of the Greenberg letter.[28] Kirchwey took this drastic step partly because the charge of fellow traveling had become so serious and she wanted to discourage it, but mainly, according to Carey McWilliams, because she was afraid of the consequences for Vayo. Though she and McWilliams always represented him as an independent, a "latter-day Don Quixote" in McWilliams' words, he was relentlessly pro-Soviet.[29] This had already led to his being detained once by immigration authorities on a visit to America, and Kirchwey was afraid that if criticism of him continued he would lose the right of reentry. Kirchwey justified her decision to go to court on the ground that in accusing *The Nation* and Vayo of being "committed" to the service of Russia Greenberg had not only libeled them but, given recent court decisions, charged them with a crime.[30]

Hardly anyone found this convincing. The *New Leader* said that in suing it for $200,000 *The Nation* was trying to stifle criticism instead of engaging in open debate.[31] Thomas Emerson, a left-wing professor of law at Yale and a friend of *The Nation*, agreed. He was on Vayo's side and thought Greenberg's politics were odious. All the same, it was wrong to sue the *New Leader*. Greenberg's letter dealt with important issues and should have been answered "in the arena of public discussion rather than by litigation." Legal action shut off debate, which was illiberal. Anyway, *The Nation* had passed up a chance to do good by refuting Greenberg's charges. To Emerson "the democratic process implies not only that participants will be reasonably tolerant but also that they will be reasonably thick-skinned."[32] Dwight Macdonald, even though a *Nation*-hater of long standing, was shocked that it would stoop so low. He told the magazine's attorney that basing a libel suit on "a one-word technicality" was "repulsive."[33]

Kirchwey remained adamant, and the suit dragged on until 1955. At that time Clifford Forster, attorney for the Committee for Cultural Freedom, which had filed an amicus curiae brief in support of the *New Leader,* contacted *The Nation*'s lawyer. He wanted to see if an out-of-court settlement could not be reached, and Kirchwey, who was handing *The Nation* to Mc-Williams, compromised. The *New Leader* paid no damages but issued a statement saying that it had not intended to defame Vayo or *The Nation.*[34] *The Nation* lost by this in several ways. It could not afford the legal costs. Important contributors defected. Robert Bendiner, after fourteen years on the staff, had left the previous fall but agreed to stay on the masthead. After the Greenberg suit he asked to have his name removed, as did Reinhold Niebuhr the famous theologian. Both had become misfits anyway owing to their anti-Communism. They resigned quietly, but the loss hurt, especially that of Niebuhr, whose prestige was at its greatest. Most of all *The Nation* lost face by this blatant effort to silence criticism, which made the magazine seem hypocritical on the issue of free speech.*

Nor did fear of legal reprisals intimidate critics. Only months after the suit was filed *The Saturday Review of Literature* published a slashing attack on *The Nation* and its British counterpart, *The New Statesman and Nation,* by Peter Viereck. He reviewed the case in detail, which, as the *SRL* had a much larger circulation than the *New Leader,* put an end to Kirchwey's hope of censoring enemies. Viereck said that the two magazines practiced the "liberalism of suicide" by urging appeasement of Stalinism. He praised *Partisan Review,* the *New Leader, Commonweal, Commentary* and *The Economist* for taking an opposite course.[36]

His essay drew hundreds of letters, as Viereck had expected, three quarters of them favorable. Twenty-five percent against still seemed high to Viereck, though he admitted that most of his friends took the big majority against *The Nation* as evidence that Stalinism had lost its hold on intellectuals. He felt all the same that such a large Stalinist minority showed the need for his

---

* The *New Leader* did not gain, either. Mary McCarthy spoke for other discriminating anti-Stalinists when she wrote that even though unjustly sued, the magazine was hopeless. "I think the *New Leader* simply cannot be converted into a responsible organ but will fight to remain a sort of partisan throwaway, with its petty satraps—Bohn, Kurt List, Chamberlin—reigning over a nothingness, like so many grand viziers."[35]

attack.*³⁷ So also did the *New Leader*, which in hailing Viereck pointed out that the *Nation* issue which came out that same week was as bad as ever, having no fewer than three offensive contributions. A Kirchwey editorial said that the United States should stop automatically rejecting Soviet overtures. Mark Gayn, a former editor of the notorious *Amerasia,* blamed neo-Nazism in Germany on the Western powers. Alexander Werth acclaimed Russia as a happy, peace-loving country.³⁸

The *New Leader* was unfair. Kirchwey's editorial did call upon the United States to take a more positive view of Stalin's peace feelers, to the extent at least of seeing where they might lead, but she showed some awareness that blame for the Cold War did not rest entirely on America's side. And it was certainly reasonable for Kirchwey to urge that the United States respond to Russian blandishments "with sober, workable proposals for settling specific differences. This would convince unbelievers, on both sides of the great divide, that we are not more afraid of a shift toward peace than of the present steady progress toward war."³⁹ The other two pieces were, however, just as bad as the *New Leader* said. Gayn's article was in the *Nation* tradition of forever detecting a Nazi revival in West Germany while ignoring ex-Nazis in the East. And *The Nation* was continuing to dish out Werth's pro-Soviet homilies as if it were still 1942.⁴⁰ Despite some concession to reality on Kirchwey's part, *The Nation* had not had a new idea in years. The old pieties still dominated, making *The Nation* a place more of worship than of stimulating debate. This was not accidental but a matter of policy.

The January 19, 1953, issue of *Time* magazine carried a story with the heading "Dissenter Eliminated." It said that Margaret Marshall, "the last top editor who opposed the *Nation*'s pink-eyed views," had been fired, ostensibly to lower costs,

---

* Viereck taught at Mount Holyoke College in the heartland of academic progressivism, which strongly influenced his views. He told Macdonald that several pro-Communist professors were influential at Smith College. Further, to his distress, Vera Micheles Dean had just been added to the faculty. He did not feel that there was any witch-hunt on campus, except the one directed against himself for criticizing *The Nation*. "McCarthyism is a menace in the extrovert world and must be fought; but in the introvert world fellow traveling still is the main menace."

actually for her politics.[41] *Time* lied, was Kirchwey's response. No it didn't, answered Marshall, though she hoped the editors meant it when they said *The Nation*'s book section would go on being independent.

> On the contrary, I would be the last to be disappointed if the editors' attempt to prove that the elimination of my job and the transfer of the book department to the jurisdiction of the editors-in-power had nothing to do with politics—combined with the Soviet Union's plunge into anti-Semitism which the most beguiled "progressive" cannot explain away—should put *The Nation* back on the track of genuine liberalism. Better late than never.[42]

Of course Marshall did not really think there would be any changes in *The Nation*'s line, and none took place. The magazine did have to economize, as its circulation had fallen to about 33,000. Firing Marshall saved a few dollars. It also removed the last critical voice, which was, perhaps, even more important. But whatever the reasons for it, the move was self-defeating. One does not, in a little magazine, raise circulation by cutting quality. Partly because of her politics Marshall had been able to enlist anti-Stalinist reviewers of note. Unwelcome in the main body of *The Nation,* they made it more interesting and diverse even from the back. Without Marshall *The Nation* was less anomalous, more boring, and still in trouble. Loans from Kirchwey's husband and Corliss Lamont only delayed matters. In 1955 Kirchwey, whose editorial decisions had all but ruined the magazine, turned it over to Carey McWilliams. This meant that its politics would not change. "The *Nation,* in other hands, is still the *Nation,*" she wrote in her unpublished history of it.[43] But McWilliams knew that in order to save *The Nation* he had to do something. Too much was written by staff members, which was costly and limiting. McWilliams sought to broaden its appeal by employing more outside contributors. He also got rid of Vayo as foreign editor.

Kirchwey urged him not to, reminding McWilliams that "Vayo has been, for the *Nation,* both a banner and a hair-shirt. He represents something very profound in our tradition of independent radicalism, and in our individual conscience," and was proof that *The Nation* could not be "politically coerced."[44] McWilliams also saw Vayo as an embodiment of the magazine's fearlessly independent leftism. But Vayo knew nothing about American politics, and his English was so bad that he wrote his contributions in Spanish, which then had to be translated. He was, accordingly, a luxury *The Nation* could no longer afford.[45] Then, too, though McWilliams did not say so, as a notorious fellow traveler he may have been more trouble than he was worth. The old guard resented these changes. Vayo told Kirchwey that everyone was now referring to *The Nation* as that "lousy paper."[46] Through energetic fund raising, the recruitment of new names and a turn toward investigative reporting, *The Nation* was saved anyway. Ten years after McWilliams assumed control it was out of debt for the first time since World War II.

The Nation, and the *New Republic* also despite its return to liberalism, no longer occupied a central position in American intellectual life. Though *Commentary,* a monthly magazine, and the biweekly *Reporter* took up some slack, it was not until *The New York Review of Books* came along that intellectuals acquired a political voice with anything like the authority progressive weeklies had once enjoyed. Their place in the early fifties was taken not by a magazine but, to a degree, by an organization—the Committee for Cultural Freedom. This was not the same group organized by Sidney Hook in 1939 to fight the Popular Front. It was new, growing out of a Congress for Cultural Freedom held in West Berlin in June 1950. The congress was a Western response to a similar meeting of intellectuals held earlier under Communist auspices in East Berlin. The idea was to unite anti-Stalinist, pacifist and nonaligned intellectuals.

A Swiss journalist reporting on the meetings in Berlin thought that two approaches dominated them. West European intellectuals talked of fighting Communism by ending social injustice, building prosperous economies and achieving European federation. Americans, Berliners and refugees from the East took a harder line. They argued that freedom "must take the political offensive, encourage the oppressed peoples enslaved within the largest and most tyrannical empire in history."[47] It was decided that as these aims were not incompatible, a permanent organization embracing them could be formed. Its sponsors included such eminent figures as John Dewey, Benedetto Croce, Bertrand Russell, Karl Jaspers, Jacques Maritain and Reinhold Niebuhr.

Its American branch, known as the Committee for Cultural Freedom, was established in 1951 and consisted at first of six hundred well-known intellectuals ranging from Dwight Macdonald and Mary McCarthy on the left through Norman Thomas, Sidney Hook and Irving Kristol to such conservatives as James Burnham and Max Eastman. It was to be a Popular Front of anti-Stalinists, something like the League of American Writers in reverse. But the extreme spread of opinion, the members agreeing only on anti-Communism, made this difficult. The immediate issue dividing the American Committee for Cultural Freedom was McCarthyism. At an early meeting Macdonald and James Farrell argued that while overseas Communism was still a cultural danger, it no longer had any influence in the United States. Here the danger was posed by witch-hunters such as McCarthy and Senator McCarran. Accordingly, the committee's chief though not exclusive target should be McCarthyism. The opposite side was led by William Phillips of *Partisan Review* and Karl Wittfogel, an Asian scholar, who wanted Communism to be the main object of attack. Others, including Hook, Clement Greenberg and Bertram Wolfe, favored a middle course. Macdonald's impression was that the "old guard" of anti-Stalinists really did not want to go after McCarthy but might be brought around in time—Phillips and Wittfogel excepted.[48]

The split was publicly dramatized on March 29, 1952, by an ACCF conference "In Defense of Free Culture" held at the Waldorf-Astoria Hotel. There were five speakers, Elmer Rice, Richard Rovere, Mary McCarthy, Professor Conway Zirkle, a scientist, and Max Eastman. According to Macdonald's notes, the first three argued that the major threat was McCarthyism, while Zirkle held that scientific inquiry was not presently in danger. The greatest sensation was caused by Eastman, once a Bolshevik sympathizer, now an ardent enemy. "Standing in all his white-maned splendor, speaking in a voice trembling with emotion and/or dramaturgy, the Grand Old Man of Ex-Radicalism poured it on."[49]

Eastman said there was no red scare in progress, as anyone old enough to remember the lynchings and repression of World War I and the Palmer Raids era should know. The real threat to cultural freedom was from the worldwide Communist conspiracy. There were excesses, he admitted, but he blamed these on the failure of liberals to be sufficiently anti-Communist. Such people had "divided loyalties," in Eastman's view, and gave aid to the enemies of freedom. He singled out the ADA, the ACLU and Freedom House, all anti-Stalinist organizations, as falling into this category. His position was "alarmingly popular" to Macdonald, especially as the meeting had been called to discuss threats to freedom generally and not just to attack Communism. Eastman was interrupted by applause seven times during his talk and got a big hand at the end, though there were some hisses too, including Macdonald's. In the discussion that followed, most criticisms were directed at Rice and Eastman, who, "in the heat of forensic strife, went much further than their original speeches."

At one point Rice accused the publisher of *Red Channels* of having "killed my friend, Mady Christians" by putting her on the blacklist. Thereupon a man arose and identified himself as E. S. Harnett, the alleged murderer. He defended his information's accuracy and said it was no business of his how the material was used. Did Rice mean to suppress his right of free speech? Harnett asked. There was no discussion of this.

For at once another average-looking citizen arose two seats away from Mr. Harnett and introduced himself as his latest victim, Philip Loeb, for years a star on "The Goldbergs" and recently fired because of pressure generated by *Red Channels*. Mr. Loeb heatedly denied any Communist leanings, now or ever, accused his neighbor of having deprived him of his livelihood (and Miss Christians of her life), and stated he had brought a libel suit against *Red Channels*.

Everyone then began shouting and calling names. The chair desperately recognized an Indian, "who took the floor with a message from the East to the assembled representatives of Western culture." As the heat rose so did Eastman's temper. He praised *Red Channels* "for cleaning the Commie termites out of radio." And Eastman defended McCarthy, saying his only faults were that he had too fine and delicate a sense of fair play and an excessive honesty and integrity of purpose. At this "a chorus of laughter and hoots arose." Eastman had gone too far. Even though he backed down somewhat, liberals never forgave him for what he had said.

The event provoked an angry letter from Richard Rovere to Arthur Schlesinger, Jr. Rovere said the only way of combating neutralism abroad was "to prove beyond a doubt that American anti-Communism is not the blind, stupid, selfish thing so many neutralists assume it to be."[50] This should be accomplished by denouncing McCarthyism loudly and often. Inviting Eastman to call McCarthy a "clear-headed patriot of freedom," as, unfortunately, he had done, was not going to win friends overseas. How could Sidney Hook say there was no hysteria in America after this? inquired Rovere. The ACCF was to meet soon, and Rovere wanted Schlesinger and others of like mind to get an anti-McCarthy resolution passed, threatening to resign if they failed. Rovere did not think Eastman, who didn't "give a damn about cultural freedom," represented a majority, but most of the committee wished to accommodate him, which was why they had to be pushed the other way.

The committee met again on April 23, Macdonald once more taking copious notes. Chairman Sidney Hook, "who was fair and able throughout," read a draft statement of policy. Macdonald began debate by asking that, in the section on present dangers to cultural freedom, McCarthy be identified by name. He argued that McCarthy was "not just a plain oldfashioned liar like Lattimore but a totalitarian liar, in [the] sense [that] his lies are so big and wholly without foundation."[51] Daniel Bell proposed as an alternative leaving the draft as it was but passing a separate resolution condemning McCarthy as a liar, particularly for calling Edmund Wilson's book *Memoirs of Hecate County* (1946) pro-Communist.

Sentiment was against both proposals. In Macdonald's notes nineteen members are listed as speaking against naming McCarthy. Many said that it would increase McCarthy's importance were they to single him out. Some believed that it would be unfair unless they also named enemies of anti-Communism.

Elliot Cohen of *Commentary* said that if McCarthy was cited "we must also mention Freda Kirchweyism and Osmond K. Fraenkelism." Diana Trilling pointed out sensibly that "it is megalomania to think that M. [McCarthy] will be dignified, or elevated to a national symbol, merely by our naming him." Philip Rahv agreed. Trilling's husband, Lionel, did not support Macdonald's resolution, but wanted the section on academic freedom strengthened. The Lattimore case was on everyone's mind, all present detesting him, and some held that if McCarthy were named Lattimore should be too. James Wechsler of the *New York Post* was alarmed to find so much support for McCarthy at a meeting of intellectuals.

William Phillips offered this formula to justify not naming McCarthy: "We are all opposed to the methods of M., but he does not represent a social force. If we denounce him in the Draft, it implies we have a social theory about McCarthyism, but this is a very complicated and subtle question, [and] cannot be taken up in a Resolution." They should also go easy on McCarthy because he had become a symbol of digging Communists out of government. In an aside Macdonald remarked to himself that Phillips was saying in effect that though McCarthy was a liar and demanded one hundred percent conformity this meant nothing, since he was not a social force. Macdonald dismissed the argument as "real mechanical Marxism." Arthur Schlesinger, Jr., was more direct. "That's the stupidest speech of the evening," Macdonald heard him say. Hook summed up things at the end. He was distressed by the intolerance shown and the extent to which members disagreed. He had been against naming McCarthy for fear it would be taken as an endorsement of Lattimore and the IPR, but the extreme anti-anti-McCarthyism of some speakers had turned him around and he now favored Bell's resolution.

Because Hook was persuasive, or out of a desire to keep the ACCF together, members did not vote as they had spoken. Macdonald's resolution failed of course, with only Rahv, Diana Trilling, Schlesinger and a few others supporting it. But though a majority had spoken against citing McCarthy, Bell's resolution calling for a separate statement of condemnation passed unanimously. Lionel Trilling's resolution that the draft statement on academic freedom be made stronger passed easily as well. But as the vote did not follow the discussion, Macdonald failed to draw comfort from it. In a final note to himself Macdonald wrote that if *The Nation* was the stronghold of anti-anti-Communism, the ACCF bore the same relation to anti-anti-McCarthyism. *The Nation* had once said that we will not know the truth about the Moscow trials for a hundred years, and in the same manner the majority on the ACCF pretended that the truth about McCarthy was obscure and hard to fathom. Like Corliss Lamont on the Soviet Union, many committee members would admit that McCarthy had defects, but not enough to matter. They seemed to Macdonald more concerned about the civil liberties of McCarthy than about those of his victims.

Macdonald stayed on the committee several more years all the same, trying to keep it, as he believed, from going off the rails. This was not easy, for the committee tended to shoot first and ask questions later. An example was its attack on the newly formed Emergency Civil Liberties Committee. Though the ECLC was the heir of the Civil Rights Congress, an undoubted Communist front, it differed from the congress. There were no acknowledged Communists among its officers and sponsors, nor was it clear at the start that it would confine itself to defending the liberties of Communists. The ACCF sent a telegram to sixteen sponsors of the ECLC anyway, asking that they break with the organization.

In a press release the ACCF justified this action by saying that Carol Foreman, the director, a majority of the ECLC's executive committee and many sponsors had long records of affiliation with Communist fronts. Foreman had been a sponsor of the notorious Waldorf Cultural and Scientific Conference for World Peace in 1949, and for ten years was president of the Southern Conference for Human Welfare. Professor Thomas I. Emerson was a past president of the National Lawyers Guild, which was on the Attorney General's list of subversive organizations. Professor Henry Pratt Fairchild was another sponsor of the Waldorf conference. Of I. F. Stone it had only to be said that "he is the author of a book which blames the Korean war on aggressive action by the South Koreans in collusion with the American military authorities."[52] Another sponsor had been the Progressive Party candidate for governor of New Jersey, and so it went.

Macdonald objected strongly. In a letter to George Counts, chairman of the ACCF, he pointed out that the committee had made no effort to get on the program of the conference on civil liberties which the ECLC was sponsoring. The charge that the ECLC was a Communist front was reckless and un-documented. The press release put out by Irving Kristol for the committee listed only past associations of officers and spon-sors, most of them predating 1950, since when many people had changed their politics. Macdonald had made inquiries him-self, and both Emerson and Foreman had told him that in 1950 they had resigned from the Progressive Party and its national committee when the pro-Communist majority blamed South Korea for the war. Macdonald did not believe in using congres-sional reports as the basis for determining loyalty. Date of membership, prominence in the proscribed organizations and other matters often made an important difference. Calling the ECLC a Communist front without getting the facts straight was both "morally wrong" and "tactically inept." Finally, it was improper for a body calling itself the Committee for Cultural Freedom to jump on another group, not for having done any-thing, but for planning a conference on civil liberties—news of which had led to the telegram's being sent.

Macdonald did not mean to say that the ECLC was not a Communist front. Talking to Foreman, whom he considered evasive, had not settled his doubts. But he was certain that going off half cocked, before the facts were known, should be avoided. James T. Farrell agreed. He wrote to Counts that mak-ing a charge without having good evidence was not "conducive to winning more people away from them," a more important object than having "good publicity releases."[53] Thus censured, the executive committee of the ACCF backed down, drafting an apology to the ECLC for having called it a Communist front, but asking for more information.[54] Its representative to the actual conference was also of two minds. He was encouraged that non-Communist disclaimers were made by I. F. Stone and others. Efforts by Stalinists to put over the Party line were rebuffed. On the other hand, the conference had a progressive flavor, leading the ACCF observer to write that though not a Communist-controlled organization the ECLC was "*in effect* a communist front," whatever that meant.[55]

Macdonald, tired of struggling with the majority, who seemed to him interested only in Communist threats to cultural freedom, resigned from the ACCF in 1954. A year later he agreed to serve as co-editor of *Encounter,* one of several magazines put out by the Congress for Cultural Freedom. This was a step that made sense at the time. *Encounter* was published in Europe and reflected the cosmopolitan view of European anti-Stalinists. Whereas the ACCF embraced conservatives, the congress was made up largely of people who were leftists or at least believed that in fighting Communism one must offer socially conscious alternatives to it. The first editors of *Encounter* were Stephen Spender, a British poet and ex-Communist, and Irving Kristol. Their collaboration had not worked out, Kristol having brought to it the views of many American anti-Communists. As Spender explained to Sidney Hook, the success of *Encounter* required the editor to be sensitive to other values.

> The last point is very important: he should be concerned not just with the wickedness of communists but also with the condition of victims, and with victimization everywhere. The concept of the defence of freedom has surely to be based on a concept of the rights of humanity and not just on a "case" held by anti-communists against communists.[56]

Kristol lacked these necessary ideas, Spender believed, hence the failure of their editorial relation. Dwight Macdonald seemed exactly the right man because no American writer better combined anti-Stalinism with the social concerns vital to European intellectuals. Before agreeing to co-edit the magazine for a year, Macdonald wanted assurances that the Congress for Cultural Freedom differed sufficiently from its American branch. He was finally satisfied that "the former is concerned with defending cultural freedom against all comers and regardless of whether Communists, fascists, or mugwumps are the parties injured, while the latter is—not."[57] He was also told that the congress did not interfere with the editorial freedom of *Encounter*. Macdonald was unconcerned about the negative response of many in the ACCF to his appointment. He told Spender that these "veteran front-line fighters against Communism are anachronisms by now anyway."[58]

This was the view also of young Michael Harrington, not yet famous as the discoverer of American poverty. In 1955 he wrote a vigorous critique of the ACCF, charging that it followed Washington's lead and seemed less an organ of cultural freedom than of "intellectual colonialism." The committee had only one requirement for membership, anti-Communism, giving it a substantial conservative membership. This explained the presence on its executive committee of Whittaker Chambers, hateful to most liberals as the person who exposed Alger Hiss. The committee had no real interest in civil liberties, he further maintained, wishing only to search out and attack the few remaining fellow travelers who sought to exploit them. Harrington cited Kristol's now infamous article on civil liberties written three years earlier, and remarked that people were calling the group "the American Committee for Cultural Accommodation." Its great weakness was a failure to combat the violations of liberty in America, "instead of querulously minimizing their extent and gravity."[59] Another crippling assumption was the ACCF's belief that it should not intervene in cases where Stalinists or alleged Stalinists were involved. This rested on Sidney Hook's argument that Stalinists as enemies of democracy had no right to democratic privileges. The trouble with this was that the assault on cultural freedom and civil liberties assumed the guise of anti-Stalinism, as when Max Schachtman, a prominent leftist, despite his many years spent fighting Communism was denied a passport. Such violations are always made easier when there is the precedent of having done it first to a Stalinist.

Harrington was most incensed with the ACCF for supporting the red scare. The worst example of this, he believed, was a long letter to the *New Republic* in 1955 from Sol Stein of the ACCF. In it Stein defended congressional investigating committees generally, and the indictment of Owen Lattimore in particular. Harrington called this letter "downright inhumane." Equally bad were the letters printed by the *New Republic* from ACCF members agreeing with Stein, though some did not. They seemed to Harrington proof that American intellectuals favored absolute freedom in Russia but limits on freedom at home.

The exchange of letters was illuminating. Stein had written to the *New Republic* to protest an article criticizing the government for indicting Lattimore on the basis of his having said to the McCarran Committee, "I am not and have never been a Communist, a Soviet agent, sympathizer or any other kind of promoter of Communism or Communist interests, and all of these nonsenses."[60] Stein agreed with the McCarran Committee that Lattimore had been "a conscious, articulate instrument of the Soviet conspiracy against the free world."[61] Accordingly, the indictment of Lattimore was just.

The *New Republic* published numerous responses to Stein's letter. David Riesman, a sociologist well known as co-author of *The Lonely Crowd* (1949), wrote that he had resigned from the ACCF because too much of its time was spent on things such as Stein's unfortunate letter, which he had urged the executive committee not to send, as it put them "behind the pursuit of an already beleaguered man, living in limbo and not permitted to teach classes," and was therefore "an act of inhumanity."[62] Richard Rovere agreed with Stein's characterization of Lattimore, but not with his "satisfied-customer view of the McCarran Committee," which Rovere considered "a mess and a menace." Herbert J. Muller objected to the search for scapegoats, arguing that whatever Lattimore's faults he had not done as much harm to America as the witch-hunters. Arthur Schlesinger, Jr., said that while he wished Lattimore had been more candid about his past sympathies, prosecuting him for them was wrong, as also Stein's letter. Norman Thomas, writing for the ACCF's executive committee, declared himself against the indictment of Lattimore. The executive committee had enjoined Stein from endorsing the indictment, which he had done, but in such a way as to make clear he took pleasure in Lattimore's judicial ordeal. Michael Straight, speaking for the *New Republic,* held the rights of an individual to be at stake.

> Owen Lattimore's scholarship is forgotten; his reputation is all but ruined; his views are automatically suspect; his influence is not so great that a Committee for Cultural Freedom is required to add its kick to those of the US Senate and the Department of Justice. We distinguish ourselves from the Kremlin when we remember that Owen

Lattimore is neither a symbol, nor a slave, but a citizen of a free nation endowed with dignity and entitled to some respect. For the Communists the root is power, for some, the root is hatred of Communism: for the rest of us (and also, I am sure, for Norman Thomas), the root remains the individual and the decency he is due.[63]

In 1967 it was revealed that the Central Intelligence Agency had secretly financed various social and cultural activities, including *Encounter*. Dwight Macdonald had heard rumors to this effect as early as 1962, but had been assured that there was no truth to them, and that the only government funds received by the Congress for Cultural Freedom were a matter of public record. Macdonald felt betrayed when it turned out that he had been lied to, and the CIA connection has since been used to discredit the ACCF on the ground that as the congress was tainted by dirty money, so must its offshoot have been.[64] It remains unclear whether the ACCF ever actually received a subsidy. It did openly receive contributions from bodies such as the Foreign Service Education Foundation (headed by Christian Herter of the State Department).[65] If in addition the ACCF took money under the table this would have been disgraceful.

Yet it must be asked what the committee did with its funds, and here the record is plain. The ACCF campaigned against Stalinism at home and abroad. It also protested McCarthyism, most notably by sponsoring a book, *McCarthy and the Communists* (1954), roundly critical of the Senator, who was shown to be giving anti-Communism a bad name.[66] And it intervened in cases where civil servants found themselves in jeopardy owing to unfounded challenges to their loyalty. Further, the committee protested against what appeared to be government endorsement of repressive, even if friendly, regimes, as when it asked the State Department not to send representatives to a UNESCO meeting in Caracas on the ground that Venezuela was run by a cruel military dictatorship.[67] It was alarmed by passport and visa abuses also, and, Harrington to the contrary, even in cases where it deplored the politics of the individual. Thus, it protested the lifting of playwright Arthur Miller's passport as a blow to cultural freedom.[68] The committee did not pretend to cherish the liberties of its opponents equally with those of its friends, and this led its most libertarian members to resign, not only in the early years but as late as 1956, when James Farrell signed off as national chairman.[69]

But it was not a McCarthyite organization, which led most of its right-wing members to resign also, especially in 1954 when it sponsored *McCarthy and the Communists*. The ACCF was, as it claimed to be, middle of the road in the fight against Stalinist culture. Later it would seem as if there never had been any need for such an organization, given the rush with which intellectuals turned against Communism. This was hardly apparent in 1950, when Stalinist culture still appeared robust. The committee's founders had no way of knowing that it would not long be required. Afterward, they did not regret what they had done. The charge of Howe and Riesman and Macdonald that it had failed to function as an ACLU of culture was beside the point. The most active members never intended that it should. They believed that the danger to cultural freedom came first from Stalinists, later from McCarthyites. They fought both, and, despite lapses of judgment and taste, their record was better than critics have been willing to admit.

The debate over McCarthyism was by no means confined to the ACCF. It preoccupied the intellectual community as a whole for much of the 1950s. Well after McCarthy's depredations began, the *New Leader* was still making light of them. Norbert Muhlen argued that McCarthy's only sin was carelessness. It was one thing to see him as practicing "slap-happy, irresponsible, vulgar and non-factual techniques," and another to wrongly see him as the leader of a movement as dangerous to America as Communism itself. There was no climate of terror, nor any rule by injustice and informer, as *The Nation* was claiming. The victims of McCarthy's attacks were not defenseless, did not disappear into prisons and were not convicted without due process. The real danger to America, wrote Muhlen, was not McCarthyism but the fight against it. If Communists

can make liberals think McCarthyism is as much of a threat to freedom and justice as Communism, if they can divert the energies of liberals from the true and worldwide danger of Stalinism into a fight against a phantom ogre, then they will have achieved very much indeed. When, ten years hence, these "non-Communist liberals" admit once again that they have been misled, it will be ten years too late—by then, they may have helped to destroy our free world.[70]

Granville Hicks quickly pointed out that though Muhlen's facts were correct, they led to a false conclusion. Anti-McCarthyism was not just a cloak for pro-Communism—though it was that too. McCarthyism was a danger, and even if *Nation*-style liberals exaggerated it this did not make the danger less real. Could anyone deny, he asked, that there was less freedom of speech than five years earlier? It was absurd to make McCarthyism a threat equal to Communism; still, in this country at this time "ignorant anti-Communism is a greater danger than Communist propaganda."[71]

This debate embraced all three positions most commonly taken by intellectuals on the issue. The anti-anti-Communists, or "non-Communist liberals," criticized by Muhlen held that McCarthyism was the only threat to American liberty and dismissed all attacks on Communism as red-baiting. Hicks's position was far more popular, taken not only by many in the ACCF but by most prominent intellectuals. Muhlen's view was that of the right-wing intellectuals, a small minority. Their case was developed by William F. Buckley and Brent Bozell in *McCarthy and His Enemies* (1954), then the most complete accounting of his years in power.

The authors maintained that in 1950 when McCarthy went on the rampage America was confused about Communism. There had been an evolution away from pro-Communism, but it had gotten only as far as anti-anti-Communism. The question then was "how might we get by our disintegrated ruling elite, which had no stomach for battle, and get down to the business of fighting the enemy in our midst?"[72] This established a level of muddle above which the book was never to rise. In fact by 1950 Communists were being purged from Hollywood, the trade-union movement and just about every other place where they had once exercised influence. The Party itself was riddled with FBI informers, as the trial of CP leaders in 1949 had shown, and was no threat to anyone. If by "ruling elite" the authors meant Truman's Administration, it could hardly be accused of indifference to Communism. It had implemented a loyalty program so extreme as to threaten liberty. And the FBI which had thoroughly penetrated the Communist Party was, of course, a branch of government headed by the very same Administration. Anti-anti-Communism was not subscribed to by government, nor even by most intellectuals, but only by a defensive minority represented by *The Nation*. This was not entirely clear at the time, hence the Committee for Cultural Freedom. But by 1954 the evidence was compelling.

Support for McCarthy rested on the misconception, which Buckley and Bozell took for granted, that domestic Communism was a powerful force in need of exposure. The authors then asked how effectively McCarthy performed this necessary task. A labored review of his career led to this box score. McCarthy had questioned the loyalty of forty-six persons, not including references to established Communists such as Hiss. Twelve of these were named only once, being already under investigation by the State Department, and ten other names were uncovered during investigations not made by McCarthy and were mentioned only to show that the loyalty program was defective. McCarthy's record as a destroyer of reputations rested, then, on twenty-four names. He did exaggerate a little, they admitted, as in calling Lattimore a top Soviet agent, but on the whole was doing extremely well. The authors wished McCarthy would stop saying his critics were either Communists or benefiting Communism, as this hurt his credibility. Otherwise he was fine, and so was liberalism, to their regret. Within six months of a campaign speech in October 1952 during which McCarthy attacked prominent liberals by name, three of them were honored: Archibald MacLeish won both the National Book Award and the Pulitzer Prize for poetry; Bernard De Voto received the National Book Award for history; and Arthur Schlesinger, Jr., was named co-chairman of Americans for Democratic Action.

McCarthy and His Enemies failed in several respects. To begin with, McCarthy was indefensible. A case of sorts could be made for other investigators. Many anti-Stalinists believed that

HUAC and even the McCarran Committee were careful enough, paid due regard to the rights of witnesses, and did not inquire except where there was reasonable suspicion. But this could not be said of McCarthy, who attacked first and looked for evidence later, dropped old allegations only to dream up new ones, bullied witnesses, and was a disgrace to the Senate and the nation. Buckley and Bozell ignored or minimized these failings, praising not only McCarthy but even Louis Budenz, most notorious of the professional witnesses.

Joseph Alsop, whose anti-Communism was never in doubt, had exposed him in 1952. Budenz was formerly editor of the Communist *Daily Worker*. After leaving the Party he testified endlessly against various people, notably Owen Lattimore. Before 1950 Budenz had never cited Lattimore in the course of some three thousand hours of talks with the FBI. In 1947 he told a State Department investigator that he had no knowledge to indicate that Lattimore was a Communist. In 1949 Budenz said to an editor of *Collier's* magazine that though Lattimore was misguided he had never acted in the way a Communist would. But after McCarthy accused Lattimore of spying Budenz went to the FBI and denounced him as a Communist, repeating the allegation to investigating committees. When his failure to name Lattimore earlier raised questions, Budenz replied that Whittaker Chambers had not been believed, either, when he fingered Alger Hiss. But the difference, as Alsop pointed out, was that Chambers had supported his claim with a mass of evidence, while Budenz offered none. Budenz almost never had proof of his charges, quoting instead from talks he supposedly had with other Communists while a Party member. They always turned out to be people who, for one reason or another, could not testify. When he cited documents, they could not be produced.

As it happened, Alsop knew from personal experience that one of the allegations Budenz made against Lattimore was false. During the war he had been on the staff of Major General Claire Chennault, former chief of the Flying Tigers and head of the Fourteenth Air Force in China. Alsop was living in Chennault's house when Henry Wallace and his party (including Lattimore) passed through during Wallace's famous visit to Asia. Thus he knew from personal experience that Lattimore and John Carter Vincent had not opposed the replacement of General Stilwell as American theater commander in China by General Wedemeyer, Budenz to the contrary, but rather had urged Wallace to back Wedemeyer. This was important because Stilwell hated Chiang Kai-shek and leaned toward supporting the Communists as the only Chinese actually fighting Japan. Wedemeyer's appointment as his successor was, therefore, "the heaviest blow that could then be struck at the Communist cause in China," a blow which Lattimore and Vincent helped strike.[73]*

One need not swallow Alsop's views on everything to take the point. Efforts to prove that China went Communist because of disloyal Americans were part of the insanity of the time, and of political opportunism by Republicans seeking to discredit the Democratic Party. The results of this were, perhaps, the most harmful of the entire red scare, as they locked America's China policy into a self-defeating course for many years. McCarthy was the worst offender, aided and abetted by the China Lobby, including Buckley and Bozell. Their book, supposedly in aid of McCarthy's case, showed the emptiness of it. No one named by McCarthy was in a position to influence State Department policy on China except John Stewart Service, and his advice, like that of nearly every authority on China, was not taken. Then, too, *McCarthy and His Enemies* failed because the authors sought to have it both ways. For purposes of building him up, McCarthy was shown as the fearless leader of a great popular movement that was turning America around. But when it came to answering liberal criticisms the authors reversed themselves, minimizing McCarthy and pointing to the vigor of liberalism as proof that he had little effect. As so often in these polemical wars, bad history and bad logic made for a bad book.

But though wrong about McCarthy, the authors did not err when they pointed to the lively opposition as evidence that the intellectual community had not been terrorized. In fact the

---

* Alsop did not suggest that Stilwell was in league with the Communists. He thought Stilwell's policy mistaken but never for a moment doubted the general's loyalty. He believed it was bad judgment, not treason, that lost China to the Communists.

country rang with denunciations of him, posing something of the same problem for sober anti-Communists as McCarthy himself did. Leslie Fiedler, a young critic and writer, remarked on this in an article written only months before McCarthy fell. Many liberals had taken the position that anyone McCarthy attacked was clearly innocent. This backfired in the case of Lattimore, who, though certainly not a Soviet agent, was shown to have been pro-Soviet. It was especially embarrassing when in the course of his testimony he tried to explain why he had defended the Moscow purge trials, or why, after he had explained to the American ambassador in Moscow that Outer Mongolia was an independent state, he had applied for a visa to it at the Russian Foreign Office. This exposed the falseness of what Fiedler called the liberal theory of "innocence by association." What of the larger claim that McCarthyism, whatever the merits of individual cases, had created an "atmosphere of suspicion, a stifling pressure of conformity"? That was debatable, too, for surely it could also be said that nothing was easier than to attack McCarthy, particularly in Eastern academic circles.

Beyond them there was a kind of anti-McCarthy popular front made up of socialists and libertarians, Old Guard and New Deal Democrats, leading spokesmen for all the major religions, and many Republicans, including apparently even the President and Vice-President of the United States. McCarthy's book *The Fight Against Communism* had not even been reviewed, while the Buckley and Bozell defense of him had received nothing but hostile notices. Virtually every major publication had editorialized against McCarthy, who was endorsed only by the Hearst and McCormick press and "back-country weeklies." This meant to Fiedler that the support for McCarthy came from the traditional reactionaries who found in McCarthy a fresh voice for old points of view. McCarthy might be defeated—most probably, Fiedler guessed, as happened, when Republicans came to see him as a liability—but the people he represented would remain.

In this larger fight against what he saw as a degenerate relic of populism, Fiedler believed that intellectuals were handicapped by their own guilty past when they had allowed Communism "to establish itself in the intellectual community as an acceptable variant of the liberal-humanistic tradition—and even more, made its recognition as such a variant the very test of political decency."[74] Hence the struggle was twofold.

> The fight against McCarthyism is more than the fight against McCarthy; it is a struggle against the distortions of the Right and the outlived illusions of the Left, against the blind resentment of the American mob and the arrogant superciliousness of the American intellectual. In this fight, each victory is only a new beginning.[75]

Fiedler's position, a more sophisticated version of Irving Kristol's, was one he took in other essays that were republished in *An End to Innocence* (1955). Many liberals resented Fiedler's argument that because they had been indifferent to the defects of Communism they were partly to blame for the success of McCarthyism. Progressives and ex-progressives were most offended, but some anti-Stalinists too. Harold Rosenberg, who did not have anything to apologize for, was angry at Fiedler just the same. Rosenberg accused Fiedler of rewriting the past so as to spread the guilt for Communist misdeeds over liberals as a whole. In Fiedler's essays on Hiss, the Rosenberg case and McCarthy it always "turns out that whoever suffered deserved what he got for not confessing and that we intellectuals with our 'shorthand' that the people cannot understand are deeply implicated."[76] Worse still,

> Fiedler's essays blend the new fake-liberal anti-Communism with that of the old fake-liberal fellow traveler to produce a "liberal" who shares the guilt for Stalin's crimes through the fact alone of having held liberal or radical opinions, *even anti-Communist ones!* For Fiedler *all* liberals are contaminated by the past, if by nothing else than having spoken the code language of intellectuals.[76]

It is not entirely clear from Rosenberg's essay why he was so upset. His politics were not strikingly different from Fiedler's. He criticized Fiedler for overgeneralizing, but responded with more of the same. Fiedler's essays were not always tightly constructed, Rosenberg wandered also. Fiedler's point that liberals were reluctant to confront their past was certainly true, as

Rosenberg, a veteran of the anti-Stalinist wars, should have admitted. Only near the end of his polemic did Rosenberg offer a clue to the reason for it. Ex-Communists had been confessing to past misdeeds, but in a way unsatisfactory to Rosenberg. Communist ideologues had hated most the "independent radical intellectuals," and had missed no chance to strike at them. But now the anti-Stalinist opposition was being forgotten, not only by ex-Communists but by liberal anti-Communists also. Perhaps this accounts for the attack on Fiedler, who by paying no attention to the old anti-Stalinists became to Rosenberg part of the conspiracy of silence burying his own past.

For liberals the most important loyalty case was that of Alger Hiss, and it led to more soul-searching, as also more defensiveness, than any other. Hiss was found guilty of having perjured himself in denying under oath that he had committed treason in the 1930s. The circumstances surrounding his case were theatrical, so much so that a documentary film about it made long afterward was received by critics as less a history than a work of art.[77] The point at issue was whether Alger Hiss, while a government employee, had passed on confidential documents to Soviet intelligence. But the case was treated from the outset as if much more were at stake. *A Generation on Trial* (1950) was the title of one account of it by the journalist Alistair Cooke. Many saw it as the acid test of the whole progressive experience. Thus years later *The Nation* would devote pages and pages to an attack on Allen Weinstein's book *Perjury: The Hiss-Chambers Case*, a scholarly work.[78] This was not because of poor scholarship—to the contrary, professionals welcomed it— but because Weinstein was convinced of Hiss's guilt. Hiss must be proven innocent, it is still believed by many, so as to establish the highmindedness and dedication to right ideals of Popular Front liberalism. Philip Rahv put it this way in reviewing Whittaker Chambers' book *Witness* (1952):

And the fierce resistance which Chambers encountered when he finally broke through with his testimony to the nation at large was essentially a symptom of the anguish of the Popular Front mind and its unreasoning anger at being made to confront the facts of political life. The importance of the Hiss case was precisely that it dramatized that mind's struggle for survival and its vindictiveness under attack. That mind is above all terrified of the disorder and evil of history, and it flees the harsh choices which history so often imposes. It fought to save Hiss in order to safeguard its own illusions and to escape the knowledge of its gullibility and chronic refusal of reality.[79]

Leslie Fiedler took this argument the farthest, engaging also in speculations about motive and psychology that Rosenberg found offensive. Fiedler began by asking why Hiss had not confessed to treason, excusing himself on the ground of good intentions. Hiss was not unique. Others, such as the Rosenbergs, also denied any guilt. This was in marked contrast to political prisoners in the old days who used their trials as opportunities for propaganda. In lying about his past, Fiedler said, Hiss was being typical. "His is, as we shall see, the Popular Front mind at bay, incapable of honesty even when there is no hope in anything else."[80] When the guilty did confess they showed moral obtuseness, according to Fiedler. Henry Julian Wadleigh admitted passing secret documents to Chambers but claimed to have been justified by history. "He finds in his own earlier activities only a certain excessive zeal, overbalanced by good will, and all excused by—Munich." Wadleigh's confession was almost as crass a lie as Hiss's denial. "He cannot, even on the dock, believe that a man of liberal persuasion is capable of wrong."

> It was this belief that was the implicit dogma of American liberalism during the past decades, piling up a terrible burden of self-righteousness and self-deceit to be paid for on the day when it would become impossible any longer to believe that the man of good will is identical with the righteous man, and that the liberal is, per se, the hero.[81]

Thus it was not treason but blindness that discredited Hiss's generation.

Certainly a generation was on trial with Hiss, on trial not, it must be noticed, for having struggled toward a better world, but for having substituted sentimentality for intelligence in that struggle, for having failed to understand the moral conditions that must determine its outcome. What is involved is not any question of all or most of the younger New Dealers having been, like Hiss, secret agents of the GPU, but of their having been so busy denying that there was a GPU or that it mattered that they could not identify an enemy of all the values in which they most profoundly believed.[82]

Fiedler held that most liberals were glad Hiss denied his guilt, thus sparing them the need to confront their own. It was this that angered him.

An exchange between Diana Trilling and Hans Meyerhoff focused the issue of liberal guilt most sharply. One of the famous cases of the McCarthy era did not involve the Senator at all but rather the Atomic Energy Commission. In 1954 the AEC removed the security clearance of J. Robert Oppenheimer, known as the "father of the atomic bomb" owing to his wartime leadership of the nuclear-weapons project. Liberals were aghast that so eminent a figure could be humiliated in this public way, and viewed the case as an example of McCarthyism minus McCarthy. Diana Trilling arrived at a different conclusion after reading the lengthy transcript of the hearings that resulted in Oppenheimer's disgrace.

This had been accomplished in two stages. First a Personnel Security Board had reviewed Oppenheimer's record. After hearings the board announced on June 2, 1954, that it had found Oppenheimer to be a loyal American, whose security clearance should be lifted anyway because he had opposed making the hydrogen bomb. On June 30 the AEC, in a report written by Chairman Lewis Strauss, reached the same end by an opposite path. The AEC declared that it had not considered Oppenheimer's position on the H-bomb, because he had a perfect right to take any stand he wished. The AEC pulled his clearance because of instances—it listed six—which revealed defects of character inappropriate to a person with access to government secrets.

Trilling agreed with most liberals that this was deplorable. A study of the transcript showed that Oppenheimer had been at a considerable disadvantage. The AEC had taken a prosecutorial role that loaded the dice against him. Whatever the AEC might say, it was evident that if Oppenheimer had not opposed the H-bomb he would never have been investigated. Trilling had supposed, in view of his past as a fellow traveler, that Oppenheimer had favored developing the strongest possible weapon for use against the enemy in wartime, but afterward opposed developing a stronger weapon, as its likely target would be the Soviet Union. There was no question about Oppenheimer's past. He had been a fellow traveler and closely associated with Communists or former Communists, including his wife, brother, and sister-in-law. He had given large sums of money to Communist causes, in payments made directly to CP representatives. By his own testimony he had not become disillusioned with the Soviet Union until 1946 or '47.

Trilling found, however, that Oppenheimer had become anti-Communist before the H-bomb decision was made, and that he opposed it for practical reasons. He feared that it would divert resources from atomic weaponry, that it might not work, that even if it did it would be less useful than atomic weapons, and that it would compromise efforts to achieve arms control. These were doubts entertained by many who had no past record of fellow traveling. As Trilling put it, neither "pacifism nor tenderness for the Soviet Union" influenced Oppenheimer's position. Accordingly, there was no basis here for removing his security clearance.

The more serious charges made by the AEC arose from certain incidents in 1943. The chief one was that Oppenheimer had lied about a request that he pass on secret information to the Soviet Union. It was issued by a member of the Communist Party and relayed to Oppenheimer by a close friend, Haakon Chevalier, an instructor in Romance languages at the University of California.* Oppenheimer rejected the overture, and informed security personnel of it. But he lied about Chevalier, saying that three different people whom he wished to leave nameless had approached him. Under pressure he finally gave Chevalier's name, having raised doubts about himself that would not go away in the vain effort to save his friend. Of the other five

---

* Chevalier, like Oppenheimer a member of the pro-Soviet left but not a Communist, denied this. He remembered only having warned Oppenheimer that such an approach had been made to him, which he had rejected as improper.

instances cited by Strauss, two were trivial and three involved discrepancies in Oppenheimer's testimony as to whether he had known certain individuals to be Communists.

Oppenheimer's defense was that he had tried to protect Chevalier out of friendship. The confusion over the point at which he learned that various people were Communists was attributed to the lapse of time. Trilling, in her most original contribution to the debate, argued that this was a poor strategy. Trilling believed that the right course would have been to tell the truth, which she understood differently. In her view Oppenheimer had withheld Chevalier's name not simply out of friendship but because of sympathy for Communism and the state of public opinion. A security officer, in the course of his testimony, recalled that during World War II he had not been able to prevent known Communists from being commissioned into the military because of interference from the White House—which he attributed to Mrs. Roosevelt. Trilling went on:

> Fairness to Dr. Oppenheimer requires that we remind ourselves that our current acute relations with Russia, of which the Oppenheimer case is only one relatively small result, would very likely never have reached their present point of crisis had not so much of the energy of liberalism been directed, in the very period in which Dr. Oppenheimer failed to report Chevalier, to persuading the American people that Russia was our great ally instead of the enemy of democracy and peace which she had already clearly demonstrated herself to be! If the dominant liberal sentiment of the time, from the White House down, could put its whole blind force on the side of protecting friends of the Soviet Union, why should Dr. Oppenheimer alone have been expected to see with the unclouded eyes of the future and promptly report his friend.[83]

The right kind of defense, then, would have reconstructed the situation as it had been in 1943. It would have admitted that Oppenheimer had a lingering sympathy for radicalism, "however ambiguous and however unconscious" it was. This would not reflect on his present loyalty and would eliminate the air of dishonesty that surrounded his position. By the same token Oppenheimer would have been more believable if he had said in

1954 that he lied about Chevalier in 1943, and also about having favored hiring a Communist named Lomanitz to work on the A-bomb because at the time he and many others did not see anything wrong with Party membership. Instead he testified during the hearings that he had not known Lomanitz was a Communist in 1943, after which evidence was brought forward indicating that he had. Revealing the truth, as Trilling understood it, would have clarified the discrepancies in Oppenheimer's testimony and created an impression of probity, unlike his actual testimony. Even so, though Oppenheimer had taken the wrong road in defending himself, there was still no reason to lift his clearance. The standards by which he was deemed a security risk were so strict that anyone might fail them. Oppenheimer had not passed on secret information during that time in his life when political sympathies made him most likely to. Why deny him clearance now when his loyalty was established? At best this seemed an act of "tragic ineptitude. In effect it constitutes a projection upon Dr. Oppenheimer of the punishment we perhaps owe ourselves for having once been so careless with our nation's security."[84]

Trilling's speculation, ingenious and plausible though it was, infuriated Hans Meyerhoff, as did the assumptions on which it rested. Meyerhoff, a contributor to *Partisan Review,* fired off an angry rebuttal. He compared Trilling's essay invidiously with an article by the Alsops on Oppenheimer denouncing the AEC's decision as a "shocking miscarriage of justice."[85] Trilling had failed on two counts, said Meyerhoff. First, she "evades or avoids any reference to anything that might possibly have any meaning for the liberal culture of our times."[86] Worse still, the significance she did find in the case "refers exclusively to the personal charges which formed the basis of the verdict by Admiral Strauss, and in such a way as to implicate the liberal tradition itself in these charges." Trilling looked only at the liberal culture in explaining public opinion in 1943, whereas the Alsops had correctly shown that not only liberals but all articulate people were pro-Russian. They had offered the example of *Time* magazine, which in that year criticized the government for sending Charles Bohlen to accompany Cordell Hull's mission to Moscow, on the ground that Bohlen was prejudiced against the Soviets.

Meyerhoff was especially incensed with Trilling for having said that had liberals not worked so hard to misrepresent Russia during the war things would be better now. He maintained that they did not have the option favored by Trilling of exposing Russia, since doing so would have been to commit "political suicide." Meyerhoff called her guess as to Oppenheimer's motive in 1943 a "far-fetched and wildly speculative" theory. If Oppenheimer had taken the course recommended by Trilling he would have been saying, in effect, that he was more guilty than he thought but should be forgiven and cleared "because, you see, the whole liberal culture of which I was a part was so much worse than anybody knew it was."[87] Meyerhoff resented Trilling's essay because it ignored the present implications of the case and focused solely on the mistakes of liberal culture in the 1930s and '40s. Perhaps, he concluded, "it is high time for some competent student of our society (without guilty feelings) to redress the historical balance in order to do justice, if not to Dr. Oppenheimer, at least to the liberal record and cause."[88]

Trilling's response was brief and pointed. She rejected Meyerhoff's charge that if a good liberal she "should have used the Oppenheimer case only as an occasion for attack upon our present-day political culture." This was the Alsop approach, with which she disagreed. Minimizing his past politics was "disrespectful to Dr. Oppenheimer and disastrous to his defense." It was also an evasion of truth not consistent with liberalism or historical fact. If Oppenheimer had not been a fellow traveler there would be no case against him. Further, there were problems with his testimony that had not been resolved. Trilling tried to do so in terms of Oppenheimer's past relation with the Communist Party. This was a fact, not something invented by herself. To ignore it as Meyerhoff wanted would be not only to evade reality but to leave the charges against Oppenheimer unanswered. "It would also mean leaving the historical truth for the reactionary forces in our society to deal with for their own purposes."[89] She chided Meyerhoff for misrepresenting Oppenheimer's effort to protect Chevalier. It involved not just one lie but a whole string of lies, which were "very inconvenient" for those wishing to defend Oppenheimer, including herself.

This habit of glossing over the truth about Communism, which Meyerhoff was urging on her, was one of the things that had discredited liberalism as a "vital cultural and political force." Experience had shown that it was "inexpedient" to deny truth "in the supposed interest of expediency." If Trilling had treated the Oppenheimer case as simply another example of McCarthyism in the fashion of Alsop she would have been wrong. The case was more than just a matter of appealing "to the base sentiments of the reactionary elements in our society."

> On the contrary, such is the force of probity and decency which still persists in American life, and this despite the upsurge of a reactionary spirit and our properly alarmed response to it, that there is a most notable difference between the charges first formulated against Dr. Oppenheimer and the charges on which he was finally judged to be a security risk. The final charges, as I have said, point straight to the testimony—to the evidence against Dr. Oppenheimer, as such evidence applies to security regulations in the matter of character and associations. They do not point to the mere fact that Dr. Oppenheimer was once a fellow-traveler and should therefore be punished.[90]

Trilling said again that the judgment against Oppenheimer was mistaken, but not attributable to any "vicious political motive." Meyerhoff needed to remember that some people who were conscientious and who opposed McCarthyism agreed with the AEC. They should not be ruled out of the liberal camp for this, though that is what Meyerhoff would presumably have done.

Trilling was right. In case after case liberal intellectuals had defended not only accused individuals such as Hiss and Lattimore, but the entire liberal record as well, including those periods when eminent liberals and progressives had in fact been misled about Communism and the Soviet Union. Meyerhoff had echoed others in saying that liberals failed to tell the truth because doing so would have been politically suicidal. It was a strange defense inasmuch as it implied that liberals knew the truth, at least by 1943, but dared not express it. Such may have been the case for liberal politicians—though even here the question was arguable. But it certainly was not true of writers and intellectuals. Max Eastman had done so that very year in his notorious article in *Reader's Digest,* when he urged Americans not to forget in their desire to cooperate with Russia that Communism was a totalitarian doctrine. Eastman suffered for this, but it was his later defense of McCarthy, not his earlier warnings against the Soviet Union, that was chiefly held against him. Trilling might have erred in not acknowledging that the false progressive stand on Russia was shared by most people in authority at the time as well as by most liberals. But for Americans as a whole pro-Soviet views were transient and lightly held, products of the war. And, in the event, it was liberal culture, not that of the whole nation, with which she was concerned.

Like other critics Trilling unfairly lumped all liberals together, doing an injustice to the anti-Stalinist minority of the 1930s and '40s which had steadfastly opposed the progressive intellectuals. And she was wrong, too, in claiming that the world would be better off if liberals had not condoned Stalinism, as they did not make foreign policy. But on the main point Trilling was certainly right. The sickness of liberalism in the fifties did not result from McCarthyism, but from its own exploitable mistakes in the past. The failure to admit this was, and to a degree remains, bad in principle and, as Trilling said, inexpedient too. The Greenberg-Meyerhoff position was that admitting past errors weakened liberals in their struggle against McCarthyism. Though Trilling did not say so, this was the line of reasoning that progressives had followed earlier in defending the Soviet Union—thereby compiling the record which McCarthyism took advantage of. In both cases liberals insisted that the cause was more important than the truth. The question, then, was whether a cause that could not face the truth was worth defending. To this many liberals had no answer.

XI

The Academy
and the Crisis of Liberalism

FOR MOST LIBERALS the issue of past failings was not so urgent as current matters of strategy. A crucial one was how to handle investigating committees. Here also, opinions varied. After the Hollywood Ten went to prison for invoking their First Amendment right not to testify, hostile witnesses usually took the Fifth Amendment. Others told all, sometimes from conviction. Granville Hicks was called by HUAC in 1953 to testify about the extent of Communism at Harvard during the 1930s. There was no reason for Hicks not to, as he had been an open member of the Party and had written at length about his experiences. In his testimony Hicks drew what appeared to him the obvious moral.

> It seems to me I have been sitting around here for two days in which it has been demonstrated that there were ten or twelve Communists at Harvard fourteen years ago and that perhaps there is one still there. Now I would honestly think, if you could just say to the public "Look that's all," instead of saying "look how much there is, isn't that terrible?" you might do a good deal to allay the fear that is sweeping over this country.[1]

Max Lerner applauded Hicks. "He showed that a man who disapproves sharply of the committee's procedures and work nevertheless can answer the questions put to him with dignity, courage, and complete candour."[2] This was right in principle and effective too. If there were more witnesses like Hicks the committee would be out of a job. Lerner's point was not entirely a matter of wishful thinking. In the 1960s when hostile witnesses began speaking up instead of hiding behind the Constitution, HUAC withered away. Though other factors were involved, it did seem that HUAC's previous success had been based in part on the ability to intimidate, and on witnesses who, by taking the Fifth, gave the impression of having much to hide. As David Caute put it: "Witness after witness fenced, dodged, hid, and looked furtive; being a Communist, or a radical, was *apparently* something to be ashamed of, something to conceal, something that, in Richard Arens' words, prevented a man from standing up for himself and being counted 'like a red-blooded American.' "[3]

But to look at the ease with which people later mocked the committee understates the hard choices facing earlier witnesses. These were spelled out by two legal experts in the worst days of the McCarthy era. Laurent Frantz and Norman Redlich were annoyed that those who took the Fifth Amendment before congressional committees were said to misuse the right not to incriminate themselves.[4] The contrary view was advanced by Alan Westin.[5] Though long and complex, the two arguments boiled down to this: Frantz and Redlich held that witnesses before congressional committees investigating disloyalty should always take the Fifth, if guilty as the best defense, if innocent to protect themselves and others from being framed or prosecuted. It was also the best way to combat McCarthyism, which gained whenever witnesses cooperated, however minimally.

Westin was not concerned with the individual's right to invoke the Fifth, which he never doubted, but rather the wisdom of doing so. To his mind witnesses ought to testify even if they were, or had been, Communists or sympathizers. Admitting the truth was hardly more risky than taking the Fifth, since as a rule in either case the same reprisals followed. And it had the advantage of enabling people to defend their political beliefs. Silence played into the hands of witch-hunters by strengthening the impression of widespread guilt and conspiracy. Full disclosure might check them, and could only reduce fear to the extent it was based on ignorance and groundless suspicion. The next-best alternative, and one requiring as much if not more courage, was to testify about oneself while refusing to speak of others without invoking immunity. This was the path taken by Arthur Miller before HUAC two years later, which resulted in a contempt citation. Westin preferred that witnesses answer all questions, arguing that it was both honorable and politically expedient.

Time would seem to have borne him out. Opportunistic legislators thrived on silent witnesses. It was those who testified that slowed the witch-hunt down. Two failures occurred. Congress was to blame for not putting the loyalty hearings in perspective. They really showed, as Hicks said, that despite the existence of Communists and sympathizers little harm was done. Communism in government did not weaken the nation. Hollywood Communism led to the making of three propaganda movies during the war, out of a total of several thousand pictures. Some hundreds of teachers had been Communists, too few to have any effect on the vast American educational system. The same was true of organized religion. Many unions had been led by Communists. These were removed, mostly by other union leaders. Public alarm was so much greater than the facts warranted in part because they were misrepresented. Headlines seldom pointed this out, reporting instead accusation, denial or the taking of the Fifth with little regard for what was significant. Politicians followed suit, or even led the way, exploiting instances of disloyalty and proclaiming dangers that did not exist. An opportunity was thereby lost of using congressional hearings to reassure the public and make evident the small risk to national security that had formerly existed.

Secondly, witnesses who refused to testify aided this process and must share the blame. Except in the rare cases where disloyalty was involved, cooperative witnesses revealed little that was scary. It was unfriendly witnesses who promoted hysteria, for their silence was always taken to mean guilt, complicity in vast schemes to overthrow the republic. This was not only because silence has always been taken as a sign of bad faith, but more particularly because Party members were instructed not to testify and it was reasonable, even if untrue, to assume that all who took the Fifth were under Communist orders. Non-Communists who refused to testify furthered the aims of the Communist Party, inflamed tempers, and strengthened the hand of unscrupulous or misguided investigators. Sometimes they compromised their own best interests. Almost always they damaged the national interest. This was a mistaken course, even when taken for laudable reasons.

Efforts today, as by Victor Navasky in *Naming Names* (1980), to canonize unfriendly witnesses only repeat the original error. Most non-Communists who kept quiet did so, it appears, with the idea of protecting themselves or their friends. This did not work usually and at best reflected a schoolyard code of ethics according to which honest declarations made one an informer or "squealer" or "stool pigeon." What the nation required was people who were not prevented from telling the truth by childish misconceptions. It did not need the lies, or implied lies, that silence represented. And it does not now need to have such conduct glorified as heroic dedication to principle. There had been real cases of disloyalty, and government had a right, however much it was abused, to act against them. Silence promoted those abuses, fueled the red scare, and obscured truth. It was the friend of McCarthyism, not the enemy as progressives believed. Trilling and Westin rightly pointed out that liberals did their own cause no good by going along. It only made them appear to be accessories to treason and a further cause for alarm.

Legislative investigations played a central role in the attacks on academic freedom that were of special concern to intellectuals. Partly this was because there were so many more professors than earlier—some 180,000 in 1950—partly also because so many intellectuals now had college or university appointments. The first generation of radical intellectuals that came of age before the World War I included almost no college teachers. Academic freedom was weak, and the university was not seen as the right place for someone with unpopular ideas. Max Eastman typified this spirit by completing all the requirements for a Ph.D. in philosophy while declining to take the degree. That there was no room in the academy for dissidents seemed proven when the University of Pennsylvania fired economics professor Scott Nearing for being a Socialist. The growth of higher education and of academic freedom changed things. By the McCarthy era it was estimated that some 1,500 college instructors had belonged to the Communist Party at one time or another. Few proclaimed their membership, but few also appear to have made a secret of their beliefs. In the Popular Front years, leftism was not seen of itself as reason for dismissal and it was rare, at better colleges and universities anyway, for faculty to suffer from politically motivated reprisals.

The Cold War, however, made scholars vulnerable on account of positions which, when originally taken, had not been seen as notably harmful or dangerous. Many professors were called before investigating committees, and somewhere between one and two hundred lost their appointments, and often their academic careers. This was especially true in New York. David Caute estimated that fifty-eight college faculty members were expelled from their jobs in the city alone.[6] Many were dismissed in California too, not only because of investigating committees but as a result of loyalty oaths which the offending professors would not sign. Few major universities escaped at least token firings, usually as a result of teachers invoking the Fifth Amendment.

Intellectuals divided over whether Communists should be allowed to teach. Though today almost any kind of political test is seen as repugnant and injurious to liberty, this was not so in the 1940s and '50s when many thoughtful people believed that Communist Party membership disqualified one as a teacher. Sidney Hook argued the case strongly. In a controversial essay he maintained that Communists by virtue of Party discipline were not free agents and therefore ineligible to teach. He was, however, concerned not so much with actual Party members, who were few in number, as with the far larger group of fellow travelers who called themselves liberals but often followed the Party line or were sympathetic to Communists and their causes. Hook believed that these people, whom he referred to as "ideological typhoid Marys," were more influential than actual Communists and posed the most difficult problem. It was not so much that they lied as that they were none too scrupulous.

I am referring to the half-conscious belief, born of political euphoria, that everything goes because one knows in one's heart that it is all in a good cause, and that in the interest of human welfare it is not necessary to put too fine a point on truth. Especially when one is dealing with the "enemy" —the enemy being anyone who disagrees on a matter of political importance. Intellectual integrity thus becomes the first victim of political enthusiasm.[7]

Hook offered in evidence a recent article by Helen Lynd. Professor Lynd was a well-known social scientist, the co-author, with her husband, of the classic *Middletown* (1929), sharing also his politics. Among the faults of her piece on academic freedom, to Hook's mind, was her use of a statement attributed to Albert F. Canwell that anyone critical of racism or economic inequality was a Communist.[8] Canwell had been chairman of a Washington State investigating committee, and Lynd used his alleged statement to show the bigotry that led to three members of the University of Washington faculty being dismissed for membership in the Communist Party. The quotation was taken from private letters sent to Lynd by individuals whom she did not name. Canwell denied having said any such thing. The anonymous accusations bothered Hook, as did the fact that Lynd attributed the firings to a desire by President Allen and the regents that an impending medical-school appropriation not be jeopardized. Hook said of such charges that "Dr. Lynd would never descend to this level in her own field of study and she would be horrified if anyone sought to defend the dismissal of Communist party teachers with methods similar to those with which she attacks it."[9]

This was typical of academic fellow travelers, according to Hook. They defended the right of the Hollywood Ten not to testify and of Communist fronts not to have to produce membership records, but said nothing when a Klan leader was sentenced to jail for the same offense. They complained that the de-Nazification program in West Germany was halfhearted but said nothing when ex-Nazis served in the Communist government of East Germany. Recently a conference sponsored by many academicians in New York voted to protect leaders of the Communist Party from the Smith Act, but howled down a resolution asking President Truman to restore the civil rights of eighteen Trotskyists convicted under that same statute. Though Paul Robeson compared the Trotskyists to Klansmen, no academic sponsor withdrew in protest.

Hook admitted it was difficult to move against Communist professors, let alone fellow travelers. Loyalty oaths were of no use. Hook was against legislation such as the Feinberg Law in New York that mandated the firing of Communist teachers. Tenure was for faculties to decide and not a proper subject of concern for state officials or university administrators. The point, as he saw it, was to punish not ideas but conspiracy or unethical conduct. Actual Party membership seemed an indication of such misconduct, Hook believed, but fellow traveling of itself was not. Here exposure and criticism were the best recourse. Hook urged professors to speak out and not allow themselves to be intimidated by charges of red-baiting.

Lynd resented being offered up as an example of unfairness and special pleading. In a letter to the editor she defended her methods, saying that the Canwell statement had been sent to her by no fewer than four informants, whose names she had given to her editor at the *American Scholar*. Hook, she pointed out, always said that colleagues alone should judge a teacher's competence, yet he seemed to be siding with the president and regents of the University of Washington. In another letter to the editor, Arthur E. Murphy of Cornell defended Lynd, asking Hook to prove his accusation that professors were the strongest and most effective fellow travelers.[10]

Hook replied with his usual directness. Lynd had not refuted his claim that she violated the normal canons of scholarship. Canwell was not the issue, nor was the legislative investigation of the University of Washington, which he deplored as he did all outside investigations of faculties. At issue was method. It was wrong of Lynd to use anonymous informants. If this were done to a Communist she would insist that the accusers come forward and face examination. Conversely, she ignored evidence in the public record that the expelled teachers had proselytized for Communist causes. Here was the double standard at work again.

Hook denied that he was calling people fellow travelers for criticizing the Washington decision. Hook knew the difference and indicated it by pointing out that Lynd herself had signed Communist-front petitions and been a sponsor of the Waldorf conference for world peace that spring. To his knowledge she had never protested on behalf of any victim of Communism. Lynd was, he implied, if not a fellow traveler at least the next thing to it. That was probably why he had chosen her article on the University of Washington as an example. Hook had not defended the president and regents as Lynd said. He had written about the Communist teacher issue in general terms only. Now he addressed the Washington case, saying that the majority of the faculty committee on tenure had voted against the firings not because it held Party membership to be allowable, but because the rules governing tenure were unclear. The committee favored revising the rules to make it plain that CP membership was grounds for dismissal, with which Hook agreed.

Hook answered with a few statistics Murphy's demand that he establish the importance of academic fellow travelers. In 1939 when a letter was published by friends of the Soviet Union attacking his Committee for Cultural Freedom, some forty of the 175 signers were academicians. Of 559 sponsors of the Waldorf peace conference in 1949 at least 110 were college and university faculty members. Five of the twelve members of the initiating committee for the Bill of Rights conference at which Paul Robeson equated the Socialist Workers Party with the Ku Klux Klan were academicians, as were almost seventy of the 360 sponsors. Hook thought Murphy ought to be worried about this, as also about the use to which Lynd put her alleged Canwell quotation. She had said that it was the "kind of thinking that supports the decision of the Regents," thereby smearing, Hook said, not only the president and the regents but a minority of the tenure committee and all who agreed with it as racists and red-baiters.* Why was Murphy not bothered by this?[11]

The position that Communists were unqualified to teach was taken by many eminent figures. In the *American Scholar* symposium to which Lynd contributed, Arthur O. Lovejoy and T. V. Smith, both leading academicians, said that Communists should not be fired, only because so few teachers were Party members that it was not worth the trouble of rooting them out.

---

* Another example that Hook might have used was Lynd's claim in her article that the real targets of the legislature were not Communist professors but anyone who might be "liberal in thought or who engages in any progressive social action." As only six members of a large faculty had been investigated, this was plainly untrue and showed the recklessness to which Hook objected.

John L. Childs, a professor at the Teachers College of Columbia University, was against allowing them on faculties not only out of principle but from experience too. He had seen Communists operate, in New York where he had been state chairman of the Liberal Party, and in teachers' unions as well. Consequently he supported the American Federation of Teachers, which held that the CP was not a party but a conspiracy and membership in it evidence of professional unfitness.[12]

Carey McWilliams took the opposite view. He was especially upset by the University of Washington case, discussing it in detail. It was wrong to expel Communist teachers as biased, since many professors were prejudiced in one way or another and yet did not lose their jobs. He feared that after the Communists were purged teachers who agreed with them on some points would go next, which was in some respects even more alarming owing to their greater numbers.[13] This was special pleading, as McWilliams identified with professors who might be in jeopardy for holding on to beliefs which he shared. A more principled critique of the Hook position was made by Irving Howe in the Trotskyist publication *New International*. Trotskyists were, by definition, anti-Stalinist and so presumably attracted by the idea of expelling Stalinists from teaching posts. But Trotskyists had also been early Smith Act victims and therefore had a stake in the fight against political tests. Howe began by arguing that one could not, as Hook did, properly discuss the issue except in reference to specific cases. At the University of Washington six professors had been brought up on charges of Communist Party membership and of personal misconduct. The second charge was dropped in all but one instance. Ultimately one professor was fired for misconduct and two for membership in the CP. The other three, all ex-Communists, were put on probation.

Howe faulted Sidney Hook for not dealing with the issues raised by the firings, by the atmosphere of intimidation created in Washington, by the punishing of individuals for past membership in the Party or for refusing to give the names of former associates. Hook's argument that Communists should be fired because they were doctrinaire did not make sense unless all doctrinaire professors were fired, which would be all but impossible and in any case horrendous. Howe went further, saying that even if teachers could be stopped from expressing their opinions it would be wrong, as students ought to be exposed to the real world and not sheltered from unpopular ideas. Hook's criticism of Stalinists as secretive would be valid were it not that openness meant penalties and usually unemployment. It also seemed to Howe that in practice Communist teachers behaved much like everyone else. Few if any were the Party-line automatons Hook made them out to be. The real issue was not whether a professor belonged to the Party but how he conducted himself. Those behaving improperly should be dismissed regardless of their politics, and, be they ever so odious, ideas alone should not be held against teachers whose actual conduct was blameless. Howe felt that the anti-Stalinist intellectuals were subordinating everything to this one cause, a bad sign even though he agreed with them on the evils of Communism.[14]

The frequency and vigor with which Hook addressed the issue resulted in much criticism of him, not only at the time but long afterward. In his autobiography Alfred Kazin described Hook as having in the 1950s "supported the firing of supposed Communist teachers on libertarian grounds."[15] Hook replied angrily that, far from urging that "supposed" Communists be removed, "I held that even membership [in the Party] is not a ground for automatic dismissal but a rebuttable presumption of unfitness warranting inquiry by a committee of a teacher's peers, not by any governmental agency, whose investigations into teachers' fitness and loyalty I vehemently opposed."[16] Hook had the better memory. The distance between himself and libertarians such as Kazin was less than might be imagined. With Howe he believed that Communist teachers should be removed only for cause, though Party membership to his mind went a long way toward establishing it. Unlike Howe, he saw no reason why students should be exposed to Communists. This was to take the free marketplace of ideas further than he wished to go. But as a practical matter Hook and Howe were close enough. Both made actual behavior the acid test, and in any given case where they agreed on conduct they might well agree on a verdict. Yet one would not have guessed this from Howe's attack, nor from Kazin's remembrance of those days. In the excitement libertarians misread Hook, imputing views to him that he did not hold. The main differences were tactical. Libertarians believed that in the emotional climate of the McCarthy era all efforts to unseat Communist teachers weakened academic freedom. Hook thought otherwise, arguing that academic freedom gained from responsible peer reviews. Hook may have been wrong but was not giving in to McCarthyism. That some who were in reality so close to his position could not see this owed something to Hook's aggressive style, but more, perhaps, to the times.

As might be expected, professors also differed over the extent to which McCarthyism was hurting them. Edward C. Kirkland, a historian, took a gloomy look in 1951. "The results of the anti-Red drive have been disastrous for higher education in America." "This reign of terror is unexampled in the history of American higher education."[17] *The Nation* often said as much. H. H. Wilson, a member of the Academic Freedom Committee of the ACLU, saw it as the civil liberty most under attack. The red scare would not end until "the last honest seeker after truth is driven out of education." Universities were bad enough to begin with. It took so long to earn tenure that by the time the average professor achieved it he had lost "the drive and incentive to be even remotely interested in challenging the status quo, and has probably been beaten out of the urge to do creative thinking and research."[18] Witch-hunting had only made things worse. The faculties were intimidated, the students apathetic. Nineteen eighty-four was close at hand.

Kalman Seigel, who had won a prize for his articles in *The New York Times* surveying freedom of thought and speech at seventy-two colleges and universities, agreed. America was facing "its most serious onslaught of intellectual vigilantism." No one was willing to discuss controversial issues in the classroom. Students were avoiding unpopular ideas and political clubs. They were afraid to use words like "liberal," "peace" and "freedom." They shunned progressive classmates. A dean of women was quoted as saying that female students avoided the "humanitarian point of view" because it was associated with Communism. A placement director at the same institution, Barnard College, said that employers regarded the "liberal girl" as an "obstructionist" and an "organizer against employer interests."[19]

The heaviest statement of alarm was Robert M. MacIver's *Academic Freedom in Our Time* (1955), a product of the American Academic Freedom Project at Columbia University that MacIver directed. Louis M. Rabinowitz subsidized this effort, to which many professors at Columbia contributed, as did a panel of advisers including heads of major libraries and presidents of famous colleges and universities. MacIver summarized at inordinate length conventional liberal thinking on the subject. He quoted approvingly from Robert M. Hutchins' testimony before the Illinois Seditious Activities Investigation Commission, which was told by Hutchins that "the miasma of thought control that is now spreading over this country is the greatest menace to the United States since Hitler."[20] MacIver held that book censorship was rampant and assaults on free speech too. William F. Buckley was a special offender. His book *God and Man at Yale* (1951) had taken a consumer's view of higher education by urging alumni and parents to see that their sons received the ideology they were paying for. Despite patches of sunshine, things looked bleak. "In fact, it is hardly an exaggeration to say that the weight of authority in the United States is now adverse to the principle of intellectual freedom. By the weight of authority we mean that the forces unfavorable to it are more effective than its defenders in making their will prevail."[21]

But the same facts could be read differently. Robert E. Fitch, a dean and professor at the Pacific School of Religion, was suspicious of charges that intellectuals had been intimidated and the life of the mind clouded by fear. He pointed out (as H. H. Wilson had said to make an opposite case) that the great majority of professors were, and always had been, apathetic. They were not victims of a new climate of fear but silent by tradition. On the other hand, the outspoken minority was as bold as ever. Hutchins and Henry Steele Commager and the rest were, if anything, louder than before. Fitch agreed with Sidney Hook that teachers were more aroused and actively resistant to infringements of academic freedom than they had ever been. The only change was a certain wallowing in despond, cries of alarm, and requests that people feel sorry for those who were too timid to speak out. Fitch recognized that McCarthyism was real and deplored it. But he attributed the decline of student activism mainly to lack of interest. Similarly, faculties were less active—except in defense of academic freedom—because of loss of faith and perhaps also from having a bad conscience about past mistakes. Could it be that if professors "lack the courage of their convictions, it is because they no longer have any great convictions? Is this why the intellectual tone of student and faculty life is 'subdued and muted'?"[22]

Paul K. Hays, a professor of law at Columbia and vice-chairman of the Liberal Party, felt the same. The AAUP, made up of 37,000 college and university teachers, had just accepted a report on "Academic Freedom and Tenure in the Quest for National Security." This document was not as bad, in his view, as some efforts to panic professors into believing that their liberties were being destroyed. It contained none of the exaggerations of Robert M. Hutchins, "whose efforts to picture the present situation as a reign of terror where no professor dares to speak out have done so much to discredit the causes for which he claims to stand."[23] It went too far even so. One statement declared that it would take great courage for a student or teacher to agree with any position taken by Russia to which the United States objected. This was nonsense, said Hays. It required no special courage to speak against German rearmament, or in favor of recognizing Red China, and thousands of students and teachers routinely did so.

The report also embraced bad principles, as in saying that no one should be kept out of an academic department dealing with national security matters simply because of past associations and beliefs, but only if involved in criminal acts or conspiracies. This was absurd, as no university hired known traitors or conspirators, and past associations and beliefs were almost the only criteria available on which to decide who should have access to national secrets. The report was, to his mind, a "collection of false platitudes" written by people who wanted to defend the rights of Communists to be university instructors without actually saying so. Thus they drew up a set of principles so broad as to cover all crimes short of murder. The AAUP would have been better off to face the issue directly and say that Communists should be allowed into the academy. Hays thought that would have made for a more honest if misguided statement.

· · · ·

Even after it ended, many professors continued to believe that the red scare had been directed chiefly against themselves, and that it had been successful. In 1955 an entire issue of the *Journal of Social Issues* was given over to anti-intellectualism, which contributors viewed as a major threat. Many felt that owing to it faculty members had betrayed their principles.[24] William L. Neumann surveyed American history texts in 1957 and discovered that out of cowardice or greed they had been rewritten to suit the new conservative and nationalistic mood. Gone were the Marxist assumptions of yesterday, as also criticisms of business and imperialism. Samuel Flagg Bemis, a noted historian of foreign affairs, had recently said at a professional meeting that at a time when American diplomacy was under attack from foreigners, scholars should not supply them with ammunition. True to his beliefs, Bemis had revised his own diplomatic-history texts to show America in a better light. Criticism of the military had disappeared from textbooks also, again on principle supposedly. Samuel Eliot Morison in his 1950 presidential address to the American Historical Association had spoken ill of the antiwar historians such as Charles Beard for failing to prepare youth for battle, a novel and repugnant mission according to Neumann. "Alas poor Clio! This muse was never meant for profit or propaganda."[25]

Four years later Professor H. Stuart Hughes of Harvard wrote that as a result of faculty cowardice an entire lost generation of students had grown up without any political knowledge. For nearly a decade "almost no fundamental issue was publicly discussed."[26] Why, he asked, at no time in the McCarthy era had liberals and intellectuals united to turn back the tide of bigotry and reaction? Hughes offered several reasons. One was that none of the cases seemed an ideal rallying point. The Hiss case turned out badly. Owen Lattimore displayed a "lack of total candor" in his replies to McCarthy. Liberals who felt this way were overscrupulous, Hughes maintained. Perfect cases seldom turn up in real life. We have to take our issues where we find them he maintained.

Another reason for lack of action was that "liberals and radicals were uneasy in their consciences. They could not spring to the defense of others because they were unsure of their own innocence." This was McCarthy's greatest triumph. He crippled

338 THE ACADEMY AND THE CRISIS OF LIBERALISM

liberals by stirring in them "the demon of self-doubt."[27] Intellectuals responded to the crisis by making all kinds of fine distinctions inappropriate to an urgent time. It was a matter of them or us, Hughes said, and intellectuals ought not to have concerned themselves with details like should a Communist be a professor. As a matter of strategy they should have defended all accused persons, since most were innocent of any crime. Intellectuals, it was true, had erred in the past, ignored the crimes of Stalin, committed the sin of "anti-anti-communism." Even so, they had done far less harm than the anti-Stalinist liberals who made the Cold War worse. These were "Sorcerer's Apprentices" who "helped unleash forces over which they had totally lost control." The result of the witch-hunt was moral debasement, "or rather a moral numbness. Most people were not corrupted by what they went through or what they saw going on around them. They were simply stunned by it."[28] So they retreated from public affairs. Students taught by such people could only be ignorant politically. The new activists would have to start from scratch.

Hughes's feeling that professors had been thoroughly intimidated was shared by most leading historians and social scientists. It was the theme of *The Academic Mind* (1958), an enormous survey conducted by Paul Lazarsfeld and Wagner Thielens, Jr. Sponsored by the Fund for the Republic, a controversial and short-lived offshoot of the Ford Foundation, the book was based on a sample of 2,451 academicians surveyed by two respected polling organizations in 1955. Historians made up twenty-eight percent of the sample, economists twenty-three percent, sociologists sixteen percent and political scientists fifteen percent. Except for literary scholars, these were the most politically conscious faculty members. Accordingly, it was plausibly argued, they would be the most sensitive to infringements on academic freedom. The authors focused on two things, "apprehension," the degree to which professors worried about their freedom, and "permissiveness," which meant having liberal or left-wing political convictions.

The study was weighted toward the most successful scholars and scientists, turning up many correlations that ought to have surprised no one in academic life. Eminence in the learned professions was related to productivity, rank being a function of publication. The most productive faculty were to be found at the largest universities and best colleges. The more distinguished the professor, the more likely he (women made up only eleven percent of the sample) was to be apprehensive. The more apprehensive a professor, the more likely to be politically active and a reader of liberal magazines.

Productivity, activism, permissiveness and apprehension went together and were concentrated in the highest-ranking institutions. For the most part the more apprehensive a professor became about pressures to conform, the more he was apt to speak out. The younger tenured faculty were inclined to be more permissive and more apprehensive than older professors, though at the best schools age made little difference. Conservative professors were unlikely to be apprehensive, save at institutions where there were loyalty scares. In such cases conservatives formed views similar to those held by the already permissive. *The Academic Mind* appeared to show that as a result of McCarthyism there was a great increase in anxiety about academic freedom, and a decline in the exercise of it except among those surveyed.

Though well-intentioned, this study had glaring faults, according to Ernest Van Den Haag. It was ambiguous as to whether social scientists actually were threatened or only felt themselves to be. The "apprehension index" was put forward as a measurement of objective risk when it might indicate only a subjective and possibly groundless alarm. It may have been that professors listed as highly apprehensive exaggerated their anxiety over the danger they faced so as to magnify their courage or minimize their timidity. Though ignored by the authors, this explained an apparent contradiction to Van Den Haag. The most apprehensive professors usually said that they would volunteer to do the things that they were afraid to do—join unpopular organizations, receive suspect magazines, protest against threats to free speech, and the like. "Should we not inquire whether some, at least, might be cherishing a romantic image of themselves as courageously defying the forces of evil?"[29] Most of the professors thought they ranked low in public esteem, he observed, whereas surveys showed the opposite was true. Perhaps the apprehensiveness of professors was equally unfounded.

To Van Den Haag the apprehensiveness index had no value,

and the permissiveness scale was almost as bad, since it recorded only "how permissive some professors were toward their own views when articulated by others." Using this standard, a Communist would come out as permissive.

> According to the interviews compiled in *The Academic Mind*, research and publication, too, were impaired, because professors turned cautious in the face of threats and attacks; they avoided controversial subjects in the classroom, secretly trimmed reference lists, even eliminated courses in comparative economics and other dangerous subjects, and avoided writing on contemporary history, Russia, Marxism, etc. The respondents do not hesitate to portray themselves and their colleagues as public heroes and private cowards. In their eagerness to indict enemies whom they despised, professors drew a self-portrait which is fortunately as unrealistic, in my opinion, as it is unattractive.[30]

Van Den Haag doubted that academic freedom had suffered in these ways. Productivity could have been measured, for example, if the authors had wished. But they failed to do so, he implied, because they knew that no such fall as was claimed actually took place. Yet the authors presented data on "patterns of caution" as if they were describing real acts instead of imaginary ones.

Van Den Haag was, perhaps, too scathing. The fear in academia was real, and there was a basis for it, too. Scores of colleges and universities experienced the red scare at first hand, and hundreds of faculty members lost their positions. This had a chilling effect. Yet, as was often noticed at the time, faculty resistance to McCarthyism was very high throughout the period. And, as *The Academic Mind* did establish beyond a doubt, the most worried professors were also the most likely to speak out. Maybe they only exercised greater prudence than before, chose their words more carefully, thought twice before signing petitions. This was not necessarily a bad thing after so many years of emotionalism and ill-considered rhetoric. There was, in any event, no reign of terror on campus, only attempts, usually blocked, to establish one.

Students were less political than they had been in the thirties and would be again in the sixties. Such apathy seems to have resulted not from cowardice or the failure of teachers to discuss issues but rather from a lack of incentive. The old issues— Republican Spain, isolation, intervention, antifascism—had died or withered or been compromised. New ones of comparable appeal had yet to take their place. If students in the fifties had a collective ambition, it was to return to normal after the long years of depression, war and ex-GI seriousness. The most apt model was the 1920s, seen as the golden age of student life, hence the numerous efforts to revive it. Hughes to the contrary, professors did reproach students for their lack of social conscience, but to little avail. It was not fear of McCarthyism, no threat to students anyway, that accounted for the "silent generation." Students were quiet for the best of reasons—they had nothing to say.

It soon became evident that libertarian fears were unwarranted. The issue of Communist teachers disappeared along with, to all intents and purposes, the Communist Party. McCarthyism passed away also, having had a less blighting effect than worried academics feared. Yet the end of McCarthyism did not comfort them as much as might be supposed. Some continued to believe there had been a reign of terror which was still being felt. Many suffered, paradoxically, from the loss of McCarthyism, as it had promoted unity even if not to the degree Hughes wished. In the wake of the red scare intellectuals were divided and demoralized, uncertain of their own roles, confused as to the meaning of recent history.

To independent leftists it seemed that liberals had betrayed their own principles during the McCarthy era. Irving Howe attended the ADA convention in 1955 and reported that though the members seemed decent and tolerant they did not command respect. The atmosphere was one of "worried complacence." Delegates suffered from collective amnesia. They denounced abuses of civil liberties by government without noting that these began under the Democrats. They voted a resolution in favor of repealing portions of the Smith Act and the Communist Control Act of 1954 without mentioning that the latter bill had been

introduced by their own Hubert Humphrey. The shallow pragmatism of the liberal mind displayed itself in a willingness to
challenge aspects of American foreign policy but never its
underlying assumptions. ADA people were schizoid on civil
liberties, wanting to take a strong stand but also to show themselves as "responsible." So for every step forward they took one
back.[31]

Murray Kempton was harsher still. Writing in *Dissent*, which
Howe and others had just founded as a voice of independent
socialism, he discussed the conversion of Harry Cain. A former U.S. senator from Washington, Cain had been appointed
to an agency thrown up by the red scare known as the Subversive Activities Control Board. Though a conservative, he had
been shocked by the abuse of individual rights he witnessed as
an SACB member and was now a forceful critic of McCarthyism. Kempton contrasted Cain's example with that of Hubert
Humphrey, who was still defending his Communist Control Act
that would send Party activists to jail for five years. Kempton
preferred Cain, even though Cain supported measures such as
the Taft-Hartley bill regulating labor unions. "He can vote for
Taft-Hartley; and, if I lived in Washington, I'd vote for him
against any sitting liberal. To hell with liberals. What good's a
man if he votes for unlimited funds to build school gymnasiums
and shuts his mouth when teachers are bullied and debased?"[32]

The opposite view was that liberals had discredited themselves not by disregarding civil liberties but by defending them
in mistaken ways. Alan Westin believed that the conduct of
liberals during the red scare had been self-defeating. When the
issue first arose, civil libertarians argued that the Communist
Party was no worse than other fringe movements and proposed
to deal with it by exposing its errors and shady practices, and
by strengthening the theory and function of democracy. This
position was destroyed by revelations that Communists had
committed espionage, fomented strikes and infiltrated government. The next phase, Westin said, was marked by investigations of the Communist penetration of government. Libertarians
met the challenge by rallying behind Alger Hiss, who turned out
to be guilty. They rallied again behind Owen Lattimore, but
hearings showed that his Institute of Pacific Relations had been
manipulated by Communists and fellow travelers. Time and

again libertarians relied on wrong history or wrong facts to represent as praiseworthy, or at least harmless, men and movements that proved to be indefensible on those grounds.

Similarly, the libertarian critique of the loyalty program in 1947 was that subversion and disloyalty posed no real problem and so no such program was needed. The famous disloyalty cases undermined this position as well. Westin believed that if Truman had not set up the loyalty program Congress would have insisted on the firing of even more government employees, or created a worse program of its own. Libertarians had erred also in saying that people who took the Fifth Amendment should not be considered loyalty risks and that guilt by association was wrong. In taking such extreme stands liberals had enabled McCarthyites to accuse them of special pleading. They had failed to be realistic, reacted to the loyalty problem mechanically, and had no reason to congratulate themselves now that the red scare was ending, as it was no thanks to them.[33]

Many, perhaps most, intellectuals did not see their plight as having any relation to their own mistakes. David Riesman and Nathan Glazer, co-authors of *The Lonely Crowd,* asked why had intellectuals fallen from their high estate? Once upon a time "a group of intellectuals led and legislated for a class of discontented people . . . and a mass of underprivileged people," but, alas, no more. The poor and discontented had been eliminated by affluence. The "ex-masses" were now conservative and had different fears than earlier. They opposed intellectuals for advocating spending programs and felt threatened by the movement for racial equality, as also by homosexuality, which was somehow associated with intellect, according to the authors. The fears of the new rich and the new middle class led to McCarthyism, and McCarthy was admired not for his supposed ends, the destruction of Communism, but rather for his means —that is, his attack on Eastern snobs and intellectuals. "As a result of all this, the left wing and liberal intellectuals, who led the masses during the New Deal and who played so effective a role in the fight against Nazism and in 'prematurely' delineating the nature of the Communist as an enemy, today find themselves without an audience, their tone and their slogans ineffectual."[34]

While this was to severely misread events and obliterate all

distinctions—intellectuals had never led the masses, never fig-
ured prominently in the New Deal, and had not as a class
perceived the evils of Communism earlier than the general
public—it reflected the feelings of many during the fifties. Part
of the fun of being a liberal or left intellectual in the previous
two decades derived from identifying at one and the same time
with the leaders and the led. For some the locus of power had
been the Soviet Union, for others the New Deal. Progressives
often related to both. In any case, anti-Stalinists excepted, an
intellectual could experience in his or her imagination both
union with "the people" and the thrilling exercise of power.
Contributors to *The Nation* and the *New Republic* wrote of the
Russian Revolution as if they had made it, of the New Deal as
if they had conceived it, and of the people as extensions of
themselves. By 1955 these illusions had collapsed. Stalinism
was dead. So was Franklin Roosevelt and the New Deal. Few
intellectuals any longer could think of themselves as being in
power, still less of enjoying unity with the masses, who, by
turning to Senator McCarthy, had seriously let the intelligentsia
down. Worse still, in the one fight that still claimed them—
protecting civil liberties—intellectuals found themselves aligned
not with the people but rather with the very establishment that
earlier was the enemy. Polls showed again and again that support for civil liberties was greatest among the educated and
affluent, community leaders, members of the upper class—in
short, Republicans.[35]

This was obscured at first by the GOP's exploitation of
Communism as a partisan issue. When Eisenhower became
President, subversion and disloyalty stopped being party issues,
and when McCarthy failed to see this, conservatives were
obliged to destroy him. Some intellectuals had predicted as
much. In the summer of 1950 while he was editing Alan Barth's
The Loyalty of Free Men, Malcolm Cowley wrote to Barth that
conservatives "had as much to do as anyone with ending the
great red scare of 1919–20, and when the present scare is
finally ended . . . it may also be by the stand against it of many
good conservatives."[36] Though this was what happened, intellectuals found their de-facto alliance with the former class
enemy to be a perverse turn harmful to the romance of politics.
Anti-Communism did not fill the need, as Riesman and Glazer

observed. Supporting Cold War measures such as the Marshall Plan and Point Four was necessary but unexciting compared to the old days when people of goodwill everywhere were united by antifascism. Emotionally, NATO was no substitute for the Popular Front.

Time had reduced the glamor of intellectual life while adding something new and repulsive, or so it seemed to many. In 1949 Dwight Macdonald wrote to Irving Kristol about the issues dividing them and said, "Like you, I dislike (and am coming to fear) the increasingly envenomed and clashing NYC intellectual atmosphere."[37] Three years later, when it had gotten worse, Arthur Schlesinger put the point more strongly in a letter to Macdonald: "There is some deep sickness in certain sectors of the New York intellectuals—particularly in the *Commentary* crowd."[38] Alfred Kazin agreed, even though he was an anti-Stalinist of long standing and a New York Jewish intellectual similar in most respects to those writing for *Commentary*. He called them the Upper West Side Hebrew Relief Association in his memoirs, and drew attention to the paradox that recognition and even some degree of affluence had not made them happy. "Politics had turned them mad," like so many others at the time.[39] Cowley went beyond this, employing mental illness not as a metaphor but as literal description. He wrote to Barth that:

> guilt, insecurity, suspicion, fear, messianism: these are the symptoms of the situation. They are also the symptoms of the medically recognized disease called paranoia. I have been impressed by how many people I know or read about have succumbed to paranoia (Robert Cantwell, Robert Lowell, Forrestal . . .). Individuals, often the most sensitive and intelligent individuals, succumb to a disease that is in this case social in its origins, almost as if they were catching the plague.[40]

Somewhere in between hysteria and nostalgia most intellectuals struggled along, trying to orient themselves and make sense of what had happened.

The state of liberalism and the status of intellectuals remained in doubt through the fifties. Arthur Schlesinger, Jr., took

a cheerful view of both. In *The Vital Center,* which appeared
first in 1949 and was reprinted in 1962, this liberal historian
and active Democrat argued that one reason why liberals had
come of age was owing to the failure of progressivism. Schlesinger called progressives "doughfaces," meaning "democratic men
with totalitarian principles." Their naïve faith in progress and
their false optimism about the perfectibility of human nature
had led them into fellow traveling, and through it into the ash-
can of history. Purged of doughfaces, the time was ripe for "a
new radicalism," by which he meant New Deal liberalism minus
illusions about Russia and Communism. Abroad, this would
entail working with the non-Communist left to contain Soviet
expansion. At home, liberalism meant a greater dedication to
civil liberties. Peter Viereck, a fierce enemy of the doughface,
also thought liberalism was in good shape. To William Buckley
and Brent Bozell, it will be remembered, liberalism was doing
all too well, judging by the ceaseless attacks upon Senator Mc-
Carthy.[41]

This was not the common view. Malcolm Cowley believed
that the liberal-left as a whole had been discredited. It had
failed to save Spain or prevent World War II. It had been used
by Communists and on discovering this had undergone a "failure of nerve" leading not to new ideas but only to loss of faith
in progress by logical or scientific methods, as also in "ourselves" as guides to progress. Intellectuals in particular had
been demoralized by history and personal experience, and
though younger novelists had not been parties to the wreck,
they acquired from it a "sort of generalized distrust of the intellect as a means of improving life on this planet." Added to it
was a fear of expressing unorthodox opinions, arising from
McCarthyism. "The result is that we are now reading novels by
intellectuals, for intellectuals, about supposedly intellectual or
at least well-educated characters, in which not a single intelligent notion is expressed about the world in which we live."[42]

Lionel Trilling was even more severe. In 1950 his collection
of essays *The Liberal Imagination* confirmed his place as the
literary scholar with most prestige among intellectuals. Though
part of the liberal tradition, he was scornful of it too. Trilling
indicted the liberal mind for drab rationalism and an emotional

shallowness that had made liberals susceptible to corrupting ideological passions. Reinhold Niebuhr, the intellectual's favorite theologian, whom both Schlesinger and Trilling had drawn on, went beyond them by criticizing not merely the dead horse of progressivism but historic American liberalism itself. In *The Irony of American History* (1952) Niebuhr pointed to unconscious weaknesses and contradictions that frustrated national designs. A crucial one was the "extravagant emphasis in our culture upon the value and dignity of the individual and upon individual liberty as the final value of life."[43] This involved contradictions, he wrote, because on the one hand "our culture does not really value the individual as much as it pretends; on the other hand, if justice is to be maintained and our survival assured, we cannot make individual liberty as unqualifiedly the end of life as our ideology asserts."[44] And yet "our social practice is frequently better than the creed. The justice which we have established in our society has been achieved, not by pure individualism, but by collective action."[45] Thus the irony cut both ways.

Niebuhr's argument was too complex for easy summation. What it amounted to in the end was not so much a call for better political thought as for a different political philosophy, a recognition of "the limits of all human striving, the fragmentariness of all human wisdom, the precariousness of all historic configurations of power, and the mixture of good and evil in all human virtue."[46] Niebuhr said that in order to combat the illusions and pretensions of Communism, Americans must discard their own. This done, the possibility arose of a political and ideological rivalry waged in civilized and Christian ways.

There is, in short, even in a conflict with a foe with whom we have little in common the possibility and necessity of living in a dimension of meaning in which the urgencies of the struggle are subordinated to a sense of awe before the vastness of the historical drama in which we are jointly involved; to a sense of modesty about the virtue, wisdom and power available to us for the resolution of its perplexities; to a sense of contrition about the common human frailties and foibles which lie at the foundation of both the enemy's demonry and our vanities, and to a sense of gratitude for the divine mercies which are promised to those who humble themselves.[47]

That such a thing was possible for America, or indeed any great nation, was Niebuhr's own illusion. What lay before us, even in the fifties, was not awe and modesty and contrition but what Senator William Fulbright would one day call the arrogance of power.

Hardly anyone could swallow the Niebuhr formula whole, but the style of his analysis, and of Trilling's also, with its emphasis on paradox, ambiguity, irony and complexity, had much appeal. It became the standard mode of discourse in the fifties, though also something of a mixed blessing, according to Daniel Bell. He attempted to analyze the problem in generational terms, contrasting the experience of the intellectuals of the 1930s, led, as it seemed to him, by Trilling and Niebuhr, with the experience of his own generation. He had in mind younger people such as Richard Hofstadter, Leslie Fiedler and Alfred Kazin, who had achieved distinction in the forties and fifties. The essay did not quite work, because both generations had gone through the same cycle, moving, as he put it, from a passionate, simplistic and hortatory leftism to a mature, sophisticated liberalism. The difference between these generations was mainly that the older one went through the change at a higher level of eminence. Further, Trilling, Niebuhr, Philip Rahv, William Phillips, Sidney Hook, Edmund Wilson and the rest had, in effect, overthrown the generation before them. In contrast, Bell and his fellows had not displaced Trilling and Niebuhr and company, but joined with them instead. They had a community of interest with their elders, even though a somewhat different history. Bell said that "ours, a 'twice-born' generation, finds its wisdom in pessimism, evil, tragedy, and despair. So we are both old and young 'before our time.' "[48] He agreed with Norman Podhoretz, who had said recently that beneath the maturity and sober, matter-of-fact acceptance of complexity lay a feeling of having been cheated of adventure, a desire for passion, the yearning for a cause. But there was no cause, nor any great enemy to struggle against as previously, only an emptiness arising from what Bell called the end of ideology.

For Irving Howe, on the other hand, the problem was not so much a matter of changed beliefs as of altered status.

> What is most alarming is not that a number of intellectuals have abandoned the posture of iconoclasm: let the *Zeitgeist* give them a jog and they will again be radical, all too radical. What is most alarming is that the whole idea of the intellectual vocation—the idea of a life dedicated to values that cannot possibly be realized by a commercial civilization—has gradually lost its allure. And it is this, rather than the abandonment of a particular program, which constitutes our rout.[49]

Howe was worried that intellectuals were no longer in opposition to it but had become pillars of American life. Prosperity had taken them out of bohemia and into the university. Lionel Trilling had written that this was a good thing, evidence that intellect was now taken seriously as a national asset and perhaps even a source of power. Howe thought otherwise, saying that the assimilation of intellectuals by government and the "pseudo-culture" meant that they had ceased to function as intellectuals.

There were numerous examples of this. Sidney Hook, Mary McCarthy, Daniel Boorstin, David Riesman, Irving Kristol, the Committee for Cultural Freedom, *Commentary* and the *New Leader*, once advocates of change, now professed a spongy liberalism. *Commentary* had perfected the art of advancing liberalism as a "strategy for adapting to the American status quo." It seemed concerned more with the threat to freedom posed by Freda Kirchwey and Arthur Miller than with that of Senator McCarthy. And the university was as bad, with its odious Ph.D. system that "grinds and batters personality into a mold of cautious routine."[50] Art had declined, too. The avant garde was all but dead, engulfed by advancing middlebrowism. America was becoming a vast cultural and political wasteland, inhabited by accommodators and bureaucrats, the frightened and the frightful, Howe appeared to think.

Howe's romantic view of the intellectual as adversary was no longer widely shared. Two years earlier, *Partisan Review* had surveyed a group of writers and intellectuals, questioning them about the end of alienation and their desire to be part of American life. To Howe's disgust, twenty-five had responded affirmatively, with only a handful—himself, Norman Mailer, C. Wright Mills—dissenting. Howe's "This Age of Conformity" was his response, an attack on his peers for their comfortable new relation to the United States. Yet Howe was not immune to altered circumstances, either. Though remaining a determined socialist, he too sank into the welcoming arms of academia, finding, perhaps not to his complete surprise, that one could, even though a professor, retain one's integrity and critical bite.

All this sounded strange later. While intellectuals complained of lack of vitality, the end of politics and ideology, conformity, and the passive student, history was about to mock them again. The sixties were to bring a new outburst of radical energy, and radical chic as well. Though led by students, the movement would affect intellectual life too, putting an end for the moment to discourse that turned on pessimism, tragedy, irony and despair. Some would become, as Howe foresaw, all too radical. Dwight Macdonald returned to politics, not in his own journal as before, but by writing a column for *Esquire,* a magazine devoted to male fashions and the last place one would look for radical jeremiads. *The New York Review of Books,* founded as an American equivalent of *The Times Literary Supplement* of London, turned into a hotbed of revolutionary enthusiasm. Intellectuals were leaders of the peace movement, and also of the movement to "dump" President Johnson.[51] In this they succeeded, opening the way to the presidencies of Nixon, Ford, Carter and Reagan, and the return of pessimism, tragedy, irony and despair.

XII

Rewriting the Past

IN THE PERIOD covered by this book the left was obliged to face four great challenges: Hitlerism, Stalinism, McCarthyism and the Vietnam War. Progressives met three of these but failed to identify Stalinism as the principal enemy of freedom and culture after World War II, while the anti-Stalinist intellectuals were on target every time. This is easily demonstrated. Their opposition to Hitler and Stalin has not been at issue. Attacks on anti-Stalinists have focused on their resistance to McCarthyism and the Vietnam War. In 1974 a study was published that shed light on both. *The American Intellectual Elite* included a survey of 110 "representative" intellectuals drawn from a pool of eight thousand contributors to serious magazines and journals.[1] These 110 were asked to list the intellectuals they believed to have the most prestige. Seventy intellectuals were so named. Of those who had been active in the early fifties almost all had been anti-McCarthy, whether inside the American Committee for Cultural Freedom (Daniel Bell, Dwight Macdonald, Mary McCarthy, Arthur Schlesinger, Jr., Philip Rahv) or out (Norman Mailer, Irving Howe, Edmund Wilson, Alfred Kazin and others). They opposed the Vietnam War also. As early as 1965 three quarters of them were against it, though most Americans still supported their government's policy. The people would turn around eventually, as over McCarthyism, but both times intellectuals got there first.

It might be supposed that this enviable record would have put the anti-Stalinist intellectuals above reproach politically. No such canonization took place, owing to one of those ironies with which history abounds. The war in Vietnam discredited anti-

Communism, which many came to see as the cause of America's misadventure. Anti-Stalinists were hurt by this backlash even though they were themselves against the war. The charge, moreover, was not just that they had been mistakenly anti-Communist in the fifties, but that by so doing they had contributed to the very war which in the sixties they would protest against. In 1967 Jason Epstein, a leading publisher, suggested as much. "Was not Kristol's form of anti-Communism . . . likely to deaden the mind and feelings so that when the war in Vietnam fell into our laps some of us would have grown too rigid to feel the stupidity and arrogance from which it evolved and which continues to sustain it?"[2] *Commentary,* without naming Epstein, said the accusation was "that the anti-Communism of the Left was in some measure responsible for, or helped to create a climate of opinion favorable to, the war in Vietnam," and asked forty anti-Stalinist intellectuals to answer the charge and two related questions.[3] Twenty-one did, and *Commentary* summarized their positions. Most rejected the idea that liberal or left anti-Communism was implicated in the war. A majority still regarded themselves as anti-Communists, though many qualified or defined their politics in a different way than earlier. Most also rejected the idea of containing Communism by military means. The biggest difference *Commentary* saw was that as a group they appeared to have stopped believing that the United States could act as a force for good in world affairs.

As always, opinions varied. A few people like Sidney Hook and Arthur Schlesinger, Jr., had not changed their minds in any important respect. A few others, such as Murray Kempton and Richard Rovere, had backed down considerably, Kempton to the point of accepting his share of the blame for the excesses of popular anti-Communism. Daniel Bell grasped the nettle, saying that he had been a member of the Committee for Cultural Freedom for fourteen years and did not feel that its accomplishments were compromised at all by secret CIA subsidies, whose existence had just been exposed. Diana Trilling was sanguine about CIA funding also, but horrified by Epstein's article, which she took on directly. It was the latest fruit of thirty years of anti-anti-Communism, to her mind, a perpetuator of the false doctrine that anti-Communism always leads to, or promotes, reaction, which had done "incalculable damage" to both the intellectual and the democratic communities. On the other hand, excessive anti-Communism had done much harm, too, she admitted, especially by supplying ammunition to the anti-antis. In the struggle between these two factions during the McCarthy era,

> what suffered the worst defeat was liberalism itself, even intelligence itself. Both liberalism and reason were deserted by the anti-Communists who could suppose that McCarthy's method of combatting Communism could be theirs. And both liberalism and reason were betrayed by the anti-anti-Communists who believed that because Communism was being fought by the wrong means, McCarthy's, it had to be protected.[4]

Robert Lowell and William Phillips seemed to agree with Trilling on this, while distinguishing between their anti-Stalinism and the anti-Communism of the mob.

Irving Howe, who had vigorously criticized both extremes in the fifties, entertained no regrets. He was glad that he and his allies had attacked Stalinism, despite the risks apparent even then. "We had the choice of telling the truth and knowing it might be exploited by the reactionaries, or of keeping silent and thereby not merely acquiescing in horrible events but allowing the reactionaries to exploit the truth all the more effectively. We chose, as best we could, to tell the truth."[5] Their candor, wrote Howe, helped maintain the intellectual health of the nation, unlike the anti-antis, who kept quiet about the crimes of Stalin and so were tarnished by them.

A year later Howe returned to this theme from a different direction. In an essay on the New York intellectuals, the modernist, mostly Jewish intelligentsia that coalesced in the thirties, he placed special emphasis on their anti-Stalinism.

> It helped destroy—once and for all, I would have said until recently—Stalinism as a force in our intellectual life, and with Stalinism those varieties of Populist sentimentality which the Communist movement of the late thirties exploited with notable skill. If certain sorts of manipulative soft-headedness have been all but banished from serious American writing, and the kinds of rhetoric once associated

with Archibald MacLeish and Van Wyck Brooks cast into permanent disrepute, at least some credit for this ought to go to the New York writers.[6]

He paid tribute to Sidney Hook, now out of favor with most intellectuals for what was seen as a wrongheaded refusal to give up Cold War myths. In the thirties, Howe maintained, Hook had been preeminent as a "spokesman for a democratic radicalism and a fierce opponent of all the rationalizations for totalitarianism a good many intellectuals allowed themselves." Hostility to all forms of tyranny, now often taken for granted, was a position that "first had to be won through bitter and exhausting struggle." It was Hook and those aligned with him who had done this. "Whatever distinction can be assigned to the New York intellectuals during the 30s lies mainly in their persistence as a small minority, in their readiness to defend unpopular positions against apologists for the Moscow trials and the vigilantism of Popular Front culture."[7]

Yet Howe still believed, as in his famous essay of the fifties "This Age of Conformity," that the New York intellectuals had compromised themselves during the McCarthy era by allowing their anti-Communism "to become cheap and illiberal." And he was still angry that so many had joined in the celebration of American life and did not lead the attack on McCarthy. He attributed this in part to complacency arising from success. Howe continued to grumble that the little band of intellectual outsiders with whom he identified had become insiders, a new establishment based on taste rather than power. This helped to explain their failure, it seemed to him, before McCarthy, as well as their failure in the sixties to attack the "new sensibility" of the new left for its antidemocratic and anti-intellectual components.

Howe's critique of the anti-Stalinist intellectuals came from within. A more sweeping and typical attack was made on them by Christopher Lasch. A professional historian, Lasch was also one of those named as belonging to the intellectual elite. But he was not a New York intellectual, nor an anti-Stalinist, nor, in his political tracts, much of a scholar. His essay "The Cultural Cold War: A Short History of the Congress for Cultural Freedom" (1969) was more polemic than history, and typical of the fashionable leftism of the sixties in being longer on indignation than on fact.[8] Lasch criticized Sidney Hook for not attacking McCarthy, and Irving Kristol for defending him. In this he was mistaken. As we saw, Hook supported the ACCF's anti-McCarthy resolution in 1952. And Kristol had not, in his notorious *Commentary* article that same year, upheld McCarthy but rather attacked liberals for shortcomings he thought benefited McCarthy. In any case, the details did not matter to Lasch, who believed that the very existence of anti-Communism pointed up the rottenness of American society and culture. He said that all talk of pluralism and the open society was "cant." There was no censorship in America, he conceded, but this was only because "intellectuals can be trusted to censor themselves, and crude 'political' influence over intellectual life comes to seem passé." Academic freedom, though real, was meaningless because academicians and intellectuals accept conditions that "have undermined their capacity for independent thought. The literary intellectuals are free, but they use their freedom to propagandize for the state." Accordingly, "the freedom of American intellectuals as a professional class blinds them to their unfreedom." These lines were written at a time when intellectuals were more outspokenly united against the policies of their government than perhaps they had ever been. This made no difference to Lasch, who suggested instead that Americans might almost envy Soviet intellectuals, who at least had no illusions about their position. "A society which tolerates an illusory dissent is in much greater danger, in some respects, than a society in which uniformity is ruthlessly imposed."[9] There was more of this kind of silliness in Lasch's essay, which was a melancholy portent of things to come.

Epstein and Lasch had fired early shots in the campaign to revise modern history along progressive lines. New-left scholars naturally wished to turn the liberal version of recent events upside down by showing the anti-Stalinists as villains, and progressives as farsighted and heroic enemies of the Cold War. This led to the writing of much bad history.[10] Surviving progressives were even more eager to show that they had been, after all, right and the anti-Stalinists wrong in the 1940s and '50s. A formula was quickly arrived at to this end. History has vindicated us, participants would say. CIA misdeeds, and the war in Vietnam even more, prove that we had the goods on American imperialism. True, we ignored the crimes of Stalin, but this was a small thing and excusable in light of our good intentions. Anyway, we injured no one by our slight mistakes, whereas liberals, through their anti-Communism, aided Joe McCarthy and led America into Vietnam.

This is the line still taken by Corliss Lamont, and tirelessly proclaimed by James Aronson and Cedric Belfrage, former editors of the *National Guardian*.[11] Their joint history of the *Guardian* is remarkably candid about strategy. Being fellow travelers, they wished to promote socialism as practiced in Communist states, but judged the American people to be unready for it and so represented themselves as independent liberals instead. One doubts that many people were fooled by this. The *Guardian* was anti-American and pro-Soviet. In the spirit of the Popular Front, it had no enemies on the left save democrats. Aronson and Belfrage remained proud of their editorial record, seeing themselves as part of the great tradition of American radicalism personified by Eugene Debs and others to whom they bore no resemblance. Their approach was not only dubious but masochistic. It led to constant attacks on them by Communists, who resented each trivial deviation from the Party's platform, and to reprisals by the government, which took a dim view of resident aliens who sided with Communist movements. Belfrage, a British subject, was deported, landing finally in Mexico, from where he issued attacks upon the ruthless disregard of human rights, particularly his own, shown by the United States.

Carey McWilliams too was of much the same mind, even though, if devotion to Soviet interests is the benchmark of leftism, somewhat to the right of Aronson and Belfrage. In his exceptionally complacent memoirs he hailed himself for fearless and lifelong devotion to principle, blaming the difficulties of himself and *The Nation* during the fifties on anti-Communist liberals and intellectuals. "What these elements could not abide was the magazine's criticism of Cold War policies of the kind that finally resulted in the Vietnam disaster and its consistent denunciation of the witch hunt which was in part a consequence, in part a cause, of these policies."[12] Even after McWilliams gave up the editorship in 1976, this remained *Nation* policy. In a special issue given over to praise of McWilliams it ran a long article acclaiming him as the hero of the McCarthy era. The author explained that McWilliams and *The Nation* were almost alone in seeing the danger of McCarthyism properly, most liberals having fought McCarthy in the wrong way. "They all accepted the proposition that communism was a dangerous disease and then sought to argue that McCarthy's methods to combat it were wrong, or that given individuals did not in fact have it."[13] Such a course was beneath *The Nation,* which "refused steadfastly to blame the extreme Left for the resurgence of reaction in the postwar era, thereby parting company with many liberals who blamed their own discomfort more on the Communists than on McCarthy."

This is rather like a homeowner refusing to assign any responsibility to the fire in his house for the damage done by firemen. *The Nation,* both then and later, held that dedication to principle obliged it to disregard the fire. Conversely, where the Soviets were concerned *The Nation* had always sacrificed principle to expediency. Though Russia and other Communist states violated all the human rights held sacred by *The Nation,* their crimes had to be passed over in the interests of a higher cause—world peace or the social revolution or whatever. It was lack of integrity that denied *The Nation* a larger audience. Abroad it practiced the double standard of morals, at home it insisted upon the harmlessness of Communists. *The Nation* was wrong here too, for Communists were a problem, even if not so great a one as was widely believed. Worse still, the magazine's position was blatantly self-serving, for *The Nation* did not want the "left" examined because it was part of that "left" and had published many things that in retrospect were compromising if not shameful. A blanket defense was the best defense, in *The Nation*'s view, and all the more so as it could be said to arise from devotion to civil liberties.

Rereading *Nation* issues from the 1940s and '50s, its panegyrist was "struck by the intensity and clarity of thought that Carey McWilliams and his colleagues brought to the issue of McCarthyism." No other publication "could equal its intensity, consistency, eloquence and uncompromising clarity of reasoning on every major civil liberties issue."[14] This was doubly self-serving, for the author, a law school dean, contributed to

The Nation during that period and was one of those whose eloquence and clarity he applauded. For over forty years *The Nation* has believed that ignoring or apologizing for violations of human rights abroad does not prevent one from effectively championing them at home, that defending one's own record is a high form of altruism. In light of these views it is not hard to see why *The Nation* has never had a very good understanding of its failures to communicate.

McWilliams and his allies recognized that no one outside the little band of *Nation* readers paid any attention to its strictures against McCarthyism, but never asked why. They attributed *The Nation*'s isolation to superior insight and virtue. During that benighted era we alone had the courage and wisdom to speak out, they always say, which not only misses the point but is in the *Nation* tradition of always missing the point. From the time of Freda Kirchwey, *Nation* editors have never faced up to the consequences of blind partisanship. Villard's *Nation* had influence not only because of quality but because it was open to varieties of liberal and left-wing opinion and because Villard himself was not entirely predictable. Kirchwey made the *Nation* one-sidedly progressive, and so, for the most part, it has remained. The post-Villard editors have taken pride in their independence, but it has been a different and narrower independence than his. *The Nation* has kept free of institutional ties and is still answerable only to itself. But it is also largely free of open-mindedness. Since Villard there has been only one right side so far as *The Nation* goes, and that one its own. *The Nation* enjoys this role, but the price of it is a complete lack of influence beyond the family circle. It hardly matters that McWilliams and *The Nation* were right about McCarthy, and many other issues too. What counts is that the magazine arrived at its conclusions first and then looked for reasons to justify them. Admirable as such consistency might be, it persuades no one not already a believer.

Unlike *The Nation,* Lillian Hellman has pressed modern history into a more personally flattering shape with brilliant results. A dramatist whose first effort, *The Children's Hour,* was a success in the 1930s, she later scored with *The Little Foxes* (1939), *Watch on the Rhine* (1941), *The North Star* (1943) and *Toys in the Attic* (1960). Well known for Broadway hits and popular screenplays, she was famous, too, for her politics. Hellman became a leftist through her liaison with Dashiell Hammett, a Communist and writer of detective stories. Her faith was strengthened by a visit to Republican Spain in 1937, and to Russia in 1944. She was especially active in the Wallace campaign of 1948 and the Waldorf "peace" conference the following year. She was called before HUAC, and took the Fifth Amendment. Hellman was blacklisted in consequence, and though Broadway, where the blacklist was not very effective, remained open to her, most of Hellman's earnings in the fifties, greatly reduced from earlier years, went to pay back taxes. She launched a second career in 1961 by teaching at Harvard and then other universities, and a third in 1969 when the first volume of her memoirs, *An Unfinished Woman,* was published. To date three volumes have appeared, all best-sellers, and it is as a memoirist that she is now best known.[15]

Hellman's success is even more remarkable than that of Dalton Trumbo. He sought only to regain his old place as a screenwriter, dismissing his former politics. Hellman not only regained fame and fortune in a different literary form but defended the political record previously held against her. She did this most effectively in the third volume of her autobiography, *Scoundrel Time* (1976), a slender, fast-paced, very engaging and spiteful work. It began with a long, fatuous introduction by Garry Wills which confused every issue. A policy of rebuilding the military was undertaken in 1947, he observed, because "America in the early 1940s fell in love with total war." Wills drew a false distinction unique to himself between the "radical" and the "ideologue." The former is superior to the latter, he maintained, because "the radical hates vicious and harmful people" and "the radical tries to uphold a private kind of honor in a rotten world."[16] Wills insisted that both Hellman and Hammett were radical in this sense, which destroyed his theory, as that meant Stalin could not be considered a vicious and harmful person, nor could denying his crimes be regarded as inconsistent with honor.

Hellman's text, though equally intemperate, was far more skillfully done. Her aim was to show how taking the Fifth Amendment elevated her above the fearful mass of mankind.

This inspired William Buckley to give her book its proper title, "The Heroism of Lillian Hellman During the Darkest Days of the Republic."[17] A secondary goal of Hellman's was to skewer liberal intellectuals for failing to defend her. She accomplished the one by a colorful narrative of the events surrounding her appearance before HUAC, the other in passages such as the following—which contains the first of two references to her pro-Soviet past.

> Simply, then and now, I feel betrayed by the nonsense I had believed. I had no right to think that American intellectuals were people who would fight for anything if doing so would injure them; they have very little history that would lead to that conclusion. Many of them found in the sins of Stalin Communism—and there were plenty of sins and plenty that for a long time I mistakenly denied —the excuse to join those who should have been their hereditary enemies. Perhaps that, in part, was the penalty of nineteenth-century immigration. The children of timid immigrants are often remarkable people: energetic, intelligent, hardworking; and often they make it so good that they are determined to keep it at any cost.[18]

Hellman put forward the odd theory that intellectuals have a duty to come to the aid of their political enemies, for enemy she was despite having associated personally with many anti-Stalinist intellectuals. But when the shoe was on the other foot there is no evidence that Hellman applied this rule to herself. She appears not to have condemned the government for prosecuting Trotskyists under the Smith Act. Victims of Stalinism in Europe had no claim on her sympathy in those days. All the same, she felt entitled to support in her hour of trial from anti-Stalinists, whose failure to give it could arise only from cowardice and lack of American roots. There was to her no chance that anyone might be anti-Stalinist on principle. It had to be a pretext for doing the comfortable thing.

Speaking of *Partisan Review* and *Commentary* she said: ". . . there were many thoughtful and distinguished men and women on both magazines. None of them, as far as I know, has yet found it a part of conscience to admit that their Cold War anti-

Communism was perverted, possibly against their wishes, into the Vietnam War and then into the reign of Nixon, their unwanted but inevitable leader."[19] Later she regretted giving them the benefit of any doubt. Having in mind that some anti-Stalinists went to conferences and wrote for magazines secretly subsidized by the CIA, she concluded that "'the step from such capers was straight into the Vietnam War and the days of Nixon." And the really shameless aspect, of course, was that none of the intellectuals had apologized for visiting war and Nixon upon the country. The anti-Stalinist intellectuals had one valid point, she admitted, making the other reference to her own dark past. "Such people would have a right to say that I and many like me took too long to see what was going on in the Soviet Union. But whatever our mistakes, I do not believe we did our country any harm. And I think they did."[20]

The objects of her anger, many of whom Hellman named, were understandably annoyed. In his review of *Scoundrel Time* Nathan Glazer pointed out that Hellman falsely accused *Partisan Review* and *Commentary* of not having attacked McCarthy. Glazer resented Hellman's charge that his side had failed to defend freedom. Who, he asked rhetorically, did the most for freedom during the Waldorf conference in 1949, the anti-Stalinists who attacked Communists for extinguishing liberty wherever they came to power, or the Hellmanites who, in the name of peace, denied or ignored this fact? He wished that Hellman would stop regarding her refusal to testify before HUAC as a moral triumph. Both at the time and in her book Hellman maintained that the only issue was should she be loyal to her friends. At the suggestion of her counsel, Abe Fortas, she had written to HUAC saying that she would testify about her own past but not that of others. As expected, this was not allowed, and Hellman took the Fifth, but only after reading an eloquent and self-congratulatory statement that was to be the basis of her later reputation. Glazer believed that Hellman had a higher duty at that time which she had failed to recognize. As an insider in the Wallace campaign, she knew that Communists had taken it over. Was she not then obliged to tell the truth about a subject of great controversy?

William Phillips, the editor of *Partisan Review,* resented

Hellman's claim that anti-Stalinist intellectuals ought to have defended her. She knew perfectly well that he and others did not aid Stalinists because they were on opposite sides.

> And just as she asks how we could not come to the defense of McCarthy's victims, one could ask her how she could not come to the defense of all those who had been killed or defamed by the Communists? How could she still be silent about the persecution of writers in Russia? Why has she not spoken up against Russian anti-Semitism or the lies about Israel?[21]

Phillips did not regret having been anti-Stalinist, only that he had pushed a valid position slightly too far. Sidney Hook, whose pen had lost nothing of its edge, had no regrets at all, meeting Hellman's polemic with one of his own. Reviewing the English edition of *Scoundrel Time,* he called it dishonest and misleading. To show this he went over her political record before 1948, which she barely mentioned. During the 1930s she had defended the Moscow trials and attacked John Dewey's Commission of Inquiry. She worked closely with the Party faction in such organizations as the League of American Writers and the Theater Arts Committee. She followed the Party line, for example, in attacking a theatrical relief committee for victims of Soviet aggression during the war with Finland, saying that "charity begins at home" and that relief was a disguised form of intervention. Yet she had been active in organizing and supporting Communist relief activities around the world.

Hellman lied frequently, according to Hook. She claimed to be the first person to invoke the Fifth for the sake of other people, though actually a number of witnesses before her had taken the same position. By her own testimony in *Scoundrel Time* she had lied to Henry Wallace. He asked her at one point how extensively the Progressive Party had been infiltrated by Communists. Hellman answered that there were Communists in the field, but did not add that they held top jobs in party headquarters as well. Her refusal to testify before HUAC involved another lie. If she was not a Communist it was wrong of her to invoke the Fifth Amendment, because answering the question would not have incriminated her. But if testifying would have incriminated her, then she lied in her book by saying that she was not a Communist. Whether she was a Party member or not—and Hook believed that she had been one and perhaps still was—refusing to testify played into HUAC's hands by creating the impression of a vast Communist conspiracy. If Hellman and others had been frank, the red threat in America would have been exposed as the small thing it was. Finally, for someone such as Hellman who had cooperated with Communists for forty years, as Hook believed she had done, "to impugn the integrity of liberal anti-Communists like Lionel Trilling and others of his circle is an act of political obscenity."[22]

Hellman ignored this slashing review, but Diana Trilling did not escape so easily. The September 28, 1976, issue of *The New York Times* reported that a forthcoming book of her essays had been dropped by the firm of Little, Brown, which also published Hellman.[23] It did so because in one of her essays, and in her introduction to the volume, Trilling defended herself and her late husband against Hellman's strictures. Trilling gave further offense by criticizing Hellman on her record and for things written in *Scoundrel Time*. When published by Harcourt Brace Jovanovich, *We Must March, My Darlings* (1977) did not seem abusive. Trilling's comments on Hellman were restraint itself compared to Sidney Hook's. Trilling was scornful of Hellman's claim to moral greatness before HUAC, saying the only difference between her and hundreds of other witnesses was that, thanks to Fortas, she had written a letter saying that she would not cut her conscience to suit this year's fashion. Trilling did accept, in a general way, some responsibility for the Vietnam War, inasmuch as all who were anti-Communist contributed to the atmosphere that made intervention possible. By the same token, she insisted, Hellman and the anti-anti-Communists had to share the blame for McCarthyism, since it was partly the failure of left-wing intellectuals to confront the truth about Stalinist oppression that enabled McCarthy to flourish.

Little, Brown explained that it had rejected Trilling for mercenary reasons. As her books were not best-sellers like Hellman's, she was expendable. Hellman claimed to have had nothing to do with the decision, and to know nothing about Trilling's manuscript except that it contained an hysterical attack upon herself. Later events cast doubt on this. In February 1980 Hellman filed a defamation suit against Mary McCarthy, Dick Cavett and the Educational Broadcasting Corporation in the amount of $2.25 million. She sought compensation for damages resulting from statements made about her by McCarthy on Cavett's show the previous month. McCarthy had called Hellman a bad and dishonest writer, and when asked what made her think so had answered, "Everything. I said in some interview that every word she writes is a lie including 'and' and 'the.' "[24]*

Intellectuals responded to the suit in accordance with their politics, except for those who knew both women and did not wish to offend either. Some did anyway. Norman Mailer cast himself in the unlikely role of peacemaker by urging Hellman to drop her suit. Richard Poirier, a professor of literature and author of a much-praised book on Mailer, rebuked him for failing to take Hellman's side. "Norman Mailer followed with a second letter on the subject of Richard Poirier, which was unfit to print although copies were sent to eight people. Lillian Hellman then wrote a letter to Norman Mailer, with copies to six people, calling off the Mailer-Hellman friendship."[26]

Irving Howe, Dwight Macdonald and other anti-Stalinists agreed with McCarthy. Diana Trilling repeated her charge that Hellman had no right to put on airs over her appearance before HUAC. "What is important is that people think of her as a heroine of culture. It's as if she's the only person who faced down the House Un-American Activities Committee, when she to jail."[27] Hellman's defenders included Victor Navasky of *The Nation*, though he believed that her course of action was mistaken—as well he might, considering *The Nation*'s experience with libel suits. Malcolm Cowley said that Hellman was not a bad writer, and regretted that Mary McCarthy was "dragging up the past" without learning anything from it. Some regarded McCarthy's charges as red-baiting. John Hersey accused Hellman's critics of having given up on reform, while she, in con-

---

* Norman Podhoretz had made the same point more delicately. Speaking of Hellman's admirers, he wrote that her "prose style—an imitation of Hammett's imitation of Hemingway, and already so corrupted by affectation and falsity in the original that only a miracle could have rendered it capable of anything genuine at this third remove—was to them the essence of honesty and distilled candor."[25]

trast, "remained alive to a changing world." He cited especially her work as a founder of the Committee for Public Justice, a civil libertarian group, and her support of particular Soviet dissidents.

Some speculated that the quarrel was over aesthetics as well as politics. In the 1930s and '40s while Hellman's plays were commercial successes they were not admired by avant-garde critics, who thought them middlebrow, unlike McCarthy's fiction, which was highly acclaimed. Meyer Schapiro, an art historian, guessed at Hellman's literary motives. "Maybe she still thinks of Mary as being a rival. She's had great success, yes, but she still hasn't made it with the people who prefer Mary's work. *Partisan Review* stood for perhaps a more accomplished style of writing and a more knowing audience than she achieved."[28] Hellman's attorney Ephraim London took the opposite view, saying that McCarthy, whose recent books had done poorly, was jealous of Hellman's achievement as a memoirist. Perhaps he did not know that McCarthy herself had written an elegant and moving autobiography, *Memories of a Catholic Girlhood* (1957).

In the event, there was no need to reach out for explanations. To old anti-Stalinists such as McCarthy everything in *Scoundrel Time* was false. They believed Hellman had compounded her original sins as a fellow traveler by writing a book that misrepresented the McCarthy era, ignored her own guilty past, and defamed the intellectuals who had been right about all the matters on which she herself had been so wrong. It was an offense to the anti-Stalinists that Hellman, who had sacrificed, so they thought, all human values to the service of tyranny, should now be acclaimed, not only by herself but by many others, as a heroine of culture and morals.

Hellman's motives too appear uncomplicated. She was the recipient of countless honors. In 1960 she was elected to the American Academy of Arts and Sciences. The National Institute of Arts and Letters made her a vice-president. Its parent group, the American Academy of Arts and Letters, invited her to become one of only fifty members. The joint Academy-Institute awarded her its gold medal. She had been given the Brandeis University Creative Arts Award and the Achievement Award of the Women's Division of the Albert Einstein College of Medicine. Colleges and universities stood in line to give her honorary degrees. *An Unfinished Woman* received a National Book Award. *Scoundrel Time* led to further honors, including the Paul Robeson Award of Actors Equity and the Lord and Taylor Rose Award, given her in recognition of her "unshakeable faith in the rights of the human being and for her unwavering crusade for personal dignity."[29]

But neither time nor laurels had diminished her fury. Judging by *Scoundrel Time,* she had been in a constant state of rage for thirty years, against the government for sending Hammett to jail and depriving her of wealth and a much-loved farm, and against all those who failed to stand by her. *Scoundrel Time* was her revenge against the anti-Stalinist intellectuals. Yet it was not, seemingly, enough. Since the fifties Hellman had represented herself as a champion of individual liberties. Recent events suggest that settling old scores was even more important to her.

For others also the witch-hunting era never died. Participants and their sympathizers rake over the old issues tirelessly. As early as 1970 at least three books had been written arguing that the Rosenbergs, who had been convicted of espionage, were really innocent victims of the Cold War. To these books was added a play by Donald Freed, *Inquest: A Tale of Political Terror,* which cast the Rosenbergs as victims of an FBI frameup that involved perjured testimony on the part of Ethel's brother and sister-in-law. Ethel and Julius were depicted as naïve, human, progressive and, above all, blameless. New York critics took the play seriously, some agreeing with its thesis despite the very considerable evidence against the Rosenbergs.[30]

Though eager to reverse the verdicts in all such trials, progressives have invested most heavily in the case of Alger Hiss. Accordingly they were outraged when Allen Weinstein, a professional historian, wrote in opposition to the dozens of books that had exonerated Hiss. Though praised by many reviewers, including even Garry Wills, as thoroughly documented and convincing book that supported Chambers' testimony, it infuriated Victor Navasky. He denounced Weinstein's *Perjury: The Hiss-Chambers Case* (1978) as one-sided and inaccurate. Navasky stopped short of proclaiming Hiss innocent, but, as the *New Republic* said, it was hypocritical of him to maintain that the case was still open when everything printed on it by *The Nation* for the last thirty years had been meant to clear Hiss. Navasky based much of his attack on statements by persons who now said that Weinstein had misrepresented or falsified remarks made in interviews with him. Weinstein replied that they were taking back what they had told him earlier.[31] Navasky called the *New Republic*'s criticism an "ad hominem diatribe" against himself, which it was not. This too was in *The Nation* tradition.[32]

Whatever the merits of individual pieces of evidence, a few essential points about the Hiss case still stand. There was a Communist underground in the 1930s, and Chambers belonged to it. He had an intimate knowledge of Hiss's life during the period in question, revealed under circumstances that make coaching seem unlikely. He also possessed copies of confidential government documents that had been made on a Hiss family typewriter. Hiss was convicted of perjury for denying any connection with the espionage this evidence suggested, and time and endless rehashes of old and new data have not undermined this verdict. Weinstein hoped that, as a scholar with no previous ties to the case, he could put an end to speculation by reviewing the evidence and providing new information gleaned from interviews and government documents obtained under the Freedom of Information Act. In this he failed, not from lack of skill— there were flaws, as might be expected in a work that ran to 656 pages including notes and bibliography, but none that imperiled his conclusions—so much as from the feeling of old and new leftists that establishing the innocence of Alger Hiss would redeem their history.

So the Hiss case goes on and on. In 1978 Hiss petitioned to have his case reviewed, and the supporting brief was published and distributed to scholars and interested parties.[33] In 1980 a documentary film on the case favorable to Hiss appeared. It was made by John Lowenthal, a former law professor. Lowenthal denied trying to show that Hiss was not guilty. He claimed rather to have established that the government had fabricated items of evidence and suppressed others that could have led to a different verdict. Lowenthal, who had done research for Hiss's attorneys at the time, told reporters that he had first considered writing yet another book, in addition to the thirty-five already published on the case, but had decided on film instead because the camera discloses something called "demeanor evidence," the way a person looks and sounds when testifying, that cannot otherwise be appreciated.[34] This was a shrewd decision, according to movie critic Vincent Canby. Hiss had "aged so well that it looks to be a sign of grace."[35] Whittaker Chambers, on the other hand, was still handicapped on film as formerly in life (Chambers died in 1961) by an unattractive appearance. If demeanor evidence were crucial, Hiss would have won easily. Of course it was not, and, as Canby also pointed out, the film was unlikely to change many minds. In the end, as in the beginning, the Hiss case was being judged not on merit but by political standards.

To some intellectuals, particularly Norman Podhoretz, the editor of *Commentary,* it seemed as if Stalinism was on the rise again. In youth he had been excited by anti-Communist liberalism, which in the late forties and early fifties was "full of the dynamism, élan and passion that so often accompany a newly discovered way of looking at things," whereas "the fellow travelers could marshal nothing but boring clichés and tired arguments."[36] But by the late fifties "revisionist" liberalism too had become "boring and stale," leading Podhoretz to want more stimulating ideas. He found them in the leftism associated to a degree with Norman Mailer and especially Paul Goodman, whose *Growing Up Absurd* (1960) "made the enterprise of radical social criticism seem intellectually viable once again." Podhoretz began running articles taking issue with American policy that filled Diana and Lionel Trilling and others with alarm, and rightly so, he was later to think.

They knew, that is, how fragile the liberal anti-Communist consensus really was and conversely how deceptive was the apparent weakness of fellow-traveling liberalism, especially among intellectuals. Intimidated by McCarthyism and discredited by Stalinism, the fellow-traveling liberals had temporarily lost their nerve, but they had by no means been converted or given up.[37]

Their revenge was gained through the next generation, Podhoretz believed. New-left leaders were scions of the "First

Families of American Stalinism," and the movement itself was an effort "by the children of McCarthy's victims to avenge their parents on the flesh of the country which had produced them." With the new left and the war in Vietnam, fellow-traveling liberalism rose again. Members had to admit they were wrong about Russia in the old days.

> But they could and did still claim to have been right about the United States—right in having blamed it for starting the cold war, and right in believing that it was fundamentally an evil country. As they had been put on the defensive in the past because of Stalin, they now sought to put the anti-Communist liberals on the defensive by focusing on the "crimes" of the United States.[38]

And they were joined in this enterprise by a larger group with no links to Stalinism, such as Jason Epstein.

Podhoretz himself became alarmed, reverting to his earlier politics, now known, not very helpfully, as "neoconservatism." The failure of Lionel Trilling, one of his mentors in college, to join wholeheartedly in Podhoretz's war against fellow-traveling liberalism and radical chic dismayed him. Podhoretz attributed it to Trilling's fear of going the way of Sidney Hook, whose prestige among intellectuals had vanished.

> For Trilling, Hook was the cautionary figure of his own generation—the one who had gone too far in the rebellion against radicalism—just as Irving Kristol was of the generation below him and as I myself, ten years younger than Kristol, was rapidly becoming for the generation below that. Trilling's fear of the fate of Sidney Hook was not nearly so great as that of William Phillips, who would have done almost anything to avoid it. But Trilling did, I believe, grow fearful enough in the late sixties to shy away from too close an identification with the antiradical position.[39]

Even after the new left collapsed *Commentary* pressed on, because its real enemies were not student demonstrators but the people and institutions on the left who had been radicalized, or in some cases re-radicalized, in the 1960s. *Commentary* went after *The New York Review,* fashionable leftist pundits such as Theodore Roszak and Kenneth Kenniston, and what Podhoretz saw as the new-liberal fellow-traveling institutions including the op-ed page of *The New York Times,* and the ACLU, which had swung left again and was now more blatantly partisan than at any time since the thirties.

Though wrong in some instances, Podhoretz was right about the trend. Even after the collapse of the new left and the decline of liberalism in the seventies intellectuals continued to give at least lip service to radical ideas. A resurgent progressivism in the middlebrow media glorified and misrepresented the victims of McCarthyism. There were documentary films in praise of Paul Robeson, the Hollywood Ten, and Hiss, of course. Dramatic films sympathized with the Rosenbergs and those blacklisted by the TV industry. The old Stalinists were worshipfully acclaimed in a book entitled *The Romance of American Communism* (1977), which hailed certain survivors for their former emotional intensity and present beauty.

Hilton Kramer denounced Vivian Gornick, the author, for being selective and caring only about "the passion for the Party and its purpose: a passion that is alleged to have conferred moral—and even, apparently, physical—superiority on those political hacks who lived by it and for it."[40] This was a work of fiction to Kramer, who called it "a travesty of some of the most hateful history of our time—a history that Miss Gornick rapturously embraces." It made him wonder why, after all that had happened, people still cherished a desire for totalitarian rule. Kramer was unfair to Gornick, a feminist and no totalitarian. She had been raised in the self-contained world of American Communism, and her book was infused with filial piety, being a loving tribute to her parents and their friends. Even so, her book was, as Kramer said, lacking in moral intelligence, as is often the case with recent treatments of Stalinists and fellow travelers. The convention is to say that they meant well and were treated unjustly. The reasons for it are slighted or ignored. One would not know from seeing films such as *The Front* or reading books like *The Romance of American Communism* that the heroes in them were apologists for Stalin's death machine.

A similar blindness afflicts those who wish to glorify the memory of Paul Robeson. The greatest black artist of his generation, Robeson was also a Stalinist. Though denying actual Party membership, he followed every twist and turn of the Party line. This presents difficulties for his admirers, who, understandably, are tempted to get around it by focusing on the man and the artist. This was the course taken by Philip Hayes Dean, whose play *Paul Robeson,* starring the noted actor James Earl Jones, opened in New York on January 19, 1978. Dean's approach made good sense dramatically, but it conflicted with the desire of black activists to exploit the memory of Robeson as a radical hero. In consequence fifty-six prominent men and women—including Alvin Ailey, James Baldwin, Coretta Scott King, Dr. Alvin F. Poussaint and Paul Robeson, Jr.—signed an advertisement just before the play opened calling it "a pernicious perversion of the essence of Paul Robeson."[41] At a forum Baldwin said that by depicting Robeson as a "misguided, tragic hero" the play misrepresented him in the interests of popular culture. It was in keeping with a plot going back to the time of Secretary of State John Foster Dulles, according to Paul Robeson, Jr., who read a memo allegedly composed by Dulles ordering that government publications describe Robeson as "talented but naive and bitter."

Members of the National Ad-Hoc Committee to End the Crimes Against Paul Robeson were also angry with Carl Stokes, a New York television newsman who had aired several stories critical of their efforts to kill Dean's play. The actor Ossie Davis condemned both Stokes and Dean for ignoring Robeson's socialism. "What this country needs," he reportedly said, "is a hero who is black and a socialist." The play ran for seventy-seven performances on Broadway. After it closed, thirty-three playwrights, members of the executive council of the Dramatists Guild, issued a statement deploring attempts to "influence critics and audiences against a play."[42] It was shown on public television the following year, arousing fresh complaints from Paul Robeson, Jr. His father's memory was now being honored frequently. Rutgers University, Robeson's alma mater, had named a building and other things after him. His name had been inscribed on a pink star in something called the Walk of Fame in Hollywood. There had been a week-long celebration in Detroit on the eightieth anniversary of Robeson's birth. But his son was not appeased. Media interest in Robeson perpetuated "the myths that my father was a political patsy, spent much of his life in self-exile and died a bitter, tragic figure. There is a desire of the establishment to now embrace a great man and clean him up so that he fits an acceptable image."[43]

Perhaps only a family member could know if Robeson was truly bitter, or whether his years in seclusion amounted to self-exile or not. But Robeson was undeniably a tragic figure because he ruined himself. His brilliant career was destroyed as a result of his persistent service to Communist causes, which earned him a Stalin Peace Prize but also a place on the blacklist. Robeson's politics could not have been more simple. In foreign affairs he held that Soviet Russia was always right and America always wrong. On civil liberties he ruled that Communists should have them but not enemies of the Party, especially Trotskyists. His civil-rights position was that white Americans were committing genocide against blacks. Robeson's politics enabled racists to claim that integration was a Communist plot, and obliged black leaders to keep their distance from him. This makes it hard to know what Robeson, Jr., and James Baldwin and the others wanted. Many feel badly today that Robeson was blacklisted and his passport taken away. Others wish to honor the artist and even the man, as Dean did in his play. But few Americans could honor his politics, which, Ossie Davis to the contrary, were Stalinist rather than socialist. Robeson went around the world endorsing a political system based on mass murder, forced labor and the denial of every human right, accusing all who criticized him for doing so of bigotry. Surely Davis did not expect, and perhaps at heart did not even want, such a record to be brought out. Yet the alternative would seem to be that chosen by Philip Hayes Dean and excoriated by Davis. For black progressives, as for whites, the past is still embarrassing.

A further illustration of the progressive dilemma was *Naming Names,* by Victor Navasky. It was about those figures in the entertainment industry who were friendly witnesses before HUAC. Navasky wished in particular, he said, to explain why show-business people were willing to inform on their friends and colleagues. The question was vital supposedly "because it promises to teach us most about the conditions under which good men do things they know or suspect to be wrong, about a political system that puts people in a position where they are encouraged to violate their values, about a republic that asks its citizens to betray their fellows."[44] This was to make too much of a question that could be answered in considerably fewer than the 427 pages Navasky allowed himself. In fact, only two out of sixteen chapters were devoted to summarizing and dismissing the reasons given by informants to justify their having named names. Navasky's real purpose was to discredit anti-Communism by showing the moral degradation to which it led.

Navasky made clear that no form of anti-Communism was acceptable to him by offering many examples. One of these was an article by Alan Westin in 1954 criticizing a pamphlet, "McCarthy on Trial," that was the transcript of an event conducted by Communists and fellow travelers. Westin objected to it as Communist propaganda, and especially as an effort by individuals, whom he named, to create a Popular Front against McCarthy for their own benefit. Westin was wrong, Navasky explained, not because his article was inaccurate but because by identifying the contributors as he did Westin put himself on the side of the witch-hunters. "Thus did a committed libertarian, accepting the labels and definitions and symbols of the cold war, use them to degrade those men whose rights one would have thought he would defend."[45] But most of those named by Westin—including Howard Fast, Albert Kahn, Mrs. Robeson, James Aronson, Angus Cameron—were well-known Party members or sympathizers. To Navasky it was bad to call a Communist a Communist because that was what witch-hunters did, because it degraded a person to be so characterized, and, finally, because it denied the person a right Westin ought to have defended, that being the right not to be correctly identified. Had this standard been widely upheld it would have been very difficult indeed to speak plainly about Communists or Communist-sponsored activities, which is what progressives wanted—and still want, it would seem.

Though *Naming Names* had a political objective, it was, for the most part, a work of moral philosophy. Navasky's chief interest was in showing how utterly corrupt and debased a thing it was to testify about friends and colleagues, and, by the same token, how brave it was to refuse. Those who, like the Hollywood Ten, invoked the First Amendment were somewhat more blessed than people who took the Fifth, but there was glory enough for all. "Whatever the motive, they did not permit the state to take over their values; they defined their own situation, and by risking self and career they emerged as moral exemplars. Tarnished exemplars, but exemplars nonetheless."[46] People who did testify, whatever their reasons, were more to be pitied than censured, except for those obdurate sinners—especially Elia Kazan—who stubbornly refused to apologize later. Navasky reserved the lowest circle of hell for such worms, or in his role as Pope Victor excommunicated them from the Church of Decent and Progressive Humanity. It was not that he failed to recognize the complex situation in which politically active show-business people found themselves. Many passages were given over to ruminations on the pros and cons of different kinds of behavior. But in the end all morality was reduced to a simple rule according to which informing was the only sin and silence the only virtue. The result was a pious work that would not help anyone make sense of the topic, still less arrive at plausible moral judgments.

Navasky's book failed out of necessity rather than from lack of intelligence, as do all apologies for Stalinists. That people suffered for being wrong may be deplorable but does not make their error less nor their conduct more impressive. *Naming Names* was bad history because it was so relentlessly one-sided and selective, and morally dubious for the same reasons. Like *Scoundrel Time*, it was written as an act of vengeance, not on Navasky's own behalf but for the sake of his political ancestors. This was most evident in Navasky's treatment of a speech by Dalton Trumbo. In 1970 Trumbo was given an award by the Screen Writers Guild and took the opportunity to reflect on the blacklisting era. Trumbo advised younger people that

it will do no good to search for villains or heroes or saints or devils because there were none; there were only victims. Some suffered less than others, some grew and some diminished, but in the final tally we were all victims because almost without exception each of us felt compelled to say things he did not want to say, to do things he did not want to do, to deliver and receive wounds he truly did not want to exchange. That is why none of us—right, left, or center —emerged from that long nightmare without sin.[47]

As a statement of the ethics involved this would seem very hard to better. But even though Trumbo is one of Navasky's heroes, and despite Trumbo's care to avoid saying that all suffered equally or were equally justified, Navasky was shocked anyway by Trumbo's statement and devoted several chapters to undermining it. His main tactic was to quote at length from Albert Maltz, who had learned nothing and forgotten nothing in all the years since the Ten were called before HUAC, and who missed the point right away by defining Trumbo's thesis as being "that everyone during the years of blacklist [sic] was equally a 'victim,'" precisely what Trumbo did not say.[48] Tiring finally of the issue, Navasky issued this bull: ". . . perhaps it is the beginning of wisdom to acknowledge that whatever their motives the resisters did the right thing, and, whatever their motives, the informers did not."[49] So much for motivation, and the intricacies of moral philosophy too.

XIII

Conclusions

DESPITE THE EFFORTS to obscure it, what has been set forth here does have a moral dimension that must be addressed. For one thing, it explains the passionate feelings of both sides. Communists and progressives believed that the urgency of their cause was so great that it excused lesser lapses, such as the crimes of Stalin. These were unfortunate accidents that had to be lied about, evaded or ignored for the sake of world revolution and/or world peace, which would ultimately redeem them. Failure to see this could only result from malice and blackest reaction. To anti-Stalinists, on the other hand, these same facts proved that revolution, so defined, was calamitous, and world peace, thus obtained, little more than the peace of the grave. Those who thought otherwise were, if not participants in evil, apologists for it, which was nearly as bad. Their judgment prevailed in the fifties and seemed likely to endure. That it has not, or at least not without challenge, arises from the vested interest surviving progressives have in their old positions, and from the continuing revulsion against anti-Communism felt by latter-day progressives, and the need of both to prove that American opponents of the Cold War have been right all along. Attempts to prove that Stalinists were justified in concealing or misrepresenting their politics are only a small part of this rhetorical campaign.

The question of which side actually had the better case is not hard to answer. Stalinists, and to a degree progressives also, maintained that the end justified the means, and they constantly employed the double standard to advance it. Liberal and left-wing anti-Stalinists, in contrast, were more scrupulous. Though they sometimes went too far, as Irving Howe, Alfred Kazin and others frequently pointed out, they tried even so to act consistently and from principle. Whereas Stalinists and most progressives were concerned only with civil liberties for their own side, anti-Stalinists generally struggled to be fair.* One need not agree with Sidney Hook's formula of "Heresy yes, Treason no," for example, as a justification for firing Communist teachers. It was an honest effort to establish the limits of dissent all the same.

A more difficult question to answer is, what consequences resulted from the great debate among intellectuals? As the anti-Stalinists won it, a possible answer is that truth and justice were served and progressives kept from doing much if any harm. This is denied by Lillian Hellman, who says that though wrong about Stalin she and her friends did no real damage, while the anti-Stalinists, by permitting or encouraging the red scare, and failing to come to the aid of victims such as herself, paved the way for Vietnam and Nixon's presidency. By this reasoning it makes no difference if one applauds distant evils, but it matters greatly if one supports a policy that is taken by government further than one wishes. Diana Trilling answered this by saying, in effect, that she would share the blame for Vietnam if Hellman would admit to helping bring on McCarthyism. This confused the issue. McCarthyism was the opposite of Hellmanism, not its extension. An apter comparison would be to say that anti-Stalinism was to Vietnam as Hellmanism to the Gulag Archipelago. But that is a responsibility which progressives will not take. Nor, for that matter, would most anti-Stalinists assume any blame for the war in Vietnam, which they vigorously opposed.

Even if we absolve both sides for the actions of Moscow and Washington there still remains a difference. The progressive intellectuals were not simply deceived about Stalin. They knew there were great evils in Soviet Russia but suppressed that information. Alexander Werth acknowledged this long afterward. He confessed to having given out what he knew were false

---

* This does not apply to anti-Communists as a whole, who were often as bad as American Communists, even if in a better cause.

figures about the number of Soviet labor camp inmates, under-stating them deliberately.

> But there was a very good reason for this. In 1948 the Cold War was at its height, and there were no end of people in Britain, and especially in the U.S., who were advocating a preventive war against Russia; and the "slave labour" (the more the better) was their pet argument. It was the "hawks" of those days who spoke of the 3–30 million "slave labourers" whom it was the Free World's sacred duty to liberate.[1]

He was unrepentant about his deception then, and unabashed that he had erred in saying Khrushchev was not anti-Semitic, that being "a very small matter." The cause came before the truth, the end, as usual, justifying the means. Nor, as we have seen, was Werth an isolated case. During the Stalin-Hitler Pact era both *The Nation* and the *New Republic* revealed that they knew much about the true state of affairs in Russia, develop-ing amnesia only after the German invasion. When the truth became inconvenient it was simply put aside. Anti-Stalinists made false statements, too, but seldom knowingly and therefore did not corrupt intellectual life. It was the progressives who subordinated truth and honesty to the "higher" needs of peace or socialism or whatever who did the most harm.

In this sense it did matter that progressives hailed the spread of democracy in Eastern Europe after the war, not to the in-habitants, who were destined to suffer whatever *The Nation* said, but to Americans. And it still matters in that intellectual life continues to endure misleading accounts of the old debate and misrepresentations of the old issues. We have seen many instances of the former; here is a sample of the latter. In *Henry Wallace, Harry Truman and the Cold War* (1976) Richard J. Walton has this to say of the Czechoslovakian coup:

> . . . but one does not have to be an admirer of Soviet treatment of its East European neighbors to notice a double standard at work. It was acceptable by American standards for the State Department and the Central Intel-ligence Agency to use extreme political pressure and spread around vast quantities of dollars to influence the

governments of France and Italy, to mention just two, but not all right for the Soviet Union to act in similar fashion on its very doorstep.[2]

To Walton the effort of one government to influence another is the same as the destruction of one government by another. The United States, having taken the one course, was therefore no different from Russia and its criticism of the Soviets for obliterating Czech freedom and independence could only be hypocritical. A step forward from the old progressivism in that Soviet misdeeds are admitted, this is still so far from being a truthful comparison as to make debate impossible.

But Walton is not necessarily typical of modern progressives. To observers like Norman Podhoretz the return of progressivism is evidence that things are almost as bad as ever, which, if so, would mean that the painful experiences recorded here had been for nothing. There is some basis for the bleak Podhoretz view, yet ground also for cautious optimism. A case in point is revisionist diplomatic history. This academic school, which began with the publication of William Appleman Williams' *The Tragedy of American Diplomacy* (1959; revised edition 1962), is deprecated by some anti-anti-Stalinists as the carrying forward of progressivism by other means. Williams and his followers do put greater blame for the Cold War on the United States, owing to its superior power after World War II and its tendency to expand, which Williams calls Open Door Imperialism. Revisionist diplomatic history is one-sided, charitable in dealing with Soviet motives, unforgiving in its indictment of American aggression, cupidity and shameless hostility to revolutions. Yet revisionism is less deplorable than bald summaries make it seem. As the democratic socialist Michael Harrington pointed out in a review of its historiography, "I was struck by the degree to which almost everyone had become a revisionist of sorts," especially in accepting Williams' thesis that Russia had acted mostly out of immediate needs, rather than from any master plan, during the Cold War.[3] Though Williams himself is vulnerable to charges of faulty reasoning and lack of evidence, the school as a whole did much to reinvigorate the history of foreign relations.[4] A growth industry itself, revisionism also stimulated a rival literature, and even what are called "post-revisionist" studies that seek to go beyond the Williams framework.[5] It has been, accordingly, both useful in its own right and a prod to further research by others. Respect for this accomplishment rather than agreement with his opinions was probably what led his colleagues to make Williams president of the Organization of American Historians in 1980. Though proceeding from what to anti-Stalinists often seem faulty assumptions, and lacking almost entirely any sense of the American national interest as having a valid claim, revisionism has raised the level of debate even so, and presented the case against American foreign policy more honestly and intelligently than progressives ever did.

On the polemical level too, modern progressivism is an improvement. *The Nation,* though still flying old flags and fighting old battles, is more self-critical than before. An instance is the essay by David Horowitz, "A Radical's Disenchantment." Horowitz, formerly an editor of *Ramparts* magazine, was concerned over the one-sidedness of that broad and ill-defined left to which he and *The Nation* belonged. It worried him that leftists were always protesting against murder and oppression in Nicaragua, Chile and South Africa, but never against the same things in Cambodia, Tibet and the Soviet bloc. Unwanted events in Russia were dismissed as irrelevant or anomalous. The great increase in Soviet power was ignored. Horowitz wondered if the left could "begin to shed the arrogant cloak of self-righteousness that elevates it above its own history and makes it impervious to the lessons of experience?"[6] A crucial question indeed, but one that was never asked by Kirchwey's *Nation.* Further, when in 1979 Joan Baez and eighty other former members of the peace movement of the sixties signed an open letter to the Communist government of Vietnam accusing it of violating human rights, *The Nation* endorsed it, despite feverish protests by leftist and progressive readers, including Corliss Lamont, who knew that all the charges were false owing to reports by Stalinists such as Wilfred Burchett.[7] These were hopeful signs, evidence that the past had not been entirely for nothing.

Against them must be set the fact that progressives are still tied to obsolete dogmas, chief among them being that Russia poses no danger and that all statements to the contrary arise from sordid motives. Nowhere was this more apparent than in responses to the Soviet occupation of Afghanistan. *The Nation* deplored this act, but it also rang familiar chimes.[8] Soviet intervention was nothing to worry about, as Afghanistan had been a Soviet client state since 1978. Soviet policy was opportunistic rather than calculated, and therefore practically harmless. It was wrong to say that Afghanistan was Russia's Vietnam. "Americans who use the Vietnam analogy are trying to debase their former foes, to equate the Marxist guerillas of the Mekong Delta with the ultraconservative tribesmen of the Hindu Kush."[9] These "primitive fundamentalist Moslem tribesmen" were an altogether lower form of life, it appeared, who did not merit the sympathy of progressive mankind.

Ronald Steel extended this argument. An accomplished scholar, as witness his splendid biography of Walter Lippmann, Steel was also a progressive and willing to square every circle if need be.[10] He too said that this country had nothing at stake in Afghanistan and that the Soviets had gained influence over it earlier, acquiring thereby, he seemed to feel, the right to do whatever they pleased. Anyway, the United States was in no position to complain, having done the same thing to the Dominican Republic in 1965. Though Steel did not mention it, progressives (and many others too) had protested the Dominican invasion instead of rationalizing it as they did the Soviet seizure of Afghanistan. Progressive minds were still free of the hobgoblin of consistency. Steel's anger was directed not at the Soviet occupation but against those who complained of it, as they could, naturally, have no valid reason for doing so. President Carter was in trouble with the voters and needed a popular issue. Henry Kissinger and other Republicans were using Afghanistan to get back into office. Neoconservatives and complaining liberals were really upset over the decline of their own status owing to the black revolt and the new left (whose disappearance Steel had failed to notice). Liberals were looking for reds under their beds out of fears stemming from the decline of American imperial power. No one could possibly imagine that Russia, with its weak economy and numerous enemies, posed any real threat to the West.[11]

This last was revealing. As an expression of alienation from the United States, progressivism has never been debatable. But as a reasoned case against American foreign policy it has depended on the conviction that, being stronger than Russia, the United States had both an obligation to forbear and the freedom to do so. Vietnam was a triumph for progressivism, as it showed the folly of unrestrained anti-Communism. By the same token Afghanistan threatened to undo progressivism as a creditable line of argument. There, for the first time, Soviet Russia used force in a land to which it had no claim and that it had not conquered during World War II. To say that the Afghans were inferior specimens, the place itself of no value and the motives of protestors unworthy were hardly convincing excuses for Soviet aggression.

American hand-wringing offered progressives targets not to be missed. Walter La Feber, one of the best revisionist historians, said of Jimmy Carter: "A President who in three years could not construct a consistent policy toward Russia now enjoys the trust of an overwhelming number of Americans because that policy has finally collapsed."[12] Though amusing, and true to an extent, La Feber's essay rested on the same old progressive assumptions—U.S. military power is always too great, U.S. foreign policy always too expansive—that Afghanistan had thrown into doubt. It would take more than sneering references to American hawks to answer questions about Soviet ambitions raised by Soviet behavior. The strategy of revisionist historians, as of progressive journalists, had been to shift attention from Russia to the United States. What the Soviets did was always explained away as a consequence of what America had done. The taking of Afghanistan, unprovoked by the United States and unjustifiable in terms of any threat to Russian security, undercut this argument, forcing progressives to say that Russia's occupation was a mere pretext for American belligerence, or even an unimportant crime against unimportant people. Such arguments did not inspire much respect.

If Afghanistan showed progressives at their worst, that was still not quite so bad as in the old days. Modern progressives did not, for the most part, acclaim the pro-Soviet faction as the democratic side, or argue that Russia had invaded Afghanistan for its own good. Something had been learned after all. There was now a more visible difference between progressives and Stalinists. Few things had contributed more to public confusion in the 1940s and '50s than the lack of a clear distinction between them. This was not due so much to the Communists, who were partisan and sectarian in the extreme after 1945, as to progressives who clung to the Popular Front idea of having no enemies on the left. Since the anti-Stalinists did not go along, this meant having in effect a policy of no enemies on the left save democrats and Trotskyists. It was hard to explain to anti-Communists how someone could defend Stalinism and still not be a Stalinist. And it was often difficult even for the politically sophisticated to tell a Stalinist from an independent radical, especially when blinded by friendship. Thus it was that Roger Baldwin insisted Corliss Lamont was not a fellow traveler, all evidence to the contrary, because he had deviated from the Kremlin line on several occasions. Progressives thought they strengthened the left by blurring the lines dividing it. But this only guaranteed that they would go down, too, when American Communism foundered.

Their mistake was perpetuated by the Englishman Godfrey Hodgson, who in his history of modern America indicted liberals for the failure of leftism. Of the postwar liberal consensus he wrote that it "condemned the United States to face the real dangers for too long without any fundamental debate. Thanks to the liberal triumph, the powerful emotions and interests that always work for conservative policies were not balanced by equally powerful forces and principles of the left."[13] Hodgson had it wrong way around. It may be that the absence of a strong left is unfortunate, but that did not result from an all-powerful liberal offensive. Stalinism collapsed in America because it was wrong, vicious and deservedly unpopular. Progressives, not seeing this, aligned themselves too closely with Stalinism to survive its inevitable disgrace. Liberalism can hardly be reproached for failing to destroy itself similarly. The left was not so valuable as to merit eternal life at all costs. Hodgson retained the old habit of excusing the left despite its errors, while liberalism could never be forgiven the sin of having been right about them. Yet progressives cannot get off the hook so easily. Anti-Stalinists must answer for their excesses, but progressives also for their greater ones. Scapegoating cannot take the place of thorough self-examination, which so far progressives have been reluctant to undertake.

Hodgson was right about one thing. Although the old left

deserved to fail, we do need a left wing of the proper kind. A left rooted in anti-Americanism and dedicated to the interests of foreign countries, which is what we have had for most of the last half century or so, benefits no one, not even itself. An ethical left that regarded the well-being of the United States as a legitimate concern would be valuable as a counter to the right —always more powerful in this country than its opposite—and as a way of making responsible dissent effective. Had there been a genuinely independent and democratic left of consequence in the 1960s, the worst national misadventures might have been avoided, or at least scaled down. That the Michael Harringtons and Irving Howes are so few is a problem that has defied the best efforts of socialists since World War I. But whatever the solution, experience makes clear that going the other way, as both the old and new lefts did, is not it. A strong left, if there is to be one, will have to be an *American* left, democratic, loyal, and with no compulsion to admire or emulate foreign tyrannies. Anything less would be flawed and, the record indicates, futile too.

As their response to Afghanistan shows, many progressives and leftists are still committed to the politics of alienation. Few any longer defend historic Stalinism, but many favor its contemporary manifestations in the third world. Progressive churchmen justify revolutionary violence with no thought given to its human costs. A writer in the *New Republic* pointed out that "under Reinhold Niebuhr's direction *Christianity & Crisis* was Protestantism's most influential journal of social responsibility. But today its editors have become apologists for Castroism, enthusiasts for guerrillas everywhere, and defenders of PLO terrorism."[14] Left intellectuals dedicated to the promotion of third-world "liberation" movements have their own research group, the Institute for Policy Studies, with offices in Washington and Amsterdam, a budget of some two million dollars, and a staff of seventy-five. Some members celebrated the Communist victories in Laos and Angola. Leaders of the IPS took out an advertisement in *The New York Times* to say that the government of Vietnam "should be hailed for its moderation and for its extraordinary effort to achieve reconciliation among all of its people."[15] This resulted from bad publicity owing to Vietnam's expulsion of Chinese citizens, and the flight of other desperate refugees known as the boat people, and was, therefore, an astonishingly blatant falsehood equal to any published by *The Nation* at its worst. One individual who had been a fellow of the IPS wrote a book applauding the Pol Pot regime in Cambodia, the bloodiest tyranny since that of Stalin, and, on a per-capita basis, even more destructive. For progressives of this type, history has been in vain.

No book about leftists can end without a word on the role and function of intellectuals. Such basic questions seldom arise when discussing homogeneous groups. But, though they are all professionals, intellectuals come from many different fields and are not easily measured. We have been concerned mainly with literary intellectuals, artists, writers, journalists and professors. Though sharing a common interest in radical politics, they were sharply divided over issues, and over their obligations as political activists. At the extremes there was little disagreement over function, the most militant holding themselves to be shapers of events. Thus, the anti-Stalinists blamed leftists and progressives for losing China, while they in turn held anti-Stalinists responsible for McCarthyism and Vietnam. Both sides were led astray by faith in the power of ideas, as also by the large role played by intellectuals in revolutions abroad. Yet the United States was not Russia or China or anything like them. Had *The Nation,* the *New Republic, Common Sense, Partisan Review,* the *New Leader, Commentary* and all who wrote for them never existed, history would have turned out the same. American intellectuals played minor roles. That so many writers were pro-Soviet during World War II made it easier for government to maintain that Russia wanted the same things as America. Government would have argued this anyway. And, by the same token, anti-Stalinist intellectuals contributed to the selling of Cold War policies that would have prospered without them. Whether as critics or cheerleaders, most American intellectuals were off the field, not players in the game of world politics, and did not score points for any team.

What intellectuals did do was less glamorous but not insignificant. They were unable to mold public opinion, as usual most Americans remaining firmly out of reach. But they influenced the views of educated people, aligning them more strongly behind U.S. foreign policy in the 1940s and '50s—during both its pro-Soviet and anti-Soviet phases—and helping turn them against America's Indochinese policy later on. In all cases, however, the marginal effect that intellectuals had makes the way they arrived at positions more significant than the positions themselves. To defend Stalinism was self-defeating, but, even worse, to set a bad example. And this was not simply unfortunate, a matter of leading innocents astray; it was to misconstrue a central purpose of the intelligentsia. Intellectuals cannot, on the record, lay claim to superior political virtue. What they can do is exemplify a better, more reasoned approach to public affairs than blind partisanship or instinctive loyalties. There never is any shortage of dogmatists, of men and women who believe in their cause or their country, right or wrong, and who are untroubled by the means used to reach a desired end. There are seldom enough reflective persons who know that the means influence the ends, and that the health of a people depends as much on how they make decisions as on the decisions themselves. When intellectuals, for whatever reasons, abandon their calling and join the zealots, they give up a role they alone can play. And in doing so not only are they as prone to error as anyone else, but they sacrifice qualities of judgment unique to themselves and precious to democracy and free culture. These are familiar lessons that, according to the evidence given here, can never be repeated enough.

All honor, then, to the real heroes we have been discussing, to Roger Baldwin, Dwight Macdonald, Sidney Hook, Mary McCarthy, Margaret Marshall, George Orwell, Diana Trilling, Edmund Wilson and the others who, often former partisans themselves, won through to the truth, insofar as we can know it, and demonstrated that being an intellectual is a function not just of mind but of character too.

Notes

[*Unpublished papers referred to in the Notes may be found in the libraries listed below.*]

The American Civil Liberty Archives are in the Princeton University Library, Princeton, NJ.

The Malcolm Cowley Papers are in the Newberry Library, Chicago, IL.

The Hollywood Democratic Committee Papers and those of Raymond Robins are in the State Historical Society of Wisconsin, Madison, WI.

The Freda Kirchwey Papers are in the Schlesinger Library of Radcliffe College, Cambridge, MA.

The Max Lerner Papers and the Dwight Macdonald Papers are in the Sterling Library of Yale University, New Haven, CT.

The Papers of F. O. Matthiessen are in the Beinecke Rare Book and Manuscript Library of Yale University, New Haven, CT.

The Upton Sinclair Papers are in the Lilly Library of Indiana University, Bloomington, IN.

The Ralph De Toledano Papers are in the Boston University Library, Boston, MA.

I. In Shock: August 24, 1939–June 22, 1941

1. Daniel Aaron, *Writers on the Left* (New York, 1961). David Caute, *The Fellow Travelers* (New York, 1973). Frank A. Warren III, *Liberals and Communism* (Bloomington, Ind., 1966).
2. Freda Kirchwey, "Red Totalitarianism," *Nation*, May 27, 1939, pp. 605–6. Sidney Hook to Freda Kirchwey, Aug. 23, 1939, Kirchwey MSS.
3. "To All Active Supporters of Democracy and Peace," *Nation*, Aug. 26, 1939, p. 228.
4. Max Eastman, "Discrimination About Russia," *Modern Monthly*,

September 1934, p. 479. Peter F. Drucker, "That Coming Nazi-Soviet Pact," *Common Sense*, March 1939, pp. 16–17; ed., "Stalin's Blast," April 1939, p. 6; "Periodicals," July 1939, p. 28.

5. Quoted in I. F. Stone, "Chamberlain's Russo-German Pact," *Nation*, Sept. 23, 1939, p. 314.

6. Louis Fischer, "Soviet Russia Today, I: Has Stalin Blundered?," *ibid.*, Dec. 30, 1939, p. 728.

7. Adam B. Ulam, *Stalin: The Man and His Era* (New York, 1973), pp. 504–21.

8. This is still the Soviet line. See Vyacheslav Dashichev, letter to the editor, *New York Times*, Sept. 20, 1979.

9. Freda Kirchwey, "Communism and Democracy," *Nation*, Oct. 14, 1939, pp. 399–401.

10. Oswald Garrison Villard, "Issues and Men," *ibid.*, Nov. 4, 1939, p. 499.

11. Freda Kirchwey, "By Fire and Sword," *ibid.*, Dec. 9, 1939, p. 640.

12. Reinhold Niebuhr, "Ideology and Pretense," *ibid.*, Nov. 9, 1939, p. 646.

13. Bruce Bliven, *Five Million Words Later* (New York, 1970), p. 323.

14. Ed., "Stalin's Munich," *New Republic*, Aug. 30, 1939, p. 89.

15. Ed., "Moscow: Berlin: America," *ibid.*, Sept. 6, 1939, p. 114.

16. Ed., "Communist Imperialism," *ibid.*, Oct. 11, 1939, p. 257.

17. Ed., "Stalin Spreads the War," *ibid.*, Dec. 13, 1940, p. 219.

18. Malcolm Cowley, *Exile's Return* (New York, rev. ed., 1951), p. 308.

19. Cowley, "Russian Turnabout," *New Republic*, June 14, 1943, pp. 800–801.

20. Cowley, "The Sense of Guilt," in *And I Worked at the Writer's Trade* (New York, 1978), pp. 133–52.

21. Cowley to J. V. Healy, Dec. 5, 1939, Cowley MSS.

22. Edmund Wilson to Malcolm Cowley, Jan. 26, 1940, in Elena Wilson, ed., *Edmund Wilson Letters on Literature and Politics, 1912–1972* (New York, 1977), p. 357.

23. Cowley, *And I Worked at the Writer's Trade*, p. 155.

24. James Wechsler, "Stalin and Union Square," *Nation*, Sept. 30, 1939, p. 344.

25. Samuel N. Harper, *The Russia I Believe In: The Memoirs of Samuel N. Harper: 1902–1941* (Chicago, 1945).

26. Carey McWilliams, *The Education of Carey McWilliams* (New York, 1979), p. 93.

27. James Wechsler, *op. cit.*

28. Max Lerner to Harold Laski, Jan. 9, 1940, Lerner MSS.

29. Upton Sinclair to S. K. Ratcliffe, Sept. 21, 1939, Sinclair MSS.

30. "Sidney Hook has been writing me, scolding me for my refusal to take a stand against the Soviet Union." Sinclair to Lewis Browne, Sept. 5, 1939, Sinclair MSS. James T. Farrell to Sinclair, Sept. 22,

1939, Sinclair MSS. There is no copy of Sinclair's response in the Sinclair papers, but it can be inferred from Farrell to Sinclair, Sept. 29, 1939, Sinclair MSS.

31. Sinclair to W. E. Woodward, Sept. 25, 1939, Sinclair MSS.

32. Sinclair to Eugene Lyons, Oct. 13, 1939, Sinclair MSS.

33. Joseph North to Upton Sinclair, Oct. 20, 1939, Sinclair MSS.

34. Sinclair to League of American Writers, Oct. 21, 1939, Sinclair MSS.

35. Sinclair to Joseph North, May 21, 1940, Sinclair MSS.

36. Quoted in Sidney Hook to the editor of *The Call*, n.d., Sinclair MSS. A copy was sent to Sinclair by *The Call*'s editor. Gerry Allard to Upton Sinclair, Oct. 31, 1939, Sinclair MSS.

37. Sinclair to TASS, June 23, 1941, and Sinclair to S. K. Ratcliffe, June 23, 1941, Sinclair MSS.

38. Sinclair to Thomas L. Harris, Oct. 27, 1943, Sinclair MSS.

39. This information is derived from the voluminous Raymond Robins papers in the State Historical Society of Wisconsin.

40. Robins to John Dewey, n.d., Robins MSS.

41. Robins to Mary Dreier, June 12, 1939, Robins MSS. His question was addressed to Alexander Gumberg, who had been Robins' interpreter during the Russian Revolution. Gumberg, though a resident of the United States, maintained close ties with the Soviet Union. See James K. Libbey, *Alexander Gumberg and Soviet-American Relations* (Lexington, 1977).

42. Robins to Salmon Levinson, May 11, 1939, Robins MSS; Robins to Mary Dreier, May 12, 1939, Robins MSS.

43. Robins to Mary Dreier, June 22, 1939, Robins MSS.

44. Robins to Mary Van Kleeck, July 25, 1939, Robins MSS.

45. Robins to Mary Dreier, August 1939, Robins MSS.

46. Robins to Mary Dreier, Sept. 15, 1939, Robins MSS.

47. Robins, Sept. 20, 1939, Robins MSS.

48. Robins, untitled statement, Nov. 7, 1939, Robins MSS.

49. Robins to Ruth and Salmon Levinson, Dec. 27, 1939, Robins MSS.

50. Robins to Claude Pepper, June 15, 1940, Robins MSS.

51. Frank N. Trager, "Frederick L. Schuman: A Case History," *Partisan Review*, Vol. VII, No. 2 (1940), p. 147.

52. Jeb Stuart Magruder, *An American Life: One Man's Road to Watergate* (New York, 1974), p. 22.

53. Frederick L. Schuman, "Machiavelli in Moscow," *New Republic*, Nov. 29, 1939, p. 159.

54. Ed., "Power Politics and People," *ibid.*, p. 155.

55. Vincent Sheean, "Brumaire: The Soviet Union as a Fascist State," *ibid.*, Nov. 8, 1939, pp. 7–9, and "Brumaire II," Nov. 15, 1939, pp. 104–6.

56. Trager, "Frederick L. Schuman," *op. cit.*, p. 144.

57. Frederick L. Schuman, "Machiavelli Gone Mad," *New Republic*, Dec. 27, 1939, p. 290.

58. Frederick L. Schuman, Lawrence Dennis, Max Lerner, "Who Owns the Future?," *Nation*, Jan. 11, 1941, p. 37.

59. *Ibid.*, p. 44.

60. Ed., "Mr. Stolberg's Glue," *New Republic*, Feb. 24, 1941, p. 261.

61. Max Eastman, *Stalin's Russia and the Crisis in Socialism* (New York, 1940).

62. Granville Hicks, "Communism and the American Intellectual," in Irving De Witt Talmadge, ed., *Whose Revolution* (New York, 1941), pp. 78–115.

63. Roger Baldwin, "Liberalism and the United Front," in Talmadge, *op. cit.*, p. 169.

64. Malcolm Cowley to Felix Frankfurter, Nov. 18, 1940, Cowley MSS.

65. For an unfriendly review of his political history up to 1940 see James T. Farrell, "The Faith of Lewis Mumford," in *The League of Frightened Philistines* (New York, 1945).

66. Lewis Mumford, "The Corruption of Liberalism," *New Republic*, April 29, 1940, pp. 568–73.

67. Archibald MacLeish, "The Irresponsibles," *Nation*, May 18, 1949, p. 622.

68. Waldo Frank, "Our Guilt in Fascism," *New Republic*, May 6, 1940, pp. 603–8.

69. Ed., "Mr. Mumford and the Liberals," *ibid.*, April 29, 1940, p. 564.

70. Malcolm Cowley to Lewis Mumford, Feb. 13, 1941, and n.d., Cowley MSS.

71. Malcolm Cowley, "Poets and Prophets," *New Republic*, May 5, 1941, p. 640.

72. Edmund Wilson, "Archibald MacLeish and 'the Word,' " *ibid.*, July 1, 1940, pp. 30–32. See also Morton Dauwen Zabel, "The Poet on Capitol Hill," *Partisan Review*, January–February 1941, pp. 2–19, and March–April, pp. 128–45.

73. Ed., "War and the New Generation," *New Republic*, July 1, 1940, pp. 7–8.

74. For example see the opinions in "On the Irresponsibles," *Nation*, June 1, 1940, pp. 678–82.

75. Irving De Witt Talmadge, *op. cit.*, p. vi.

76. Malcolm Cowley, "Faith and the Future," in Talmadge, *op. cit.*, p. 164.

77. Lewis Corey, "The Need Still Is: A New Social Order," in Talmadge, *op. cit.*, pp. 248–73.

78. Max Lerner, "Reflections on a Harsh Age," *New Republic*, March 3, 1941, p. 304.

79. George Seldes, "1940 Political Buncombe Campaign," *In Fact*, Oct. 7, 1940, p. 1. His autobiography is *Tell the Truth and Run* (Greenberg, N.Y., 1953).

80. George Seldes, "Roosevelt and Labor," *In Fact*, Nov. 18, 1940, p. 1.
81. Seldes, "The Truth About England: Kennedy's Report to President Roosevelt," *ibid.*, Jan. 13, 1941, p. 1.
82. *In Fact*, May 26, 1941, p. 1.
83. George Seldes, editorial, *In Fact*, June 9, 1941, pp. 1–2.
84. See Carl Friedrich Joachim, "The Poison in Our System," *Atlantic Monthly*, June 1941, p. 668.
85. George Soule, "If Germany Wins," *New Republic*, April 22, 1940, p. 526.
86. Ed., "The Lesson of Norway," *ibid.*, May 13, 1940, pp. 626–28.
87. Ed., "Do We Need Conscription?," *ibid.*, Sept. 2, 1940, p. 294.
88. Ed., "Roosevelt's Mandate," *ibid.*, Nov. 11, 1940, pp. 647–48.
89. Ed., "Why We Need Britain," *ibid.*, Jan. 6, 1941, pp. 7–8.
90. For example, "Democratic Defense," *ibid.*, Feb. 17, 1941, a 32-page supplement.
91. Ed., "Does It Mean War?," *ibid.*, March 17, 1941, pp. 358–59.
92. Ed., "Face the Facts," *ibid.*, May 12, 1941, p. 651.
93. Ed., "Five Minutes to Twelve," *ibid.*, May 19, 1941, p. 683.
94. Ed., "Should We Declare War?," *ibid.*, July 21, 1941, pp. 72–73.
95. Ed., "For a Declaration of War," *ibid.*, Aug. 25, 1941, pp. 235–38.
96. Freda Kirchwey, "What Next?," *Nation*, June 22, 1940, pp. 743–44.
97. Oswald Garrison Villard to Freda Kirchwey, June 13, 1940, Kirchwey MSS. Oswald Garrison Villard, "Issues and Men," *Nation*, June 19, 1940, p. 757.
98. Freda Kirchwey, "Escape and Appeasement," *ibid.*, June 19, 1940, pp. 773–74.
99. Freda Kirchwey to Jacob Billikopf, Oct. 29, 1941, Kirchwey MSS.
100. Quoted in ed., "The Shape of Things," *Nation*, Nov. 2, 1940, p. 406.
101. Freda Kirchwey, "Now We Must Act," *ibid.*, May 24, 1941, pp. 600–602. Kirchwey, "How to Invade Europe," *ibid.*, May 31, 1941, pp. 625–27.

II. THE "PEOPLE'S WAR" BEGINS: 1941–1943

1. Ralph B. Levering, *American Opinion and the Russian Alliance, 1939–45* (Chapel Hill, 1976), pp. 33–34.
2. Irving Howe and Lewis Coser, *The American Communist Party: A Critical History* (New York, 1962).
3. Ed., "Party Zig-zag," *New Republic*, July 7, 1941, p. 4.
4. Thomas L. Pahl, "G-String Conspiracy, Political Reprisal or Armed Revolt? The Minneapolis Trotskyite Trial," *Labor History* (Winter 1967), pp. 30–51.

5. Michael R. Belknap, *Cold War Political Justice: The Smith Act, the Communist Party, and American Civil Liberties* (Westport, Conn., 1977). Alan M. Wald, *James T. Farrell: The Revolutionary Socialist Years* (New York, 1978).

6. Joseph R. Starobin, *American Communism in Crisis, 1943–1957* (Cambridge, Mass., 1972), p. 47. John Gates, *The Story of an American Communist* (New York, 1958), p. 127.

7. Levering, *op. cit.*, p. 43.

8. Ed., "Americans and Russia," *New Republic*, Jan. 15, 1940, p. 71.

9. Ed., "The Soviet-Nazi Partnership," *ibid.*, May 26, 1941, p. 716.

10. Ed., "One Day That Shook the World," *ibid.*, June 30, 1941, pp. 871–72.

11. Max Lerner, "Russia and the War of Ideas," *ibid.*, July 7, 1941, p. 17.

12. *Ibid.*, p. 18.

13. Samuel Grafton, "The Uneasy Collaboration," *New Republic*, July 14, 1941, p. 52.

14. Bruce Bliven, "Russia's Morale—and Ours," *ibid.*, Sept. 1, 1941, pp. 273–75.

15. Roger Baldwin, "The Question of Liberty," *ibid.*, Nov. 17, 1941, p. 651.

16. John Scott, "Administrators at Work," *ibid.*, p. 656.

17. Max Lerner, "Homage to a Fighting People," *ibid.*, Nov. 17, 1941, pp. 643–44.

18. Freda Kirchwey, "The People's Offensive," *Nation*, Oct. 11, 1941, p. 323.

19. Ed., "Ethics of Aid to Russia," *ibid.*, Oct. 11, 1941, p. 325.

20. Quoted in "In the Wind," *ibid.*, Nov. 8, 1941, p. 455.

21. Malcolm Cowley, "A Personal Record," in *And I Worked at the Writer's Trade* (New York, 1978).

22. Alfred Kazin, *New York Jew* (New York, 1978), p. 21.

23. George Soule, "The Lessons of Last Time," *New Republic*, Feb. 2, 1942, p. 170.

24. *Ibid.*, p. 182.

25. Max Lerner, "The People's Century," *ibid.*, April 17, 1941, p. 466. The offending editorial was Henry Luce, "The American Century," *Life*, Feb. 17, 1941, pp. 61–65.

26. Ed., "Is It an Anglo-Saxon War?," *New Republic*, Sept. 21, 1942, pp. 333–34. See, for example, Freda Kirchwey, "The People's Revolution," *Nation*, April 25, 1942, pp. 561–62.

27. Michael Straight, "Is It a People's War?," *New Republic*, Nov. 16, 1942, pp. 633–35.

28. Michael Straight, "The Planner's Look Backward," *ibid.*, Nov. 23, 1942, p. 666.

29. For example, Arthur Schlesinger, Jr., "War and Peace in American History," *ibid.*, Sept. 21, 1942, pp. 337–40.

30. For reviews of books with this theme see Ralph Bates, "Study in Reconstruction," *ibid.*, March 30, 1942, pp. 433–34; and Irwin Edman, "What Brave New World," *ibid.*, Oct. 19, 1942, pp. 504–5.

31. Alan R. Sweezy, "Unite on the Left," *ibid.*, Nov. 16, 1942, p. 648.

32. Ralph Bates, "Need We Fear Russia?," *Nation*, Jan. 17, 1942, p. 61.

33. Bates, "Can We Learn from Russia?," *New Republic*, July 13, 1942, p. 58.

34. Joachim Joesten, "The Soviet Defense," *Nation*, Jan. 24, 1942, p. 98.

35. *Ibid.*, p. 100.

36. An excerpt from it is Alexander Werth, "Russia Behind the Lines," *ibid.*, April 18, 1942, pp. 454–57.

37. Alexander Werth, *Moscow War Diary* (New York, 1942).

38. *Ibid.*, p. 52.

39. *Ibid.*, p. 91.

40. *Ibid.*, p. 102.

41. *Ibid.*, p. 103.

42. *Ibid.*, p. 135.

43. Ed., "Our Bolshevik Friends," *Common Sense*, December 1942, p. 415.

44. J. Alvarez del Vayo, "1942 or Never," *Nation*, April 25, 1942, pp. 480–83.

45. Robert Bendiner, "Why the Cow Is Sacred," *ibid.*, Aug. 15, 1942, p. 192.

46. Freda Kirchwey to I. F. Stone, Jan. 27, 1942, Kirchwey MSS.

47. Bruce Bliven, "Where Do We Go from Here," *New Republic*, Dec. 21, 1942, p. 813.

48. Levering, *op. cit.*

49. TRB, "The Communist Party," *New Republic* (June 22, 1942), p. 859.

50. Bert Cochran, *Labor and Communism: The Conflict That Shaped American Unionism* (Princeton, 1977).

51. Ed., "The U.S.S.R.," *Life*, March 29, 1943, p. 20.

52. Joseph E. Davies, "The Soviets and the Post-War," *ibid.*, March 29, 1943, p. 50.

53. Quoted in Howe and Coser, *op. cit.*, p. 228.

54. Ed., "The Shape of Things," *Nation*, Aug. 28, 1943, p. 228. The statement was, of course, first made by the pro-Soviet journalist Lincoln Steffens just after the Bolshevik Revolution. For a view similar to that of Rickenbacker see William L. Batt, "Our Relations with Russia," in Bruce Bliven and A. G. Mezerik, *What the Informed Citizen Needs to Know* (New York, 1945), p. 44.

55. Quoted in Howe and Coser, *op. cit.*, pp. 432–33.

56. Ralph Barton Perry, "American-Soviet Friendship: An Invitation to an Agreement," *New Republic*, April 4, 1943, pp. 433–37.

57. Ed., "Our Russian Ally," *Collier's*, Dec. 18, 1943, p. 86.

58. Paul Willen, "Who 'Collaborated' with Russia," *Antioch Review*, September 1954, pp. 259–83.

59. Reinhold Niebuhr, "Russia and the West," *Nation*, Jan. 16, 1943, p. 83.

60. Niebuhr, "Russia and the West—II," *Nation*, Jan. 23, 1943, pp. 124–25.

61. Niebuhr's temperate letter was described by Bates as "an all too characteristic tirade . . ." Ralph Bates, "Russia, Reformation, and Revolution," *Nation*, April 3, 1943, pp. 492–93; Reinhold Niebuhr, letter to the editor, *ibid.*, April 10, 1943, p. 537; Ralph Bates, "Russia and the Comintern," *ibid.*, May 8, 1943, p. 679.

62. "Why Did Stalin Do It?," *ibid.*, June 12, 1943, pp. 834–37.

63. "Malcolm Cowley, Russian Turnabout," *New Republic*, June 14, 1943, p. 801.

64. Max Lerner, "The End of the Comintern," *PM*, May 23, 1943.

65. Lerner, "After the Comintern," *New Republic*, June 7, 1943, p. 755.

66. *Reader's Digest*, July 1943, pp. 1–14.

67. Max Lerner, "Answering Max Eastman," *PM*, July 1, 1943.

68. Maurice Hindus, *A Traveler in Two Worlds* (New York, 1971).

69. Hindus, *Mother Russia* (New York, 1943), p. 165.

70. *Ibid.*, p. 394.

71. Henry Pratt Fairchild to Max Lerner, July 1, 1943, Lerner MSS.

72. Robert Lynd to Dwight Macdonald, March 31, 1945, Macdonald MSS.

73. Lynd to Macdonald, June 6, 1945, Macdonald MSS.

74. Bernard Pares, *Russia and the Peace* (New York, 1944), p. 21.

75. *Ibid.*, p. 32.

76. Pares, "On the Fear of Russia," *New Republic*, April 19, 1943, pp. 498–502.

77. Pares, *Russia and the Peace*, p. 33.

78. Harry F. Ward, "What Is Soviet Democracy?," *New Masses*, Nov. 13, 1945, p. 6.

79. Richard Lauterbach, *These Are the Russians* (New York, 1945), p. 330.

80. *Ibid.*, p. 352.

81. Travers Clement, "A Socialist Explains," *Nation*, Nov. 20, 1943, p. 596.

82. Edmund Stevens, *Russia Is No Riddle* (Greenberg, N.Y., 1945), p. 176.

83. Max Lerner, "On Rumors of Stalin's Death," *PM*, Oct. 23, 1945.

84. Edgar Snow, *The Pattern of Soviet Power* (New York, 1945), p. 212.

85. Bennett A. Cerf and Eugene Lyons, "Our Crime and His Punishment," letters to the editor, *New Leader*, Sept. 22, 1945, p. 14.

86. Markoosha Fischer, "American Correspondents in Moscow," *Common Sense*, December 1945, p. 34.

87. Ed., "Choices at Moscow," *Nation*, Oct. 16, 1943, p. 423.

88. Ralph Bates, letter to the editor, *ibid.*, Nov. 13, 1943, p. 568.

89. Fritz Sternberg, "How Britain Finances the War," *New Republic*, July 17, 1944, p. 71.

90. Liston M. Oak, "Remission to Moscow," *New Leader*, Nov. 6, 1943, p. 4.

91. Freda Kirchwey, "Stalin and Badoglio," *Nation*, March 24, 1944, p. 352.

92. Quoted in Liston M. Oak, "Remission to Moscow, II," *New Leader*, Nov. 13, 1943, p. 2.

III. THE REVIVAL OF ANTI-STALINISM

1. Joseph P. Davies, *Mission to Moscow* (New York, 1941).

2. Margaret Marshall, "Mr. Davies's Revelations," *Nation*, Jan. 31, 1942, p. 118.

3. Ed., "Strategy of Whitewash: 'Mission to Moscow,'" *New Leader*, September 1942.

4. T. R. Greene, "'Mission to Moscow' Adviser Was Soviet Film Propagandist," *New Leader*, Oct. 3, 1942, p. 1.

5. Albert Goldman to Dwight Macdonald, Jan. 2, 1943, Macdonald MSS.

6. James Loeb, Jr., to Dwight Macdonald, May 20, 1943; Roger Baldwin to Dwight Macdonald, May 14, 1943; James Burnham to Dwight Macdonald, May 15, 1943. Macdonald MSS.

7. "Mission to Moscow," *New Leader*, 1943.

8. John Dewey and Suzanne La Follette, letter to the editor, *New York Times*, May 9, 1943.

9. Matthew Low, "Submission to Moscow," *New Leader*, May 1, 1943, p. 2. See also the issues of May 8 and May 29 for additional responses to the film.

10. Manny Farber, "Mishmash," *New Republic*, May 10, 1943, p. 636.

11. James Agee, "Films," *Nation*, May 22, 1943, pp. 749–50.

12. Dwight Macdonald, letter to the editor, *ibid.*, June 19, 1943, p. 873.

13. "Mr. Agee Talks Back," *ibid.*, June 19, 1943, pp. 973–74.

14. Arthur Upham Pope, *Maxim Litvinoff* (New York, 1943), p. 484.

15. William Henry Chamberlin, "Where the News Ends," *New Leader*, Aug. 22, 1942, p. 5.

16. David J. Dallin, *The Real Soviet Russia* (New Haven, 1944), p. 11.

17. *Ibid.*, p. 30.

18. Ralph Bates, "The Challenge of History," *New Republic*, Jan. 17, 1944, pp. 90–91.

19. For example, Sidney Hook, "The Rebirth of Political Credulity," *New Leader*, Jan. 1, 1944, p. 4.

20. Dwight Macdonald, "Koestler: Some Political Remarks," *Politics*, February 1944, pp. 4–5. On his personal history see Dwight Macdonald, *Memoirs of a Revolutionist* (New York, 1957).

21. Dwight Macdonald, "Why Politics?," *Politics*, February 1944, p. 7.

22. Ed., "The Shape of Things to Come," *ibid.*, June 1944, p. 132.

23. *Ibid.*

24. Kingsley Martin, *Harold Laski (1893–1950): A Biographical Memoir* (New York, 1953), p. 182.

25. George Orwell to Dwight Macdonald, July 23, 1944, Macdonald MSS. *Politics* had disposed of Laski's book in a brief, savage review by Louis Clair (February 1944), pp. 27–28.

26. George Orwell, unpublished review of *Faith, Reason, and Civilization*, Macdonald MSS.

27. Orwell to Dwight Macdonald, Sept. 5, 1944, Macdonald MSS.

28. Louis Fischer, "Laski Should Know Better," *Common Sense*, August 1944, p. 291.

29. Louis Fischer, "Laskiology," in *The Great Challenge* (Port Washington, 1971; lst ed., 1946), p. 220.

30. *Ibid.*, p. 236.

31. Ordway Tead, *Survey Graphic* (December 1944), p. 508; Kingsley Martin, *New Statesman and Nation*, March 18, 1944; *Times Literary Supplement*, March 18, 1944, p. 134.

32. Dwight Macdonald, " 'Here Lies Our Road?' Said Writer to Reader," *Politics*, September 1944, pp. 247–51.

33. Ed., "Mr. Fry and Russia," *New Republic*, April 16, 1945, p. 508.

34. Ed. and Varian Fry, "More About Russia," *ibid.*, May 21, 1945, pp. 710–11.

35. Reinhold Niebuhr, "Will America Back Out," *Nation*, Jan. 13, 1945, pp. 42–43.

36. For example, Louis Fischer to Freda Kirchwey, Nov. 19, 1942, Kirchwey MSS.

37. "Louis Fischer Resigns," *Nation*, June 2, 1945, pp. 631–33. Fischer's letter of resignation was dated May 7, 1945.

38. "Louis Fischer Elaborates," *ibid.*, June 23, 1945, p. 706.

39. Granville Hicks, "The *PM* Mind," *New Republic*, April 16, 1945, pp. 514–16.

40. Ed., "Mr. Hicks and the Liberals," *ibid.*, April 23, 1945, p. 544.

41. Kenneth G. Crawford, "The Double Talk of the Liberals," *Common Sense*, May 1945, p. 9.

42. Max Lerner, "The Irresponsibles," *PM*, June 5, 1945.

43. "From the Readers on Lerner's 'Irresponsibles,' " *PM*, June 14, 1945.

44. "From Max Lerner in Reply to the Readers," *PM*, June 14, 1945.

45. Kenneth G. Crawford, "The Totalitarian Liberals," *New Leader*, June 9, 1945, p. 8.

46. For another attack on Lerner see ed., "The Irresponsibles," *Common Sense*, July 1945, pp. 5–6.

47. Ed., "Unreal Realism," *ibid.*, November 1945, p. 18.

48. Ralph B. Levering, *American Opinion and the Russian Alliance, 1939–1945* (Chapel Hill, 1976), p. 197.

49. James M. Burns, *Roosevelt: The Soldier of Freedom* (New York, 1970), p. 350.

50. William C. Bullitt, "The World from Rome," *Life*, Sept. 4, 1944, pp. 94–96.

51. Ed., "Queer Doings in the Luce Press," *New Republic*, Sept. 18, 1944, p. 352.

52. Gaetano Salvemini, "Mr. Bullitt's 'Romans,' " *ibid.*, Oct. 2, 1944, pp. 423–26.

53. Max Lerner, "The Crusade of William C. Bullitt," *PM*, Sept. 6, 1944.

54. George Seldes, "National Magazines in Service of Fascism," *In Fact*, Sept. 18, 1944.

55. Liston M. Oak, "Bullitt Throws a Bombshell," *New Leader*, Sept. 9, 1944, p. 2.

56. *Ibid*. See also William Henry Chamberlin, "Bullitt, 'Pravda,' and Lerner," *New Leader*, Sept. 16, 1944, p. 8.

57. Louis Fischer to Lewis Gannett, April 16, 1945, Fischer MSS.

58. William L. White, *Report on the Russians* (New York, 1945), p. 61.

59. *Ibid.*, pp. 139–40.

60. William Henry Chamberlin, "A Self-Revealing List," *New Leader*, March 31, 1945, p. 16. John Chamberlain, "The Gang-Up on Bill White," *ibid.*, April 14, 1945, p. 5.

61. Walter Lippmann, *U. S. Foreign Policy: Shield of the Republic* (Boston, 1943), p. 143.

62. *Ibid.*, p. 166.

63. Max Lerner, "Foreign Policy—For What?," *PM*, June 15, 1943.

64. Alfred M. Bingham, "Lippmann's Realpolitik," *Common Sense*, July 1943, p. 262.

65. Kingsley Martin, "A New Holy Alliance," *New Statesman and Nation*, Sept. 11, 1943, p. 172.

66. Carl L. Becker, *How New Will the Better World Be? A Discussion of Post-War Reconstruction* (New York, 1944), p. 70.

67. Malcolm Cowley, "Peace and the Pundits," *New Republic*, April 10, 1944, p. 504.

IV. THE "PEOPLE'S WAR" FALTERS: 1943–1945

1. Max Lerner, "Opinion," *PM*, March 18, 1943.

2. Ed., "Helping Soviet Russia," *New Republic*, April 12, 1943, pp. 460–61.

3. Max Lerner, "The Russian–Polish Break," *PM*, April 27, 1943.

4. Max Lerner to Felix Frankfurter, Feb. 6, 1943, Lerner MSS.

5. Ed., "The Poles and the Russians," *New Republic*, May 10, 1943, pp. 623–24.

6. Marcin Rylski, "Poland and Russia," *Nation*, Oct. 9, 1943, p. 410.

7. Max Lerner, "Polish Boundaries and American Opinion," *PM*, Jan. 6, 1944.

8. W. R. Malinowski, "Uprising in Warsaw," *Nation*, Sept. 23, 1944, pp. 347–48.

9. Ed., "From Warsaw to Paris," *New Republic*, Sept. 11, 1944, pp. 295–96.

10. Jerome Davis, "Russia's Postwar Aims," *ibid.*, Sept. 4, 1944, p. 276.

11. Ralph B. Levering, *American Opinion and the Russian Alliance, 1939–1945* (Chapel Hill, 1976).

12. Max Lerner, "The Case of the Missing 16 Poles," *PM*, May 7, 1945.

13. Lerner, "The Trial of the Poles," *PM*, June 22, 1945.

14. Charles E. Bohlen, *Witness to History, 1929–1969* (New York, 1973), p. 219.

15. I. F. Stone, "Anti-Russian Undertow," *Nation*, May 12, 1945, p. 535.

16. Malcolm Cowley, "The End of the New Deal," *New Republic*, May 31, 1943, p. 732. I. F. Stone agreed: "Prospects for the New Year," *Nation*, Jan. 2, 1943, pp. 7–8.

17. Max Lerner, "Tired Radicals, 1943," *PM*, Feb. 16, 1943.

18. Lerner, "Russia: Guesswork and Fact," *PM*, March 8, 1943.

19. Lerner, "Russia Faces Europe," *PM*, March 11, 1943; "Russia as a World Power," *PM*, March 14, 1943, repeats the point.

20. Heinz H. F. Eulau, "Russia's Political Offensive," *New Republic*, Oct. 18, 1943, pp. 509–12.

21. I. F. Stone, "F.D.R.'s Victory," *Nation*, Nov. 13, 1943, p. 546. See also Archibald MacLeish, "The Moral Front," *ibid.*, Dec. 4, 1943, pp. 660–63.

22. Ed., "Four Men Reshape the World," *New Republic*, Dec. 13, 1943, p. 835.

23. William Henry Chamberlin, "The Double Standards of the Liberals," *New Leader*, Nov. 27, 1943, p. 8.

24. Ed., "The New Deal Must Go On," *New Republic*, Jan. 3, 1944, p. 6.

25. Malcolm Cowley, "The Happiness Boys," *ibid.*, p. 26.

26. Ed., "Russia in Europe," *ibid.*, Jan. 24, 1944, p. 105.

27. Bruce Bliven, "The Hang-Back Boys," *ibid.*, March 6, 1944, pp. 305–7.

28. Daniel Bell, "Bruce Bliven—Don Quixote of Liberalism," *New Leader*, March 4, 1944, p. 4.

29. Advertisement, *New Republic*, Sept. 4, 1944, p. 287.

30. Anon., "Washington," *Atlantic*, February 1944, p. 21.

31. Heinz H. F. Eulau, "Russia and the Balkans," *New Republic*, April 3, 1944, p. 462.
32. *Ibid.*, p. 463.
33. Anna Louise Strong, "Failure of a Mission," *Nation*, Aug. 19, 1944, p. 206.
34. Max Lerner, "On the Russian Victories," *PM*, April 17, 1944.
35. Ed., "Russia in the Alliance," *New Republic*, June 22, 1944, p. 844.
36. Julio Alvarez del Vayo, *Give Me Combat* (Boston, 1973).
37. Julio Alvarez del Vayo, "Goodby to the Revolution," *Nation*, July 15, 1944, p. 67.
38. Julio Alvarez del Vayo, "V-Day and Revolution," *Nation*, March 17, 1945, p. 306.
39. Max Lerner, "The Enigma of FDR," in *Public Journal: Marginal Notes on Wartime America* (New York, 1945). This essay was made up of three columns that appeared in April and June 1944.
40. Max Lerner, "Spokesman, Not Prophet," *PM*, Jan. 19, 1944.
41. From the telecast *Bill Moyers' Journal*, WNET-TV, May 29, 1980.
42. Bruce Bliven, "The Liberals After Chicago," *New Republic*, Aug. 7, 1944, pp. 152–54.
43. *In Fact*, Nov. 6, 1944, p. 1.
44. Ed., "The World After the War," *New Republic*, Jan. 1, 1945, pp. 3–5.
45. Ed., "The Crimean Conference," *ibid.*, Feb. 19, 1945, pp. 243–44.
46. Ed., "The Crimean Charter," *ibid.*, Feb. 26, 1945, p. 278.
47. *Nation*, Feb. 17, 1945, pp. 174–75.
48. Quoted in "What the Liberals Said About Yalta," *Common Sense*, April 1945, p. 38.
49. Reinhold Niebuhr, "Is This 'Peace in Our Time?,' " *Nation*, April 7, 1945, p. 383.
50. Ed., "Criticism from the Internationalists," *New Republic*, April 30, 1945, pp. 606–7; see also "The Question of Sovereignty," pp. 607–8.
51. Ed., "Plus and Minus at San Francisco," *New Republic*, July 2, 1945, p. 4.
52. Ed., "The Potsdam Decisions," *ibid.*, Aug. 13, 1945, p. 173.
53. Ed., "The Soviet-Chinese Treaty," *ibid.*, Sept. 13, 1945, p. 268.
54. Ed., "Conflict in London," *ibid.*, Oct. 1, 1945, pp. 422–23.
55. Bertram D. Wolfe, "Poland: Acid Test of a People's Peace," *Common Sense*, March 1945, p. 5.
56. Louis Fischer, "The Partitioning of Peace," *ibid.*, April 1945, p. 6.
57. Irwin Ross, "America's Palace Diplomacy," *ibid.*, June 1943, p. 193.
58. Ed., "Lost Victory," *ibid.*, September 1943, pp. 328–39.

59. Ed., "Liberalism on the Loose," *ibid.*, April 1944, p. 151.
60. Ed., "Timing," *ibid.*, January 1945, p. 3.
61. Ed., "The Curse of Realism," *ibid.*, March 1945, p. 4.
62. Athan G. Theoharis, *The Yalta Myths* (Columbia, Mo., 1970).

V. IN THE POSTWAR

1. Ed., "Good News From Moscow," *New Republic*, Jan. 7, 1946, p. 304.
2. Ed., "A World Made for War," *ibid.*, March 4, 1946, pp. 299–300. See also Philip Morrison, "Beyond Imagination," *ibid.*, Feb. 11, 1946, pp. 177–80; ed., "America, UN and the Atom," *ibid.*, June 17, 1946, pp. 851–52; George Soule, "The Atom and World Policy," *ibid.*, p. 877.
3. Irving Brant, "Eyewitness in Poland," *ibid.*, Jan. 7, 1946, pp. 15–18.
4. Kenneth Syers, "Letter from Poland—The New Underground," *ibid.*, Sept. 16, 1946, pp. 325–26.
5. Title of ed., *ibid.*, March 18, 1946, pp. 363–64.
6. TRB, "A New Policy Toward Russia," *ibid.*, March 11, 1946, p. 348. Ed., "Vandenberg on the UNO," *ibid.*
7. Ed., "Stalin's Speech," *ibid.*, Feb. 18, 1946, pp. 235–36.
8. Ed., "Failure in Iran," *ibid.*, April 29, 1946, p. 601.
9. Irving Brant, "What Russia Wants," *ibid.*, June 3, 1946, pp. 794–96.
10. Paul M. Sweezy and Lewis S. Feuer, "Has Colonialism a Future?," *ibid.*, Nov. 25, 1946, pp. 687–.
11. Harold Laski, "My Impressions of Stalin," *ibid.*, Oct. 14, 1946, pp. 478–49.
12. Joseph and Stewart Alsop, "The Liberals and Russia: A Program for Progressives," *ibid.*, Sept. 16, 1946, p. 323.
13. Max Lerner, "Who Can Build the New World?," *ibid.*, pp. 323–24.
14. Ed., "A New Deal with Russia," *ibid.*, Dec. 23, 1946, p. 806, and Dec. 30, p. 901.
15. Henry Wallace, "The UN—Our Hope," *ibid.*, July 21, 1947, pp. 12–13.
16. Stephen Laird, "Report from Warsaw," *ibid.*, Feb. 3, 1947, pp. 18–19.
17. Owen Lattimore, "The Czech Exception Disproves the Rules," *ibid.*, Sept. 22, 1947, p. 7.
18. Henry Wallace, "The Fight for Peace," *ibid.*, March 24, 1947, p. 12.
19. William Walton, "Men Around Marshall," *ibid.*, Sept. 22, 1947, pp. 15–19.
20. Ed., "Marshallism Gains," *ibid.*, June 30, 1947, p. 5.
21. Henry Wallace, "Too Little, Too Late," *ibid.*, Oct. 6, 1947, pp. 11–12.

22. Alexander Kendrick, "Back to Prewar in the USSR," *ibid.*, Dec. 22, 1947, p. 11.

23. Seymour Nagan, "How to Get On with the Russians," *ibid.*, Sept. 15, 1947, pp. 24–26.

24. Michael Straight, "Fixing the Blame for the Cold War," *ibid.*, Sept. 15, 1947, p. 10.

25. *Ibid.*, p. 11.

26. Alexander Kendrick, "The 9-Power Communist Pact," *ibid.*, Oct. 13, 1947, p. 9.

27. Michael Straight, "The Communist Answer," *ibid.*, Oct. 20, 1947, p. 11.

28. Harold J. Laski, "A Socialist Looks at the Cold War," *ibid.*, Oct. 27, 1947, p. 11.

29. J. Alvarez del Vayo, "Report from Moscow," *Nation*, Aug. 17, 1946, pp. 175–78; "Intermezzo in Berlin," Aug. 31, p. 526; "The People's Front," Nov. 9, p. 557.

30. Alexander Werth, "What Russia Wants," *ibid.*, Dec. 14, 1946, pp. 687–88.

31. Walter Duranty, "The Soviets Clean House," *ibid.*, Nov. 2, 1946, pp. 499–500.

32. Reinhold Niebuhr, "Europe, Russia, and America," *ibid.*, Sept. 14, 1946, p. 288.

33. Max Lerner, "The Stalin Statement," *PM*, Sept. 25, 1946.

34. Freda Kirchwey, untitled speech, Jan. 12, 1947, Kirchwey MSS.

35. J. Alvarez del Vayo, "The People's Front," *Nation*, Jan. 11, 1947, p. 41; Jan. 18, p. 70; Jan. 25, p. 96.

36. Freda Kirchwey, "Manifest Destiny, 1947," *ibid.*, March 22, 1947, p. 317.

37. Kirchwey, "To the Greeks, Bearing Gifts," *Nation*, March 29, 1947, pp. 347–49. See also Elliott Roosevelt, "A Plea to America," same issue, p. 352.

38. Freda Kirchwey, "Bundles for Europe Without Strings," *Nation*, Nov. 22, 1947, pp. 546–48.

39. Harold J. Laski, "Is Europe Done For?," *ibid.*, pp. 548–50. I. F. Stone, "ERP Goes to Congress," *ibid.*, Dec. 27, 1947, pp. 696–97.

40. Freda Kirchwey, "What America Wants," *ibid.*, May 3, 1947, p. 506.

41. Freda Kirchwey, "Liberals Beware," *ibid.*, April 5, 1947, pp. 384–85. This was in answer to a review of a saber-rattling book by James Burnham. Arthur Schlesinger, Jr., "World War III," *Nation*, April 5, 1947, pp. 398–99.

42. Freda Kirchwey, "Political Justice in Eastern Europe," *ibid.*, Oct. 11, 1947, pp. 369–71.

43. Alexander Werth, "Poland Today I. Reconstruction and Progress," *ibid.*, Aug. 9, 1947, pp. 137–38.

44. Michael Sayers and Albert E. Kahn, *The Great Conspiracy: The Secret War Against Soviet Russia* (Boston, 1946).

45. Frederick L. Schuman, *Soviet Politics at Home and Abroad* (New York, 1953), p. 583. This is a later printing of the 1946 edition.

46. *Ibid.*, p. 583.

47. Heinz Eulau, "New Beginning," *New Republic*, Feb. 11, 1946, pp. 191–93.

48. William Henry Chamberlin, "Academic Dr. Jekyll and Mr. Hyde," *New Leader*, March 16, 1946, p. 13.

49. Richard E. Lauterbach, *Through Russia's Back Door* (New York, 1947), p. 205.

50. Edgar Snow, *Stalin Must Have Peace* (New York, 1947), p. 173.

51. Claude Pepper to Raymond Robins, May 4, 1947, Robins MSS.

52. Robins to Pepper, May 4, 1947, Robins MSS.

53. Pepper to Robins, May 5, 1947, Robins MSS.

54. Agnes Smedley to Robins, June 16, 1947, Robins MSS.

55. *Ibid.*, Dec. 4, 1947, Robins MSS.

56. *Ibid.*, Dec. 11, 1947, Robins MSS.

57. Sherwood Eddy to Robins, Sept. 19, 1947, Robins MSS.

58. Jerome Davis to Robins, April 16, 1949, Robins MSS.

59. Frederick L. Schuman, "The Devil and Jimmy Byrnes," *Soviet Russia Today*, December 1947, p. 7.

60. *Ibid.*, p. 33.

61. Schuman to Robins, Dec. 11, 1947, Robins MSS. A letter expressing thanks.

62. Pepper to Robins, n.d. but probably December 1947, Robins MSS.

63. Jessica Smith to Robins, Dec. 14, 1947, Robins MSS.

64. *Ibid.*, Dec. 23, 1947, Robins MSS.

65. Fred Porter, "Reorganization of Foreign Policy Association," *New Leader*, April 19, 1947, p. 4.

66. Frederick Lewis Allen, letter to the editor, *New Leader*, May 17, 1947, p. 15.

67. Vera Micheles Dean, *Soviet Russia: 1917–1933* (New York, 1933).

68. Dean, *The United States and Russia* (Cambridge, Mass., 1947), p. 73.

69. *Ibid.*, p. 143.

70. Chester Bowles to Max Lerner, Dec. 29, 1947, Lerner MSS. *Book Review Digest* listed nine reviews of her book, none of them critical.

71. Ed., "Those 'Ethical' Publishers," *New Masses*, May 14, 1946, p. 15.

72. Ed., "The 'Liberal' Fifth Column," *Partisan Review*, 1946, No. 3, pp. 279–80. The editorial was written by William Barrett, but it expressed also the feelings of his colleagues William Phillips, Philip Rahv and Delmore Schwartz (William Barrett, *The*

Truants: Adventures Among the Intellectuals [Garden City, N.Y., 1947]).

73. *Ibid.*, p. 288.

74. Ed., "The 'Liberal' Fifth Column: A Discussion," *Partisan Review*, 1946, No. 5, p. 612.

75. Mark Schorer, "Art and Dogma," *New Republic*, Nov. 11, 1946, p. 646.

76. Kenneth Rexroth to Dwight Macdonald, n.d., 1946, Macdonald MSS. Irving Howe, "The Thirteenth Disciple," *Politics*, October 1946, pp. 329–34.

77. Dwight Macdonald to George Orwell, Dec. 2, 1946, Macdonald MSS.

78. Anon., "Kenneth Leslie and 'The Protestant,'" *New Leader*, March 9, 1946, p. 5.

79. For example, Daniel Seligman, "Communists Organize the Women," *ibid.*, June 29, 1946, p. 5.

80. Norbert Muhlen, "Submission to Moscow: A Fellow-Travelog in the Empire of the Mind," *ibid.*, Oct. 12, 1946, p. 12.

81. Harold Arthur Lehrman, *Russia's Europe* (New York, 1947), p. 299.

82. *Book Review Digest* (1947), p. 532.

83. Clifton Brock, *Americans for Democratic Action* (Washington, D.C., 1962).

84. William E. Bohn, "ADA in the 'Liberal Press,'" *New Leader*, Jan. 18, 1947, p. 2.

85. Eleanor Roosevelt to Max Lerner, Jan. 19, 1947, Lerner MSS.

86. Lerner to Eleanor Roosevelt, Jan. 22, 1947, Lerner MSS. See also Lerner to Arthur Schlesinger, Jr., Jan. 23, 1947, Lerner MSS.

87. William E. Bohn, "A Theory to Explain the 'Liberals,'" *New Leader*, April 12, 1947, p. 4, wrestles with this contradiction.

88. Freda Kirchwey, "Mugwumps in Action," *Nation*, Jan. 18, 1947, pp. 61–62.

89. Freda Kirchwey to Ralph Bates, n.d. but probably late January 1947, Kirchwey MSS.

90. Jeanne Levey to Freda Kirchwey, Jan. 22, 1947, Kirchwey MSS.

91. James Wechsler, "Did Truman Scuttle Liberalism?," *Commentary*, March 1947, pp. 222–27.

92. Brock, *op. cit.* See, for example, the *Atlantic* reports "Europe," June 1947, pp. 3–7, and "Washington," November 1947, pp. 9–12.

93. Walter Lippmann, "The Rivalry of Nations," *Atlantic*, February 1947, pp. 27–30.

94. Norbert Muhlen, "Red Baiters and Radio Baiters," *New Leader*, Feb. 15, 1947, p. 5.

95. Donald Harrington, "Unitarians Reject Party-Line Dictation," *ibid.*, June 14, 1947, p. 4.

96. Ed., "A Publisher Retracts," *ibid.*, Nov. 15, 1947, p. 10.

VI. THE RISE AND FALL OF HENRY WALLACE

1. Henry Wallace, "Beyond the Atlantic Charter," *New Republic*, Nov. 23, 1942, pp. 667–69.
2. John Morton Blum, ed., *The Price of Vision: The Diary of Henry A. Wallace 1942–1946* (Boston, 1973), p. 664.
3. Ed., "Wallace—a World Leader," *New Republic*, Sept. 23, 1946, p. 340.
4. Ed., "After the Wallace Dismissal," *ibid.*, Sept. 30, 1946, pp. 395–97.
5. Freda Kirchwey, "A New Popular Front," *Nation*, Dec. 2, 1944, pp. 677–78.
6. Bert Cochran, *Labor and Communism: The Conflict That Shaped American Unions* (Princeton, 1977), p. 232.
7. *Ibid.*, p. 233.
8. Oliver Carlson, "Hybrid Henry in Hollywood," *New Leader*, May 31, 1947, p. 5.
9. David T. Bazelon, "The Faith of Henry Wallace," *Commentary*, April 1947, p. 319.
10. James Wechsler, "The Liberals' Vote and '48," *ibid.*, September 1947, p. 217.
11. John Dewey, "Henry Wallace and the 1948 Election," *New Leader*, Dec. 27, 1947, p. 1. Chester Bowles thought so, too: Bowles to Max Lerner, Dec. 29, 1947, Lerner MSS.
12. Walter K. Lewis, "CP and Third Party Movement," *New Leader*, Aug. 23, 1947, p. 4.
13. Henry Wallace, "My Alternative for the Marshall Plan," *New Republic*, Jan. 12, 1948, pp. 13–14.
14. Michael Straight, "ERP: Aid to Peace . . . or Road to War?," *ibid.*, March 15, 1948, pp. 11–12.
15. Quoted in Curtis D. MacDougall, *Gideon's Army* (New York, 1965), p. 332.
16. *Ibid.*, p. 333.
17. E.g., Allen Yarnell, *Democrats and Progressives: The 1948 Presidential Election as a Test of Postwar Liberalism* (Berkeley, Calif., 1974).
18. Clifton Brock, *Americans for Democratic Action* (Washington, D.C., 1962), p. 75.
19. John Leslie, "Lee Pressman as Portent: Profile of a Party-Line Unionist," *New Leader*, April 18, 1948, p. 3.
20. Blum, *op. cit.*, p. 115.
21. Lillian Hellman, "They Will Be Good, Strong Hands," a talk given to Women for Wallace on Feb. 10, 1948, and circulated by them in pamphlet form.
22. Joseph R. Starobin, *American Communism in Crisis, 1943–1957* (Cambridge, Mass., 1972), p. 182.
23. "Text of Debate on 'Vermont Amendment' at Founding Con-

vention of Progressive Party," pp. 2–3, Hollywood Democratic Committee MSS.

24. Quoted in MacDougall, *op. cit.*, p. 688.

25. Dwight Macdonald, *Henry Wallace: The Man and the Myth* (New York, 1948), pp. 24–25.

26. *Ibid.*, p. 28.

27. *Ibid.*, p. 65.

28. *Ibid.*, p. 77.

29. Henry A. Wallace, *Soviet Asia Mission* (New York, 1946), p. 20.

30. *Ibid.*, p. 84.

31. Eleanor Lipper, *Eleven Years in Soviet Prison Camps* (Chicago, 1951), p. 267.

32. *Ibid.*, p. 116.

33. Dwight Macdonald to James Loeb, Jr., March 11, 1948; Loeb to Macdonald, March 20, 1948; Macdonald to Loeb, April 22, 1948, Macdonald MSS.

34. John Dewey, "Wallace vs. a New Party," *New Leader*, Oct. 30, 1948.

35. Gardner Jackson, "Henry Wallace: A Divided Mind," *Atlantic*, August 1948, p. 30.

36. James Wechsler to Dwight Macdonald, April 25, 1947, Macdonald MSS.

37. C. B. Baldwin, letter to the editor, *Atlantic*, August 1948, p. 16.

38. Ed., "Truman as Leader," *New Republic*, May 17, 1948, p. 26.

39. Ed., "The East–West Crisis," *ibid.*, Oct. 11, 1948, p. 506.

40. Helen Fuller, "The Funeral Is Called Off," *ibid.*, July 26, 1948.

41. Ed., "1948: The New Beginning," *ibid.*, Sept. 27, 1948, p. 32.

42. TRB, "Washington Wire," *ibid.*, June 21, 1948, p. 3.

43. TRB, "Washington Wire," *ibid.*, June 28, 1948, pp. 3–4, and Nov. 15, 1948, pp. 3–4; ed., "Damn the Torpedoes," *New Republic* Nov. 15, 1948.

44. Freda Kirchwey, "Socialist Union or Holy Alliance?," *Nation*, Jan. 31, 1948, p. 117.

45. I. F. Stone, "Toward World War III," *ibid.*, Feb. 7, 1948, p. 148.

46. Freda Kirchwey, "Prague—a Lesson for Liberals," *ibid.*, March 6, 1948, pp. 265–66.

47. Kirchwey, "Masaryk," *Nation*, March 20, 1948, p. 317.

48. Kirchwey, "Journey Among Creeds—II," *ibid.*, Nov. 13, 1948, pp. 546–48.

49. Ed., "The Shape of Things," *ibid.*, July 31, 1948, p. 113.

50. Robert Bendiner, "Two and Two Make Four," *ibid.*, Nov. 13, 1948, pp. 540–42.

51. Dwight Macdonald, "The Wallace Campaign," *Politics*, Summer 1948, pp. 178–88.

52. Max Lerner, "The Risen Phoenix," *New York Star*, Jan. 1, 1948, reprinted in *Actions and Passions: Notes on the Multiple Revolution of Our Time* (New York, 1949), p. 249.

53. Lerner, "The Lessons of the Czechoslovak Coup," March 11, 1948, *loc. cit.*, p. 325.

54. Lerner, "Henry Wallace: A Portrait in Symbols," Feb. 1, 1948, *loc. cit.*, p. 228.

55. Lerner, "The Ordeal of Henry Wallace," *New York Star*, July 25, 1948. What turned out to be a premature obituary of Lerner's own career is Daniel Seligman, "Profile of Max Lerner," *New Leader*, Nov. 27, 1948, p. 9.

56. Dwight Macdonald, "USA vs. USSR," *Politics*, Spring 1948, p. 77.

57. Walker K. Lewis, "Bronx Cheer for Wallace," *New Leader*, Nov. 20, 1948, p. 4.

58. Charles H. Martin, "The Southern Conference for Human Welfare and 'The Decade of Hope,' 1938–1948," an unpublished paper.

59. R. Fahan, "What Makes Henry Run," *New International*, February 1948, pp. 54–57.

60. Quoted in MacDougall, *op. cit.*, p. 509.

61. Harold J. Laski, "Truman's Task in Europe," *New Republic*, Dec. 20, 1948, pp. 10–12.

62. Edgar Snow, "Will Tito's Heretics Halt Russia?," *Saturday Evening Post*, Dec. 18, 1948, pp. 23–.

VII. THE ECLIPSE OF PROGRESSIVISM

1. Norman Podhoretz, *Breaking Ranks* (New York, 1979), p. 21.

2. Alexander Werth, "Brave New World in Czechoslovakia," *Nation*, Feb. 19, 1949, p. 209. Diana Trilling, letter to the editor, *ibid.*, March 12, 1949, p. 315.

3. Werth, letter to the editor, *New Statesman and Nation*, June 19, 1948, p. 500.

4. Reinhold Niebuhr, "The Long Cold War," *Nation*, Oct. 21, 1950, p. 369.

5. The event was modeled on a similar congress held by Stalinists and a few others in Warsaw the previous year. Bryn J. Hovde, "The Congress of Intellectuals," *New Leader*, Dec. 11, 1948.

6. Dwight Macdonald, "The Waldorf Conference," *Politics*, Winter 1949, pp. 32A–32D. All quotations are from his "Notes on the Waldorf Conference," Macdonald MSS.

7. See Joseph P. Lash, "Weekend at the Waldorf," *New Republic*, April 18, 1949, pp. 10–14; William Barrett, "Culture Conference at the Waldorf," *Commentary*, May 1949, pp. 487–93; and all the New York newspapers.

8. Freda Kirchwey, "Battle of the Waldorf," *Nation*, April 2, 1949, pp. 377–78.

9. Tom O'Connor, "News Tailored to Fit," *ibid.*, April 16, 1949, p. 440.

10. Dwight Macdonald, letter to the editor, *ibid.*, May 28, 1949, pp. 624–25.
11. Sidney Hook, letter to the editor, *ibid.*, April 30, 1949, p. 511. Freda Kirchwey's reply followed this.
12. Margaret Marshall, "Notes by the Way," *ibid.*, April 9, 1949, pp. 419–20.
13. Ed., "The 'Liberal' Fifth Column," *Partisan Review*, Summer 1946, p. 280.
14. Dwight Macdonald, "The Wallace Campaign: An Autopsy," *Politics*, Summer 1948, pp. 178–88.
15. Philip Rahv, "Disillusionment and Partial Answers," *Partisan Review*, 1948, No. 5, p. 526.
16. Max Lerner, "The New Machiavellis," *New York Post*, March 14, 1950; "Pax Teutonica," May 26, 1952; "A Man for Our Age," July 27, 1952; "Remington and Hiss," Nov. 26, 1954.
17. A fact sheet prepared in 1951 lists the lectures that had been canceled or were in doubt, Lerner MSS.
18. Dwight Macdonald, "The Responsibility of Intellectuals," *Politics*, April 1945, reprinted in Dwight Macdonald, *Memoirs of a Revolutionist* (New York, 1957), p. 101.
19. *Ibid.*, p. 103.
20. Granville Hicks, "The PM Mind," *New Republic*, April 16, 1945, p. 516.
21. Quoted in John Rackliffe, "Notes for a Character Study," in Paul M. Sweezy and Leo Huberman, eds., *F. O. Matthiessen: A Collective Portrait* (New York, 1950), p. 92.
22. Henry Nash Smith, "American Renaissance," *ibid.*, p. 60.
23. Leo Marx, "The Teacher," *ibid.*, p. 37.
24. Paul M. Sweezy, "Labor and Political Activities," *ibid.*, pp. 61–75.
25. George Abbott White, "Ideology and Literature: *American Renaissance* and F. O. Mattheissen," in George Abbott White and Charles Newman, eds., *Literature in Revolution* (New York, 1972), pp. 430–500.
26. John Lydenberg, ed., "Political Activism and the Academic Conscience: The Harvard Experience 1936–1941," a symposium at Hobart and William Smith Colleges on Dec. 5 and 6, 1975, printed by the colleges, p. 80.
27. *Ibid.*, p. 6.
28. *Ibid.*, p. 83.
29. Leo Marx, *op. cit.*, p. 42.
30. Kenneth S. Lynn, "Teaching: F. O. Matthiessen," *American Scholar*, Winter 1976–77, p. 93.
31. Alfred Kazin, *New York Jew* (New York, 1971), p. 168. Kazin explains the difference between his two sketches of Matthiessen in this way: Writing just after his death, Kazin was moved by the violence of it, and angry over the attacks on Matthiessen that continued beyond his suicide, especially those of a right-wing Boston

columnist. In the 1970s Kazin had a better perspective. "I was more scornful of his rich-man's political slumming, which I had seen directly for myself, I was also not *more* scornful of his political naïveté—but certainly angrier about the Soviet seizure of Czechoslovakia in 1968—than I would have expected to be when I wrote for the Memorial volume." Finally, "remembering that even Silone, who should have known better, had described Matthiessen as a victim of the cold war, I wanted to describe the instability for what it was." Alfred Kazin to William L. O'Neill, June 22, 1981.

32. F. O. Matthiessen, *From the Heart of Europe* (New York, 1948), p. 52.

33. *Ibid.*, pp. 143 and 187.

34. *Book Review Digest*, 1948, p. 562.

35. William Phillips to Dwight Macdonald, July 22, 1948, Macdonald MSS.

36. Irving Howe, "The Sentimental Fellow-Traveling of F. O. Matthiessen," *Partisan Review*, 1948, No. 10, p. 1127.

37. Franz Hollering, "The Head and Heart," *Nation*, Sept. 1, 1948, pp. 293–94.

38. Harold J. Laski to F. O. Matthiessen, Sept. 7, 1948; Theodore Spencer to FOM, Aug. 4, 1948, praised the book. FOM to Louis Untermeyer, Dec. 21, 1949, expressed thanks. A number of people sent blurbs for *From the Heart of Europe* to its publisher. They included Robert M. Lynd, Paul M. Sweezy and Dr. Rudolf Kurac, Consul General of Czechoslovakia. Matthiessen MSS.

39. F. O. Matthiessen to *Partisan Review*, Oct. 12, 1948; FOM to *Saturday Review of Literature*, n.d.; FOM to Henry Luce, Sept. 18, 1948, Matthiessen MSS.

40. Joseph Alsop to F. O. Matthiessen, Sept. 16, 1948, Matthiessen MSS.

41. John Finch to F. O. Matthiessen, Sept. 25, 1949, Matthiessen MSS.

42. Vladimir C. Kocina to F. O. Matthiessen, n.d., Matthiessen MSS.

43. Pete Steffens to F. O. Matthiessen, Matthiessen MSS.

44. Ella Winter to F. O. Matthiessen, 1949, Matthiessen MSS.

45. *Ibid.*, Sept. 17, 1949, Matthiessen MSS.

46. John Conway, who was then at Harvard, heard Matthiessen say this and repeated it to me on Dec. 15, 1979.

47. Ernest J. Simmons in Sweezy and Huberman, *op. cit.*, p. 137.

48. Harry Levin, "The Private Life of F. O. Matthiessen," *New York Review of Books*, July 20, 1978, pp. 42–46.

49. Arthur Bowron, "The Making of an American Scholar," in Sweezy and Huberman, *op. cit.*

50. May Sarton, *Faithful Are the Wounds* (New York, 1955), p. 197.

51. Paul M. Sweezy in Sweezy and Huberman, *op. cit.*

52. John Crowe Ransom to F. O. Matthiessen, Dec. 1, 1947,

Matthiessen MSS. Ransom explained that Rahv could not be prevented from teaching at a summer session at the Kenyon School of English, as the offer had already been made. Matthiessen, with Ransom and Lionel Trilling, was a senior fellow of the program, which was supported by a grant from the Rockefeller Foundation.

53. Giles B. Gunn, *F. O. Matthiessen: The Critical Achievement* (Seattle, 1975), p. 188.

54. An undated two-page statement written between 1949 and 1951, Robins MSS.

55. Claude Pepper to Raymond Robins, May 13, 1949. The transcript is "Radio Speech No. 5 . . . Senator Claude Pepper . . . February 22, 1949," Robins MSS.

56. Pepper to Robins, May 23, 1949, Robins MSS.

57. Robins to Pepper, June 5, 1949, Robins MSS.

58. Robins to Mary Dreier, May 3, 1950, Robins MSS.

59. Pepper to Robins, Dec. 8, 1950, and Robins to Pepper, Dec. 12, 1950, Robins MSS. Claude Pepper to William L. O'Neill, Feb. 4, 1982.

60. Mary Dreier to Robins, Sept. 8, 1950, Robins MSS.

61. Freda Utley, *Odyssey of a Liberal* (Washington, D.C., 1970), p. 200.

62. *Ibid.*, p. 201.

63. "Army Withholds Spy Data Backing," *New York Times*, Feb. 12, 1949. The report had been issued two days earlier.

64. Agnes Smedley, press release, Feb. 11, 1949, Robins MSS.

65. Typescript, Agnes Smedley, letter to the editors of the *New York Herald Tribune*, Feb. 14, 1949, Robins MSS.

66. Agnes Smedley to Raymond Robins, Feb. 12, 1949, Robins MSS.

67. *Ibid.*, Feb 17, 1949, Robins MSS.

68. *Ibid.*, Feb. 19, 1949, Robins MSS.

69. *Ibid.*, Aug. 23, 1949, Robins MSS.

70. *Ibid.*, Sept. 6, 1949, Robins MSS.

71. *Ibid.*, n.d. but probably May 5, 1950, Robins MSS.

72. Mary Dreier to Robins, May 19, 1950, and Harold L. Ickes to Robins, n.d., Robins MSS.

73. Anna Louise Strong to Robins, Oct. 9, 1949, Robins MSS. *The Nation* agreed: ed., "Anna Louise Strong," Feb. 26, 1949, p. 228.

74. Jerome Davis to Robins, April 20, 1949, Robins MSS.

75. Anna Louise Strong to Robins, Sept. 1, 1949, Robins MSS.

76. *Ibid.*, March 5, 1949, Robins MSS. Her punctuation here and below.

77. *Ibid.*, May 17, 1949, Robins MSS.

78. *Ibid.*, May 24, 1949, Robins MSS.

79. *Ibid.*, n.d. but probably fall 1949, Robins MSS.

80. *Ibid.*, October 9, 1949, Robins MSS.

81. *Ibid.*, November 20, 1949, Robins MSS.

82. Anna Louise Strong to "Dear Friends," March 4, 1950, Robins MSS.

83. Corliss Lamont to Robins, May 23, 1950, Robins MSS. The others included Henry Wallace, Dr. John Kingsbury, Mary Van Kleeck, Harlow Shapley, Edgar Snow, I. F. Stone, Albert Rhys Williams, Maurice Hindus, Walter Duranty, Richard Lauterbach and Ella Winter.

84. Anna Louise Strong to Robins, July 17, Aug. 12, Aug. 19 and Aug. 27, 1950, Robins MSS.

85. *Ibid.*, Oct. 26, 1950, Robins MSS.

86. *Today*, March–April, 1951.

87. Leo Huberman to Robins, May 8, 1950, Robins MSS.

88. Louis Adamic to Robins, Oct. 27, 1949, Robins MSS.

89. Edward L. Young to Robins, April 5, 1949, Robins MSS.

90. Minutes of the Executive Committee of the NCASP, April 6, 1949, Hollywood Democratic Committee MSS.

91. John A. Kingsbury to Robins, March 22, 1950, Robins MSS.

92. C. V. Bradley to Robins, April 6, 1950, Robins MSS.

93. Willard Uphaus to Robins, April 16, 1951, Robins MSS.

94. Robins to Freda Kirchwey, April 5, 1951, Robins MSS.

95. Scott Nearing to Robins, Sept. 8, 1950, Robins MSS.

96. Albert E. Kahn to Robins, Oct. 26, 1950, Robins MSS.

97. Jerome Davis to Robins, April 9, 1951.

98. Robins to Mary Dreier, Sept. 26, 1949, Robins MSS.

99. Dreier to Robins, April 18, 1950, Robins MSS.

100. Andrew Roth, "Korea's Impending Explosion," *Nation*, August 13, 1945, p. 153.

101. David J. Dallin, "Unite the Two Koreas," *New Leader*, July 8, 1950, p. 4.

102. *Ibid.*, and Lewis Corey, "We Must Free All Korea," *New Leader*, June 18, 1951, pp. 2–4.

103. Ed., "Korea: Final Test of the UN," *New Republic*, July 3, 1950, pp. 5–6; "To Put Our Own House in Order," July 10, 1950, pp. 5–6; "The UN Goes to War," July 17, 1950, pp. 5–7.

104. TRB, "Washington Wire," *New Republic*, July 10, 1950, p. 3, and July 24, 1950, p. 3.

105. Fletcher Pratt, "A Long, Tough Fight," *ibid.*, July 24, 1950, pp. 11–13.

106. Harold L. Ickes, "Once More We Fight for Time," *ibid.*, July 31, 1950, p. 17.

107. Ed., "The Assembly Takes Over," *ibid.*, Sept. 18, 1950, pp. 5–6, and "The Terms for Peace," Oct. 19, 1950, pp. 5–6.

108. Ed., "Communism vs. Democracy," *ibid.*, Oct. 9, 1950, p. 20.

109. Ed., "The Crisis in Greece," *ibid.*, Dec. 18, 1950, p. 11.

110. Ed., "What Sort of Help for Indo-China?," *ibid.*, May 22, 1950, pp. 5–6.

111. Ed., "The Choice in Indo-China," *ibid.*, Oct. 20, 1950, p. 5.

112. Max Lerner, "The Formosa Folly," *New York Post*, Jan. 3,

1950, and "Mao, Bao Dai, Ho and Tito," March 20, 1950.

113. Lerner, "America Now Virtually at War," June 28, 1950.

114. Lerner, "Power Tells," Sept. 18, 1950.

115. Lerner, "The Plunge," Oct. 2, 1950.

116. Lerner, "Dance of Death," Nov. 29, 1950, and "The Great Chastening," Dec. 13, 1950.

117. Lerner, "Ten Facts About Korea," June 25, 1952.

118. Lerner, "The Great Chastening," Dec. 13, 1950.

119. J. Alvarez del Vayo, "The Economic War," *Nation*, Sept. 2, 1950, pp. 203–05.

120. Alexander Werth, "What Russia Tells Itself," *Nation*, Sept. 9, 1950, pp. 226–27.

121. Alexander Werth, "British Thoughts on War," *ibid.*, March 10, 1951, p. 224.

122. Edgar Snow, "The New Phase—Undeclared War," *ibid.*, pp. 220–23.

123. Mary Dreier to Raymond Robins, June 26, 1950, Robins MSS.

124. *Ibid.*, July 28, Aug. 11 and Sept. 29, 1950.

125. *Ibid.*, Oct. 28, 1950.

126. *Ibid.*, Nov. 1, 1950.

127. Cedric Belfrage and James Aronson, *Something to Guard: The Stormy Life of the National Guardian, 1948–1967* (New York, 1978), p. 12.

128. *Ibid.*, p. 94.

129. *Ibid.*, p. 107.

130. Demaree Bess, "Did Stalin Make a Sucker Out of You?," *Saturday Evening Post*, May 12, 1951, pp. 24–.

131. Ronald Radosh, "Something to Guard," *New Republic*, Feb. 17, 1979, pp. 34–37.

132. Louis Jay Herman, "Stalinism in 'Socialist' Clothing," *New Leader*, Feb. 25, 1950, p. 4.

133. Ed., "Reply to Mr. Bittelman," *Monthly Review*, November 1951, pp. 212–20, an answer to one such attack.

134. Leo Huberman and Paul M. Sweezy," Where We Stand," *ibid.*, May 1949, p. 102, and ed., "The Soviet Bomb," November 1949, pp. 193–94.

135. Ed., "Review of the Month," *ibid.*, August 1950, p. 115.

136. Howard Kaminsky, "Freedom Under Socialism," *ibid.*, November 1950, pp. 345–53.

137. Ed., "Freedom Under Socialism: A Comment," *ibid.*, December 1950, pp. 394–96.

138. Shamus O'Sheel, "Reflections on Freedom Under Socialism," *ibid.*, February 1951, pp. 464–67.

139. John A. Bachrach, "Soviet Freedom: Fact or Fiction?," *ibid.*, p. 476.

140. Arthur K. Davis, "Freedom Under Socialism: Summary and Comment," *ibid.*, May 1951, p. 24.

141. Joshua Kunitz, "The Jewish Problem in the USSR," *ibid.*, March 1953, pp. 402–13, and April 1954, pp. 454–72.
142. Ed., "On Trials and Purges," *ibid.*, March 1953, p. 389.
143. *Ibid.*, p. 394.
144. *Ibid.*, p. 396.
145. Lewis Coser and Irving Howe, "Authoritarians of the 'Left,' " *Dissent*, Winter 1955, p. 45.
146. Irving Howe, "Russia and the *Monthly Review*," *ibid.*, Fall 1956, p. 435.

VIII. THE BLACKLIST

1. Leo C. Rosten, *Hollywood: The Movie Colony, The Movie Makers* (New York, 1941).
2. Raymond Chandler, "Writers in Hollywood," *Atlantic*, November 1949, p. 52. See also Ch. VII in Hortense Powdermaker, *Hollywood, the Dream Factory* (Boston, 1950).
3. Quoted in Rosten, *op. cit.*, p. 309.
4. Philip Dunne in *Take Two: A Life in Movies and Politics* (New York, 1980) argues on the basis of his long experience in it that the Screen Writers Guild was never controlled by Communists.
5. See the "History" of the Hollywood Democratic Committee prepared by the staff of the Wisconsin State Historical Society, and the typescript "Hollywood Democratic Committee Background," HDC MSS.
6. Anon., "Glamor Pusses," *Time*, Sept. 9, 1946, p. 24. Joan La Cour to Jo Grant, Dec. 13, 1946, HDC MSS.
7. "Sculptor J. Davidson Here on P.C.A. Mission," *Los Angeles Times*, Feb. 4, 1947.
8. James Roosevelt to Professor R. G. Tyler, April 17, 1946, HDC MSS.
9. James Roosevelt to Jo Davidson, July 9, 1946, and a later undated telegram, HDC MSS.
10. James Roosevelt to John Cromwell, July 27, 1946, HDC MSS.
11. "Olivia de Haviland Unmasks L. A. Reds," *Los Angeles Herald-Express*, Sept. 5, 1958.
12. Alice P. Barrows to Joy Darwin, April 21, 1948, HDC MSS.
13. Mayor Fletcher Bowron to George Pepper, April 5, 1949, HDC MSS.
14. Christopher Isherwood to the Organizers of the Cultural and Scientific Conference for World Peace, April 7, 1949, HDC MSS.
15. "Seven Others Arrested in Wild Fight," *Culver City Star News*, Oct. 8, 1945.
16. "Here's Full Text of Brewer Press Statement," *The Hollywood Closeup* (Bulletin of the IATSE), Nov. 1, 1945.
17. Eric Bentley, ed., *Thirty Years of Treason: Excerpts from Hearings Before the House Committee on Un-American Activities, 1938–1968* (New York, 1971), p. 86.

18. Gordon Kahn, *Hollywood on Trial* (New York, 1948), p. 11.
19. Elmer Rice, "The M.P.A. and American Ideals," *Saturday Review of Literature*, Nov. 11, 1944, p. 18; Morrie Ryskind, "A Reply to Elmer Rice About the M.P.A.P.A.I.," *ibid.*, Dec. 24, 1944, pp. 9–10, followed by Rice's untitled reply, p. 10.
20. Ring Lardner, Jr., "30 Years After the 'Hollywood Ten,' " *New York Times*, March 18, 1978; Lester Cole, "Hollywood 10: A Survivor's Update," *ibid.*, April 7, 1978.
21. Dunne, *op. cit.*
22. There are descriptions and excerpts from testimony in Bentley, *op. cit.*; Walter Goodman, *The Committee: The Extraordinary Career of the House Committee on Un-American Activities* (London, 1969); Kahn, *op. cit.*; and Robert Vaughn, *Only Victims: A Study of Show Business Blacklisting* (New York, 1972).
23. Kahn, *op. cit.*, p. 74.
24. *Ibid.*, p. 103.
25. Dore Schary, *Heyday: An Autobiography* (Boston, 1979), p. 163. Dunne, *op. cit.*
26. Vaughn, *op. cit.*
27. Richard English, "What Makes a Hollywood Communist," *Saturday Evening Post*, May 19, 1951.
28. Quoted in Bentley, *op. cit.*, p. 405.
29. Victor Lasky, "The Case of the Hollywood One," *New Leader*, Aug. 6, 1951, pp. 14–15.
30. Sterling Hayden, *Wanderer* (New York, 1963), p. 392.
31. Edward G. Robinson and Leonard Spigelgass, *All My Yesterdays* (New York, 1973), p. 193.
32. "American Civil Liberties Union Report of Special Committee to Investigate the Charges Against Merle Miller's *The Judges and the Judged*," July 14, 1952, ACLU MSS.
33. "Merle Miller Statement," May 22, 1952, ACLU MSS.
34. Minutes, Board of Directors Meeting, July 21, 1952, ACLU MSS.
35. Patrick Murphy Malin to Board Members, Oct. 8, 1952, ACLU MSS. The newspaper story was by Frederick Woltman in that day's *New York World-Telegram*.
36. Edward L. Bernays to Alan Reitman, Oct. 10, 1952, ACLU MSS.
37. For example, Mary Sperling McAuliffe, *Crisis on the Left: Cold War Politics and American Liberals, 1947–54* (Amherst, 1978).
38. The following are examples. Alan Reitman to Victor Riesel, June 5, 1952, ACLU MSS, asking for information about Riesel's claim in the *New Leader* that a band of fellow travelers was keeping anti-Communist entertainers out of work. Patrick Murphy Malin to Frank Reel, July 23, 1952, asking about a similar story in the *New York World-Telegram and Sun*. A memo by Alan Reitman, July 20, 1952, summarizes a long conversation he had with a Lois Wilson, who alleged that she had been blacklisted for

her anti-Communism but would not give particulars, such as the names of persons who had failed to hire her.

39. Ralph De Toledano, letter to the editor, *New York Times*, April 10, 1952, ACLU MSS, a typewritten copy.

40. Morrie Ryskind to Alan Reitman, Sept. 14, 1954, ACLU MSS.

41. Louis Berg, "How End the Panic in Radio-TV? The Demagogic Half-Truth vs. the 'Liberal' Half-Lie," *Commentary*, October 1953, p. 17.

42. *Ibid.*, p. 319.

43. *Ibid.*, p. 323.

44. *Ibid.*, p. 325.

45. For a remarkably complete accounting of the fate of blacklisted persons see David Caute, *The Great Fear* (New York, 1973).

46. Quoted in Jon Nordheimer, "Dalton Trumbo, Film Writer, Dies: Oscar Winner Had Been Blacklisted," *New York Times*, Oct. 11, 1976.

47. Bruce Cook, *Dalton Trumbo* (New York, 1977); Helen Manfull, ed., *Additional Dialogue: Letters of Dalton Trumbo, 1942–1962* (New York, 1970).

48. Dalton Trumbo to Nelson Algren, July 15, 1951, *ibid.*, p. 214.

49. Dalton Trumbo to Murray Kempton, March 5, 1957, *ibid.*, p. 393.

50. Gabriel Miller, "Two Alvah Bessies: the Innocent and the Embittered," *Los Angeles Times*, Nov. 27, 1977.

51. W. H. Auden, "Poet and Politician," *Common Sense*, January 1940, pp. 23–24.

52. Ring Lardner, Jr., "My Life on the Blacklist," *Saturday Evening Post*, Oct. 14, 1961, p. 43.

53. Alvah Bessie, *Inquisition in Eden* (New York, 1965).

54. Ed., "Mr. Ferrer and Mr. Chaplin," *Nation*, Jan. 31, 1953, p. 90.

55. *Ibid.*

56. Anon., "Hollywood Meets Frankenstein," *Nation*, June 28, 1952, p. 631.

57. Hilton Kramer, "The Blacklist and the Cold War," *New York Times*, Oct. 3, 1976.

58. "Comments on the Blacklist," *ibid.*, Oct. 17, 1976; "Blacklisting—The Debate Continues," *ibid.*, Nov. 7, 1976.

59. Bentley, *op. cit.*, p. 204.

60. Manfull, *op. cit.*, p. 43.

61. Caute, *op. cit.*, p. 491.

62. Quoted in Clayton R. Koppes and Gregory D. Black, "What to Show the World: The Office of War Information and Hollywood, 1942–45," *Journal of American History*, June 1977, p. 92.

63. *Ibid.*, p. 95.

64. Ted Enright, "Mealy-Mouthed Martyrs," *The New International*, July 1948, p. 160.

65. Pauline Kael, "Raising Kane—I," *New Yorker*, Feb. 20, 1971, p. 60.
66. *Ibid.*, p. 61.
67. *Ibid.*, p. 64.
68. *Ibid.*, p. 66.
69. Quoted in Donal Henahan, "A 'Ruptured Duck' That Just Will Not Fly," *New York Times*, Aug. 15, 1976.
70. *Ibid.*
71. Quoted in Caute, *op. cit.*, p. 490.
72. Adolphe Menjou to Ralph De Toledano, Aug. 21, Sept. 15, April 2 and April 9, 1951, De Toledano MSS.
73. Albert Maltz, "Moving Forward," *New Masses*, April 9, 1946, p. 8. Maltz was referring to Max Eastman's *Artists in Uniform* (1934), an early exposé of the regimentation of writers in Soviet Russia.
74. *Ibid.*, p. 10.
75. Ingrid Winther Scobie, "Jack B. Tenney and the 'Parasitic Menace': Anti-Communist Legislation in California, 1940–1949," *Pacific Historical Review*, May 1944, pp. 188–211.
76. See the many copies of statements and depositions by movie people in the De Toledano MSS.
77. Quoted in Bentley, *op. cit.*, p. 495.
78. *Ibid.*, p. 497.
79. Victor Navasky, *Naming Names* (New York, 1980). This book is discussed in chapter XII.

IX. CHINA: PROGRESSIVE PARADOX

1. "The Pacific War," *Atlantic Monthly*, July 1943, p. 13.
2. Ed., "The Moral Crisis of the War," *New Republic*, Feb. 8, 1943, pp. 163–65.
3. Ed., "Democracy in China," *ibid.*, Sept. 27, 1943, p. 412.
4. Ed., "Impasse in Chungking," *Nation*, Sept. 25, 1943, p. 341.
5. Ed., "What About China?," *ibid.*, Aug. 21, 1943, p. 200.
6. Maxwell S. Stewart, "Cross-Currents in China," *ibid.*, Sept. 24, 1943, p. 346.
7. Heinz H. F. Eulau, "China's Hour of Decision," *New Republic*, Oct. 9, 1944, p. 453.
8. *Ibid.*, p. 454.
9. Richard Watts, Jr., "The Chinese Giant Stirs," *New Republic*, May 28, 1945, pp. 733–36.
10. "The Pacific War," *Atlantic Monthly*, December 1944, pp. 8–13. See also Maxwell S. Stewart, "China's Zero Hour," *Nation*, Nov. 25, 1944, pp. 637–39.
11. An early example is Langdon Warner's review of Edgar Snow, *People on Our Side* (1944), *Atlantic Monthly*, October 1944, p. 129.

12. Michael Schaller, *The U. S. Crusade in China, 1938–1945* (New York, 1979).

13. Richard Watts, Jr., "Old American Hand," *New Republic*, Feb. 5, 1945, p. 182.

14. Edgar Snow, "China to Lin Yutang," *Nation*, Feb. 17, 1945, p. 180.

15. Lin Yutang, "China and Its Critics," *ibid.*, March 24, 1945, p. 324.

16. Edgar Snow, "China to Lin Yutang-II," *ibid.*, March 31, 1945, p. 359.

17. Snow, *Journey to the Beginning* (New York, 1958), p. 14.

18. David Caute, *The Fellow-Travellers: A Postscript to the Enlightenment* (New York, 1973), p. 364.

19. Edgar Snow review of Owen Lattimore, *Solution in Asia*, in *New York Times Book Review*, Feb. 25, 1945, p. 3.

20. Owen Lattimore review of Harrison Forman, *Report from Red China*, in *Atlantic Monthly*, April 1945, p. 133.

21. Owen Lattimore, "The International Chess Game," *New Republic*, May 28, 1945, p. 733.

22. William Mandel, "The Russian Bear Looks East," *ibid.*, May 28, 1945, pp. 739–41.

23. Richard Watts, Jr., "Sabotaging Chinese Unity," *New Republic*, March 18, 1946, pp. 374–76.

24. "The Far East," *Atlantic Monthly*, October 1946, pp. 8–13.

25. Theodore H. White, "Lost: American Policy in China," *New Republic*, Dec. 16, 1946, pp. 796–98.

26. John Fairbank review of *Thunder Out of China*, in *New York Times Book Review*, Oct. 27, 1946, p. 1.

27. David Halberstam, *The Powers That Be* (New York, 1979).

28. Agnes Smedley, "We're Building a Fascist China," *Nation*, August 31, 1946, pp. 236–38.

29. John K. Fairbank, "Our Chances in China," *Atlantic Monthly*, September 1946, pp. 37–42.

30. Ed., "Gambler's Choice in China," *New Republic*, July 21, 1947, p. 15.

31. Robert P. Martin, "A Chinese Village Goes Red," *ibid.*, Nov. 24, 1947, pp. 14–18.

32. Walter L. Briggs, "Is China Different?," *ibid.*, June 28, 1948, p. 15.

33. Ed., "The Shape of Things," *Nation*, Dec. 25, 1948, p. 710.

34. Response to "Old China Hand" in letters-to-the-editor section, *Atlantic Monthly*, October 1948, pp. 20–21.

35. John King Fairbank, "Toward a New China Policy," *Nation*, Jan. 1, 1949, pp. 5–8.

36. "China," *Atlantic Monthly*, January 1949, p. 10.

37. *Ibid.*, p. 11.

38. E. J. Kahn, Jr., *The China Hands: America's Foreign Service Officers and What Befell Them* (New York, 1975).

39. Ed., "The Shape of Things," *Nation*, Aug. 13, 1949, p. 146.

40. John K. Fairbank, "America and the Chinese Revolution," *New Republic*, Dec. 5, 1949, p. 223.

41. Owen Lattimore, "Our Failure in China," *Nation*, Sept. 5, 1949, p. 223.

42. Ed., "Living with the Chinese Communists," *New Republic*, Dec. 12, 1949, pp. 5–7.

43. Ed., "Not Time for Secret Diplomacy," *ibid.*, Jan. 16, 1950, p. 5.

44. Harold L. Ickes, "Truman's Formosa Policy," *ibid.*, Jan. 23, 1950, p. 17.

45. Ed., "The Truman Doctrine Is Dead," *ibid.*, p. 7.

46. "Washington," *Atlantic Monthly*, March 1950, pp. 4–8.

47. "China," *ibid.*, April 1950, pp. 5–10.

48. Max Lerner, "The Air Is Poisoned," *New York Post*, May 23, 1950.

49. John K. Fairbank, "China," *Atlantic Monthly*, November 1950, p. 24.

50. *Ibid.*, p. 25.

51. "Washington," *ibid.*, March 1950, pp. 4–8.

52. Owen Lattimore, *Ordeal by Slander* (Boston, 1950), p. 27.

53. *Ibid.*, p. 87.

54. "A Fool or a Knave," *Time*, April 17, 1950, p. 22.

55. Willard Shelton, "McCarthy's Vicious Retreat," *Nation*, April 15, 1950, pp. 341–42.

56. Earl Latham, *The Communist Controversy in Washington: From the New Deal to McCarthy* (Cambridge, Mass., 1966).

57. "Sixth Round," *Time*, June 27, 1955, p. 18.

58. Freda Utley, "The Triumph of Owen Lattimore," *American Mercury*, June 1955, p. 25.

59. Utley, *Odyssey of a Liberal* (Washington, 1970), p. 212.

60. *Ibid.*

61. *Ibid.*, p. 249.

62. *Ibid.*, p. 304.

63. William L. O'Neill, *The Last Romantic: A Life of Max Eastman* (New York, 1978).

64. Utley, *Odyssey*, p. 215.

65. John T. Flynn, *The Lattimore Story* (New York, 1953), p. 103.

66. *Ibid.*, p. 3.

67. Owen Lattimore to Edward Carter, July 10, 1938, quoted in John N. Thomas, *The Institute of Pacific Relations: Asian Scholars and American Politics* (Seattle, 1974), p. 40.

68. T. A. Bisson, "China's Part in a Coalition War," *Far Eastern Survey*, July 14, 1943, pp. 135–41.

69. Harold C. Hinton, "The Spotlight on Pacific Affairs," *Commonweal*, April 25, 1952, p. 65.

70. Anon., "Reading Lattimore," *Reporter*, June 6, 1950, pp. 13–15.

71. Richard L. Walker, "Lattimore and the IPR," *New Leader*, March 31, 1952, S12–S16.
72. Owen Lattimore, *The Situation in Asia* (Boston, 1949), p. 97.
73. David J. Dallin, "A Chinese Tito?," *New Leader*, April 30, 1949, p. 2. See also David J. Dallin, "Mao No Tito: U.S. Must Act," *ibid.*, May 7, 1949; "Writings of Owen Lattimore Reflect Pro-Soviet Views," May 13, 1950, p. 11. In the same vein is Karl A. Wittfogel, "How to Checkmate Stalin in Asia," *Commentary*, October 1950, pp. 334–41.
74. David J. Dallin, "Myth of Chinese 'Titoism' Revived," *New Leader*, Aug. 27, 1951, p. 13. See also "Alsops Reply to Dallin on Chinese Titoism," Oct. 8, 1951, p. 26, and Dallin's rejoinder, pp. 26–27.
75. Henry Wallace, "My Mission to China," *ibid.*, Nov. 16, 1951, pp. 2–3. This was in response to David J. Dallin, "Henry Wallace and Chinese Communism," Oct. 22, 1951, p. 14. A further statement was David J. Dallin, "The Meaning of Wallace's Trip," Nov. 16, 1951, p. 5.
76. Granville Hicks, "Lattimore and the Liberals," *ibid.*, May 28, 1950, p. 17.
77. "Ideas Can Be Dangerous," *Time*, April 17, 1950, pp. 29–30.
78. John K. Fairbank, "Dangerous Acquaintances," *New York Review of Books*, May 17, 1979, pp. 30–31.

x. The Question of Liberal Guilt

1. Arthur M. Schlesinger, Jr., "What Is Loyalty?," *New York Times Magazine*, Nov. 2, 1947.
2. Norbert Muhlen, "Hysteria in America?," *New Leader*, June 26, 1948, p. 6.
3. E.g., Athan Theoharis, *Seeds of Repression: Harry S. Truman and the Origins of McCarthyism* (Chicago, 1971).
4. Irving Kristol, "Flaying Off the Broomstick," *Commentary*, April 1951, p. 402.
5. Kristol, " 'Civil Liberties,' 1952—A Study in Confusion," *ibid.*, March 1952, p. 229.
6. *Ibid.*
7. *Ibid.*, p. 231. Henry Steele Commager was a distinguished American historian, Alan Barth and Zachariah Chafee well-known civil libertarians.
8. *Ibid.*, p. 234.
9. *Ibid.*
10. *Ibid.*, p. 236.
11. See "Letters From Readers," *Commentary*, May 1952, pp. 491–500, and Arthur M. Schlesinger, Jr., letter to the editor, *ibid.*, July 1952, pp. 83–84.
12. Alan F. Westin, "Our Freedom—and the Rights of Communists," *ibid.*, July 1952, p. 38.

13. Irving Kristol, letter to the editor, *ibid.*, July 1952, p. 86.

14. David Rees, *Harry Dexter White: A Study in Paradox* (New York, 1973).

15. Philip Rahv, *Essays on Literature and Politics 1932–1972*, ed. Arabel J. Porter and Andrew J. Dvosin (Boston, 1978), p. 332. This essay appeared first in the May–June 1952 issue of *Partisan Review*.

16. Elizabeth Hardwick to Dwight Macdonald, Feb. 23, 1949, Macdonald MSS.

17. Dwight Macdonald to Elizabeth Ames, March 3, 1949, Macdonald MSS.

18. Harvey Breit, John Cheever, Eleanor Clark, Alfred Kazin, Kappo Phelan to Dwight Macdonald, March 21, 1949, Macdonald MSS.

19. Alfred Kazin, *New York Jew* (New York, 1978), p. 205.

20. Malcolm Cowley to Kenneth Burke, May 2, 1949, Cowley MSS.

21. Cowley to Elizabeth Ames, March 11, 1949, Cowley MSS.

22. Cowley to Phil, April 13, 1951, Cowley MSS.

23. Elizabeth Ames to Dwight Macdonald, Sept. 12, 1953, Macdonald MSS. Macdonald had not known about Lowell's history of mental illness and therefore took what he heard from the poet at face value; Macdonald to William L. O'Neill, Nov. 25, 1981.

24. Granville Hicks, "The Liberals Who Haven't Learned," *Commentary*, April 1951, p. 329.

25. Freda Kirchwey, letter to the editor of *Commentary*, April 16, 1951, Kirchwey MSS. Freda Kirchwey, "The Cohorts of Fear," *Nation*, April 14, 1951, pp. 339–41.

26. Critical of them are Bernard De Voto, "The Ex-Communists," *Atlantic*, February 1951, pp. 61–65, and Hannah Arendt, "The Ex-Communists," *Commonweal*, March 20, 1953, pp. 595–99. A defense of the ex-Communists is William E. Bohn, "For Twenty-five Years," *New Leader*, Jan. 21, 1950, p. 2.

27. Clement Greenberg, letter to the editor, *New Leader*, March 19, 1951, pp. 16–18.

28. Ed., "The *Nation* Sues Us," *New Leader*, April 2, 1951, p. 2.

29. Carey McWilliams, *The Education of Carey McWilliams* (New York, 1979), p. 150.

30. Ed., "Why the *Nation* Sued," *Nation*, June 2, 1951, pp. 504–5.

31. Ed., "Why Did the *Nation* Sue?," *New Leader*, June 11, 1951.

32. Thomas I. Emerson to Freda Kirchwey, June 13, 1951, Kirchwey MSS.

33. Dwight Macdonald to Daniel Bell, Aug. 24, 1951, Macdonald MSS.

34. R. Lawrence Siegel to Freda Kirchwey, Feb. 7 and May 31, 1955, Kirchwey MSS.

35. Mary McCarthy to Dwight Macdonald, summer 1951, Macdonald MSS.

36. Peter Viereck, "Sermons of Self-Destruction," *Saturday Review of Literature*, Aug. 8, 1951, p. 6.

37. Peter Viereck to Dwight Macdonald, n.d. but probably 1952, Macdonald MSS.

38. Daniel James, "The Liberalism of Suicide," *New Leader*, Aug. 27, 1951, pp. 14–17.

39. Freda Kirchwey, "Proof of the Pudding," *Nation*, Aug. 18, 1951, pp. 122–23.

40. Mark Gayn, "Stormtroopers in Mufti," *Nation*, Aug. 18, 1951, pp. 125–27, and Alexander Werth, "The Soviet Peace Bid," pp. 131–33.

41. "Dissenter Eliminated," *Time*, Jan. 19, 1953, p. 62.

42. Margaret Marshall, letter to the editor, *Nation*, Feb. 7, 1953, p. 135.

43. Freda Kirchwey, "The *Nation*—1918 to 1955," p. 25, Kirchwey MSS.

44. Freda Kirchwey to Carey McWilliams, Aug. 18, 1955, Kirchwey MSS.

45. McWilliams, *op. cit.*, p. 194.

46. J. Alvarez del Vayo to Freda Kirchwey, Jan. 25, 1956, Kirchwey MSS.

47. François Bondy, "Berlin Congress for Freedom," *Commentary*, September 1950, pp. 245–51, and Francis Bond, "Freedom Has Now Taken the Offensive," *New Leader*, July 8, 1950, pp. 6–7.

48. Dwight Macdonald to Mary McCarthy, March 18, 1952, Macdonald MSS.

49. Dwight Macdonald, "Notes on the Conference, 'In Defense of Free Culture,' called by the Am. Comm. for Cultural Freedom, at the Waldorf-Astoria Hotel, March 29, 1952," Macdonald MSS.

50. Richard Rovere to Arthur Schlesinger, Jr., March 20, 1952, Macdonald MSS.

51. Dwight Macdonald, "Notes on Meeting of Committee for Cultural Freedom at the Columbia Club, April 23, 1952," Macdonald MSS.

52. American Committee for Cultural Freedom, news release, Jan. 21, 1953, Macdonald MSS.

53. Dwight Macdonald to George Counts, n.d.; James T. Farrell to George Counts, Feb. 3, 1953, Macdonald MSS.

54. "Draft of a communication to be sent to the Emergency Civil Liberties Committee by the executive committee of the Committee for Cultural Freedom," n.d., Macdonald MSS.

55. Oliver Snyder, "A Report on the Session of the Emergency Civil Liberties Conference, Jan. 31," ACCF MSS.

56. Stephen Spender to Sidney Hook, June 5, 1955, Macdonald MSS.

57. Dwight Macdonald to Stephen Spender, June 6–20, 1955, Macdonald MSS.

58. *Ibid.*, June 2, 1955, Macdonald MSS.

59. Michael Harrington, "The Committee for Cultural Freedom," *Dissent*, Spring 1955, p. 116.

60. Quoted in Brian Gilbert (pseudonym), "New Light on the Lattimore Case," *New Republic*, Dec. 27, 1954.

61. Sol Stein, letter to the editor, *New Republic*, Feb. 14, 1955, pp. 20–22.

62. "Lattimore, McCarran and the Due Process of Law," *New Republic*, Feb. 28, 1955, p. 21.

63. *Ibid.*, p. 23.

64. John C. Hunt to Dwight Macdonald, Feb. 1, 1962; Dwight Macdonald to Michael Josselson, March 30, 1967, Macdonald MSS. See also Dwight Macdonald, "Politics," *Esquire*, June 1967.

65. Christian Herter to Sidney Hook, July 8, 1951, ACCF MSS.

66. James Rorty and Moshe Decter, *McCarthy and the Communists* (New York, 1954).

67. Sol Stein to John Foster Dulles, Nov. 14, 1955, ACCF MSS.

68. American Committee for Cultural Freedom, news release, March 31, 1954, ACCF MSS.

69. James T. Farrell to Norman Jacobs, Aug. 28, 1956, ACCF MSS.

70. Norbert Muhlen, "The Phantom of McCarthyism," *New Leader*, May 21, 1951, p. 18.

71. Granville Hicks, "Is McCarthyism a Phantom?," *ibid.*, June 4, 1951, p. 7.

72. William F. Buckley, Jr., and L. Brent Bozell, *McCarthy and His Enemies* (Chicago, 1954), p. 4.

73. Joseph Alsop, "The Strange Case of Louis Budenz," *Atlantic*, April 1952, p. 32.

74. Leslie Fiedler, "McCarthy," *Encounter*, August 1954, p. 18. The theory that McCarthy was some kind of populist, or appealed to populism, was common at the time. It is put to rest in Michael Rogin, *The Intellectuals and McCarthy* (Cambridge, Mass., 1967).

75. Fiedler, "McCarthy," *op cit.*, p. 21.

76. Harold Rosenberg, "Couch Liberalism and the Guilty Past," *Dissent*, Autumn 1955, pp. 320–21.

77. Vincent Canby, "A Documentary: 'Trials of Alger Hiss,' " *New York Times*, March 9, 1980.

78. Allen Weinstein, *Perjury: The Hiss-Chambers Case* (New York, 1978).

79. Philip Rahv, "The Sense and Nonsense of Whittaker Chambers," in *op. cit.*, p. 323.

80. Leslie Fiedler, "Hiss, Chambers, and the Age of Innocence," *Commentary*, August 1951, p. 110.

81. *Ibid.*, p. 111.

82. *Ibid.*, p. 118.

83. Diana Trilling, "The Oppenheimer Case: A Reading of the Testimony," *Partisan Review*, November–December 1954, p. 629.

84. *Ibid.*, p. 635.

85. Joseph and Stewart Alsop, "We Accuse!," *Harper's*, October

1954, pp. 24–25. It was expanded into a book with the same title.
86. Hans Meyerhoff, "Through the Liberal Looking-Glass Darkly," *Partisan Review*, Spring 1955, p. 240.
87. *Ibid.*, p. 244.
88. *Ibid.*, p. 248.
89. Diana Trilling, "A Rejoinder to Mr. Meyerhoff," *ibid.*, Spring 1955, p. 249.
90. *Ibid.*, p. 251.

XI. THE ACADEMY AND THE CRISIS OF LIBERALISM

1. Eric Bentley, ed., *Thirty Years of Treason: Excerpts from Hearings Before the House Committee on Un-American Activities, 1938–1968* (New York, 1971), p. 662.
2. Max Lerner, "When Is a Professor a Man?," *New York Post*, March 1, 1953.
3. David Caute, *The Great Fear* (New York, 1978), p. 103.
4. Laurent Frantz and Norman Redlich, "Does Silence Mean Guilt?," *Nation*, June 6, 1953, pp. 471–77.
5. Alan F. Westin, "Do Silent Witnesses Defend Civil Liberties?," *Commentary*, June 1953, pp. 537–46.
6. Caute, *op. cit.*
7. Sidney Hook, "Academic Integrity and Academic Freedom," *Commentary*, October 1949, pp. 329–39.
8. Helen M. Lynd, "Truth at the University of Washington," *American Scholar*, Summer 1949, pp. 346–53.
9. Hook, *op. cit.*, p. 332.
10. Helen M. Lynd, letter to the editor, *Commentary*, December 1949, pp. 594–95, and Arthur E. Murphy, pp. 596–98.
11. Sidney Hook, letter to the editor, *ibid.*, pp. 598–601.
12. Arthur O. Lovejoy, "Communism versus Academic Freedom," *American Scholar*, Summer 1949, pp. 332–37, and T. V. Smith, "Academic Expediency as Democratic Justice," pp. 342–46; John L. Childs, "Communists and the Right to Teach," *Nation*, Feb. 26, 1949, pp. 230–33.
13. Carey McWilliams, "The Test of a Teacher," *Nation*, March 5, 1949, pp. 270–73.
14. Irving Howe, "Intellectual Freedom and Stalinists," *New International*, December 1949, pp. 231–36.
15. Alfred Kazin, *New York Jew* (New York, 1978), p. 188.
16. Sidney Hook, letter to the editor, *New York Times Book Review*, April 12, 1981.
17. Edward C. Kirkland, "Do Antisubversive Efforts Threaten Academic Freedom?," *Annals of the American Academy of Political and Social Science*, May 1951, p. 138.
18. H. H. Wilson, "Academic Freedom and American Society," *Nation*, June 28, 1952, pp. 658–59.

19. Kalman Seigel, "Style Noted: the Campus Strait-Jacket," *ibid.*, pp. 661–63.
20. Quoted in Robert M. MacIver, *Academic Freedom in Our Time* (New York, 1955), p. 35.
21. *Ibid.*, p. 266.
22. Robert E. Fitch, "The Fears of the Intelligentsia," *Commentary*, October 1954, p. 334.
23. Paul R. Hays, "Academic Freedom and Communist Teachers," *ibid.*, June 1956, p. 550.
24. *Journal of Social Issues*, 1955, No. 3.
25. William L. Neumann, "Historians in an Age of Acquiescence," *Dissent*, Winter 1957, p. 69.
26. H. Stuart Hughes, "Why We Had No Dreyfus Case," *American Scholar*, Fall 1961, p. 474.
27. *Ibid.*, p. 476.
28. *Ibid.*, p. 478.
29. Ernest Van Den Haag, "McCarthyism and the Professors," *Commentary*, February 1959, p. 181.
30. *Ibid.*, p. 182.
31. Irving Howe, "The ADA: Vision and Myopia," *Dissent*, Spring 1955, pp. 107–12.
32. Murray Kempton, "Cain and Humphrey," *ibid.*, Autumn 1955, p. 123.
33. Alan F. Westin, "Libertarian Precepts and Subversive Realities," *Commentary*, January 1955, pp. 1–9.
34. David Riesman and Nathan Glazer, "The Intellectuals and the Discontented Classes," *Partisan Review*, Winter 1955, p. 58.
35. Nathan Glazer and Seymour Martin Lipset, "The Polls on Communism and Conformity," *The New American Right* (New York, 1955).
36. Malcolm Cowley to Alan Barth, draft copy, summer 1950, Cowley MSS.
37. Dwight Macdonald to Irving Kristol, May 21, 1949, Macdonald MSS.
38. Arthur Schlesinger, Jr., to Dwight Macdonald, April 29, 1952, Macdonald MSS.
39. Kazin, *op. cit.*, p. 185.
40. Malcolm Cowley to Alan Barth, Aug. 10, 1949, Cowley MSS.
41. Arthur Schlesinger, Jr., *The Vital Center* (Boston, 1962). Peter Viereck, *The Shame and Glory of the Intellectuals: Babbitt Jr. vs. the Rediscovery of Values* (Boston, 1953). William F. Buckley, Jr., and L. Brent Bozell, *McCarthy and His Enemies* (Chicago, 1954).
42. Malcolm Cowley, *The Literary Situation* (New York, 1954), p. 57.
43. Reinhold Niebuhr, *The Irony of American History* (New York, 1952), p. 7.
44. *Ibid.*, p. 8.
45. *Ibid.*, p. 10.

46. *Ibid.*, p. 13.
47. *Ibid.*, p. 174.
48. Daniel Bell, "The Mood of Three Generations," in *The End of Ideology: On the Exhaustion of Political Ideas in the Fifties* (rev. ed., New York, 1961), p. 300.
49. Irving Howe, "This Age of Conformity," *Partisan Review*, 1954, No. 1, p. 11.
50. *Ibid.*, p. 27.
51. See William L. O'Neill, *Coming Apart: An Informal History of America in the 1960s* (Chicago, 1971).

XII. REWRITING THE PAST

1. Charles Kadushin, *The American Intellectual Elite* (Boston, 1974).
2. Jason Epstein, "The CIA and the Intellectuals," *New York Review of Books*, April 20, 1967, p. 18.
3. "Liberal Anti-Communism Revisited," *Commentary*, September 1967, pp. 31–79.
4. *Ibid.*, p. 74.
5. *Ibid.*, p. 49.
6. Irving Howe, "The New York Intellectuals: A Chronicle and a Critique," *Commentary*, October 1968, p. 33.
7. *Ibid.*
8. It appears in Christopher Lasch, *The Agony of the American Left* (New York, 1969).
9. *Ibid.*, p. 111.
10. A growing historical literature blames liberal politicians and intellectuals for the rise of McCarthyism. Examples are: many of the essays in Robert Griffith and Athan Theoharis, eds., *The Specter: Original Essays on the Cold War and the Origins of McCarthyism* (New York, 1974); Robert Griffith, *The Politics of Fear: Joseph R. McCarthy and the Senate* (Lexington, Ky., 1970); Mary Sperling McAuliffe, *Crisis on the Left: Cold War Politics and American Liberals, 1947–54* (Amherst, Mass., 1978); Athan Theoharis, *Seeds of Repression: Harry S. Truman and the Origins of McCarthyism* (Chicago, 1971).
11. Corliss Lamont, *Voice in the Wilderness* (Buffalo, N.Y., 1975). James Aronson, *The Press and the Cold War* (Indianapolis, 1970). Cedric Belfrage, *American Inquisition, 1945–1960* (Indianapolis, 1973). Cedric Belfrage and James Aronson, *Something to Guard: The Stormy Life of the National Guardian 1948–1967* (New York, 1978).
12. Carey McWilliams, *The Education of Carey McWilliams* (New York, 1979), p. 145.
13. Norman Redlich, "McCarthy's Global Hoax," *Nation*, Dec. 2, 1978, p. 612.

14. *Ibid.*
15. Doris V. Falk, *Lillian Hellman* (New York, 1978).
16. Garry Wills in Lillian Hellman, *Scoundrel Time* (Boston, 1976), p. 29.
17. William F. Buckley, Jr., "Who Is the Ugliest of Them All?," *National Review*, Jan. 21, 1977, p. 102.
18. Hellman, *op. cit.*, p. 39.
19. *Ibid.*, p. 83.
20. *Ibid.*, p. 150.
21. William Phillips, "What Happened in the Fifties," *Partisan Review*, 1976, No. 3, p. 339.
22. Sidney Hook, "Lillian Hellman's *Scoundrel Time*," *Encounter*, February 1977, p. 91.
23. Alfred Kazin, "The Legend of Lillian Hellman," *Esquire*, August 1977, discusses the incident.
24. Quoted in Michiko Kakutani, "Hellman–McCarthy Libel Suit Stirs Old Antagonisms," *New York Times*, March 19, 1980.
25. Norman Podhoretz, *Breaking Ranks* (New York, 1979), p. 317.
26. John Leonard, "What Do Writers Think of Reviews and Reviewers?," *New York Times*, Aug. 7, 1980. The public exchange consisted of Norman Mailer, "An Appeal to Lillian Hellman and Mary McCarthy," *New York Review of Books*, May 11, 1980; and Richard Poirier, letter to the editor, *ibid.*, June 15, 1980, pp. 33–34.
27. Quoted in Kakutani, *op. cit.*
28. *Ibid.*
29. "Lillian Hellman Gets Lord & Taylor Award," *New York Times*, Nov. 10, 1977. A long list of awards and honors is in Falk, *op. cit.*
30. Allen Weinstein, "Agit-Prop & the Rosenbergs," *Commentary*, July 1970, p. 25.
31. Victor Navasky, "The Case Not Proved Against Alger Hiss," *Nation*, April 8, 1978, pp. 393–401. Editors and Allen Weinstein, " 'Perjury,' Take Three," *New Republic*, April 15, 1978, pp. 16–21.
32. Victor Navasky, letter to the editor, *ibid.*, May 13, 1978. See also Weinstein's response on p. 38, and also Victor Navasky, "New Republic, New Mistakes," *Nation*, May 6, 1978, pp. 523–25; "The Hiss–Weinstein File," *ibid.*, June 17, 1978, pp. 718–24. John Chabot Smith, author of a book defending Hiss, also took *The Nation*'s view, "The Debate of the Century (cont'd.)," *Harper's*, June 1978, pp. 81–85.
33. *In Re Alger Hiss* (New York, 1979), ed. Edith Tiger with an introduction by Thomas I. Emerson.
34. Robert Blair Kaiser, "Film About Hiss Trials Revives Controversy," *New York Times*, Feb. 26, 1980.
35. Vincent Canby, "A Documentary: 'Trials of Alger Hiss,' " *ibid.*, March 9, 1980.
36. Norman Podhoretz, *Breaking Ranks: A Political Memoir* (New York, 1979), p. 21.

37. *Ibid.*, p. 173.
38. *Ibid.*, p. 254.
39. *Ibid.*, p. 300.
40. Hilton Kramer, "Beautiful Reds," *New York Times Book Review*, April 2, 1978, p. 29.
41. "Controversy Over Robeson Play Continues in Forum on His Image," *New York Times*, May 14, 1978.
42. "33 Playwrights Protest 'Censure' of 'Robeson,' " *New York Times*, May 18, 1978.
43. Quoted in Earl L. Cunningham, "PBS to Air Play About Paul Robeson," *Rutgers Alumni Magazine*, September 1979, p. 2.
44. Victor S. Navasky, *Naming Names* (New York, 1980), p. xv.
45. *Ibid.*, p. 325.
46. *Ibid.*, p. 423.
47. *Ibid.*, pp. 387–88.
48. *Ibid.*, p. 389.
49. *Ibid.*, p. 406.

XIII. CONCLUSIONS

1. Alexander Werth, letter to the editor, *New Statesman*, Oct. 13, 1967, p. 468.
2. Richard J. Walton, *Henry Wallace, Harry Truman and the Cold War* (New York, 1976), p. 204.
3. Michael Harrington, "After Afghanistan," *Dissent*, Spring 1980, p. 138.
4. See J. A. Thompson, "William Appleman Williams and the 'American Empire,' " *Journal of American Studies*, Vol. 7, No. 1, pp. 91–104; and Warren Kimball, "The Cold War Warmed Over," *American Historical Review*, October 1974, pp. 1119–36.
5. Arthur M. Schlesinger, Jr., "The Cold War Revisited," *New York Review of Books*, Oct. 25, 1979, pp. 46–52.
6. David Horowitz, "A Radical's Disenchantment," *Nation*, Dec. 8, 1979, p. 59.
7. The original *Nation* editorial was by Aryeh Neier in the issue of June 23, 1979. An editorial note reaffirming it, together with many angry letters, appeared in the issue of July 14–21, 1979.
8. Ed., "The Russians Have Come," *Nation*, Jan. 5–12, 1980, p. 1.
9. Fred Halliday, "Wrong Moves on Afghanistan," *ibid.*, Jan. 26, 1980, p. 70.
10. Ronald Steel, *Walter Lippmann and the American Century* (Boston, 1980).
11. Steel, "The Absent Danger," *New Republic*, Aug. 16, 1980, pp. 19–22.
12. Walter La Feber, "The Politics of Déjà Vu," *Nation*, March 15, 1980, p. 289.

13. Godfrey Hodgson, *America in Our Time* (Garden City, N.Y., 1976), p. 98.
14. Charles Krauthammer, "Holy Fools," *New Republic*, Sept. 9, 1981, pp. 10–13.
15. Quoted in Joshua Muravchik, "The Think Tank of the Left," *New York Times Magazine*, April 26, 1981.

Index

Abramovich, Ralph, 53–54
Abt, John, 144
Academic Freedom in Our Time (MacIver), 335
Academic Mind, The (Lazarsfeld and Thielens), 338–40
Acheson, Dean, 129, 170, 184, 200, 262, 263, 264, 282
Action in the North Atlantic, 246
Adamic, Louis, 194
Afghanistan, Soviet invasion of, 381–82
Agee, James, 77–78
Airborne Symphony, The, 245–246
Algren, Nelson, 236
Allen, Frederick Lewis, 131
Almanac Singers, 37
Alsop, Joseph, 117–18, 180, 280, 311, 312n
Alsop, Stewart, 117–18, 280
Amalgamated Clothing Workers, 144, 146
Amerasia, 274–75
America as a Civilization (Lerner), 171
America First Committee, 41
American Association of University Professors (AAUP), 336
American Civil Liberties Union (ACLU), 31, 45, 138, 228–230, 232, 299, 370
American Committee for Cultural Freedom (ACCF), 14, 297–308, 352
  anti-McCarthy work of, 307–308, 355
  anti-Stalinist work of, 307, 308
  CIA linked to, 307, 352
  Harrington's critique of, 305
American Federation of Teachers, 332
American Inquisition, 1945–1960 (Belfrage), 206
American Intellectual Elite, The (Kadushin), 351
American Intellectuals for Freedom (AIF), 164, 165, 166–67
American Labor Party, 145–46, 158
American Legion, 239–40
American Newspaper Guild, 140–41
American Peace Mobilization, 35–36
American Renaissance: Art and Expression in the Age of Emerson and Whitman (Matthiessen), 173–74
American Scholar, 330, 331
Americans for Democratic Action (ADA), 138–40, 147, 158, 299, 341–42
  Communists banned from, 138–139
  at Democratic convention, 154
  founding of, 138
  Macdonald rejected by, 152
  PCA rivalry with, 139, 140
American Unitarian Association, 140
American Veterans Committee, 231–32
Ames, Elizabeth, 290–91

Angell, Ernest, 228–29
anti-Stalinists, 75–79
    Cultural and Scientific Con-
        ference penetrated by, 164,
        165
    Lerner attacked by, 171
    in *Mission to Moscow* contro-
        versy, 75–78
    Nation's views attacked by,
        84–85
    New Leader as forum for, 135
    in popular press, 88
    pro-Soviet books attacked by,
        81–84
    revisionist histories of, 354–
        356
    revolution denounced by,
        376–77
    Soviet conduct linked to re-
        vival of, 98–115
    Vietnam War era backlash
        against, 351–52
    Wallace opposed by, 145
    White's *Report on Russia* in
        support of, 90–92
    as World War II minority, 59
Aronson, James, 203–4, 206,
    356
Arts, Sciences and Professions
    Council (ASP), 217
Arts, Sciences and Professions
    Council of the Progressive
    Citizens of Southern Cali-
    fornia (ASP-PCA), 217
Asphalt Jungle, 226
Atlantic, 106, 140, 153, 255,
    259, 261, 262, 264–65, 266
Atlantic Charter, 105
Atomic Energy Commission
    (AEC), 317–18
Auden, W. H., 237
Austin, Warren, 131

Bachrach, John A., 208
Baez, Joan, 380
Baldwin, C. B., 144, 153–54
Baldwin, James, 372
Baldwin, Roger, 31, 48, 76, 78,
    383

Balkans, Soviet presence in, 137
Bao Dai, 199, 265
Barth, Alan, 285, 287, 289, 344
Bates, Ralph, 54, 62–63, 73, 79
Battle Hymn of China (Smed-
    ley), 186
Bazelon, David T., 145
Becker, Carl, 95–97, 115
Belfrage, Cedric, 191, 203–4,
    206, 356
Bell, Daniel, 80, 106, 300, 348,
    352
Bemis, Samuel Flagg, 337
Bendiner, Robert, 157, 294
Berg, Louis, 231, 232, 233
Berlin Blockade, 154, 156
Bernal, J. D., 218
Bernays, Edward L., 229
Bernstein, Leonard, 245–46
Bessie, Alvah, 237–38, 239, 243
Biberman, Herbert, 222
Biddle, Francis, 44, 45
Bingham, Alfred, 94
Bisson, T. A., 253–54, 274, 275
blacklist, 223–41
    of anti-Communists, 230
    Cogley's report on, 233–34
    entertainers on, 234, 239
    Fifth Amendment claims re-
        sulting in, 224–25
    humiliation caused by, 239–40
    Kramer's essay on, 240–41
    Miller's report on, 228–30,
        231, 232
    in motion picture industry,
        223–28, 232–33, 239, 240
    names selected for, 233
    number of people on, 239
    producers' role in, 223–24
    as punitive, 233
    in radio industry, 228, 239
    Stalinism as motivation for,
        249, 251
    tactics for circumvention of,
        236–37, 238–39
    in television industry, 228, 239
    testimony as means of re-
        moval from, 225–28
    writers on, 234, 236–39

Blair, Anita, 203
Blitzstein, Marc, 245–46
Bliven, Bruce, 18, 34, 51, 119
  on anti-Stalinists, 106
  on Soviet war morale, 47–48
  State Department criticized
    by, 58
Bohlen, Charles, 120, 320
Book Review Digest, 137
Borgese, G. A., 111
Bowles, Chester, 41, 138
Bozell, Brent, 309–11, 312, 313,
  346
Brave One, The (Trumbo), 237
Brecht, Bertolt, 221
Brewer, Roy, 218–19, 226, 241
Bridge on the River Kwai, The,
  238
Bridges, Harry, 205
Broun, Heywood, 21
Browder, Earl, 43, 59
Buckley, William F., 309–11,
  312, 313, 335, 346, 359
Budenz, Louis, 268, 292, 311–12
Bullitt, William C., 88, 90
Burchett, Wilfred, 380
Burnham, James, 76
businessmen, Soviet Union as
  viewed by, 60–61
Business Week, 228
Byrnes, James, 130, 131, 143

Cain, Harry, 342
Call, The, 23
Cambodia, Pol Pot regime in,
  385
Canby, Vincent, 368
Cantor, Eddie, 144
Canwell, Albert F., 329
Capra, Frank, 241
Carter, Edward C., 273, 274,
  275
Carter, Jimmy, 381, 382
Caute, David, 248, 325, 328
Cavett, Dick, 364
Central Intelligence Agency
  (CIA), 307, 325, 361
Cerf, Bennett, 71, 78

Chamberlain, John, 44, 91
Chamberlain, Neville, 26, 67
Chamberlin, William Henry,
  91, 105, 127
Chambers, Whittaker, 259, 273,
  286, 305, 311, 315–16, 366,
  367, 368
Chandler, Raymond, 213
Chaplin, Charlie, 240
Chart for Rough Water (Frank),
  33
Cheever, John, 290
Chennault, Claire, 311
Chevalier, Haakon, 318–20
Chiang Kai-shek, 53, 162, 199,
  252, 253, 254–55, 259,
  261–62, 312
Chicago Tribune, 197
Childs, John L., 332
Childs, Marquis, 138
China:
  Communist vs. Nationalist
    conditions in, 256
  in Korean War, 266
  Kuomintang party (KMT) in,
    253, 255, 258, 260
  progressives' views on, 252–
    253, 282–83
  Roosevelt's policies on, 252–
    253, 255, 257, 280
  Soviet relations with, 258–59
  State Department report on,
    190–91, 262–63
  Truman's policies on, 261,
    262, 264
China at War (Utley), 271
China Lobby, 254, 261, 262,
  264, 266, 270, 272, 274,
  312
China Story, The (Utley), 270
China Today, 273
China Weekly Review, 257
Chinese Conquer China, The
  (Strong), 191
Chou En-lai, 257
Christian Century, 111
Christian Science Monitor, 179
Churchill, Winston, 45, 46, 52,
  80–81

Citizens Committee for Motion Picture Strikers, 218
Civil Rights Congress, 302
Civil Rights Defense Committee, 44–45
Clark, Eleanor, 290
Cogley, John, 233–34, 247
Cohen, Elliot, 301
Cohn, Roy, 272
Cole, G. D. H., 53–54
Cole, Lester, 221–22, 223–24
Collective Portrait, 183
Collier's, 61, 311
Comintern, 62–63
Commager, Henry Steele, 335
Commentary, 139, 145, 161, 228–29, 231, 279, 285, 294, 297, 345, 349, 352, 355, 360–61, 368–70
Committee for a Democratic Far Eastern Policy, 191, 275
Committee for Public Justice, 365
Committee for the First Amendment, 223
Committee of One Thousand, 223
Committee to Defend America by Aiding the Allies, 36
Common Sense, 15, 57, 82, 86, 87, 94, 111, 113–14
Commonweal, 294
Communist Control Act (1954), 341–42
Communist Party:
  as backbone of Progressive movement, 147
  college instructors in, 327–28
  FBI infiltration of, 309–10
  Great Britain supported by, 44
  HUAC policies of, 221, 326
  on Korean War, 203
  membership figures for, 43, 135
  in motion picture industry, 214, 215–16, 220, 241–42, 243, 244, 247–48, 250
  national organizations controlled by, 135
  in NCPAC, 143–44
  New Republic views on, 59
  in 1948 elections, 158–59
  as obstacle to U.S.–Soviet friendship, 59
  in red scare of 1940–41, 43–44
  Stalin-Hitler Pact and, 43
  strikes barred by, 43–44
  SWP prosecution endorsed by, 45
  Wallace supported by, 147–148, 156–57
Compass, 192, 202, 203
Conference of Studio Unions (CSU), 218
Congress for Cultural Freedom, 297–98, 304, 307
Congress of Industrial Organizations (CIO), Political Action Committee (PAC) of, 143
conscription bill, 39
Cooke, Alistair, 240, 315
Copland, Aaron, 218
Corey, Lewis, 35
Coser, Lewis, 210
Coughlin, Father Charles E., 29
Counts, George, 303
Cousins, Norman, 166–67
Cowley, Malcolm, 18, 97n, 103, 179, 344, 346, 364
  on Comintern dissolution, 63
  on liberal intellectuals, 31–32
  Mumford reviewed by, 33–34
  political life abandoned by, 51
  in Popular Front, 19–20
  on U.S.–Soviet alliance, 105–6
  in Yaddo affair, 291
Crawford, Kenneth, 59, 86, 87
Croly, Herbert, 17, 18
Cromwell, John, 216
Crossfire, 222
Crossman, Richard, 183
Cultural and Scientific Conference for World Peace (1949), 163–68, 194, 302, 330, 331

Cultural and Scientific Conference for World Peace, *cont.*
  AIF penetration of, 164, 165, 166–67
  ASP work in, 217
  Kirchwey on, 165–66, 167–68
  Marshall on, 167–69
  participants in, 164–65
  State Department actions against, 164, 165, 166
Curran, Joe, 35–36
Czechoslovakia, Communist takeover of, 146, 156, 378–379

Daily Worker, 14, 197, 248, 273, 311
Dallin, David J., 78–79, 162–63, 197, 279–80
Da Silva, Howard, 224, 247
Daughter of the Earth (Smedley), 186
Davidson, Jo, 144, 215–16
Davies, John, 271, 277
Davies, Joseph E., 60, 61, 64, 75–76, 77
Davis, Arthur K., 208
Davis, Bette, 144
Davis, Elmer, 242, 280–81
Davis, Jerome, 130, 189, 195
Davis, Ossie, 371, 372
Dean, Philip Hayes, 371, 372
Dean, Vera M., 131–33
Defiant Ones, The, 238
De Haviland, Olivia, 215, 216–217
de Kruif, Paul, 21
De Lacey, Hugh, 149
Del Vayo, J. Alvarez, *see* Vayo, J. Alvarez Del
De Mille, Cecil B., 228
Democratic Party, 154, 198, 312, 341
Dennis, Lawrence, 29
Design for Power (Schuman), 53
Destination Tokyo, 243
De Toledano, Ralph, 229–30, 247

Deutscher, Isaac, 292
De Voto, Bernard, 310
Dewey, John, 25, 44, 76, 145, 152–53
Dewey, Thomas E., 155
Dies Committee, 219
Disney, Walt, 219
Dissent, 210–11, 342
Dmytryk, Edward, 220, 225–26
Dodd, Bella, 268
Dominican Republic, U.S. invasion of, 381
Dorner, Hannah, 144, 194
Douglas, Helen Gahagan, 129
Douglas, Kirk, 238
Douglas, Melvyn, 213
Douglas, Paul, 154
Dream We Lost, The (Utley), 271
Dreier, Mary, 25, 185–86, 188, 195–96, 202–3
Dreiser, Theodore, 36
Dubinsky, David, 138
Du Bois, W. E. B., 164, 205
Dulles, John Foster, 131, 371
Dumbarton Oaks Conference, 111, 113
Dunne, Philip, 222, 223, 230
Duranty, Walter, 15, 55, 122
Durdin, Tillman, 272
Dwell in the Wilderness (Bessie), 237
Dynamics of War and Revolution, The (Dennis), 29

Eastman, Max, 15, 31, 56, 61, 64, 76, 164, 165, 183, 272, 298–300, 322–23, 327
Economist, 294
Eddy, Sherwood, 130
Einstein, Albert, 144
Eisenhower, Dwight D., 344
Eisler, Gerhart, 219
Eisler, Hanns, 219, 249
Emergency Civil Liberties Committee (ECLC), 302, 303
Emerson, Thomas I., 293, 302, 303
Encounter, 304, 307

End Poverty in California (EPIC) platform, 22
End to Innocence, An (Fiedler), 314
Epstein, Jason, 352, 355
Esquire, 350
Eulau, Heinz H. F., 104, 106–7, 127, 134, 254
Europe, Russia and the Future (Cole), 53
European Recovery Program (ERP), 120, 156–57
Exile's Return (Cowley), 19
Exodus, 238

Fadayev, A. A., 164, 165, 167
Fairbank, John, 259–60, 261, 263, 265–66, 282
Fairchild, Henry Pratt, 66, 302
Faith, Reason, and Civilization (Laski), 81–84
Faith for the Living (Mumford), 32
Faithful Are the Wounds (Sarton), 182
Farber, Manny, 77
Far Eastern Survey, 254, 273, 274
Farrell, James T., 22, 44, 76, 248, 298, 303, 308
Fast, Howard, 164
Federal Bureau of Investigation (FBI), 290, 311
  Communist Party infiltrated by, 309–10
Federal Communications Commission, 229
Feinberg Law, 330
Ferrer, José, 225, 239–40, 247
Fiedler, Leslie, 313–15, 316–17
Field, Frederick Vanderbilt, 268, 273, 275
Fight Against Communism, The (McCarthy), 313
Finch, John, 180
Finland, Soviet invasion of, 19, 43, 55, 67
Fischer, Louis, 16, 63, 82–83, 85, 90, 113

Fitch, Robert E., 335–36
Fitzgerald, Albert J., 146
Flynn, John T., 272–73
Forced Labor in Russia (Dallin and Nicolaevsky), 162–63
Ford, Henry, 41
Ford Foundation. 233
Foreign Policy Association (FPA), 131
Foreign Service Education Foundation, 307
Foreman, Carl, 238
Foreman, Carol, 302, 303
Forrestal, James, 120
Forster, Clifford, 293–94
Forsythe, Robert, 21
Fortas, Abe, 268, 361
Fortune, 80
Fortune poll, 60–61
Four Freedoms, 121
Fox, Edward Whiting, 176
Frank, Waldo, 33, 44–45
Frankfurter, Felix, 99
Frantz, Laurent, 325
Freed, Donald, 366
Freedom House, 299
Freidel, Frank, 80
Friendly Persuasion, 238
Fritchman, Stephen H., 140
From the Heart of Europe (Matthiessen), 178, 182
Front, The, 240, 370
Fry, Varian, 84
Fulbright, William, 348
Fund for the Republic, 338
Fur Workers Union, 43

Gallup polls, 43, 45, 223
Garfield, John, 225
Gates, John, 45
Gayn, Mark, 295
Geer, Will, 224, 234
Generation on Trial, A (Cooke), 240, 315
Glazer, Nathan, 343, 344–45, 361
God and Man at Yale (Buckley), 335

God That Failed, The (Crossman), 183
Goldman, Albert, 76
Goodman, Paul, 368
Gornick, Vivian, 370
Grafton, Samuel, 47
Great Britain, U.S. aid to, 39–40, 44
Great Conspiracy, The (Sayers and Kahn), 125, 133, 141, 195
Great Fear, The (Caute), 248
Greenberg, Clement, 45, 292–293, 298
Growing Up Absurd (Goodman), 368
Guthrie, Woody, 37, 246

Hallinan, Vincent, 205
Hammett, Dashiell, 359, 366
Hardwick, Elizabeth, 290
Harnett, E. S., 299
Harper, Samuel N., 21
Harriman, Averell, 120
Harrington, Michael, 305, 379
Harvard University, 175–77, 324
Hayden, Sterling, 226, 239
Hayford, James, 149
Hays, Paul K., 336
Hearst, William Randolph, 36, 118
Hellman, Lillian, 144, 358–66
  on anti-Stalinists, 360–61, 377
  background of, 358–59
  Hook on, 362–63
  before HUAC, 225, 359, 360, 361, 362–63, 364
  McCarthy sued by, 364–65
  Scoundrel Time by, 240, 241, 359–63, 365, 366
  Trilling's dispute with, 363–364, 377
  in Women for Wallace, 148
Henahan, Donal, 245–46
Henderson, Leon, 138
Henreid, Paul, 215
Henry Wallace, Harry Truman and the Cold War (Walton), 378–79

Hersey, John, 364–65
Hesseltine, William B., 80
Hicks, Granville, 21, 31, 85–86, 172, 280–81, 292, 309, 324, 326
Hidden History of the Korean War, The (Stone), 202
Hillman, Sidney, 143–44, 145
Hindus, Maurice, 55, 61, 64–66
Hinton, Harold C., 275–76
Hiss, Alger, 170, 281, 286, 305, 311, 315–17, 337, 342, 366–68, 370
history, revisionist, 379–80, 382
Hobart and William Smith Colleges symposium (1975), 175–76
Ho Chi Minh, 265
Hodgson, Godfrey, 383–84
Hollywood Anti-Nazi League, 213
Hollywood Democratic Committee (HDC), 214, 218, 235
Hollywood Independent Citizens Committee of the Arts, Sciences and Professions (HICCASP), 216–18, 235
Hollywood on Trial (Cole and Lardner), 222, 240, 243
Hollywood Reporter, 226
"Hollywood Ten," 217, 220–24, 225, 234, 235, 242, 243, 249
  see also House Committee on Un-American Activities; motion picture industry
Hollywood Writers Mobilization, 235, 244
Hook, Sidney, 14, 22, 76, 204, 328–34, 352, 355, 377
  in ACCF, 298, 300, 301, 305
  AIF organized by, 164, 165
  at Cultural and Scientific Conference, 164, 165, 166–67
  Hellman's book reviewed by, 362–63
  Howe on, 354
  prestige lost by, 369

Sinclair attacked by, 23–24
on teachers as Communists,
    328–31, 333
Hoover, Herbert, 264
Hoover, J. Edgar, 227
Hornbeck, Stanley, 275
Horowitz, David, 380
House Committee on Un-Ameri-
    can Activities (HUAC),
    175, 219–28, 249–50
in blacklist rehabilitations,
    225–28
disintegration of, 324–25
Fifth Amendment claims be-
    fore, 221, 224–25, 324,
    325–27, 359, 360
First Amendment claims be-
    fore, 221–22
Hellman before, 359, 360,
    361, 362–63, 364
Hicks's testimony before, 324
Los Angeles hearings of, 219
motion picture industry inves-
    tigated by, 219–28
MPA cooperation with, 219–
    220
press coverage of, 223
producers' cooperation with,
    223–24
progressives investigated by,
    250–51
public opinion on, 223
as punitive measure, 225
receptive climate for, 219
Stalinism as inspiration for,
    249, 250–51
unfriendly witnesses before,
    220–23
writers before, 225
Howe, Irving, 135, 179, 210,
    211, 308, 364, 377
on ADA, 341–42
on anti-Stalinism, 353–54
on Hook, 354
on intellectuals, 349–50, 354
on teachers as Communists,
    332–33
How New Will the Better World
    Be? (Becker), 95–97

HUAC
    see House Committee on Un-
        American Activities
Huberman, Leo, 148, 194, 206
Hughes, H. Stuart, 337–38
Hull, Cordell, 320
Humphrey, Hubert H., 152, 342
Hungary, Soviet control of, 124–
    125
Huston, John, 223, 226
Hutchins, Robert M., 335, 336

Ickes, Harold L., 188, 198, 202,
    215, 264
Independent Citizens Committee
    of the Arts, Sciences and
    Professions (ICCASP),
    144–45, 214
Independent Voters Committee
    of the Arts and Sciences
    (IVCAS), 144
Indochina, progressives' policy
    on, 199
In Fact, 36–37, 89–90, 205
Inner Asian Frontiers of China
    (Lattimore), 276, 277
Inquest: A Tale of Political
    Terror (Freed), 366
Institute for Policy Studies
    (IPS), 384–85
Institute of Pacific Relations
    (IPR), 269, 273, 274–76,
    342
International Alliance of The-
    atrical Stage Employees and
    Moving Picture Machine
    Operators of the United
    States and Canada
    (IATSE), 218–19, 235
Iran, Soviet withdrawal from,
    117
Irony of American History, The
    (Niebuhr), 347–48
Isherwood, Christopher, 217–18
Italy, Badoglio regime in, 72–73

Jackson, Gardner, 153
Jacoby, Annalee, 259

Japan, in war with China, 254,
255, 258
Japan's Feet of Clay (Utley),
271
Jarrico, Paul, 224
Joesten, Joachim, 55
Johnny Got His Gun (Trumbo),
235
Johnson, Gerald W., 277
Johnson, Lyndon, 350
Johnston, Eric, 90, 223
Joliot-Curie, Frédéric, 281
Jolson Story, The, 224
Journal of Social Issues, 337
Judges and the Judged, The
(Miller), 228, 229, 231,
232, 233
Jungle, The (Sinclair), 22
Justice Department, U.S., 270

Kael, Pauline, 244–45
Kahn, Albert, 141, 195
Kaminsky, Howard, 207–8
Katyn Forest massacre, 91, 98–
99, 172
Kazan, Elia, 374
Kazin, Alfred, 51, 76, 177–78,
241, 290, 291, 333, 345,
377
Kempton, Murray, 236–37, 342,
352
Kendrick, Alexander, 120, 121
Kennan, George, 120
Kennedy, Joseph P., 36
Kenniston, Kenneth, 370
Khrushchev, Nikita, 162
Kingsbury, John A., 194
Kirchwey, Freda, 14, 16–17, 41,
62, 72, 73–74, 108, 143,
358
ADA criticized by, 139
Cold War editorial by, 295
on Cultural and Scientific
Conference, 165–66, 167–
168
on Czech takeover, 156
in Fischer's resignation, 85
Hicks dismissed by, 292
in *Nation* suit, 294

in NCPAC, 143, 144
Soviet aid favored by, 50
State Department criticized
by, 58
on Truman Doctrine, 123–25
Vayo defended by, 293
on Wallace, 156–57
Kirkland, Edward C., 334
Kissinger, Henry, 381
Koestler, Arthur, 80, 103
Kohlberg, Alfred, 274
Korean War, 196–206
China in, 266
Communist position on, 203,
205
Dreier on, 202–3
fellow travelers vs. progres-
sives on, 203
outbreak of, 196–97
Roth's reports on, 196–97
United Nations in, 197, 198,
200
U.S. intervention in, 197–98
Kramer, Hilton, 240–41, 370
Kristol, Irving, 284–89, 304,
305, 355

La Feber, Walter, 382
La Follette, Suzanne, 77
Lamont, Corliss, 192, 205, 296,
356, 380, 383
Lardner, Ring, Jr., 221, 222,
238–39
Lasch, Christopher, 354–55
Lash, Joseph P., 21
Laski, Harold, 21, 81–84, 117,
121–22, 124, 159
Lasky, Victor, 240
Lattimore, Owen, 119, 150, 201,
264, 266–82, 301, 313, 337,
342
background of, 266–67
Budenz's testimony against,
268, 311–12
Communist China favored by,
258, 279
Davis's defense of, 280–81
Flynn's book on, 272–73
indictment of, 269–70

at IPR, 273–76
on Korea, 278–79
Kristol on, 286, 288
McCarran Committee investigation of, 269, 273–74, 275, 276, 277
McCarthy's charges against, 252, 267, 268–69, 272–73, 281
New Leader on, 279, 280
press coverage of hearings on, 268–69
as scholar, 276–78
State Department work by, 267, 277
Stein on, 305–6
Time on, 281–82
Tydings Committee testimony of, 267–68, 269, 277
Lattimore Story, The (Flynn), 272
Lattimore the Scholar (Johnson), 277
Laughton, Charles, 249
Lauterbach, Richard, 69, 127
Lawson, John Howard, 222, 235, 246, 248
Lazarsfeld, Paul, 338
League of American Writers, 23, 362
League of Professional Groups for Foster and Ford, 27
Lees, Robert, 224
Lehman, Herbert L., 131
Lehrman, Hal, 136–38
Lend-Lease aid, 39, 112
Lerner, Max, 21–22, 29, 105, 107, 144
    ADA criticized by, 138–39
    Alsops answered by, 118
    anti-Stalinists attacked by, 86–87
    Bullitt's article criticized by, 89, 90
    on Comintern dissolution, 63–64
    Eastman refuted by, 64, 66
    after German invasion of Soviet Union, 46–47

in Germany, 171–72
on HUAC, 324–25
on Katyn Forest massacre, 98–99, 172
on Korean War, 199–200, 265
as liberal, 170–71
Lippmann's book reviewed by, 93–94
on Mumford-MacLeish thesis, 35
"People's Century" proposed by, 52
as *PM* writer, 99
on Polish government-in-exile, 100, 101–2
on Roosevelt's foreign policy, 109
on Schuman, 30
Soviet war effort supported by, 46–47, 49
on U.S.–Soviet relations, 103–4, 122–23
on Wallace, 109, 157–58
Levin, Harry, 176
Lewis, John L., 43
Liberal Imagination, The (Trilling), 346–47
Liberty Under the Soviets (Baldwin), 48
Life, 59–60, 88
Limelight, 240
Lindbergh, Charles, 41
Lin Yutang, 255–57
Lipper, Eleanor, 151
Lippmann, Walter, 17, 92–95, 96, 115, 140, 264
Loeb, James, Jr., 76–77, 138, 152
London, Ephraim, 365
Lonely Crowd, The (Riesman), 306, 343
Los Angeles Times, 218
Lovejoy, Arthur O., 331
Lovett, Robert, 120
Lowell, Robert, 164, 290, 291, 353
Lowenthal, John, 367–68
Loyalty of Free Men, The (Barth), 285, 289, 344

Loyalty of Free Men, The, cont.
  loyalty program, 284, 288–89,
    310, 343
Luce, Henry, 52, 88–89, 180,
    259
Lynd, Helen, 329, 330–31
Lynd, Robert, 67, 179
Lynn, Kenneth, 177
Lyons, Eugene, 22, 71
Lyons, Leonard, 239–40

MacArthur, Douglas, 197, 200
McCarran Committee, 269,
    273–74, 275, 276, 277,
    306, 310
McCarthy, Joseph:
  ACCF criticisms of, 307
  Buckley and Bozell on, 309–
    311, 312, 313
  Kristol on, 285, 286
  Lattimore case and, 252, 267,
    268–69, 272–73, 281
  liberals' denunciations of,
    312–13
  Muhlen's defense of, 308–9
  State Department investigated
    by, 267, 269
  Westin on, 287
McCarthy, Mary, 45, 164, 165,
    294n, 298, 364–65
McCarthy and His Enemies
  (Buckley and Bozell), 309–
    311, 312
McCarthy and the Communists,
    307, 308
Macdonald, Dwight, 76, 79–81,
    84, 134, 161, 179, 204, 345,
    350, 364
  in Committee for Cultural
    Freedom, 298, 299, 300,
    301–2, 303–4, 308
  on Cultural and Scientific
    Conference, 164, 165, 166
  as *Encounter* editor, 304–5,
    307
  on Lerner, 171–72
  Lynd on, 67
  in *Mission to Moscow* contro-
    versy, 76, 77–78

on *Nation* suit, 293
Politics founded by, 79–80
shift in views of, 134, 135
on Wallace, 149–50, 151–52,
    154, 157, 158
in Yaddo affair, 290, 291
MacIver, Robert M., 335
MacLeish, Archibald, 32, 33,
    34–35, 37, 38, 310
McWilliams, Carey, 21, 202,
    284–85, 289, 293, 296–97,
    332, 356–58
Magruder, Jeb Stuart, 27
Mailer, Norman, 164, 165, 364,
    368
Maltz, Albert, 222, 226, 243,
    248, 375
Manchester Guardian, 81
Mao Tse-tung, 162, 189, 257,
    265
Marcantonio, Vito, 35–36, 153
Marshall, George C., 120, 282
Marshall, Margaret, 45, 75–76,
    167–69, 295–96
Marshall Plan, 120, 124, 146
Martin, Kingsley, 83, 94–95,
    201
Marx, Leo, 174, 177
Masaryk, Jan, 156, 179
Mathewson, Rufus, 176
Matthiessen, F. O., 45, 173–83,
    194, 218
  American Renaissance by,
    173–74
  background of, 173
  at Cultural and Scientific
    Conference, 165
  on Czechoslovakia, 180–81
  death of, 173, 182, 183
  From the Heart by, 178–80
  personal life of, 173, 181,
    182–83
  political life of, 174
  as teacher, 174, 176–78, 182
Maxim Litvinoff (Pope), 61, 66
Maxwell, Stewart, 253
Memoirs of Hecate County
  (Wilson), 300
Memories of a Catholic Girl-

hood (McCarthy), 365
Men in Battle (Bessie), 237
Menjou, Adolphe, 219, 230, 247
Meyerhoff, Hans, 317, 320–22
Middletown (Lynds), 329
Miller, Arthur, 225, 235, 307, 325–26
Miller, Merle, 228, 229, 231–33
Miller, Perry, 175
Mills, C. Wright, 80
Mission to Moscow (Davies), 61, 75–76
Mission to Moscow (film), 75–78, 220
Montgomery, Robert, 219
Monthly Review, 177, 194, 205, 206–11
   Communist government supported by, 207–8
   on Korean War, 207
   readers of, 208–9
   on Soviet purges, 209–10
Morison, Samuel Eliot, 337
Moscow War Diary (Werth), 55
Mother Russia (Hindus), 65
Motion Picture Academy, 238
Motion Picture Alliance for the Preservation of American Ideals (MPA), 219–20
Motion Picture Democratic Committee (MPDC), 213
motion picture industry, 212–28
   anti-Communists in, 219–20, 230, 247
   Communists in, 214, 215–16, 220, 241–42, 243, 244, 247–48, 250
   HUAC investigations of, 219–228
   Kael's view of ethics in, 244–245
   OWI guide for, 242–43
   Popular Front in, 213, 217
   power centralized in, 212
   progressive Democrats in, 214–15
   pro-Soviet films in, 220
   Stalinism in, 248–49
   unionization of, 213, 218–19, 247
   writers in, 213–14, 225
   see also blacklist
Motion Picture Industry Council, 225
Motion Picture Producers Association, 223
Motion Pictures, U.S. Bureau of, 243
Moulin Rouge, 239–40
Muhlen, Norbert, 135, 308–9
Muller, Herbert J., 306
Mumford, Lewis, 32–33, 34–35, 37, 38
Murphy, Arthur E., 330, 331
Murphy, George, 219
Murray, Philip, 143
Murrow, Edward R., 80
Muste, A. J., 164

Naming Names (Navasky), 327, 372–75
Nation, The, 14–15, 18, 29, 30, 31, 155, 161, 268, 302, 334, 344, 378, 380
   on Afghanistan invasion, 381
   on blacklisting, 240
   Browder's attack on, 59
   on China, 253, 260–61, 262, 263
   on Cultural and Scientific Conference, 165–66, 167
   Fischer's resignation from, 85
   on Hiss case, 315, 367
   on Korean War, 201–2
   under McWilliams, 296–97, 356–58
   Marshall fired from, 295–96
   Matthiessen's book reviewed in, 179–80
   Mission to Moscow film reviewed by, 77–78
   New Leader sued by, 291–94
   "people's war" supported by, 52
   on Polish government-in-exile, 99

Nation, The, cont.
  after Progressive defeat,
    161–62
  Soviet aid favored by, 50
  on Soviet purges, 122
  on Stalin-Hitler Pact, 14,
    16–17
  State Department criticized
    by, 58
  on Truman Doctrine, 123–25
  U.S. entry into war favored
    by, 40–41
  Viereck's attack on, 294–95
  on Wallace, 156–57
  on Warsaw uprising, 100
  on Yalta Agreement, 111
National Ad-Hoc Committee to
  End Crimes Against Paul
  Robeson, 371
National Citizens Political Action Committee (NCPAC),
  143, 144, 145, 217, 218
National Committee for Peace-
  ful Alternatives, 203
National Council for the Arts,
  Sciences and Professions,
  168
National Council of American-
  Soviet Friendship (NCASF),
  24, 192, 194, 203
National Geographic, 151
National Guardian, 191, 203–5,
  356
  Aronson's and Belfrage's book
    on, 356
  founding of, 203–4
  on Korean War, 205
  pro-Soviet views in, 204–5
National Labor Relations Board,
  213
National Lawyers Guild, 218,
  302
National Maritime Union, 43
Nation Associates, 139
Navasky, Victor, 327, 364, 366–
  367, 372–75
Nearing, Scott, 195, 327
Neumann, William L., 337
New Critics, 175

New International, 158–59, 332
New Leader, 53–54, 71, 76, 86,
  106, 248
  on American Labor Party,
    145–46
  on Bullitt article, 90
  on China, 279–80
  fellow travelers' activities
    reported in, 135–36, 140
  Foreign Policy Association
    attacked by, 131
  on Korean War, 197
  on McCarthyism, 284, 308–9
  Miller's report attacked in,
    228
  in *Mission to Moscow* film
    protest, 76, 77
  on *Monthly Review*, 206
  Nation attacked by, 295
  Nation's suit against, 291–94
  on Pressman, 147
  on progressives' double stan-
    dard, 105
  Wallace attacked by, 152–53
New Masses, 21, 23, 69, 105,
  133, 235, 237, 248
New Republic, 17–19, 20, 27,
  28, 31, 32, 81, 105, 107–8,
  179, 297, 344, 378, 384
  on anti-Stalinists, 45–46
  Browder's attack on, 59
  on Bullitt article, 89
  on China, 253, 259, 260, 264
  circulation of, 51, 106, 161
  on Communist Party, 59
  conscription endorsed by, 39
  on Dumbarton Oaks Con-
    ference, 111
  on execution of Polish leaders,
    98
  Fry's resignation from, 84
  Great Britain supported by,
    39–40, 44
  Hicks's criticisms of, 85–86
  on Hiss case, 366–67
  on Indochina, 199
  on Iranian-Soviet relations,
    117
  on Korean War, 198–99

Lerner's critique of, 49
Mission to Moscow film reviewed by, 77
Mumford-MacLeish thesis debated in, 33, 34–35
on Norway invasion, 38
Partisan Review attack on, 133
"people's war" supported by, 52
on Polish government-in-exile, 99
on Polish socialism, 116, 117
political shift in, 198–99
on Potsdam Agreement, 112
after Progressive defeat, 161–162
Roosevelt endorsed by, 39
on Soviet foreign policy, 104, 105
Soviet–U.S. comparisons in, 47–48
Soviet war effort supported by, 46, 47–48, 50
Stalin-Hitler Pact denounced by, 45–46
Stein's letter in, 305–6
on Truman Doctrine, 119–20
Truman endorsed by, 154–55
U.S. entry into war favored by, 40
on U.S.–Soviet relations, 105, 106, 118–19, 120–21
Wallace as editor of, 119, 143
Wallace supported by, 142, 154
on Warsaw uprising, 100–101
on Yalta Agreement, 110–11
New Statesman and Nation, The, 136, 163, 294
Newsweek, 247
New York Herald Tribune, 179, 190, 282
New York Post, 171, 260
New York Review of Books, 297, 350, 370
New York Times, 15, 28, 41, 77, 80, 166, 179, 206, 229, 240, 257, 259, 282, 334, 363, 370
New York Times Magazine, 103
New York World-Telegram, 147
Nicolaevsky, Boris, 162–63
Niebuhr, Reinhold, 17, 62, 85, 111, 122, 138, 163, 294, 347–48
Nineteen Eighty-Four (Orwell), 208
Nixon, Richard, 266
Norris, George W., 144
North, Joseph, 23
North Star, 220
Norway, German invasion of, 38

Oak, Liston M., 73
Objective Burma, 243
O'Connor, Tom, 166
Odets, Clifford, 218
Office of War Information (OWI), 242–43
Olson, Culbert, 214
One World (Willkie), 93
Oppenheimer, J. Robert, 317–22
Ordeal by Slander (Lattimore), 269, 277
Ornitz, Samuel, 222
Orwell, George, 80, 81–82, 208
Oumansky, Constantine, 25

Pacific Affairs, 266, 273, 274, 276, 277–78
Pares, Bernard, 61, 68–69
Parks, Larry, 224–25, 226
Partisan Review, 27, 28, 80, 133–35, 168, 169, 179, 289, 294, 349–50, 360–61, 365
Part of Our Time (Kempton), 236–37
Pattern of Soviet Power, The (Snow), 70, 127
Patton, James, 144
Pauling, Linus, 217
Paul Robeson (Dean), 371
Peace Week, 43
People's Century, concept of, 52

People's World, 238
Pepper, Claude, 26, 128–29, 131, 184–85
Pepper, George, 217
Perjury: The Hiss-Chambers Case (Weinstein), 315, 366
Perry, Ralph Barton, 61
Phillips, William, 179, 298, 301, 353, 361–62
Pinchot, Gifford, 144
Pitzele, Merlyn S., 228, 229
Place in the Sun, A, 238
PM, 59, 64, 85, 86, 89, 90, 99, 133–34, 157, 161, 171
Podhoretz, Norman, 161, 348, 364*n*, 368–69, 370, 379
Poirier, Richard, 364
Poland:
  arrests in, 101–3
  government-in-exile of, 99–100
  Katyn Forest massacre in, 91, 98–99
  Soviet invasion of, 20–21, 67, 100
  Warsaw uprising in (1944), 100–101
Politics, 67, 79–80, 135, 152, 169–70
Pope, Arthur Upham, 58, 61, 66–67, 78
Popular Front:
  in motion picture industry, 213, 217
  music in, 245–46
  second form of, 58–59
Porter, Fred, 131
Potsdam Agreement, 112
Pratt, Fletcher, 198
Pravda, 89, 90
Preminger, Otto, 238
Press and the Cold War, The (Aronson), 206
Pressman, Lee, 144, 147, 149, 153
Pride of the Marines, The, 243
Progressive, 86
Progressive Citizens of America, 138, 139, 140, 145

Progressive Citizens of Southern California, 217
Progressive Party, 24, 147, 156
  on Korean War, 205
  nationalization called for by, 148
  in Soviet connection, 158–59, 160
  Vermont Resolution rejected by, 148–49
Protestant, 135
public opinion:
  on Allied difficulties, 88
  on civil liberties, 344
  on Finland invasion, 43
  on German invasion of Soviet Union, 45
  on HUAC investigations, 223
  on Soviet post-war cooperation, 60–61
  on Soviets as allies, 58–59
  Soviet victory over Germany favored in, 45
  on U.S. intervention in war, 40
  on U.S.–Soviet conflicts, 135

Rabinowitz, Louis M., 335
Radio Writers Guild, 244
Radosh, Ronald, 206
Rahv, Philip, 10, 169, 182, 289, 301, 315–16
Rand, Ayn, 219
Randolph, A. Philip, 76
Rankin, John E., 61, 222
Rauh, Joseph, 138
Reader's Digest, 61, 64, 322–23
Reagan, Ronald, 219, 226, 230
realism, progressive, 87–88
Real Soviet Russia, The (Dallin), 78–79
Red Channels, 228, 231, 233, 299–300
Redlich, Norman, 325
Red Star Over China (Snow), 61, 257
Reed, John, 183
Religion and Labor Foundation, 195

Reporter, 161, 276, 297
Report on Blacklisting (Cogley), 233–34
Report on Russia (White), 90
Republican Party, 198, 312, 344
Reuther, Walter, 138
Rexroth, Kenneth, 135
Rice, Elmer, 220, 298, 299
Rickenbacker, Edward V., 60, 74
Riesel, Victor, 227–28
Riesman, David, 306, 308, 343, 344–45
Robeson, Paul, 35–36, 239, 329, 331, 370–72
Robeson, Paul, Jr., 371–72
Robins, Raymond, 24–27, 128–131, 183–96
  Pepper's relations with, 184–186
  progressives' correspondence with, 194–96, 202, 203
  pro-Soviet views of, 183–84
  Smedley's correspondence with, 187–88
  Strong's relations with, 189, 190, 191, 192, 193–94
Robinson, Edward G., 215, 225, 226–28, 230, 233, 247, 250
Rogers, Lela, 230
Rogge, O. John, 187, 205–6
Romance of American Communism, The (Gornick), 370
Roosevelt, Eleanor, 138, 139
Roosevelt, Franklin D., 36, 37, 52, 242
  Browder's letters to, 59
  China policies of, 252–53, 255, 257, 280
  HDC support for, 215
  Nation endorsement of, 41, 139–40
  New Republic endorsement of, 39, 139–40
  in Socialist Workers Party persecution, 44
  State Department relations with, 58

  U.S.–Soviet relations and, 108–9
  Wallace dropped by, 109–10
  Welles forced out by, 104–5
  at Yalta, 114
Roosevelt, James, 215–16
Roosevelt, Theodore, 24, 25
Roper polls, 59
Rosenberg, Ethel, 366, 370
Rosenberg, Harold, 314–15
Rosenberg, Julius, 366, 370
Rosinger, Lawrence, 275, 282
Rosten, Leo, 212–13, 214
Roszak, Theodore, 370
Rotarian, 61
Roth, Andrew, 196–97
Rovere, Richard, 21, 298, 300, 306, 352
Russia and Postwar Europe (Dallin), 78–79
Russia and the Peace (Pares), 68
Russia at War (Werth), 57
Russian Peasant and the Revolution, The (Hindus), 64–65
Russia's Europe (Lehrman), 136–38
Ryskind, Morrie, 219, 220, 230

Salt, Waldo, 224
Salvemini, Gaetano, 89
Sandburg, Carl, 36
Sarton, May, 182
Saturday Evening Post, The, 36, 61, 70, 127–28, 205, 225–226, 235, 239, 257
Saturday Review of Literature, 137–38, 220, 294
Sayers, Michael, 141
Schachtman, Max, 305
Schapiro, Meyer, 365
Schine, David, 272
Schlesinger, Arthur, Jr., 164, 240–41, 284, 300, 301, 306, 310, 345–46, 352
Schorer, Mark, 134–35
Schultz, Lillie, 139
Schuman, Frederick L., 27–30, 53, 126–27, 130–31, 149,

Schuman, Frederick L., *cont.*
164, 205, 218
Scott, Adrian, 222
Scott, John, 48–49, 54
Scoundrel Time (Hellman),
240, 241, 359–63, 365, 366
Screen Actors Guild (SAG),
213
Screen Writers Guild (SWG),
213, 214, 218, 220, 235,
241–42, 244, 247
Seeger, Pete, 37, 205, 234, 239
Seigel, Kalman, 334
Seldes, George, 36–37, 89–90,
110, 205
Serge, Victor, 80
Service, John, 275, 277, 312
Shapley, Harlow, 144, 218, 223
Sheean, Vincent, 28
Sheen, Fulton, 61
Sillen, Samuel, 248
Sinclair, Upton, 22–24, 212
Situation in Asia, The (Latti-
more), 278
Smathers, George, 185
Smedley, Agnes, 129, 164, 186–
188, 259, 290
books by, 186
charges against, 187–88
pro-Chinese views of, 187–88
Smith, Harold J., 238
Smith, Henry Nash, 173–74
Smith, Jessica, 131, 190
Smith, T. V., 331
Smith Act (1940), 44, 45, 341–
342, 360
Snow, Edgar, 61, 257–58, 279
background of, 257–58
on Communist China, 257,
258, 282
on Eastern Europe, 70–71
on Lin Yutang, 255–56
on Soviet Union, 127–28,
201–2
on Stalin, 70–71
on Yugoslavia, 159
Socialist Party, 23
Socialist Workers Party, 44–45,
331

Social Science Research
Council, 229
Sokolsky, George, 227–28
Solution in Asia (Lattimore),
258, 267, 278
Something to Guard (Aronson
and Belfrage), 206
Sondergaard, Gale, 224, 247
Song of Russia, 220
Soule, George, 18, 34, 51–52,
119
Southern Conference for Human
Welfare, 158, 302
Souvarine, Boris, 56
Soviet Asia Mission (Wallace),
150–51
Soviet Council, 273–74
*Soviet Politics at Home and
Abroad* (Schuman), 126,
130
Soviet Russia Today, 127, 130,
131, 190
Soviet Union:
Afghanistan invaded by, 381–
382
Badoglio regime accepted by,
72–73
China's relations with, 258–59
collectivized farming in, 65
in Czechoslovakia takeover,
146–47
Finland invaded by, 19, 43,
55, 67
Five-Year Plan in, 55, 65–66
German invasion of, 45, 49,
79
Hungary under control of,
124–25
in Korean War, 203
labor camps in, 66, 99, 162–
163
Poland invaded by, 20–21, 67,
100
purges in, 48–49, 122, 209–10
support for Germany in, 49,
79
U.S. businessmen's attitudes
toward, 60–61
U.S. mass media glorification

of, 59–60, 61
U.S. public opinion on, 58–59
war effort in, 58–59, 78
Spanish Civil War, 62
Spartacus, 238
Speaking Frankly (Byrnes), 130
Spender, Stephen, 304
Stalin, Joseph:
  Comintern dissolved by, 62–63
  Oumansky appointed by, 25–26
  progressives' opinions manipulated by, 13, 14
  purges under, 48–49
  Strong expelled by, 189
  at Yalta, 114
Stalin-Hitler Pact, 13–18, 24, 45–46, 79
  Communist Party affected by, 43
  Nation's response to, 14, 16–17
  New Republic's response to, 18–19, 45–46
  publication of documents on, 155–56
Stampp, Kenneth, 80
Starobin, Joseph, 45, 148
State Department, U.S., 58, 76, 166, 282, 311, 312
  China white paper published by, 190–91, 262–63
  Cultural and Scientific Conference visas denied by, 164, 165, 166
  Lattimore's work in, 267, 277
  McCarthy's charges against, 267, 269
Steel, Johannes, 153, 202
Steel, Ronald, 381
Steffens, Lincoln, 183
Steffens, Pete, 180
Stein, Sol, 305–6
Stevenson, Adlai, 170
Stokes, Carl, 371
Stone, I. F., 15, 58, 102–3, 104, 111, 124, 155–56, 202, 205, 302, 303

Strachey, John, 281
Straight, Dorothy, 18
Straight, Michael, 52–53, 119, 121, 306–7
Straight, Willard, 18
Strauss, Lewis, 317
Stripling, Robert, 219
Strong, Anna Louise, 50, 107, 113, 188–94, 208
  on China white paper, 190–91
  North Korean reports by, 192
  pro-Chinese views of, 189
  Soviet expulsion of, 188–90
  on Soviet Union, 192–93
Subversive Activities Control Board (SACB), 342
Survey Graphic, 83
Sweezy, Alan R., 53, 54
Sweezy, Paul, 148, 182, 206, 211
Swing, Raymond Gram, 254

TASS, 24
Taylor, Glenn, 149
Teamsters Union, 44
Teheran Conference, 106
Tenney, Jack B., 249
Theater Arts Committee, 362
Thermidor concept, 79
Thielens, Wagner, Jr., 338
Thomas, Norman, 41, 76, 86, 87, 138, 158, 204, 306
Thunder Out of China (Jacoby and White), 259
Time, 180, 215, 259, 268, 281, 295–96, 320
Time to Speak, A (MacLeish), 33
Tobin, Daniel J., 44
Tragedy of American Diplomacy, The (Williams), 379
Tresca, Carlo, 44
Trilling, Diana, 161–62, 301, 321–23, 327, 368, 377
  on anti-Communism, 352–53
  Hellman's dispute with, 363–364, 377

Trilling, Diana, *cont.*
on Oppenheimer case, 317–
318, 319, 320, 321–23
Trilling, Lionel, 10, 134, 301–
302, 346–47, 349, 368, 369
Trotsky, Leon, 25, 56, 60, 68
Trotskyists, 44–45, 134, 329,
332, 360, 372
Truman, Harry S., 119, 140
China policies of, 261, 262,
264
Korean War policies of, 197,
198, 200
loyalty order of, 284, 288–
289, 310, 343
Pepper's opposition to, 128–
129
progressives' support for,
154–55, 157
Sinclair's support for, 24
as Vice President, 110
Wallace dismissed by, 143
Truman Doctrine, 119–20, 123–
125, 128–29, 158, 264
Trumbo, Dalton, 234–39, 243,
248, 359
background of, 235
blacklisting of, 236–37
in "Hollywood Ten," 217,
234–35
HUAC testimony of, 222, 236
Navasky on, 374–75
political activities of, 235–36
Robinson's association with,
227
on screenwriters, 213–14
on SWG, 241–42
Tugwell, Rexford, 149
Tydings Committee, 267, 269,
276, 277, 281

Unfinished Woman, An
(Hellman), 359, 366
Union for Democratic Action
(UDA), 138
United Front, 194
United Nations, 87, 88, 111–12,
116
in Korean War, 197, 198, 200

United States and Russia
(Dean), 132–33
*United States Foreign Policy:
Shield of the Republic*
(Lippmann), 92
universities, 327–41
academic freedom in, 327
anti-intellectualism in, 337
apprehensiveness in, 338–40
Communists in, 327–28
investigating committees in,
328
McCarthyism's impact on,
334–36
political dismissals from, 328,
332
student apathy in, 341
Untermeyer, Louis, 165
Uphaus, Willard, 195
Utley, Freda, 186, 268, 270–72,
281

Valtin, Jan, 141
Van Den Haag, Ernest, 339–40
Van Kleeck, Mary, 205
Vayo, J. Alvarez Del, 58, 62–63,
108, 122, 123, 161, 201,
205, 292, 293, 296–97
Versailles Treaty, 112
Viereck, Peter, 294–95, 346
Vietnam War, 351–52, 356, 377,
382
Vigil of a Nation, The (Lin
Yutang), 255
Villard, Oswald Garrison, 14,
17, 41, 358
Vincent, John Carter, 260, 277,
312
Vital Center, The (Schlesinger),
346

Wadleigh, Henry Julian, 316
Wallace, Henry, 64, 129, 142–
154, 157–60, 202, 217,
311–12
anti-Stalinist opposition to,
145
in China, 280

"common man's war"
supported by, 52
Communist support for, 147–
148, 156–57
criticisms of, 151–54
on Czechoslovakia, 146–47
electoral defeat of, 158–60
Lerner on, 109, 157–58
Macdonald on, 149–50, 151–
152
Marshall Plan rejected by, 146
Matthiessen's work for, 174–
175
as *New Republic* editor, 119,
143
organizational support for
presidential campaign of,
143–44
in PCA, 140
PCA support for, 145
platform of, 149–50, 156
red-baiting of, 146–47
Siberia visited by, 150–51
Soviet Asia Mission by, 150–
151
on Soviet Union, 142–43
on Truman Doctrine, 120
Truman's dismissal of, 143
as Vice President, 109–10
Walton, Richard J., 378–79
Ward, Harry, 69, 205
Warner, Jack, 219
Warner Brothers, 76, 78
Warren, Earl, 214
Warsaw Pact, 121
Warsaw uprising (1944), 100–
101
Watts, Richard, 254, 255
Wechsler, James, 20–21, 139–
140, 145, 153, 301
Weinstein, Allen, 315, 366, 367
Welles, Orson, 245
Welles, Sumner, 58, 88, 104–5
We Must March, My Darlings
(Trilling), 363
Werner, Max, 202

Werth, Alexander, 55–57, 122,
125, 161–62, 163, 201,
295, 377–78
Westin, Alan, 287, 325, 327,
342–43, 373
Weyl, Walter, 17
White, George Abbot, 174–75
White, Harry Dexter, 288
White, Theodore, 259, 282
White, William Allen, 36
White, William L., 90–92
Wilde, Cornel, 215
Willen, Paul, 61
Williams, William Appleman,
379–80
Willkie, Wendell, 36, 39, 41, 64,
93, 150–51, 268
Wills, Garry, 359, 366
Wilson, Edmund, 18, 20, 34, 45,
76, 300
Wilson, H. H., 334
Wilson, Michael, 238
Wilson, Woodrow, 38
Winter, Ella, 180–81
Witch Hunt (McWilliams),
284–85
Witness (Chambers), 315–16
Wittfogel, Karl, 298
Wolfe, Bertram, 113, 164, 298
World Council of Churches, 122
World War I, 37–38
World War II, 43–74, 98–115
*see also specific organizations
and periodicals*

Yaddo retreat, 290–91
Yale Daily News, 173
Yale Literary Magazine, 173
Yalta Agreement, 101, 110–11,
114
Yorty, Sam, 227–28
Young, Nedrick, 238

Zilliacus, Konni, 204
Zirkle, Conway, 298